Racist America

This second edition of Joe R. Feagin's *Racist America* is extensively revised and thoroughly updated, with a special eye toward racism issues cropping up constantly in the Barack Obama era. This tenth-anniversary edition incorporates many dozens of new research studies on U.S. racial issues that significantly extend and update the first edition's major chapters. It accents exciting new and provocative concepts, especially the white racial frame and systemic racism, that Feagin developed in recent Routledge books. The author has also added readable, perceptive discussions of numerous studies in new research areas such as environmental racism, race and health, and antiracist strategies, as well as in all other research areas covered in the first edition. He has thoroughly edited and polished the book to make it much more readable for undergraduates, including eliminating repetitive materials, simplifying endnotes, adding headings and more cross-referencing, and adding a glossary and many new and interesting examples, anecdotes, and narratives about contemporary racism, including at the opening of all chapters.

Joe R. Feagin is Ella C. McFadden Professor at Texas A&M University. Feagin has done research on racism and sexism issues for 45 years and has served as the Scholar-in-Residence at the U.S. Commission on Civil Rights. He has written 56 scholarly books and nearly 200 scholarly articles in his research areas, and one of his books (*Ghetto Revolts*) was nominated for a Pulitzer Prize. His recent books include *Systemic Racism* and *Two Faced Racism: Whites in the Backstage and Frontstage*. He is the 2006 recipient of a Harvard Alumni Association lifetime achievement award and was the 1999–2000 president of the American Sociological Association.

TITLES OF RELATED INTEREST

The Integration Debate: Competing Futures for American Cities edited by Chester Hartman and Gregory Squires

Operation Gatekeeper and Beyond: The War On Illegals and the Remaking of the U.S.–Mexico Boundary by Joseph Nevins

The White Racial Frame: Centuries of Racial Framing and Counter-Framing by Joe R. Feagin

Yes We Can? White Racial Framing and the 2008 Presidential Election by Joe R. Feagin and Adia Harvey Wingfield

The Internet and Social Inequalities by James C. Witte and Susan E. Mannon

Racist America

Roots, Current Realities, and Future Reparations

Second Edition

Joe R. Feagin

 Routledge
Taylor & Francis Group

NEW YORK AND LONDON

First published 2000
by Routledge

This edition published 2010
by Routledge
270 Madison Ave, New York, NY 10016

Simultaneously published in the UK
by Routledge
2 Park Square, Milton Park, Abingdon, Oxon OX14 4RN

Routledge is an imprint of the Taylor & Francis Group, an informa business

© 2000, 2010 Taylor & Francis

Typeset in Minion by Wearset Ltd, Boldon, Tyne and Wear
Printed and bound in the United States of America on acid-free paper by
Sheridan Books, Inc.

Trademark Notice: Product or corporate names may be trademarks or registered
trademarks, and are used only for identification and explanation without intent to
infringe.

Library of Congress Cataloging in Publication Data
A catalog record has been requested for this book

ISBN10: 0-415-99206-0 (hbk)
ISBN10: 0-415-99207-9 (pbk)
ISBN10: 0-203-89425-1 (ebk)

ISBN13: 978-0-415-99206-0 (hbk)
ISBN13: 978-0-415-99207-7 (pbk)
ISBN13: 978-0-203-89425-5 (ebk)

To Roy Brooks, Hernán Vera, and Ronald Takaki

Contents

Preface

In the fall of 2006 prominent white comedian Michael Richards, once part of the popular television show *Seinfeld*, was caught on camera yelling racist slurs, including "nigger," at black customers in his audience during a comedic performance. According to the *New York Times*, Richards yelled at one black audience member: "Shut up! Fifty years ago, we'd have you upside down..." as part of his commentary. Later he apologized, with an explanation that "I work in a very uncontrolled manner onstage. I do a lot of free association."[1]

In the spring of 2007 popular radio talk show host Don Imus made similarly blatant racist comments about a successful black women's basketball team. He laughingly called these talented college students "nappy-headed hos." Famous for barbed comments, Imus brought harsh emotion-laden framing of black women usually reserved for locker-room banter into the public frontstage. Imus was briefly fired, but white executives soon had him back on the radio. Surveys indicated that the overwhelming majority of African Americans thought he should have been fired for his racist remarks, but only 47 percent of whites agreed. Apparently, a large proportion of white Americans do not see such verbal racist attacks as particularly serious.[2] Blatantly racist incidents like these still routinely erupt across a country that many people now wishfully describe as "post-racial" or "no longer racist."

Anthropologist Jane Hill has examined how and why many whites come to define racist outbursts by white celebrities and politicians as not serious, as just "gaffes" that do not reveal a deeper racist framing of the protagonists. Her research makes clear the central role of the English language in embedding and perpetuating the old and very deep white racial framing of U.S. society. The widespread character of this "gaffe" racism, and the way such events get discussed obsessively and circulated extensively around the society, are one indication that the old-fashioned **racism** of the past has not disappeared and been replaced by a new post-racial society.[3]

In verbal attacks on black Americans, these prominent white entertainers used emotion-laden racist words, imagery, and commentary that is not new, but was taken out of a centuries-old white-racist framing of black Americans. Such views of black Americans are as old as this country, dating back to the days of slavery and Jim Crow **segregation**. Such views and actions stemming from them today reveal the important aspects of the societal racism we examine in this book—the negative images of black men and women dancing in white heads, the white racial framing that legitimates antiblack images, the commonplace discriminatory practices of whites, the arrogance of white power, and the white-dominated institutions that allow or encourage such racist practices.

In the United States, racist thought, emotion, and action are structured into the rhythms of everyday life. They are lived, concrete, advantageous for whites, and painful for those who are not white. Each major part of the life of a white person or a person of color is shaped directly or indirectly by this country's **systemic racism**. Even a person's birth and parents are often shaped by racism, since mate selection is limited by racist pressures against interracial marriage. Where one lives is frequently determined by the racist practices of landlords, bankers, and others in the real-estate profession. The clothes one wears and what one has to eat are affected by access to resources that varies by position in the U.S. racial hierarchy. When one goes off to school, her or his education is shaped by contemporary racism—from the composition of the student body to the character of the curriculum. Where one goes to church is often shaped by racism, and it is likely that racism affects who one's political representatives are. Even getting sick, dying, and being buried may be influenced by systemic racism. Every part of the life cycle, and most aspects of one's life, are shaped by the racism that is integral to the foundation and continuing operation of the United States.

One of the great tragedies today is the inability or unwillingness of most white Americans to see clearly and understand fully this racist reality. Among whites, including white elites, there is a commonplace *denial* of personal, family, and group histories of racism. Most do not see themselves or their families as seriously implicated in racial **oppression**, in the distant past or the present. Referring to themselves, most will say fervently, "I am not a racist." Referring to ancestors, many will say something like, "My family never owned slaves" or "My family never benefited from segregation." Assuming racial **discrimination** to be a thing of the past, many assert that African Americans are "paranoid" about racism and often give them firm advice: forget the past and move on, because "slavery happened hundreds of years ago." Most do not wish to discuss issues of contemporary racial framing and discrimination.

Over the last few decades, numerous white commentators have suggested that white racism is no longer a serious problem. Thus, one analysis of white attitudes on public policy matters concludes that "racism is not built-in to the American ethos," while another book boldly proclaims "the end of racism."[4] This line of argument about a post-racial society has become more popular since Senator Barack Obama's pathbreaking election as president in 2008. The post-racial perspective now articulated by mainstream commentators often includes the idea that contemporary black politicians like President Obama have an obligation to be racial healers who do not articulate a civil-rights enforcement agenda and whose elections prove racism is no longer a serious barrier to societal achievement for Americans of color. Thus, the business newspaper, *The Wall Street Journal,* asserted after Obama's election that

> A man of mixed race has now reached the pinnacle of U.S. power only two generations since the end of Jim Crow. This is a tribute to American opportunity, and it is something that has never happened in another Western democracy—notwithstanding European condescension about "racist" America.

The editorial continued with the assertion that: "One promise of his victory is that perhaps we can put to rest the myth of racism as a barrier to achievement in this splendid country. Mr. Obama has a special obligation to help do so."[5]

Such unwillingness to face current racist realities is not healthy for the present or future of the United States. It has been said that a major task for the residents of the former Communist nations of Eastern Europe is to forget the falsified past once taught them and to learn the hard facts about that oppressive past. In this process, old heroes often become villains, and old villains become heroes. One can say the same about white (and some other) Americans and U.S. history. Few mainstream media presentations or school textbooks provide full and accurate accounts of the history or current status of racial oppression in the United States.

The great scholar of the Africa diaspora C.L.R. James argued that the oppressive situation of African Americans is the number-one problem of racism in the contemporary world. If the problem of white racism cannot be solved in the U.S., it cannot be solved anywhere.[6] In this book I focus primarily on this critical case of white-on-black oppression in the United States. One reason is practical: given limited space, this focus means I can dig deeper into the development, structure, processes, and likely future of one major case of racism. My decision is also theoretically motivated. I will show that white-on-black oppression is in important respects the *archetype* of racial oppression in North America. For example, African Americans were the only racial group specifically singled out several times in the U.S. Constitution for subordination within the new U.S. nation. James Madison, the leading theorist of the Constitution, openly noted that, from a white point of view, "the case of the black **race** within our bosom ... is the problem most baffling to the policy of our country."[7]

A few decades later, white-on-black oppression would be central to the bloodiest war in U.S. history, the Civil War. Within this white-dominated society, African Americans have been subordinated and exploited by whites in much larger numbers than any other racial group. Over nearly four centuries, tens of millions of African Americans have had their labor and wealth regularly taken from them. In contrast to other groups, their original languages, cultures, and family ties were substantially obliterated by their being torn from Africa, and the oppression faced under slavery and segregation was extremely dehumanized, racialized, and systematic. No other racially oppressed group, and there have been numerous others, has been so central to the internal economic, political, and cultural structure and evolution of the North American society—or to the often obsessively racist frame developed by white Americans over many generations. Thus, it is time to put white-on-black oppression fully at the center of a comprehensive study of the development, meaning, and reality of this country.

In this book I develop an antiracist theory and analysis of the white-on-black oppression that is now nearly four centuries old. Theory is a set of ideas designed to make sense of the empirical and existential reality around us. Concepts delineating and probing racism need to be clear and honed by everyday experience, not framed from an ivory tower. Here I accent concepts, in language understandable to the non-specialist, that can be used for an in-depth analysis of this still-racist society. These concepts are designed to help readers probe beneath the many defenses and myths about "race" to our painful racist realities. They are useful in countering inaccurate assessments of the society's racialized history and institutions. A critical theory of racism can help us better understand the numerous racialized dimensions of our everyday lives.

We need an antiracist theory not only to explain the operation of the racist system but also to envision possibilities for change. Antiracist theory attempts to facilitate agency, the movement of human actors to bring change in spite of oppression. Since at least the time of Karl Marx, antioppression analysts have viewed the relationship between structures of oppression and human agency as dialectical. Structures of domination shape everyday existence, but an insightful understanding of these structures and their recurring contradictions can assist people in forcefully resisting racial oppression. It is hard to be optimistic in times of continuing oppression, but some contradictions—especially everyday resistance by those oppressed—can provide a source of optimism because they suggest significant possibilities for human societal change.

Systemic racism is about everyday experience. People are born, live, and die within the racist system. Much recent social-science research helps to unmask the workings of the deep structures of this persisting system. My conceptual perspective is informed not only by the research of others but also by numerous field-research projects that I and my colleagues have undertaken in recent years. These projects have entailed hundreds of in-depth interviews with African Americans and other Americans of color in various walks of life about daily encounters with racial hostility and discrimination.

Staying in contact with the lived experience of seasoned veterans of racism enables an analyst to move beyond the mental construction of race to the concrete reality, daily trials, and accumulating burdens of everyday racism. Black Americans and other people of color often experience the societal world differently from white Americans, and this experience can be an important guide for conceptualizing the structures, processes, and future of U.S. racism. My colleagues and I have also spent much time interviewing more than 300 white Americans on their racial views and issues of public policy. I also draw on these interviews in understanding white perspectives and actions.

Currently, we have theoretical traditions that are relatively well developed in regard to the systems of class- and gender-oppression in the U.S. and other Western countries. There is a well-developed Marxist tradition with its many important conceptual contributions. The Marxist tradition provides a powerful theory of social oppression centered on such key concepts as class struggle, worker exploitation, and alienation. Marxism identifies the basic social forces undergirding class oppression, shows how human beings are alienated in class relations, and points toward activist remedies for oppression. Similarly, in feminist analysis there is a diverse and well-developed conceptual framework targeting key aspects of gendered oppression. Major approaches accent the social construction of sexuality, the world gender order, and the strategy of consciousness-raising. Feminist theorists and activists have argued that at the heart of institutional sexism is the material reality of human reproduction and sexuality, the latter including how a woman is treated and viewed sexually by men and how she views herself. Systemic sexism is a concept that is now well-developed. Moreover, in both the Marxist and feminist traditions, there are well-developed theories of group resistance and change.

In the case of racist oppression, however, we do not as yet have as strongly agreed-upon concepts and well-developed theoretical traditions as we have for gender and class oppression. Of course, numerous researchers, writers, and activists have focused their analytical and theoretical tools on the deep structure of North American racism now for more than a century. In this book I draw heavily on some of these important analysts, past and present—including Frederick Douglass, W.E.B. Du Bois, Oliver Cox, Kwame Ture, Anna Julia Cooper, and Bob Blauner, among numerous others. Each of these analysts has probed various aspects of this country's racist history and institutions, and some tried to define basic concepts for the analysis of institutionalized antiblack racism. Beginning more than a century ago, these scholars and activists began a paradigm shift in conceptualizing and analyzing racism and **antiracism**. As yet, however, there is no widely used term for this antioppression paradigm, and I propose that we choose the terms "antiracist theory" and "antiracist strategy" for this ever-growing antioppression tradition.

Today, the dominant social-science paradigm, seen in much mainstream scholarship on "race," still views racism as something in decline and/or as tacked on to an otherwise healthy American society. One variant of this perspective portrays the problem as one of scattered white bigots betraying egalitarian institutions—the theme developed well by Gunnar Myrdal and his contemporary followers (see Chapter 8, pp. 277–278). Another variant in the mainstream approach accents "intergroup relations" or "race relations," the array of intergroup relations and conflicts in society, with whites seen as only one group among many others having more or less equal impact or resources on an increasingly level playing field. As I will show in this book, however, the central problem is that, from the beginning, European American institutions were racially hierarchical, white-racist, and undemocratic. For the most part, they remain so today.

Nicolaus Copernicus started a revolution in astronomy by putting the sun at the center of the solar system. Begun some time ago by Frederick Douglass and W.E.B. Du Bois, a revolution in the analysis of U.S. racism is gradually developing, one that views the U.S. social system as imbedding racism *at its core.* The conceptual framework developed in this book places the reality, development, and crises of systemic racism at the heart of U.S. history and society. Here I develop a theoretical approach centered on the concept of *systemic racism,* viewed as a centuries-old *foundation* of North American society. A systemic racism approach sees white-on-black oppression as the persisting foundation of this society, one in place since the seventeenth century and persisting to the present day. White-on-black oppression, and other white-on-non-white oppression, has been the central racial reality of this country now for four centuries.

Systemic racism involves both the deep structures and the surface structures of racial oppression. It includes the complex array of antiblack practices, the unjustly gained political-economic power of whites, the continuing economic and other resource inequalities along racial lines, and the emotion-laden racist framing created by whites to maintain and rationalize their privilege and power. It thus encompasses the white-racist ideologies, attitudes, emotions, images, actions, and institutions of this society. This racism is a material, social, and ideological reality and is indeed systemic, which means that the racist reality is manifested in all major institutions. If you break a three-dimensional hologram into separate parts and shine a laser through any one part, you can project the whole three-dimensional image again from within that part. Like a hologram, each major part of U.S. society—the economy, politics, education, religion, the family—reflects the fundamental realities of systemic racism.

Many Americans, especially white Americans, view racism as just an individual matter, as something only outspoken bigots engage in. Yet racism is much more that an individual matter. It is both individual and systemic.

Systemic racism is perpetuated by a broad **social-reproduction** process that generates not only the recurring patterns of racial discrimination within institutions and by individuals but also a deeply alienating racist relationship—on the one hand, the racially oppressed, and on the other, the racial oppressors. These two groups are created by the racist system, and thus have different group interests. The former resists and seeks to overthrow the system, while the latter seeks to maintain it. Thus, in dialectical fashion oppression creates contradictions that can bring change. The great inequality of socioeconomic resources across the color line regularly leads to subtle or overt resistance by Americans of color.

While racism directed at Americans of color is a core characteristic of U.S. society, it is not the only major type of institutionalized oppression. I do not claim here that an antiracist theory can explain everything about societal oppression. Indeed, I reject a reductionist analysis that tries to reduce all oppressions to one type. A pluralistic analysis of oppression is necessary. Indeed, class-structured capitalism, sexism, bureaucratic authoritarianism, and heterosexism are all important parts of the webbed package of oppressions internal to U.S. society. As I proceed, I will note some aspects of other oppressions as they intersect and interact with racial oppression at various points in this book.

As we move on into the twenty-first century, people of color are now more than 80 percent of the world's population and are gradually becoming a demographic majority in the U.S. Today, Americans of color constitute more than half the population of four of the country's largest cities—New York, Los Angeles, Chicago, and Houston. They will soon make up more than half the population in large areas of the country, including the largest states. Americans of color are now a majority in California, Texas, Hawaii, and New Mexico. Sometime in the 2040s, whites will almost certainly become a statistical minority in the U.S. population. Over the next decade or two, this impressive demographic change will likely bring great pressures for change in the ordinary racist practices and institutions of this country. Moreover, as the world's peoples of color, such as in China and India, become ever-more influential in international politics and economics, yet other pressures are likely to be put on U.S. political-economic institutions to treat all people of color with greater fairness and justice.

We need an international perspective on the systemic racism that plagues the United States. Adopting an international human-rights perspective gives one a place from which to critically assess human rights, social justice, and racial equality in a powerful nation-state like the United States. There is a growing international view of what are fundamental human rights, which include rights extending well beyond the civil rights ideally guaranteed by U.S. laws. Drawing on this international viewpoint, one can argue that people are entitled to equal treatment because they are human beings, not because they are members of a particular nation-state. According to the United Nation's 1948 Universal Declaration of Human Rights, which the U.S. government signed, fundamental human rights are rooted in the inherent dignity of each human being, are inalienable and universal, and are acquired at birth by "all members of the human family." This Declaration asserts the principle of non-discrimination and equality and lists three fundamental rights: life, liberty, and personal security. The right to a life free from racial discrimination and oppression is clearly enunciated in international law and morality. Today, the United States stands judged by international human rights doctrine and law as still quite unjust and inegalitarian in its racial structures and contours.

Acknowledgments

Lives are much like symphonies, with a grand assortment of people having effects on how we grow and develop. I am indebted to my late parents Frank and Hanna Feagin for showing me that respect for others was possible even as I grew up in a sea of blatant racism in the South. I am especially grateful to my friends Connie and Preston Williams and Melvin and Zeta Sikes for teaching me, in ways small and large, what the black experience in America means in many of its complexities, pains, frustrations, and joys. I am also indebted to my graduate school professors, Tom Pettigrew and Gordon Allport, who introduced me to the study of U.S. racism.

In the preparation of this book, I especially relied on Hernán Vera, Sharon Rush, Bernice Barnett, Gideon Sjoberg, and Roy Brooks for their friendship and encouragement, for vital discussions, and for reviews of various chapters. I am especially indebted to Louwanda Evans, Brittany Slatton, Rosalind Chou, and Ruth Thompson-Miller for extensive library work and/or summaries of research studies that helped me with this second edition's revisions. I am also in debt to Louwanda Evans for extensive reworking of the index for this edition. I would also like to thank the following scholars for their willingness to read and discuss ideas and research in this manuscript over an extended period of years: Nestor Rodriguez, Jessie Daniels, Terence Fitzgerald, Pinar Batur, Leland Saito, Karyn McKinney, Leslie Houts Picca, Eileen O'Brien, Adia Harvey Wingfield, Jennifer Mueller, Glenn Bracey, Athena Griffith, Chris Chambers, Kristen Lavelle, Rodney Coates, Ken Bolton, Charity Clay, Carla Edwards, Jim Button, William Smith, Greg Squires, Ken Nunn, Mel Sikes, Karen Pyke, Earl Smith, Ray Allen, Christiana Otto, Joseph Rahme, T.R. Young, Tim Wise, Michelle Dunlap, Hsiao-Chuan Hsia, Claire Jean Kim, Sidney Willhelm, Steve Rosenthal, Nancy DiThomaso, John Liu, Kerri Vitalo, Margaret Ronkin, and Laurel Tripp. I would also like to express my gratitude to the hundreds of black women and men, and many other women and men of color, now in two-dozen different field studies and many other consultations, who have explained to my colleagues and me how systemic racism still operates in their everyday lives.

1

Systemic Racism
A Comprehensive Perspective

We the people of the United States, in order to form a more perfect union, establish justice, insure domestic tranquility, provide for the common defense, promote the general welfare, and secure the blessings of liberty to ourselves and our posterity, do ordain and establish this Constitution for the United States of America.

Preamble, U.S. Constitution

The American idea is the nation's holiday garb, its festive dress, its Sunday best. It covers up an everyday practice of betraying the claims of equality, justice, and democracy.

John Hope Franklin

The year is 1787, the place Philadelphia. Fifty-five men are meeting in summer's heat to write a constitution for what will be called the "first democratic nation." These pathbreaking founders create a document so radical in breaking from monarchy and feudal institutions that it will be condemned and attacked in numerous European countries. These determined radicals are all men of European origin, and most are well-off by the standards of their day. Significantly, at least 40 percent have been or are slaveowners, and a significant proportion of the others profit as merchants, shippers, lawyers, and bankers from the trade in slaves, commerce in slave-produced agricultural products, or supplying provisions to slave-holders and slave-traders.[1] The man who pressed hard for this convention and chairs it, George Washington, is one of the very richest men in the colonies because of the hundreds of black men, women, and children he has long held in bondage. Washington and his colleagues create the first "democratic" nation, yet one for whites only. In the preamble to their bold document, the white founders cite prominently "We the People," but this phrase does *not* encompass the fifth of the population that is enslaved or the large indigenous population.

1

Laying a Racist Foundation: the United States

Many historical analysts have portrayed slavery as only a minor matter at the 1787 Constitutional Convention. Yet slavery was central, as a leading participant, James Madison, made clear in his notes on convention debates. Madison accented how the convention was scissored across a slave/not-slave divide among the new states.[2] Southern and northern regions were gradually diverging in their politico-economic frameworks. Slavery had once been of some importance in most areas, but by the late 1700s and early 1800s the northern states were moving away from chattel slavery as a part of their local economies, and some were seeing a growing abolitionist sentiment. Even so, a great many northern white merchants, shippers, and consumers still depended on products produced by southern and border-state slave plantations, and many merchants sold manufactured goods to the slave plantations. Northern shipbuilders and bankers were also central to the slavery economy.

Debates Influenced by Slavery

While all delegates to the Constitutional Convention agreed that the new government should protect private property, and thus existing economic inequality, this white male elite had a right-wing, a center, and a left-wing. The small left-wing, with its strong views on equality and popular revolution, was closest to the general population, and some of its members had dominated the writing of the more radical Declaration of Independence. At the Constitutional Convention, however, the center and the right-wing had more influence. The right-wing even included 21 delegates who desired some form of monarchy. The left-wing and center were able to successfully counter this desire for monarchy, for that seemed unacceptable to the majority of the population. In numerous provisions the final document was oriented to political liberty: there was agreement on rejecting religious tests for office and an established religion, on protecting freedom of debate in Congress, and on protecting citizens from much arbitrary government. Even so, many conservative and center delegates at the convention were anti-democratic in their thinking, fearing "the masses." Thus, the left-wing of this white elite was unable to add a specific list of individual rights to the Constitution, and some states did not ratify the new document until their populations were persuaded that a democratic Bill of Rights would be added.[3]

The trade in, and enslavement of, people of African descent was an important and divisive issue for the convention. Almost all of these prominent, generally well-educated men accepted the view that people of African descent could be the chattel property of others—and were not human beings with citizens' rights. At the heart of the Constitution was protection of the property and wealth of the affluent bourgeoisie in the new nation, including property in those enslaved. There was near unanimity on the idea, as delegate Gouverneur Morris (New York) put it, that property is the "main object of Society." For the founders, freedom meant the protection of unequal accumulation of property, particularly property that could produce a profit in the emerging capitalist system. This was not just a political gathering with the purpose of creating a major new bourgeois-democratic government; it was also a meeting to protect the racial and economic interests of men with substantial property and wealth in the colonies. As historian Herbert Aptheker has put it, the Constitution was a "bourgeois-democratic document for the governing of a slaveholder-capitalist republic."[4]

The harsh reality of slavery conditions and the often death-dealing slave trade hung over the convention like a demonic specter. Slavery intruded on important debates, perhaps most centrally on debates over representation in Congress. Northern and southern delegates vigorously argued the matter and reached the famous three-fifths compromise on counting those enslaved for the purpose of *white* representation. Article 1 speaks only of three groups in the new nation: "free persons," "Indians not taxed," and "all other persons." The "other" persons were those enslaved, mostly of African descent. Whether free or enslaved, African Americans were not to be citizens or voters, yet 60 percent of their number could be counted to enlarge white representation in the states. Interestingly, the earlier Articles of Confederation had used the term "white" in setting the formula for enumerating the country's population. The new Constitution made use of the Confederation's language in this regard but without the word "white."[5]

One delegate from Pennsylvania, James Wilson, questioned the three-fifths compromise; he did not see

> on what principle the admission of blacks in the proportion of three-fifths could be explained. Are they admitted as Citizens? Then why are they not admitted on an equality with White Citizens? Are they admitted as property? Then why is not other property admitted into the computation?[6]

The answer, however, was clear. Enslaved blacks were to be counted as human beings only when it suited whites to do so. Otherwise, they were just white property. Some framers of the Constitution realized that they were divesting black people of their humanity. After the convention, the *Federalist Papers* supported the compromise thus:

> Let the case of the slaves be considered as it is in truth, a peculiar one. Let the compromising expedient of the Constitution be mutually adopted, which regards them as inhabitants, but as debased

by servitude below the equal level of free inhabitants; which regards the slave as *divested of two fifths of the man.*[7]

The new country formed by European Americans in the late eighteenth century was openly viewed as a white republic. These founders sought to build a racially based republic in the face of monarchical opposition and against those people on the North American continent they defined as inferior. James Madison, who himself enslaved many black Americans, put it this way: "Next to the case of the black race within our bosom, that of the red on our borders is the problem most baffling to the policy of our country."[8]

The concerns of slaveholders would appear again and again in debates over taxation, the presidency, commerce, and other matters. For example, there were two days of debates over the importation of enslaved Africans into the colonies. A compromise was reached and placed in Article 1, Section 9. This section allowed the brutal trade to continue until at least 1807.[9] At the convention a few delegates spoke critically of chattel slavery or the slave trade. George Mason, himself a prominent Virginia slaveholder, blamed the slave trade on the greed of British merchants. He noted the threat of slave uprisings and argued that slavery made poor whites lazy. As Mason saw it, "every master of slaves is born a petty tyrant." Strikingly, however, Mason did not mention slavery's impact on those in chains.[10] He and delegate Elbridge Gerry (Massachusetts) would later refuse to sign the document, in part because of its slavery provisions. Yet their objections were not moral but political. Mason feared that the continuing slave trade would make the new United States "more vulnerable" and less capable of defense.[11] Not one of the 55 delegates advocated that the abolition of slavery and freedom for all Americans should be an integral part of the new Constitution. On key votes most northern delegations voted with southern delegations, in part because the trade in enslaved workers and slave-produced products was generally of economic benefit to northern traders and merchants.

The "Most Prominent Feature"

In one of the vigorous debates touching on slavery, the wealthy Gouverneur Morris noted cogently that "domestic slavery is the most prominent feature in the aristocratic countenance of the proposed Constitution."[12] By the end of the summer of 1787 there were at least seven sections where the framers had the system of slavery clearly in mind:

1. Article 1, Section 2, which counts slaves as three-fifths of a person;

2. Article 1, Sections 2 and 9, which apportion taxes on the states using the three-fifths formula;

3. Article 1, Section 8, which gives Congress authority to suppress slave and other insurrections;

4. Article 1, Section 9, which prevents the slave trade from being abolished before 1808;

5. Article 1, Sections 9 and 10, which exempt goods made by slaves from export duties;

6. Article 4, Section 2, which requires the return of fugitive slaves; and

7. Article 4, Section 4, which stipulates that the federal government must help state governments put down domestic violence, including slave uprisings.[13]

The founders were generally aware of the oppressiveness of the slavery from which they profited. In spite of their freedom to speak, read, and do business in the colonies, they and other whites often described their *own* sociopolitical condition as one of actual or potential "slavery." Ironically, many publications of the revolutionary period compared whites' colonial conditions under the British king to black enslavement. As early as 1774, George Washington noted the crisis over colonists' rights in this way:

> The crisis is arrived when we must assert our rights, or submit to every imposition, that can be heaped upon us, till custom and use shall make us tame and abject slaves, as the blacks we rule over with such arbitrary sway.[14]

One convention delegate, John Dickinson, expressed the common view: "*Those* who are *taxed* without their own consent, expressed by themselves or their representatives, are *slaves. We are taxed* without our own consent, expressed by ourselves or our representatives. We are therefore— SLAVES."[15] Dickinson was at one time the largest slaveholder in Philadelphia. Dickinson, Washington, and other white leaders described slavery as creating people who would be cowardly and inferior.

Generally, the founders viewed Americans from Africa as slaves by *natural law*. Natural law was also used to explain why the white male founders and their compatriots could subordinate two other large groups—white women and Native Americans. White women were not directly mentioned in the Constitution, and their legal rights under local and national laws were limited. In Article 1 of the Constitution, the section dealing with Congress regulating interstate and foreign commerce adds relations with "Indian tribes," indicating that indigenous peoples were not generally seen by the founders as part of their new nation. Until the mid- to late-nineteenth century, indigenous societies were generally viewed as separate nations, with some whites advocating treaty-making, land purchases, and the "civilizing" of indigenous Americans while others pressed for land theft, extermination, or removal of all indigenous Americans to the distant western areas.[16]

A House Founded on Racism

Antiblack racism is centrally about the lived experiences and interactions of black and white Americans. Historical events reflect and embed the tangible realities of everyday life—the means of concrete oppression and the means of symbolizing and thinking about that oppression. Every day in the U.S. many politicians, columnists, teachers, lawyers, executives, and ordinary Americans cite the U.S. Constitution, and the founders' actions, as the glory of U.S. society. The founders' decisions and understandings still shape our lives in many ways.

An "Agreement with Hell"?

The U.S. Constitutional Convention, the first such in the democratic history of the modern world, laid a strong base for the new societal "house" called the United States. Yet, from the beginning, this house's foundation was fundamentally flawed. While most Americans have thought of this document and the sociopolitical structure it created as keeping the nation together, in fact this structure was created to maintain racial separation and oppression at the time and for the foreseeable future. The framers reinforced and legitimated a system of racial oppression that they thought would ensure that whites, especially men of means, would rule for centuries.

The system they created was riddled with social contradictions that have surfaced repeatedly over the course of U.S. history. By the 1840s, for example, many black and white abolitionists were aggressively protesting slavery and the constitutional document undergirding it. Before this period there had been white antislavery advocates—black Americans, of course, had advocated abolition from the beginning—but large-scale action against the slavery system did not take place until the nineteenth century. At one 1843 meeting of the Massachusetts Antislavery Society, a resolution was adopted: "Resolved, that the Compact which exists between the North and the South is a 'covenant with death, and an agreement with hell'—involving both parties in atrocious criminality—and should be immediately annulled." At a gathering in Massachusetts on July 4, 1854, the eminent abolitionist William Lloyd Garrison burned a copy of the U.S. Constitution, uttering the words: "So perish all compromises with tyranny."[17]

The "Normality" of Slavery

Then, as now, this was not the prevailing view. Indeed, in the first two centuries of the new country most European Americans, in spite of a professed ethic of liberty, implemented or accepted the brutal subordination of black Americans and the driving away or killing of indigenous peoples. Religious leaders like Cotton Mather, the famous Puritan, and William Penn, a Quaker and founder of Pennsylvania, owned black Americans. The founder of U.S. psychiatry, Dr. Benjamin Rush, owned a black American. Men of politics like Thomas Jefferson, George Washington, Alexander Hamilton, Patrick Henry, Benjamin Franklin, John Hancock, and Sam Houston enslaved black Americans. Ten U.S. presidents (Washington, Jefferson, James Madison, James Monroe, Andrew Jackson, John Tyler, James Polk, Zachary Taylor, Andrew Johnson, and Ulysses S. Grant) at some point enslaved African Americans.[18]

Many at the head of the new United States supported, or were not uncomfortable with, the idea of a *permanent* slave society. Even the first Republican president, Abraham Lincoln, often called the "Great Emancipator," was willing to support a constitutional amendment making slavery permanent in the existing southern states if that would prevent a civil war. Such a projected pro-slavery amendment was supported by many Republicans and was actually approved by the U.S. Congress in early 1861. Indeed, from the 1780s to the Civil War period, some slaveholders articulated grand visions of expanding the U.S. slavery system across the continent and the globe.[19]

The combination of white freedom and black enslavement seems radically contradictory. Historian William Wiecek notes that "the paradox dissolves when we recall that North American slavery was racial. White freedom was entirely compatible with black enslavement."[20] Indeed, the work of those enslaved brought the wealth and leisure that whites, especially in the ruling elite, could use to pursue their own liberty. Various U.S. analysts have argued that it is unfair to judge early white enslavers by contemporary standards. However, not only were there many outspoken black opponents of slavery in this early era, there were numerous opponents of slavery among whites. For example, one of the most wealthy slaveowners in the colonies, Robert Carter III, freed all 500 of the African Americans he enslaved, for he had come to view slavery as "contrary to the principles of religion and justice."[21] Robert Carter was well-known to Thomas Jefferson, James Madison, and George Washington, the most prominent slaveholders among the founders. They just ignored the views and examples before them *in their own time.* In addition, the founders themselves sometimes exhibited guilt over slavery. James Madison himself argued that it would be wrong to state openly in the Constitution the "idea that there could be property in men."[22] As a result, the words "slave" and "slavery" do not appear there, but are replaced with euphemistic terminology in the U.S. Constitution's sections dealing with the slavery system.

Into the mid-nineteenth century, most whites—in the elites and among ordinary folk—participated directly in slavery or the economic trade around slavery, or did not object to those who did so. The antihuman savagery of slavery was considered *normal* in what was seen as a white republic. This point must be understood well if one is to probe deeply into the origins, maintenance, and persistence of racist patterns and institutions in North America. The savvy W.E.B. Du Bois put this forcefully in summing up European **colonialism** in the Americas and elsewhere, saying:

> There was no Nazi atrocity—concentration camps, wholesale maiming and murder, defilement of women and ghastly blasphemy of childhood—which the Christian civilization of Europe had not long been practicing against colored folk in all parts of the world in the name of and for the defense of a Superior Race born to rule the world.[23]

A Continuing Foundation

European colonialism and imperialism eventually reached much of the globe and created a *global racial order*, which has had severe consequences for the world's peoples for centuries. The U.S. Constitution, which embraced slavery and imbedded the global racist order in the U.S., remains the nation's legal, political, and—to a substantial degree—moral foundation. Its openly racist provisions, though overridden by later constitutional amendments, have not been deleted. At no point has a new, truly democratic Constitutional Convention been held to replace this document with one created by representatives of all the people, including the great majority of the U.S. population not represented at the 1787 Convention. Moreover, the racist spirit and impact of the original document persists today. Even as they live in, and often maintain, a racist system, most white Americans still do not see slavery, legal segregation, or contemporary racism as part of the nation's continuing foundation. At the most, the majority see racist institutions as something in the distant past, something tacked on to a great nation for a short time, and something non-systemic. From their perspective the serious racism that may have once intruded into the U.S. house has been substantially eradicated.

Conceptualizing Systemic Racism

A Rich Conceptual Tradition

The black intellectual tradition is a rich source for developing a more accurate and systemic view of this U.S. house of racism. Drawing on analyses of Frederick Douglass, W.E.B. Du Bois, Oliver Cox, Anna Julia Cooper, Kwame Ture, among others, I accent here a conceptual framework understanding this white racism as centuries-long, deep-lying, institutionalized, and systemic. As I suggested in the Preface, systemic racism includes a diverse assortment of racist practices: the unjustly gained economic and political power of whites; the continuing resource inequalities; the rationalizing white-racist frame; and the major institutions created to preserve white advantage and power.

Frederick Douglass was one of the first analysts to develop a conceptual approach accenting institutionalized racism. In 1881, speaking about the ubiquitous impact of racist prejudice and discrimination, he argued that

> in nearly every department of American life [black Americans] are confronted by this insidious influence. It fills the air. It meets them at the work-shop and factory, when they apply for work. It meets them at the church, at the hotel, at the ballot-box, and worst of all, it meets them in the jury-box ... [the black American] has ceased to be a *slave of an individual*, but has in some sense become *the slave of society*.[24]

No longer did a small group of slaveholders hold black Americans in chains; the *total racist society* held them in bondage. This broad conception of racism permeated Douglass's later speeches and writings. By the late 1800s and early 1900s, drawing on the black experience and intellectual tradition, W.E.B. Du Bois was working from a conceptual perspective viewing U.S. society as pervaded by racism across major institutions. He was probably the first social scientist to analyze the emergence of the dominant idea of whiteness and of a white-racist order extending beyond the United States. Writing of the years around 1900, Du Bois argued:

> White supremacy was all but world-wide. Africa was dead, India conquered, Japan isolated, and China prostrate.... The using of men for the benefit of masters is no new invention of modern Europe.... But Europe proposed to apply it on a scale and with an elaborateness of detail of which no former world ever dreamed.[25]

In this era, Anna Julia Cooper and Ida B. Wells-Barnett, important black activists and sociological thinkers, articulated not only an antiracist perspective, but also a clear view of character of white oppression of black men and women. As Wells-Barnett put it, black Americans have faced the "unbridled power exercised for two and a half centuries, by the white man over the

Negro," which during the Reconstruction and segregation eras after the Civil War showed itself in the "acts of conscienceless outlawry" called lynchings.[26]

The first extended analysis of U.S. society as a system of racism was probably that of Oliver Cox, who provided in the 1940s a book-length argument showing how sustained labor exploitation of black Americans created a centuries-old structure of "racial classes." In the case of African Americans, the white elite decided "to proletarianize a whole people—that is to say, the whole people is looked upon as a class—whereas white proletarianization involves only a section of the white people."[27] By the 1960s black activists and scholars were developing the institutional-racism perspective further. Drawing on Du Bois, Kwame Ture and Charles Hamilton demonstrated in empirical and theoretical detail the importance of institutionalized racism—patterns of racism built into this society's major institutions, the discriminatory patterns involving much more than actions of scattered bigots. Moreover, by the late 1960s a few white scholars and analysts were also moving in the direction of accenting institutional racism. These race-critical black and white analysts saw racism as much more than demons in white minds, for white racism entails a complex array of racialized relationships developed over many generations and imbedded in all major societal institutions.[28]

Historically, the social-science study of racial oppression has often been identified by such terms as "intergroup relations" or "race relations." These somewhat ambiguous and euphemistic phrases are accented by many analysts who prefer to view an array of racial groups as more or less responsible for the U.S. "race problem." Such terminology, however, can allow the spotlight to be taken off the whites who have most centrally created and maintained the system of racism. In the North American case, systemic racism began with European colonists enriching themselves substantially at the expense of indigenous peoples and the Africans they imported for enslavement. This brutally executed enrichment was part of the new society's foundation.

In the rest of this chapter we will examine briefly some key aspects of systemic racism, including:

1. the patterns of **unjust impoverishment** and **unjust enrichment** and their transmission over time;
2. the resulting vested group interests and the alienating racist relations;
3. the costs and burdens of racism;
4. the important role of white elites;
5. the rationalization of racial oppression in a white-racist framing; and
6. the continuing resistance to racism.

Undeserved Impoverishment and Enrichment

Analyzing Europe's extensive colonization of Africa, Du Bois demonstrated that extreme poverty and degradation in the African colonies was "a main cause of wealth and luxury in Europe. The results of this poverty were disease, ignorance, and crime. Yet these had to be represented as natural characteristics of backward peoples."[29] The unjust and brutal exploitation of African labor and land had long been downplayed in most historical accounts of European affluence. By bringing the unjust impoverishment of Africa back into the picture, Du Bois provided evidence that this impoverishment was directly and centrally linked to European prosperity and affluence. A similar connection needs to be made between the immiseration and impoverishment of African Americans and the enrichment and prosperity of European Americans.

Several scholars have suggested extending the idea of *unjust enrichment*, an idea taken from the Anglo-American legal tradition, to discuss the reality and impact of racial oppression.[30] Unjust enrichment is an old legal term associated with relationships between individuals. One legal dictionary defines the concept as "circumstances which give rise to the obligation of restitution, that is, the receiving and retention of property, money, or benefits which in justice and equity belong to another."[31] This legal concept encompasses not only the receiving of benefits that justly belong to another but also the obligation to make restitution for that injustice. This idea can be extended beyond individual relationships envisioned in the traditional legal argument to the unjust theft of labor or resources by one group, such as white Americans, from another group, such as black Americans. I suggest here the parallel idea of *unjust impoverishment* to describe the conditions of those who suffer such oppression. For many generations the exploitation of African Americans has redistributed income and wealth earned by them (as slave laborers or segregated workers) to generations of white Americans, leaving the former relatively impoverished as a group and the latter relatively privileged and affluent as a group.

Occasionally, some influential white Americans have been able to see some of the scale of this unjust enrichment for African Americans. Thus, in his brief Second Inaugural Address in 1865, not long before he was assassinated, President Abraham Lincoln made this perceptive commentary on whites' ill-gotten wealth and its consequences. He noted that, at the beginning of the Civil War,

> One-eighth of the whole population were colored slaves ... localized in the southern part of it. These slaves constituted a peculiar and powerful interest. All knew that this interest was somehow the cause of the war.... It may seem strange that any men should dare to ask a

just God's assistance in wringing their bread from the sweat of other men's faces, but let us judge not, that we be not judged.[32]

Lincoln here clearly noted the way in which some whites' prosperity had been generated off the sweat of black faces.

Racial Classes with Vested Group Interests

Understanding how this undeserved impoverishment and enrichment gets transmitted and institutionalized over generations of white and black Americans is an important step in developing an adequate conceptual framework for U.S. racism. Black labor was widely and unjustly used for building up the wealth of this white-dominated country from the 1600s to at least the 1960s—the slavery and Jim Crow segregation periods. Black Americans as a group were proletarianized to build up white prosperity. Racial classes (groups) are the rungs on the racist ladder and have divergent group interests.

Arising in Middle English, the word "interest" (literally "to be between") originally meant a share in something. A *group interest* can now be seen as a relation of being objectively concerned in something, of having a stake in something. Thus, whites are strong *stakeholders* in a centuries-old hierarchical structure of opportunities, wealth, and privileges that stems from a long history of racial exploitation and oppression. The interests of the white racial group have included not only a concrete interest in labor and other exploitation during the slavery and segregation periods, but also a concrete interest later on in maintaining the substantial economic and other social privileges inherited from white ancestors.

The racial hierarchy, initially created by the white ruling class, provided benefits to most white Americans. From the seventeenth century onward, the farms and plantations run with enslaved laborers brought significant income and wealth to many white Americans, and not just to their owners. These enterprises multiplied economic development for many whites inside and outside the farms' and plantations' immediate geographical areas (see Chapter 2, pp. 51–53). Ordinary whites, for the most part, bought into the identity of whiteness, thereby binding themselves collectively to the white racial group.

Slavery's impact extended well beyond the economy. Each major institutional arena in the country was controlled by whites and was linked to other major arenas. As we have seen, the new Constitution and its "democratic" political system were grounded in racist thinking and practices of white men, many with strong ties to slavery. Those who dominated the economic system also crafted the political system. Likewise the religious, legal, educational, and media systems were interlinked with the slavery economy and polity. Woven through each institutional area was a broad racist framing centered on rationalizing white-on-black domination and assertively creating positive views of whites and whiteness.

Alienated Racist Relations

Systemic racism involves recurring and unequal relationships between groups and individuals. At the macro-level, large-scale institutions—with their white-controlled normative structures—routinely perpetuate racial subordination and inequalities. These institutions are created and recreated by routine actions at the everyday micro-level by particular individuals. People do not experience "race" in the abstract but in concrete recurring relationships with one another. Individuals, whether perpetrators of discrimination or recipients of discrimination, are caught in a web of alienating racist relations. These socially imbedded relations distort what could be positive and egalitarian relationships into alienated relationships. The racist system categorizes and divides human beings from each other and severely impedes the development of a common consciousness and solidarity. It fractures human nature by separating those socially defined as the "superior race" against those socially defined as the "inferior race." Life under a system of racism involves an ongoing struggle between racially defined human communities—one seeking to preserve its unjustly derived status and privileges and the other seeking to resist or overthrow its continuing oppression.[33]

The alienation associated with racial oppression extends to yet other areas. In the case of black Americans, that which should most be their own—control over their lives and work—is that which is substantially taken away from them by systemic racism. There is a parallel here to the alienation described by analysts of class and gender oppression. In Karl Marx's analysis of capitalism, the workers' labor, that which in one sense is most their own, is that which is most taken away from their control by the capitalist employer. The worker is separated from control over, and thus alienated from, his or her work. In addition, feminist theorists have shown that at the heart of a sexist society is an alienating reality of dehumanized sexuality. Women are separated by intentional and institutional sexism from personal control over how their own sexuality is defined. To lose significant control over one's own life choices, body definition, future, and even self, is what social subordination imposes. Thus, racial oppression forces a life-long struggle by black Americans, as a group and as individuals, to attain their inalienable human rights.[34]

In some theorizing about contemporary inequalities, racial matters have been more or less reduced to issues of class, as in some neo-Marxist work, or to issues of socioeconomic status, as in some work of William Julius Wilson. Many analysts have argued that racism is of declining importance.[35] These positions have been rigorously contested. Michael Omi and Howard Winant have shown with much evidence that "race" cannot be reduced to ethnicity or class, but is an "autonomous field of social conflict, political organization and cultural/ideological meaning."[36]

However, even among those analysts who take contemporary racism seriously, such as Omi and Winant and Robert Miles,[37] there is a bit too much emphasis on the ideological construction of race and/or the formation of racial meanings and identities. While these are certainly important aspects of systemic racism (see Chapters 3 and 4), they are not necessarily the most important. As is clear in chapters that follow, the conceptual framework I accent here is grounded in an understanding of the concrete material advantages whites have gained unjustly over centuries of slavery, segregation, and contemporary racism.

Systemic racism is not just about the construction of racial images, attitudes, and identities. It is centrally about the creation, development, and maintenance of white privilege, economic wealth, and sociopolitical power over nearly four centuries. It is about hierarchical interaction and dominance. The past and present worlds of racism include not only racist relations at work but also the racist relations that black Americans and other Americans of color encounter in trying to secure adequate housing, consumer goods, and public accommodations for themselves and their families. As Cornel West has put it, "Categories are constructed. Scars and bruises are felt with human bodies, some of which end up in coffins. Death is not a construct."[38]

Patterns of Undeserved Enrichment and Impoverishment

Not long ago, Senator Bob Dole, a Republican presidential candidate, spoke in a television interview of "displaced" white men who compete with black workers because of **affirmative action**. He said that he was not sure that "people in America" (he meant "whites") should be paying a price for discrimination that occurred "before they were born." He was candid, saying, "We did discriminate. We did suppress people. It was wrong. Slavery was wrong." Yet Dole added that he was not sure any compensation for this damage was now due.[39] Whites' questioning of the relevance of our racist past to our present society is now commonplace.

Sources of White Wealth: A Vignette

Consider four young children coming into certain North American colonies in the early 1700s. An African brother and sister are ripped from their homes and imported in chains into Virginia, the largest slaveholding colony. Their African names being ignored, they are renamed "negro John" and "negro Mary" (no last name) by the white family that purchased them from a slave ship. This white (Smith) family has young twins, William and Priscilla. Their first and last names are those given to them by their parents, and they never wear chains. The enslaved children are seen and named as "black" by the Smith family, while the twins will live as "white."

What do these children and their descendants have to look forward to? Their experiences will be very different as a result of the system of racist oppression. William's and Priscilla's lives may be hard because of the physical environment, but they and their descendants will likely build lives with an array of personal choices and the passing down of significant social resources. As a girl and later as a woman, Priscilla will certainly not have the same privileges as William, but her life is more likely to be economically supported and protected than Mary's. Indeed, John and Mary face a stark, often violent existence, with most of their lives determined by the whims of the slaveholder who has stolen not only their labor but their lives. They will never see their families or home societies again. They can be radically separated at any time, a fate much less likely for William and Priscilla. From their labor and other enslaved labor some wealth will be generated for the Smith family and passed to later generations. Unlike the white twins, John and Mary will probably not be allowed to read or write and will be forced to replace their African language with English. Where they work and sleep will be substantially determined by whites. As they grow, major decisions about their personal and family relationships will be made by whites. Mary will face repeated sexual threats, coercion, and violence at the hands of male overseers and slaveholders, perhaps including William. Moreover, if John even looks at Priscilla the wrong way, he is likely to be punished severely.

If John and Mary are later allowed to have spouses and children, they will face a much greater infant mortality rate than whites. And their surviving children may well be taken from them, so that they and later generations may have great difficulty in keeping the full memory of their ancestors, a problem not faced by William and Priscilla. If John or Mary resist oppression, they are likely to be whipped, put in chains, or have an iron bit put in their mouths. If John is rebellious or runs away too much, he may face castration. John and Mary will have to struggle very hard to keep their families together because the slaveholders can destroy them at any moment. Still, together with other black Americans, they build a culture of resistance carried from generation to generation in oral traditions. Moreover, for many more generations John's and Mary's descendants will suffer similarly severe conditions as the property of white families. Few if any of their descendants will see freedom until the 1860s.

The end of slavery does not end the large-scale oppression faced by John's and Mary's descendants. For four more generations after 1865 the near-slavery called legal or de facto segregation will confront them, but will not racially restrict the lives of descendants of William and Priscilla.

The later black generations will be unable to build up significant resources and wealth; they will have their lives substantially determined by the white enforcers of Jim Crow segregation. Where they can get a job, where they can live, whether and where they can go to school, and how they can travel will still be substantially determined by whites. Many will face brutal beatings or lynchings by whites, especially if they resist oppression. They will likely have inherited no wealth from many generations of enslaved ancestors, and they are unlikely to garner much in the way of resources themselves to pass along to later generations. From the early 1700s to the 1960s, John and Mary and their descendants have been at an extreme economic, political, and social disadvantage compared to William and Priscilla Smith and their descendants. The lives of these African Americans have been significantly shortened, their opportunities severely limited, their inherited resources all but non-existent, and their families pressured by generations of well-organized white oppression.

The desegregation era of the 1960s did renew hopes for major changes in the racist system. But the changes came at a great price. For example, the parents of black children were forced to watch them be spat upon by howling mobs of whites seeking to stop racial desegregation. Since the **civil rights movement** forced an end to legal segregation in the 1960s, John's and Mary's descendants have had more opportunity to control their lives and to garner socioeconomic resources. Yet they too have faced large-scale discrimination in employment, housing, and other societal arenas because the 1960s' civil rights laws have often been unenforced. Descendants of William and Priscilla Smith have not faced such racial discrimination, nor have the many whites whose families came into the country after the end of slavery or legal segregation. Over the many generations since the early 1700s, John's and Mary's descendants have usually been unable to build up the economic, educational, and cultural resources necessary to compete effectively with typical white individuals and the significantly greater socioeconomic resources they mostly enjoy.

From this brief vignette we can begin to see how racial oppression is economically and systematically constructed. Unjust impoverishment for John and Mary and undeserved enrichment for William and Priscilla become bequeathed inheritances for many later generations. Undeserved impoverishment and enrichment are at the heart of colonial land theft from indigenous societies and the brutal slavery system targeting people of African descent. Over time this ill-gotten gain has been used and invested by white colonizers and their descendants to construct a prosperous white-dominated country. Today there is often a denial in the white population that African Americans have contributed substantially to American (or Western) development and civilization. However, the facts are clear: the slavery system provided much stimulus for economic development and generated critical surplus capital for the new nation. As we will see in Chapter 2, without the enslaved labor of millions of black Americans, there might well not be a prosperous United States today.

Extorting More Resources: Legal Segregation

Once in place, oppressive institutions have demonstrated great social inertia and persistence. When the Civil War and the Thirteenth Amendment to the U.S. Constitution put an end to African American enslavement, systemic racism soon took the form of officially sanctioned segregation. Like slavery, widespread segregation was implemented under the cover of law. Extensive Jim Crow segregation of free African Americans—in employment, housing, the justice system, and politics— had already been invented in the North in the 1700s and early 1800s. It was firmly in place there when southern elites adopted it.[40]

The Thirteenth Amendment abolished slavery but did not abolish the new racial barriers faced by those formerly enslaved. After the Civil War, the status of being enslaved by an individual master was replaced by a condition of being a "slave to white society," in the North and the South. Access to significant wealth-building resources was for the most part not open to the technically "free" African Americans. In contrast, whites coming of age in the century between the end of slavery and the 1960s—including recent immigrants—were mostly able to accumulate significant family resources or individual opportunities, unfairly and very disproportionately, because there was little or no black competition for many important socioeconomic resources and opportunities. As we will see later, these resources and opportunities included, among other things, decent-paying jobs, quality educations, good farm land, oil leases, airline routes, radio and television frequencies, and good housing areas. The new barriers of racial segregation were regularly enforced by individual whites and organized white violence, including police brutality, house burnings, beatings, and lynchings.

Contemporary Racism: More Enrichment and Impoverishment

With the end of Jim Crow segregation in the 1960s came some changes in the operation of systemic racism. For the first time African Americans had, at least officially, access to many areas of the economy and larger society off-limits to them for centuries. However, the political and legal changes of the contemporary era have by no means eradicated white-imposed racism as the foundation of the U.S. "house." Since the 1960s, racial oppression has persisted in the form of widespread discrimination against African Americans and numerous other Americans of color—often in violation of U.S. civil rights laws. To make matters worse, these laws have often been weakly enforced. Some continuing oppression of black Americans is more covert or subtle than in the past, and this can make racist practices more difficult to see for those who are not the targets. Nonetheless, racism is still systemic and webbed across all sectors of this society. Whites still dominate almost every major organization and most major resources, be they economic, political, educational, or legal. And official violence against African Americans can still be seen in recurring instances of police malpractice and brutality.

In Chapters 5–7, I provide much detail in regard to the current racial discrimination targeting African Americans and its advantages for whites. Here we can briefly note one example: like the legally segregated economy of the 1950s, the contemporary economy channels many black Americans into certain types of jobs and away from other types of employment. Many do not have access to good-paying jobs—or face unemployment—because of intentional discrimination in the job market or because of the use of certain screening barriers by white employers that reflect the lack of access by black workers to white-dominated job networks or to adequate job training or educational programs. Today, many low-wage service and unskilled menial jobs are held by African Americans or other people of color who regularly service white managers, white employers, or white skilled workers. As Iris Young explains, "These jobs entail a transfer of energies whereby the servers enhance the status of those served."[41] In addition, even those black workers who do secure good-paying jobs still face numerous other discriminatory hurdles such as hostile workplace climates and discrimination in promotions. Over time, thus, employment discrimination has serious consequences that take the form of yet more undeserved impoverishment for black workers and their families, and yet more unfair enrichment for white workers and their families. Today, the mechanisms of racial discrimination and de facto segregation continue to operate in major areas of U.S. society.

Social Reproduction: Transmitting Wealth over Generations

How does prior wealth and privilege, however gained in one generation, translate into wealth and privilege for later generations? And what are the main forms of socioeconomic resources that are transmitted? More generally, how is the societal system of racial inequality reproduced as a whole? An inter-temporal perspective on racial discrimination and related oppression is critical to a comprehensive understanding of the development and structure of U.S. society. I accent here the concept of the *social reproduction* of racial oppression.

For systemic racism to persist across many human generations, it must reproduce well and routinely the necessary socioeconomic conditions. These conditions include substantial control by whites of major economic resources and possession of the political, police, and ideological power to dominate subordinated racial groups. Systemic racism is perpetuated by social processes that reproduce not only racial inequality but also the fundamental racist relation—on the one hand, the racially oppressed, and on the other, the racial oppressors. This alienated relationship, which undergirds the racial hierarchy, is reproduced across all areas of societal life, from one neighborhood to the next, from one generation to the next.

The perpetuation of systemic racism requires an *inter-temporal* reproducing of a variety of important organizational structures and institutional and ideological processes. These structures and processes are critical to sustaining racial inequalities. Reproduced over time are racially structured institutions, such as economic institutions that embed the exploitation of black labor and the legal and political institutions that protect that exploitation and extend oppression into other arenas of societal life. Each new generation inherits the established organizational structures that protect unjust enrichment and unjust impoverishment. Important too is the reproduction from one generation to the next of the interpretive and ideological apparatus, the **white racial frame** (see below, pp. 25–26) that rationalizes and legitimates racial oppression.

By the 1700s, slavery was well-entrenched and profitable for a great many whites, including slaveholders and those servicing or trading with slave farms and plantations. After the initiation of slavery, the next step was its perpetuation and maintenance, not only in terms of meeting the internal requirements but also in terms of countering challenges. Much effort went into reinforcing and expanding this oppressive system. Numerous laws were passed; courts were used to sustain it. Slave insurrections had to be protected against, so white patrols were created to police those enslaved. The political system, including its founding documents, was shaped in response to the need to protect this slavery economy. This oppressive political-economic system was succeeded, in the late nineteenth century, by the near-slavery of Jim Crow.

For many generations this deeply imbedded system of racial inequality has been regularly reproduced. Today, most whites underestimate the degree to which the United States remains a very racist society. They underestimate the extent of white racial privileges and resources and the degree to which these privileges and resources have been passed down from their predecessors. Social inheritance mechanisms are imbedded in society and disguised to make inter-temporal inheritance appear fair. Each new generation of whites has inherited an array of racial privileges and resources. Over time, the majority of whites inherit some economic resources—often in the form of house equity or family savings—or other resources such as access to job training or a good education.

For example, recent Federal Reserve studies show huge differentials in household wealth between white and black families (see Chapter 6,

p. 20). White families' net worth is now about *ten-times* that of black families' net worth, with much of that in housing equities built up over generations of discrimination severely limiting black access to housing and other socioeconomic resources. For example, almost all the home mortgages provided on a large scale to soldiers returning after World War II went to white soldiers and their families. Mortgage and other housing discrimination was commonplace and open until the late 1960s. And much housing discrimination has continued, if often more subtly and covertly, since that decade. Most significantly, the white wealth built up in these housing equities has often been passed along to children and grandchildren.[42]

Even the relatively poor immigrants from southern and eastern Europe in the early 1900s were, within a generation or so, defined as "white." Although they faced some initial discrimination, they and their descendants benefited greatly from the far more extensive racial discrimination then restricting black Americans. These new whites often participated in that antiblack discrimination. In a generation or two, they or their descendants were able to move up economically, politically, and socially. This is a striking societal result, given the fact that the average black American then (as now) had ancestors going back several more generations in this country's history than these relatively new white Americans.[43]

Not only do most whites today benefit from inheritance of some, or a lot of, economic and cultural wealth from ancestors who profited from slavery or legal segregation, but most also benefit from contemporary racist patterns—the job, housing, political, educational, and other discrimination that still gives them and their children significant advantages over black Americans. While white Americans vary by class and gender in the scale of these **white privileges** and inherited wealth, most in all walks of life have benefited to some degree from white privileges and resources (see Chapter 6, pp. 190–200). Note too that the vital resources inherited by a great many whites over time also include educational and other cultural wealth. Edward Ball, a slaveholder's descendant, has noted, "If we did not inherit money, or land, we received a great fund of cultural capital, including prestige, a chance at an education, self-esteem, a sense of place, mobility, even (in some cases) a flair for giving orders."[44] Interestingly, Ball is one of several white descendants of powerful slaveholding families who have recently acknowledged the substantial inheritances they gained from their slaveholding ancestors.

The Extraordinary Costs and Burdens of Racism

Unjustly gained wealth and privilege for whites is often linked directly to undeserved immiseration for black Americans. This was true for many past generations, and it remains true for today's generations. What does it cost to be black in the United States? Government reports regularly repeat the grim statistics: the average black person has *a life expectancy four to six years (female/male) less* than the average white person. An average black family earns *less than two-thirds the income* of an average white family— *and has about 10 percent of the economic net worth* of an average white family. These data signal the cumulative cost of white racism for black Americans.

Acts of oppression are not just immediately harmful, but carry long-term effects. In the social-science literature, much has been made of the impact of historical racism on black families, subculture, or values, sometimes as part of a blame-the-victim perspective. At least as important is the impact of systemic racism on the social, economic, political, and educational resources and opportunities available to black individuals and families for ten-to-fifteen generations. If the members of a group suffer serious bars to securing the resources necessary for achievement and mobility, this not only restricts their own achievements but also shapes the opportunities of descendants for generations to come.[45]

When men and women of color do not have significant and equivalent access to inherited savings or other economic resources, or to cultural capital such as a good education, or to important job skills because of blatant or subtle discrimination, they usually cannot prosper like more privileged whites. And they and their descendants will likely have a serious and persisting disadvantage relative to whites. Thus, researchers have shown that the cumulative lack of wealth for black families often has a serious impact on children. One recent analysis examined the amount of time that the average black, white, and Latino child is likely to spend growing up in a substantially impoverished neighborhood. The study estimated that the average black child spends about half his or her first 18 years in such impoverished neighborhoods. This compares to about 40 percent of these years for average Latino children, but only 5 percent of these years for average white children. Being born in such an impoverished neighborhood was found to be the most determinative factor for spending much of one's youth there. Parental mobility in and out of such neighborhoods was a factor, but not as important as just being born there.[46]

The value of having money and other economic resources in hand is critical, for once a group is far ahead in terms of resources it is very difficult for another group without access to those resources, or even with modest new resources, to catch up, even over a substantial period of time. When entry to employment, education, or business is blocked by slavery, legal segregation, or widespread informal discrimination today, African Americans have infinite entry costs. Even if these racial barriers are removed at some later point, and African Americans are finally allowed to enter once exclusively white societal arenas, they will likely enter with more significant resource and operational problems, including higher personal or business costs, than whites who have not faced massive discrimination in the past or present (see Chapter 6, pp. 200–212). Moreover, for African Americans and other Americans of color, everyday racism generally involves not only living with fewer socioeconomic resources, but also enduring the consciousness that grows out of and reflects on racially oppressive conditions.

Most theories about U.S. racial matters do not take seriously enough the existential perspective of the oppressed others, their everyday experiential intelligence. When black men, women, and children speak of being black in a country largely controlled at the top by whites, they typically do not speak in abstract concepts learned from books, but rather voice accounts of encounters with whites. Take this account from an interview with a black woman, a dental assistant, who describes a black child's experience:

> [An] incident happened to my girlfriend's daughter about a month or so ago. She's in a Christian school. And the teacher told the kids that black, black children are born with their sin. And the little girl went home and she asked her mother, she said, "Sit down," and told her mother. She said, "I just wish I was white." And she's only nine, she's nine.… And [the] little girl had said what the teacher had said, and she said, "Black people were born of sin, let's pray for the black people." And now the little girl is really scarred, but you don't know how scarred … and that kind of stuff makes you angry. You take a little child that doesn't know anything about prejudice, and this is the way you plant it … in all these little white children's heads.[47]

The white teacher in this religious elementary school appears to be drawing on one of the oldest explanations of black inferiority, the mythological story of Noah condemning his black son Ham's descendants to be the servants of whites (see Chapter 3, p. 63). We see here the operation of the racialized hierarchy of power—the perhaps unthinking use of a white person's power to cause a black child and the adults who love her much damage.

We see too that racism is a *lived* experience. Racist relations recur frequently in the lives of most black Americans. Whites generate much pain, frustration, stress, and anger. We see the white-generated alienation of a black child from herself, and perhaps from her community. Racism means that what should be most her own, the control of her self and identity, is what is often taken away. This account suggests that theories of racial oppression should take seriously the life experiences and experiential intelligence of black Americans and other Americans of color. They know well the oppressive world that hits them in the face on a routine basis. This gives them a well-developed knowledge base from which they can develop sophisticated, and usually collective, understandings of racism.

White Elites and Ordinary Whites: The Public Wage of Whiteness

European and European American elites began the large-scale exploitation of the labor of African Americans and the land of Native Americans. Ever since, white elites have acted aggressively to create or maintain the social, economic, and political organizations and institutions, as well as conceptual framing, that reflect their interests. The actions of white economic elites—originally composed of slaveholders, traders, and merchants, but later of industrialists and other entrepreneurs—and political elites are critical for the creation and maintenance of the racist system. White elites crafted and reworked the system at critical junctures in U.S. history, and were central to its rationalization. Significantly, the makeup of those drafting the U.S. Constitution is similar to the demographic makeup of those who still disproportionately dominate the top positions in most sectors of U.S. society today.

For several centuries, most whites not in the elites have accepted the society's racist hierarchy because of their access to the privileges, opportunities, and cultural resources associated with being white and because they have bought heavily into a white-racist framing of society. Thus, white workers have accepted what W.E.B. Du Bois once called the "public and **psychological wage**" of whiteness, instead of the greater economic wages and better working conditions they might have had if they had joined over the last century in strong worker and other organizations with black workers.[48] In the United States, unlike in numerous European capitalist countries, class consciousness among white workers has to a substantial degree been lessened by a strong racial consciousness (see Chapter 6, pp. 215–216).

By the late seventeenth century many in the colonial elites were concerned about the resistance of white laborers and small farmers to elite rule. Critical to the development of the colonial economic system was the problem of labor. At first, the farmers who worked on a large scale made use of significant numbers of white laborers, the property-less European immigrants who were often indentured servants. These white servants and laborers revolted a number of times against social class oppression. Sometimes they were joined by enslaved African Americans, as in Nathaniel Bacon's Rebellion in 1676, against the elite administration of the colonies. Indeed, the possibility of such biracial coalitions was a serious concern among white elites. Out of this fear was born, at least in part, the extension to property-less whites of certain privileges of whiteness, as well as an extensive racist framing rationalizing white superiority. The creation of a system in which only Americans of color could be enslaved was coupled with accenting racial solidarity across the white economic classes.[49]

Just after the Civil War, the elite-crafted social and ideological arrangements that deflected white workers' class consciousness were threatened by the new freedom for ordinary blacks and small white farmers that emerged with the destruction of slavery and the implementation of more democratic governments in the South during the era called Reconstruction. On occasion, blacks and some whites joined again in mutual-aid organizations, such as militant farmers' organizations working for better farming conditions in the late nineteenth century. It was not long, however, before the old elites in the South recovered their positions by aggressively buying off ordinary white farmers and workers with a renewed racist framing of society that made whites of all classes feel racially superior, as well as by the use of violence against African Americans and some white political activists.[50]

This history is important to understanding how systemic racism was perpetuated over time. To a substantial degree, social-class oppression is obscured by the elites' use of a white-racist framing of society and by white workers' fully accepting that framing and the concrete advantages they viewed as stemming from it. Thus, for the most part, white labor leaders in the union movements that expanded from the mid-1800s to the 1960s collaborated in maintaining the system of black workers' exclusion and white workers' racial privileges. White union leaders were often outspoken in their ideological racism and commitment to racially exclusionary barriers. In addition, we should consider some shifts in the last half of the nineteenth century in the views and allegiances of numerous white women who had been active in the abolitionist movements and outspoken against slavery earlier in the century. Once slavery was abolished, and the movement for women's rights accelerated in the late nineteenth century, numerous white leaders in this women's movement dismissed the significant concerns of black women and developed racially segregated political interests and organizations. The majority of the white female leaders in this feminist political movement accepted white racial privileges and the new racist theories of U.S. imperialism at the turn of the twentieth century with little or no questioning.[51]

In later chapters we will observe the intensity of white identity and white-racist attitudes in many aspects of U.S. history and society. A common racial identity has persisted for centuries across class and gender lines. In contrast, there is no similar trans-racial world of workers in which all workers hold a strong and common class identity and loyalty across the racial line. Nor is there a trans-racial world of gender where all women (or all men) hold a strong common identity and loyalty across the color line. Historically, most white workers and most white women have been uninterested in building unity of identity and protest with, respectively, black workers or black women across the color line.

The White Racial Frame: Rationalizing Racial Oppression

Historically, most whites have not been content to exploit African Americans and other Americans of color and then to just admit candidly that such action is crass exploitation for their own individual or group advantage. Instead, white Americans have developed a strong racial frame that interprets and defends white privileges and advantaged conditions as meritorious and accents white virtues as well as the alleged inferiority and deficiencies of those people of color who are oppressed.

In recent decades, cognitive, neurological, and social scientists have developed the idea of a perspectival frame that gets imbedded in individual minds (in the brain's neural networks) and helps people interpret and deal with situations encountered in everyday lives. In their everyday rounds, people use multiple frames, but the one I accent here is the dominant, white-created racial frame that provides an over-arching and racialized worldview extending across divisions of class, gender, and age. Since the seventeenth century, this powerful *white racial frame* has provided the vantage point from which whites and others have regularly viewed and interpreted this society. This broad racial framing includes at least these important dimensions:

1. racial **stereotypes** (a verbal–cognitive aspect);
2. racial narratives and interpretations (integrating cognitive aspects);
3. racial images (a visual aspect) and language accents (an auditory aspect);
4. racialized emotions (a "feelings" aspect); and
5. inclinations to discriminatory action.[52]

As we will see in detail in Chapters 3 and 4, this dominant racial frame includes a socially imbedded set of racial stereotypes, images, and emotions that are widely accepted and critical to maintaining the subordination of black Americans and other Americans of color. Over centuries now, this strong framing has had a very positive orientation to whites and whiteness and a negative orientation to the racial "others" who are oppressed. Early on, this over-arching framing assertively accented a positive view of white superiority, virtue, and moral goodness. Whites have rationalized U.S. society's dominant racial hierarchy by defining "superior" groups who are "justifiably" dominant and "inferior" groups who "deserve" their lower place in society. For most whites, this dominant racial frame is more than one perspectival frame among many. Indeed, it is a worldview that has routinely defined a way of being and acting, a broad perspective on life, and one that provides the language and interpretations that structure, normalize, and make sense out of much in this society. Moreover, almost all Americans, of various racial and other backgrounds, are indoctrinated to some extent in elements of this white racial frame, from their earliest years.

Once developed and imbedded in human minds, the white racial frame did become, and still is, a *concrete force* in Western and global history. Today, as in the past, the impoverishment and enrichment stemming from centuries of slavery, legal segregation, and contemporary racism are rationalized by this extensive framing with its racial myths, prejudices, stereotypes, narratives, and images. We have noted previously how the founders' myths about liberty co-existed with the extreme exploitation and subordination of Native Americans and African Americans. White elites have long been indispensable for this myth-making process, for they have long created or reformulated the central legitimizing frame by means of the mass media, schools, workplaces, legislatures, and churches.

The Central Idea of Whiteness

In the first extended analysis of whiteness, the pioneering book *Darkwater* (1920), sociologist W.E.B. Du Bois noted that

> the discovery of personal whiteness among the world's people is a very modern thing.... The ancient world would have laughed at such a distinction ... we have changed all that, and the world in a sudden, emotional conversion has discovered that it is white and by that token, wonderful![53]

The early articulations of whiteness as a defense of white power and privilege came from slaveholders and others who sought to rationalize slavery. The generally darker skin (early called "black") of Africans was used by white slaveholders and other whites as an early marker of subordinated status. The skin-color imagery was part of a larger conceptual framing among Europeans that had long before viewed most aspects of "blackness" in negative terms, as relating to the devil and darkness. By the late-1600s whiteness, in contrast, stood for "civilization" and advanced "culture" among Europeans and European Americans.[54]

According to Benjamin Franklin, a liberal U.S. founder, the ideal of the virtuous American was grounded in whiteness. "[T]he number of purely white people in the world is proportionably very small," he said. "Why increase the sons of Africa, by planting them in America, where we have so fair an opportunity, by excluding all blacks and tawneys, of increasing the lovely white and red?"[55] Even the political liberals among the founders, those opposed to importing more enslaved Africans, held strong antiblack images and saw their preferences for "lovely white" people as quite normal and natural.

Aggressive Biological Racism

By the late eighteenth century, a virulently racist framing of society had been created, and it came to dominate most white views on "race" for the next two centuries. Images of "lovely whiteness" were soon wedded to a very strong biological racism, a deterministic view that saw white Americans as the biologically and intellectually "superior race" and black Americans as the biologically and intellectually "inferior race." Influential scholars and intellectuals like Immanuel Kant in Europe and Thomas Jefferson in the U.S. lent their authority to the aggressive notion of a hierarchy of "races" (see Chapter 3, pp. 69–70). This reinvigorated biological racism developed by leading Western intellectuals in the late 1700s was spread by newspapers, pamphlets, and pulpits of the day to the general population. Over the course of the eighteenth and nineteenth centuries a strong biological view of a hierarchy of races came to accompany older antiblack views accenting black inferiority in culture, religion, and civilization. As we will see in later chapters, in the early twentieth century the developing motion picture, radio, magazine, and television industries further accelerated the spread of this racist framing of African Americans to all corners of U.S. society and, eventually, the globe.

Today, numerous social scientists and many popular analysts view racism as mainly about racial attitudes, as personal prejudices "directed at people because of their race."[56] They focus on the micro-level of the bigoted individual. Although this conventional perspective recognizes some relational aspects of U.S. racism, it frequently overlooks the point that the prejudices held by individuals are still rooted firmly in an extensive *system* of racism. As Oliver Cox put it, "race prejudice is not an individual idiosyncrasy; it is a social attribute. Ordinarily the individual is born into it and accepts it unconsciously, like his language, without question." Antiblack prejudices have been socially perpetuated as a way of stigmatizing black Americans "as inferior so that the exploitation of either the group itself or its resources or both may be justified."[57] Today, as in the past, antiblack attitudes are deeply imbedded in European American culture and are part of the well-developed white-racist framing that has dominated white society for centuries now.

Resisting Systemic Racism

A comprehensive theory of systemic racism should encompass the dialectical idea that oppression creates the seeds of its own destruction. Historical analysis indicates that racist oppression regularly breeds resistance. Racist structures heavily shape the lives of human beings, but when human agents gain a solid understanding of weaknesses in these structures of oppression, they can use that knowledge to rebel, sometimes successfully.

The social process that reproduces systemic racism has major contradictions. One important contradiction is that racially subordinated groups like black Americans have for some time been allowed access to certain limited resources so that they can survive and be useful to the economy. However, when they have secured some resources beyond subsistence, they have often increased their individual and collective resistance to oppression. Human beings have a unique ability to reflect on their own circumstances and to create, in association with others, a collective consciousness that can lead to social change. Thus, because black women and men have long been at the center of the racist system, their protest consciousness has great potential for re-making or destroying that onerous system. Periodically, changes in the racist system have been forced by the antiracist consciousness and organizational efforts of African Americans. We see evidence of this in the many conspiracies to revolt, and periodic insurrections, of enslaved African Americans that took place between the mid-1600s and the 1850s (see Chapter 8, p. 269). In addition, in the decades before the Civil War, hundreds of thousands of black and white abolitionists organized actively against slavery, thereby helping to bring it down.

Continuing resistance to systemic racism could again be seen in the rise of the Niagara movement and the National Association for the Advancement of Colored People (NAACP) in the early 1900s, which built a strong tradition of legal action and educational efforts against Jim Crow segregation and other racial discrimination (see Chapter 8, pp. 270–272). These movements laid the basis for later civil rights movements that brought some changes in the operation of systemic racism by the 1960s and 1970s. Over their long and arduous history in North America, African Americans have created or participated in many resistance organizations, some of which are still working actively to end systemic racism.

From the beginning, black Americans, as well as other Americans of color, have generally been the theorists of their own experiences with systemic racism, as they have made clear in a long history of antidiscrimination manifestos and protests. In each period of overt struggle by black Americans against racism, the renewed development of antiracist perspectives is often viewed by white Americans with great alarm. Black protest against oppression has encompassed not only overt confrontation with the dominant group but also the development of a critical perspective on the surrounding racist world, an antiracist framing generated from daily fighting domination. Nothing is a clearer thread running through the tapestry of U.S. history than recurring African American struggles against racial oppression.

Conclusion

The United States can be seen in metaphorical terms as a "house" of racism, one with a political-economic foundation firmly built during the first two centuries of colonial development. While many of the founders asserted in the Declaration of Independence and elsewhere that "all men are created equal," they did not mean literally what they said. Their equality and liberty framing was conditional and hypocritical, for it excluded black Americans, indigenous peoples, and white women. The real U.S. foundation was crafted to create wealth and privilege for those transplanted Europeans who stole the lands of the indigenous peoples and enslaved African labor. In this process, Europeans and European Americans came to frame themselves and their society as a "white" republic.

Since this house of racial domination was created, it has periodically been remodeled. We observe remodeling in the Reconstruction period after the Civil War and again during and after the 1950s–1960s civil rights movement. When progressive changes have come in the racist system, white elites—always with debate and divisions among themselves—have typically worked to make the least significant changes possible under conditions of mass protest. Never have elites been interested in changes that would be substantial enough to build a new non-racist foundation and political-economic structure. Thus, under pressure from black and white abolitionists, and reacting to the impact of the Civil War, the liberal wing of the white leadership finally saw to it that slavery was abolished in the 1860s by an amendment to the U.S. Constitution. However, in spite of this constitutional eradication of slavery, no new constitutional convention was called so that a new governing document could be democratically written with the participation of all Americans, including those newly freed from enslavement. Moreover, the white elites created, in the North and South, a new system of near slavery called Jim Crow segregation. Every major sector of U.S. society—the economy, politics and the law, education, and the media—was still run by and for whites, with the elites generally making the most important decisions.

When black protest movements in the 1960s forced the white leadership to again consider significant societal changes, this elite made modest changes in the racist system. They passed important civil rights laws and issued major court decisions against formal segregation, but over the next few decades they also saw to it that the enforcement of antidiscrimination laws and regulations would mostly be weak. Legal segregation ended, but little compensation for past oppression was provided, and informal patterns of racial discrimination persisted on a large scale. Most antidiscrimination programs have only been intended as modest efforts designed to fit some black Americans, other people of color, and white women into the Procrustean bed of historically white institutions. Today, most such institutions remain, mostly or disproportionately, white-male-controlled in their normative structures and white male in terms of those who hold top decisionmaking positions.

2
Slavery Unwilling to Die
The Historical Development of Systemic Racism

Historian Charles Joyner describes the Atlantic slave trade as it was actually experienced:

> Slaves who were herded into the slave ships, into the dark, landed on unsanded plank floors, chained to their neighbors, their right foot shackled to the left foot of the person to their right. Their left foot shackled to the right foot of the person to their left. About 18 inches or less below, another layer of slaves on another unsanded plank floor. Every time the waves came you could see them and prepare for them, you just slid across these unsanded floors. There was no fresh air, no light. The slaves had no way of knowing where they were going [or] when, if ever, they would get there. And indeed it was a long trip.[1]

This country was thus born in blood and violence against non-European "others." This grim historical reality must be understood well if we are to comprehend contemporary racism and current interracial relations. As the European colonists gradually established permanent settlements in North America, they intentionally drove off or killed the indigenous inhabitants and routinely took their lands by force or treachery. These colonists and their descendants enriched themselves by what was often a process of **genocide** directed against indigenous peoples. Soon, too, they or their descendants enslaved Africans to work these appropriated lands.

Land Theft and Genocide: Indigenous Americans

Article 2 of the United Nations Convention on the Prevention and Punishment of Genocide defines genocide as "acts committed with intent to destroy, in whole or in part, a national, ethical, racial, or religious group." These acts specifically include "causing serious bodily or mental harm" and "deliberately inflicting on the group conditions of life calculated to bring about its physical destruction in whole or in part."[2] From the late 1400s to the first decades of the 1900s, the European colonizers and their descendants periodically, and often deliberately, inflicted conditions of life that brought about the physical devastation, in whole or in part, of numerous indigenous societies across the Caribbean islands and North and South America. Indeed, the intentional attacks on indigenous peoples—and the devastating effects of European diseases—are estimated to have cost as many as 90 million casualties—the largest case of human destruction in recorded history. The brutal and exploitative practices of whites were not aberrations or occasional; they were common practice in European colonialism.[3]

The English colonists on the Atlantic coast relied on indigenous peoples to survive the first difficult years. Soon, however, these Europeans turned on the indigenous inhabitants. As early as 1637, a war with the Pequots in New England ended when a white-led force massacred several hundred in a village. The 1675–1676 King Philip's War with the Wampanoag society and its allies, precipitated by encroachment and other actions of the colonists, resulted in substantial losses on both sides. The Native American leader, Metacom (King Philip), was "captured, drawn, and quartered: his skull remained on view on a pole in Plymouth as late as 1700."[4] Some Indian survivors were sold as slaves by the European colonists who, ironically, saw themselves as a "civilized" people dealing with "savage" peoples. For some time European colonists enslaved some Native Americans as part of their initial attempts to find exploitable labor. In the mid-eighteenth century, about 5 percent of those enslaved in several colonies were Native American.

James Madison commented that the stereotyped "red race" was second only to the "black race" in the racist concerns of whites. What should be done with these people who stood in the way of European lust for the land and riches of the Americas? Few European colonizers made an effort to understand the attempts of indigenous peoples to protect themselves from European invaders. While some leaders like Benjamin Franklin and Thomas Jefferson occasionally expressed admiration for Indian societies (even viewing them as "the white men of America"), most whites more than balanced their admiration with great hostility, negative imagery, and savage actions.[5]

Until the mid-nineteenth century, the majority of indigenous societies maintained substantial political and cultural autonomy. Europeans were frequently forced by the strength of indigenous societies to negotiate with them for land and other resources. A process of gradual encroachment became the rule. Europeans would move into Native American lands (often violating agreements or treaties), Native Americans would respond with defensive violence, colonial or U.S. troops would put the rebellion down, and a new treaty securing much or all of the stolen land for whites would be made. There was often some pretense of negotiation and legal treaty-making. However, by the 1830s—with slaveholding President Andrew Jackson's decision to expel Cherokees and other Native American groups from the eastern states by force (the famous "trail of tears" that cost at least 4,000 lives)—Native American societies increasingly faced a policy of overt displacement from white areas to western "reservations" or renewed attacks designed to eliminate whole indigenous societies. Even the pretense of legality was gradually disappearing. By 1831 the U.S. Supreme Court had redefined indigenous societies as "domestic dependent nations."[6]

In the infamous 1857 *Dred Scott* decision, the U.S. Supreme Court showed that leading whites viewed the situations of Native Americans and African Americans as different. Indians, Chief Justice Roger Taney asserted, had

> formed no part of the colonial communities, and never amalgamated with them in social connections or in government. But although they were uncivilized, they were yet a free and independent people, associated together in nations or tribes, and governed by their own laws.... But they may, without doubt, like the subjects of any other foreign Government, be naturalized by the authority of Congress, and become citizens of a State, and of the United States; and if an individual should leave his nation or tribe, and take up his abode among the white population, he would be entitled to all the rights and privileges which would belong to an emigrant from any other foreign people.

Whites, the leading white judge asserted, had long viewed Native American groups as separate nations, though less civilized than whites. In contrast, in this decision about the status of an enslaved black American, the white judges viewed black Americans not as a nation to be negotiated with, but rather as "beings of an inferior order, and altogether unfit to associate with the white race, either in social or political relations; and so far inferior, that they had no rights which the white man was bound to respect."[7] Whites' racist views of indigenous societies often allowed for more independence or freedom, albeit as groups only beyond white borders and as individuals only if assimilated. Moreover, over the centuries, most Indian societies confronted whites on their own turf, with much strength arising from their indigenous cultural and geographical resources.

Native Americans lost their ability to make treaties with the U.S. government in 1871. Over the next several decades, federal policies forced many of the surviving indigenous Americans onto federally supervised reservations. With some oscillation, federal policies allowed whites to take yet more Native American land and pressured Native Americans to assimilate to white ways. By 1890, with most forced onto reservations, the number of Native Americans in North America had decreased to about 250,000, sharply down from an estimated 15 million people when Europeans arrived in the late 1400s. The brutal and bloody actions and consequences of European conquests do often fit the United Nations definition of genocide.

Slavery and Modern Capitalism

In the Spanish colonies in Mexico and South America, indigenous Americans were usually the major source of labor, and thus were central to the internal development of these colonial societies. This was not true for the English. As Benjamin Ringer notes,

> except for the early days when trade with the Indian was important for the survival of the English settler, the Indian played virtually no significant role in the internal functioning of the colonial society, but a crucial role in defining its frontier.[8]

Africans, on the other hand, did play a very central role in the functioning of colonial society. By the early 1700s people of African descent had become a major source of labor for the white-run colonies.

The North American colonies developed two modes of production. One type was the subsistence economy of small-scale farmers, who were European immigrants or their descendants. Early on, the North American colonies became places to dump surplus peasants and workers displaced by the reorganization of European agricultural economies. Alongside this subsistence farming was a profit-making commercial economy, much of it rooted in the slave trade, slave farms and plantations, and the commercial businesses essential to the burgeoning slavery economy. Slavery in the Americas became a large-scale commercial and capitalistic, market-centered operation, which distinguished it from slavery in the ancient world.[9]

With much farm land available for new European immigrants, colonial entrepreneurs and development companies frequently could not secure enough white laborers, particularly for large-scale agriculture. At first, larger landowners made use of white indentured servants, but these laborers could be difficult to secure or to control. The enslavement of African women, men, and children not only stemmed from a desire for profit but also from a concern with developing a scheme of social control that maintained bond-labor against the resistance of those enslaved. The color and cultural differences of Africans typically made them easier for whites to identify for purposes of enslavement and control.

The Legal Establishment of Slavery

The first Africans brought into the English colonies were bought by the Jamestown colonists from a Dutch-flagged ship in 1619. Laws firmly institutionalizing slavery were not put in place in the English colonies until the mid-seventeenth century. Yet, even during the earliest decade, the 1620s, the Africans for whom we have records were already treated differently from English colonists. As early as 1624, one court case made clear that a "negro"—note the early naming of Africans and the lowercase spelling—could testify in court only because he was a convert to Christianity. A "negro" status was then socially and legally inferior to a European colonist's status.[10] Historians have shown that Christianity in this colonial period, as later, was dogmatic and Eurocentric in "**ideology**, organization, and practice."[11] As we see in this 1624 example, already central to this Eurocentric viewpoint was the idea that every person must become a Christian to have legal rights. Indeed, many apologists for the enslavement of African Americans, from the seventeenth century to the present day, have argued that one of the virtues of slavery was bringing Christianity to the enslaved.

The degradation of slavery was already clear. In one 1671 declaration Virginia's General Assembly put "sheep, horses, and cattle" in the same category as "negroes." Colonial laws early attempted to prevent black men and women from running away; there were barbaric laws encompassing the whipping, castration, or killing of rebellious slaves. Slavery was more than a system of coerced labor. Enslaved black men, women, and children were legally subjugated in or excluded from major societal institutions including the economic, legal, and political institutions.[12]

As we saw previously, in the 1770s and 1780s the white group interest in the slavery system was recognized in the defining documents of the new nation. The draft Declaration of Independence, prepared mostly by Jefferson, originally contained language accusing the British king of pursuing slavery, of waging

> cruel war against human nature itself, violating its most sacred rights of life and liberty in the persons of a distant people who never offended him, captivating them and carrying them into slavery in another hemisphere, or to incur miserable death in the transportation thither.[13]

Such accusations against the British king were hypocritical, since at least half the signatories to the Declaration, including Jefferson, were slaveholders or significantly involved in the slavery economy. Because of pressure from slaveholding interests in the South and slave-trading interests in the North, this critique of slavery was omitted from the final Declaration of Independence.

Slavery and Commercial Capitalism

While a number of factors played an important role in the expansion of commercial capitalism in the Americas, slavery was one of the most consequential. Between the early 1600s and the 1820s, at least eight million Africans were forcibly brought to the Americas, while in contrast only 850,000 European immigrants came during the same period. For each person put on a slave ship, many others lost their lives while chained and waiting for ships, in slave raids, or from disease. Others died on the ships. The total number who died is unknown, but has been estimated to be 30 to 50 million. Two-thirds were men, often young men, a reality that caused a sharp decrease in African population growth, and thus in economic development in Africa over subsequent centuries. In many parts of the Americas, enslaved African labor was far more important than European labor in building up the wealth of white enslavers and other whites linked to the slavery economy. Involved in this economic growth was an array of European participants on both sides of the Atlantic, including slaveholders, slave-traders and merchants, intellectuals, ministers, and government officials. The trade in enslaved Africans was begun by the Portuguese and the Spanish as they early developed overseas empires, but the English (by 1707 the "British") and English American colonists soon joined in the barbaric Atlantic trade in human beings.[14]

A principal objective of English colonization of North America was to secure raw materials and markets for English goods. Once land was taken from indigenous societies, the European colonizers' search for labor soon led to the pre-existing African slave trade, which became critical to the full exploitation of the land. Larger farms and plantations using enslaved Africans were generally profitable and produced a range of agricultural products for the international market—sugar, tobacco, rice, indigo, and, by the late 1700s, cotton. Plantation owners demanded larger numbers of workers, and the number of those enslaved grew rapidly—from about 60,000 in the early 1700s to several million by the 1860s. By the 1770s, about 40 percent of the population in southern areas was African American. In the North there were also significant numbers of enslaved and free African Americans. In the late eighteenth century, African Americans reached their highest proportion of the population (about one-fifth), before or since, in what was by then the United States.[15]

Variations in Plantation Capitalism

In important respects the variant of capitalism developing in southern agricultural areas was different from the capitalism developing in northern urban areas. For most southern slaveholders there was more to slavery than profit-making. As Jefferson and other leading slaveholders emphasized, an agricultural society was to be preferred to an urban society. In their view the gentleman's life necessitated owning black men, women, and children for social status as well as profit. One of the ironies of the slavery system is the accent that these "gentlemen" and their "ladies" put on values such as chivalry and personal and family honor, even as they practiced social barbarism.[16]

In the decade preceding the Civil War, one-quarter of the white families in southern and border states legally owned nearly four million black men, women, and children. These families, especially those who enslaved the most African Americans, were the most influential in controlling the regional economy and politics. Ordinary whites provided the infrastructure of the slavery system—providing transport, growing foodstuffs, policing slaves, running local governments, and providing many of the skilled trades. The white slaveholding oligarchy maintained its dominance over the non-slaveholding white majority not only by these critical economic ties but also by propagating a white-supremacist framing of society and by providing certain types of white privilege to all whites. Most whites accepted the reality of slavery because "it provided not only an escalator by which they might one day rise, but also a floor beneath which they could not fall."[17]

What was the position of white women in this system? Whatever their class level, they were generally under the control of husbands and fathers. They had far fewer rights than white men and suffered significantly from much patriarchal oppression. Working-class women, the majority of white women, provided most of the household labor that supported male workers and farmers. Women in affluent families also played a direct role in maintaining the racist system. One prominent analysis notes that white

> mistresses, even the kindest, commonly resorted to the whip to maintain order among people who were always supposed to be on call; ... among people whose constant presence not merely as servants but as individuals with wills and passions of their own provided constant irritation along with constant, if indifferent, service.[18]

Among social scientists there is debate as to whether the southern slavery system was capitalistic or just a unique enclave economy imbedded in a larger capitalistic market system. However, scholars generally agree on two points:

1. the larger slaveholders were clearly oriented to making profits off their enslaved laborers; and
2. these slaveholders always oriented themselves to trading within a capitalistic world-market system.

Whatever other social values (for example, feudalistic or aristocratic inclinations) they may have held, the larger plantation owners were early capitalists.[19]

Slavery in the North

Northern merchants and manufacturers were often active in the slave trade or had other economic ties to slave plantations. At the time of the American Revolution, the slave trade was, in Lorenzo Greene's detailed analysis, the "very basis of the economic life of New England; about it revolved, and on it depended, most of [the region's] other industries."[20] Greene lists 160 prominent slaveholding families in the area. Slavery-linked businesses included those dealing in sugar, molasses, and rum, as well as those dealing with shipbuilding and shipping. Leading textile manufacturers were "active participants in the slave trade or active in commercial and industrial endeavors that were closely intertwined with the slave[ry] trade."[21] Numerous northern industrialists were strong supporters of southern slaveholders, and most colluded in the slavery system that buttressed their industries. Northern manufacturers, farmers, and professionals often bought black laborers or servants for their families.

Significant numbers of black Americans were enslaved in northern areas into the 1800s. The colony of Massachusetts Bay had been the first to legalize slavery, and by the mid-1600s there were strict slavery laws throughout the northern colonies. By the 1720s more than one-fifth of New York City's population was black, with most of this black population enslaved. New York City's famous Wall Street area was one of the first large colonial markets where whites bought and sold enslaved black Americans. This savage business lasted in New York City until 1862, even after the Civil War had begun.[22]

White northerners sometimes responded to black attempts to break the bonds of slavery like white southerners—with barbaric brutality. In 1712, for example, there was a major slave revolt in New York City; in retaliation, whites hung, starved, or roasted to death at least 15 of the estimated 70 African Americans who participated in the revolt. In New York state, where slaves made up 7 percent of the population in 1786, even a partial emancipation statute was not passed until 1799. And that statute only freed enslaved children born after July 4, 1799, and only when they reached their mid-twenties. All enslaved black Americans there did not become free until the 1850s. In Massachusetts, famous for its abolitionists, it was not until the 1780s that pressures from the white populace forced the abolition of slavery there. Even so, it was not a recognition of black civil rights but pressure from white workers, who objected to competing with enslaved laborers, that played the major role in forcing slavery's abolition. Moreover, in northern states where black workers and their families were emancipated, they faced intensive Jim Crow segregation and discrimination in jobs, housing, and public accommodations. The early enslavement of black Americans in the North became part of a deep and early systemic racism that facilitated later patterns of institutional racism in the North.[23]

Most white northerners, including religious leaders, did not support immediate emancipation of enslaved African Americans in the South until the first battles of the Civil War made this expedient. Prior to the Civil War, many whites in all regions felt that slavery could not be abolished because of its economic importance to the larger society.[24]

Unjust Immiseration: Terrible Costs for Africans and African Americans

The Barbarity of Slavery

Unjust enrichment for whites brought great immiseration for blacks. Considering the number of people killed or maimed, and the scale and time involved, the enslavement of Africans is one of the most savage aspects of European and North American history. According to those enslaved, the slavery system was hellish and deadly beyond description. Once captured, enslaved Africans were often taken to slave corrals in Africa where they were chained, branded, and held for shipping. The horrors of this Atlantic "Middle Passage" included seriously inadequate food and water, beatings, and epidemics.[25] On the Atlantic voyage, as we saw in the opening quote, those enslaved were usually chained in close quarters, and often in death-dealing conditions. In recent research Stephanie Smallwood summarizes the profit-making that came from this horrific trade:

> Slaves became, for the purpose of transatlantic shipment, mere physical units that could be arranged and molded at will—whether folded together spoonlike in rows or flattened side by side in a plane. Because human beings were treated as inanimate objects, the number of bodies stowed aboard a ship was limited only by the physical dimensions and configuration of those bodies.[26]

The conditions of those enslaved at the points of destination in North America were also brutal and oppressive. William Wells Brown, son of a white slaveowner and enslaved black woman, reported on what happened to an assertive black man named Randall. One day a white overseer, Grove Cook, got three friends to help subdue Randall. As Brown explains:

> He refused to go; whereupon he was attacked by the overseer and his companions, when he turned upon them, and laid them, one after another, prostrated on the ground. [One man] drew out his pistol, and fired at him, and brought him to the ground by a pistol ball. The others rushed upon him with their clubs, and beat him over the

head and face, until they succeeded in tying him. He was taken to the barn, and tied to a beam. Cook gave him over one hundred lashes with a heavy cowhide, had him washed with salt and water, and left him tied during the day. The next day he was untied, and taken to a blacksmith's shop, and had a ball and chain attached to his leg.[27]

Brown recounts that this brave man was forced to work hard in the fields with the chain on him and that the slaveowner was pleased with the sadistic cruelty of his overseer. Brown observed numerous beatings and killings of black men and women by whites during years of enslavement. The surviving narratives of those enslaved are filled with accounts of chains, mutilation, whippings, and starvation.[28]

The Rape of Enslaved Women

Once fully instituted, the arrangements of slavery became much more than a machine for generating wealth. They constituted a well-developed system for the social and sexual control of men and women. During slavery, and later under legal segregation, many African and African American women were sexually coerced and raped by white men, including sailors, slave-masters, overseers, and employers. Such sexual violence symbolized white male power to everyone in local communities. Under the North American system, the children resulting from coerced sexual relations were automatically classified as black, even though they had European ancestry. Indeed, it is estimated today that at least three-quarters of "black" Americans have at least one "white" ancestor.[29] No other U.S. racial group's physical makeup has been so substantially determined by the sexual coercion and depredations of white men. Patricia Williams, a black law professor, has described the case of Austin Miller, the 35-year-old white lawyer who bought her 11-year-old great-great-grandmother, Sophie. By the time Sophie was 12, Miller had made her pregnant with the child who was Williams's great-grandmother Mary. Sophie's child became a house servant to Miller's white children. Williams's great-great-grandfather was one of a large number of white men who sexually coerced black women or sexually molested black children.[30]

Numerous surviving narratives from enslaved women have accounts of such sexual exploitation by white men. For example, in 1850 a prosperous Missouri farmer, Robert Newsom, bought Celia, then a 14-year-old, and soon thereafter attacked her. Over the next five years, Newsom sexually attacked her many times, fathering children by her. In summer 1855, when Newsom came to Celia's cabin to attack her again, she hit him with a stick, and he died. In a travesty of justice, Celia was convicted in a Missouri court of the "crime" and hung in December 1855. Black women typically had no redress for such brutal crimes against them.[31]

Like Miller and Newsom, many of these white oppressors were respectable men in their communities. One was Thomas Jefferson. In his forties he coerced the young enslaved teenager Sally Hemings into his bed. That he fathered at least one child with her has now been confirmed by DNA testing, and it is likely he fathered other children by her. Yet in his lifetime Jefferson, a leading racist intellectual, never admitted to this interracial relationship.[32] Indeed, until the DNA evidence showed the likelihood of this exploitative relationship, most white historians and commentators denied that Jefferson could have had children with an enslaved woman. As the first professional biographer of Jefferson, James Parton, put it in 1874, "If Jefferson was wrong, America is wrong. If America is right, Jefferson was right."[33]

One of the most oppressive aspects of U.S. racism lies in this sexual thread, which weaves itself through various manifestations of systemic racism to the present. White men often coerced and raped African American women with impunity during the country's first three centuries. Given that most such men also proclaimed themselves virtuous and religious, such sexual attitudes and actions clearly contradicted their expressed morality. The tensions between this image of themselves as virtuous and their sexualized actions toward black women—often coupled with a denial at the conscious level of these feelings—seem to have led to a projection of many white men's sexual desires onto black men, thereby constructing the latter as "oversexed."[34]

Given this early projection of white men's desires onto black men, one can perhaps better understand certain lasting aspects of U.S. racism— the obsession of many white men (and women) with the black man as a rapist (see Chapter 4, p. 67) and the extraordinarily brutal and often sexualized attacks on black men in thousands of lynchings and other violent attacks on black men over the last century and a half of U.S. history.

African Immiseration

African societies paid a heavy, often catastrophic, price for the Atlantic slave trade. For several centuries many of the African continent's young people were ripped from its shores, thereby damaging the future development of the continent. Tens of millions of Africans were enslaved or died in the slave trade, so some argue that the term "black holocaust" seems appropriate for this savage process.[35]

Over time, this Atlantic trade in human beings had serious negative effects on social institutions in parts of Africa, a destruction that greatly facilitated later European exploitation and colonization of that continent. Recall Du Bois's argument that African colonization is usually downplayed in mainstream histories of European development, wealth, and affluence.

Yet any serious understanding of the development of European wealth must center on early and late African colonialism, for the labor and mineral resources of Africans were taken to help create European prosperity. Similarly, much African immiseration today is ultimately linked to the creation of white prosperity over the course of North American history.

Some scholars and popular writers have accented the role of Africans in this Atlantic slave trade, often in order to play down the European role. One must put this African participation in perspective. Europeans were not enslaved by Africans, and virtually all Africans enslaved in the Americas were taken from Africa by European traders and sold to Europeans, usually in the Americas. This trade began when European ships arrived seeking commerce with African societies, whose economies were not centered in profit-making from enslavement. As Europeans grew in power, African societies were played off against each other. The European intruders built 600 slave ports for their bloody slave trade, and engaged in at least 300 battles with Africans as part of the enslavement process. In some cases Africans were kidnapped directly by Europeans. In many other cases African social and political leaders, who had at first traded African goods for European goods, ran out and, pressed by the Europeans, turned to trading people held in servitude.[36]

This theft of millions of able-bodied Africans in the Atlantic slave trade, plus the loss of tens of millions who died in the enslavement process, together with the past and present-day theft of African mineral and other resources, likely account for a significant amount of the poverty and degradation seen across the African continent in recent centuries, indeed to the present day.

A Distinctive Form of Human Slavery

The enslavement of Africans in the Americas was not only more extreme than slavery in most African societies, but also more oppressive than slavery in ancient societies such as the Roman Empire. In the Americas the Europeans applied slavery, as Du Bois reminds us, "on a scale and with an elaborateness of detail of which no former world ever dreamed. The imperial width of the thing—the heaven-defying audacity—makes its modern newness."[37] Unlike Roman slaves, North American slaves were generally forbidden by law to read or write. An essential feature of North American slavery was the denial of human liberties. Those enslaved

> could own nothing; they could make no contracts; they could hold no property; nor traffic in property; they could not hire out; they could not legally marry ... they could not appeal from their master; they could be punished at will.[38]

Even the English language became an important weapon for subordinating enslaved Africans. The latter were from many different societies, but were forced to learn the language of their oppressors. Voluntary immigrants to the United States have been allowed to retain much more of their home languages and have generally kept more of the home culture associated with those languages. In the destruction of African languages and their replacement by English we see how extensive the system of racial oppression is. Enforced adaptation to English not only marked the movement of early English colonizers across the lands of conquest, but also marks today—such as in attacks on Spanish or Ebonics—similar attempts to maintain white cultural dominance over those who are racially subordinated.[39]

Ill-gotten Gains: Wealth and Prosperity from Slavery

American slavery was a system created, supported, and financed by a large number of the leading political, business, and intellectual figures in the country's early centuries. Consider just one major enterprise of the early eighteenth century, the famous British South Sea Company. This was an official company set up to transport enslaved Africans overseas. Stockholders included the leading physical scientist Isaac Newton, major authors like Jonathan Swift and Daniel Defoe, and the founder of the Bank of England, the Earl of Halifax. They included many members of the House of Lords and of the House of Commons. Many aristocrats held stock.[40] Clearly, the leading men of Britain were directly and financially involved in the Atlantic slave trade. Similarly, many leading Americans, including George Washington, Thomas Jefferson, Patrick Henry, George Mason, and James Madison, profited greatly from slavery or the slave trade. These esteemed founders saw North American slavery as an honorable, wealth-generating business activity.

Building the Wealth of Britain and Continental Europe

The British merchants of the eighteenth century recognized the centrality of slavery in building the wealth of their powerful nation. In the 1740s one business pamphleteer wrote about Britain's wealth this way:

> The most approved Judges of the Commercial Interests of these Kingdoms have ever been of the opinion that our West-India and African Trades are the most nationally beneficial of any we carry on. It is also allowed on all Hands, that the trade to Africa is the Branch which renders our American Colonies and Plantations so advantageous to Great Britain: that Traffic only affording our Planters a constant supply of Negro Servants for the Culture of their Lands in the Produce of Sugars, Tobacco, Rice, Rum, Cotton, Fustick, Pimento, and all other our Plantation Produce: so that the

extensive Employment of our Shipping in, to, and from America, the great Brood of Seamen consequent thereupon, and the daily Bread of the most considerable Part of our British Manufactures, are owing primarily to the Labour of Negroes; who, as they were the first happy instruments of raising our Plantations: so their Labour only can support and preserve them, and render them still more and more profitable to their Mother-Kingdom. The Negroe-Trade therefore, and the natural consequences resulting from it, may be justly esteemed an inexhaustible Fund of Wealth and Naval Power to this Nation.[41]

This remarkable summary accurately accents the primary role of the "labour of Negroes" to British shipping and manufacturing, and thus to an "inexhaustible fund of wealth" for whites in Britain and its American colonies.

Economic trade generated by British and French plantations in the Americas was the source of much of the capital for the commercial and industrial revolutions of the two countries. British and French industry, shipping, naval and merchant marine development, banking, and insurance were significantly stimulated by or grounded in the labor of enslaved Africans in their respective colonies. From the early 1700s to the mid-1800s a large proportion of major agricultural exports in world trade were produced by enslaved people of African descent. British port cities became prosperous as centers for the trade in Africans, and British industrial cities became prosperous in part because of the manufacturing of goods with materials from slave plantations. Textile manufacturing was the core industry of the Industrial Revolution, and most cotton was grown by enslaved laborers. Moreover, circulating through banking enterprises, the profits from growing international trade—much of it related to the slave trade and trade in slave-produced products—provided a substantial part of the large-scale investments in ever-expanding British industry, growth that in turn led to many new technologies and products of the Industrial Revolution.[42]

Slavery and Economic Development in the Americas

It is also unlikely that the American colonies and, later, the United States would have seen the dramatic agricultural and industrial development of the eighteenth and nineteenth centuries without the blood and sweat of those enslaved. Much of the wealth generated between the early 1700s and the 1860s came from the slave trade and the labor of enslaved men, women, and children on plantations and in other profit-making enterprises. In the seventeenth century, the famous triangular trade emerged between Europe, Africa, and the North American colonies.

Europe and America provided ships and agricultural exports, while Africa provided enslaved laborers. Sugar plantations in the West Indies "became the hub of the British Empire, of immense importance to the grandeur and prosperity of England," and it was the African laborers who made the West Indies the "most precious colonies ever recorded in the whole annals of imperialism."[43] A major economic bridge between Europe and the overseas colonies in this period was this extensive slave–sugar complex. The Caribbean plantations also spurred mainland development. Much of the oats, corn, flour, fish, lumber, soap, candles, and livestock exported by the continental American colonies went to the West Indies plantations. In 1770 no less than three-quarters of all New England exports of foodstuffs went to the West Indian plantations or to Africa. A substantial proportion of the wealth of the New England and Middle Atlantic colonies came from the trade with slave plantations in the southern colonies and the Caribbean.[44]

From the early 1700s to the mid-1800s much of the surplus capital and wealth of North America came directly, or by means of economic multiplier effects, from the slave trade and slave plantations. With the growing demand for textiles, U.S. cotton production expanded between the 1790s and the beginning of the Civil War. Cotton was shipped to British and New England textile mills, greatly spurring the wheels of British, U.S., and international commerce. By the mid-nineteenth century New England cotton mills were industrial leaders in value added, and second in number of employees, in the United States. Without slave labor there would probably not have been a successful textile industry, and without that cotton textile industry—the first major U.S. industry—the United States would have been unlikely to become a major industrial power when it did.[45] In the first half of the nineteenth century northern merchants, bankers, and shipping companies became "closely tied to cotton. New York became both the center of the import trade and the financial center for the cotton trade."[46] Slave-grown cotton became ever-more central to the economy and accounted for about half of all exports, and thus for a large share of the profits generated by exports.

In the North profits from the cotton economy and sale of products to slave plantations stimulated the growth of investment in financial and insurance enterprises, other service industries, and various manufacturing concerns, as well as, by means of taxes, of investment in government infrastructure projects. Cotton-related activities were an important source of economic expansion before the Civil War, and most cotton was grown by enslaved Americans. Their agricultural production undergirded much national economic development and the U.S. market revolution. One biographer has concluded there was not a New England "merchant of any prominence who was not then directly or indirectly involved in this trade."[47] As the nineteenth century progressed, sons and grandsons of earlier traders in slaves and slave-related products became the economic captains of the textile and other major industries in the North.

British and New England manufacturers' demand for cotton fueled the demand for more enslaved workers and more Native American land. The leading cotton states—Mississippi, Alabama, and South Carolina—were substantially carved out of Native American lands, and as the cotton system expanded westward, the lands of more indigenous societies were taken, usually by force or threat of force. Moreover, labor was perhaps the most critical factor in U.S. economic production in the eighteenth and nineteenth centuries, and enslaved African Americans often filled that demand. In the decade before the Civil War the dollar value of those enslaved was estimated by one leading planter to be $2 billion—a figure then *exceeding* the total value of all northern factories.[48]

Not only did the southern agricultural system provide cotton for the textile mills of the North, but profits from the cotton trade also helped to generate demand for northern manufactured products and, increasingly, for western foodstuffs. The coerced labor of black men, women, and children built up profits used by many slaveowners for luxurious living, further investments in various enterprises, and deposits in banks. Such capital—and related capital generated in international trade in slave-produced products—could be used or borrowed by merchants, shippers, railroad executives, and other industrialists in the North or South. Thus, the economic prosperity and industrial development of Western nations, including the U.S., were grounded to a substantial degree in the slavery system of the Atlantic basin.[49]

The Wealth of Powerful Slaveholders

In the century prior to the Civil War the slaveholding oligarchy of southern and border states controlled a huge share of the resources and riches of the country. By the early nineteenth century the slaveholders owned much of the country's most productive land and the agricultural produce for export. They owned a large proportion of the livestock, warehouses, plantation buildings, and processing mills, as well as large numbers of enslaved workers. The South was the most economically prosperous and politically powerful region from the mid-1700s to the 1850s.[50]

The theft of Indian land and enslavement of Africans became the foundation of prosperity for many white families. George Washington, chair of the Constitutional Convention and first U.S. president, was one of the very wealthiest Americans of his day. Owner of more than 36,000 acres, he held substantial securities in banks and land companies. By 1783 his accounting showed he enslaved 216 black Americans. Reading his records, one sees that he viewed black men, women, and children primarily as economic investments, like farm animals whose purpose was to bring him monetary profit. Enslaved black workers made possible his luxurious lifestyle. As Fritz Hirschfeld has documented:

> Slaves washed his linens, sewed his shirts, polished his boots, saddled his horse, chopped the wood for his fireplaces, powdered his wig, drove his carriage, cooked his meals, served his table, poured his wine, posted his letters, lit the lamps, swept the porch, looked after the guests, planted the flowers in his gardens, trimmed the hedges, dusted the furniture, cleaned the windows, made the beds, and performed the myriad domestic chores.[51]

Though Washington said he was opposed to violent brutality against those enslaved, his actions contradicted his stated view. Overseers were allowed to use flogging, and he vigorously pursued enslaved runaways.

Similarly, the principal author of the Declaration of Independence, Thomas Jefferson, was wealthy because he owned 10,000 acres of land and because, by the early 1800s, he held 185 African Americans in bondage. He enslaved several hundred people over his lifetime. His extravagant lifestyle was made possible by these African American workers. While Jefferson was sometimes critical of slavery, he rarely freed those he enslaved. Thus, the intellectual who is still seen as a principal progenitor of U.S. liberty, who penned the phrase "all men are created equal," was a major Virginia slaveholder. He fathered at least one child whom he kept enslaved, and he too chased down fugitive slaves and had them severely whipped.[52]

Slaveholders and the U.S. Government

Without the capital and wealth generated by enslaved black Americans, it is possible that there would not have been an American Revolution and, thus, a United States. One of history's great ironies is the fact that the Declaration of Independence's "all men are created equal" did not apply to African Americans, yet the American victory in the struggle against Great Britain was possible substantially because the wealth generated by the slavery system and its economic spin-offs was available to help finance and support the American Revolution. A significant proportion of the money amassed or borrowed to fight that revolution came, directly or indirectly, from capital generated by the slave plantations and trade in slaves and slave-produced products. Money borrowed from northern sources often had its ultimate origin in the slavery constellation, as did some of the money borrowed from overseas. France's involvement in the American Revolution was essential to its successful outcome, and, as Edmund Morgan has shown, the "single most valuable product with which to purchase assistance was tobacco, produced mainly by slave labor.... To a large degree it may be said that Americans bought their independence with slave labor."[53]

The political structure established after the revolution continued to reflect the elite interest in slavery and in controlling African Americans, whether enslaved or free. The mainstream view of the U.S. government sees it and its actions as set, from its first decades, in the context of "democracy"—as the result of competing group interests jockeying for position through democratic political mechanisms.

A contrasting view sees the early U.S. government as very undemocratic and as central to the creation of systemic racism and the perpetuation of a racial hierarchy. Historically, white male elites have worked through local and federal governments to create social institutions serving their interests. In the early development of the U.S. government, white women, African Americans, and Native Americans had no direct representation. The white male ruling class created a racialized government, which played a central role in defining who was "black" and "white" and what the benefits of being in each racial class were. For most African Americans—and Native Americans forced onto reservations—this took the form of a type of police state. The standard dictionary definition of "police state" is "a political unit characterized by repressive governmental control of political, economic, and social life usually by an arbitrary exercise of power by police."[54]

Slavery dominated U.S. politics in many ways between the making of the U.S. Constitution and the beginning of the Civil War. For 50 of the first 64 years of the new nation the U.S. president was a slaveowner. Chief Justices of the U.S. Supreme Court for most of the period up to the Civil War, John Marshall and Roger B. Taney, were slaveholders, as were numerous others on that high court. In the decades after the U.S. Constitution was put into place, the slavery system continued to shape legal and political decisions in major ways, including the building up of constitutional law in numerous federal-court decisions such as the *Dred Scott* decision discussed in Chapter 3. For decades few major decisions made by the federal legislative and judicial branches went against the interests of the country's slaveholding oligarchy, and foreign and domestic policies generally did not conflict with the interests of major slaveholders. For example, George Washington's presidential administration even loaned money to French slaveholders in Haiti to put down a major slave uprising on that island.[55]

By the 1850s a major schism in the white ruling class, between southern planters and growing numbers of northern industrialists with little economic interest in slavery, was becoming clear in political battles over such issues as expansion of slavery into western lands. Fearful of its economic and political future, the South's slaveholding oligarchy eventually moved to secede from the union. The victory of the North in the subsequent Civil War marked the arrival of northern industrialists and merchants as a dominant force in the U.S. economy and government.[56]

The Emergence of Jim Crow: Slavery Unwilling to Die

Group Terrorism by White Americans

After the Civil War, in the late 1860s and early 1870s, the Reconstruction period came to the South as a breath of fresh air. Federally enforced Reconstruction policies were precipitated by southern whites' unwillingness to make major changes in the treatment of freed slaves or to prevent the unrepentant leaders of the old Confederacy from again assuming autocratic power. A brief period of limited federal military occupation resulted. Prior to the 1860s black Americans had not generally been allowed to vote at any level of government. Now the Thirteenth, Fourteenth, and Fifteenth Amendments to the U.S. Constitution abolished slavery, asserted the civil rights of black Americans, and officially guaranteed black men (but not women) the right to vote. During Reconstruction new state constitutional conventions included black delegates, although in most states white southerners predominated. For a time southern governments were mostly controlled by ordinary whites who had not been active leaders in the Confederacy, and black Americans gained a measure of personal and political freedom, although considerable Jim Crow segregation already existed. During the Reconstruction era these biracial state governments brought much needed political reforms to the South, including significant prison reform and the first public education.[57]

Today there is little recognition, in the media or many history textbooks, of the scale and barbarousness of the white terrorism that brought an end to the often progressive Reconstruction governments and, with that, any hope for political or economic equality for black Americans. Sometimes, this southern terrorism even gets positive coverage. The early 1900s movie *The Birth of a Nation*, still considered a classic film by movie experts, aggressively celebrates the very hostile and racist Ku Klux Klan view of Reconstruction. Moreover, the recurring release of pro-slavery movies (for example, the 1930s *Gone with the Wind* movie was re-released in the late 1990s) signals how unconcerned or ill-informed the white majority still is about the country's sometimes savagely racist history.

What mainstream U.S. movies should cover, but never have, is how the South's white elite, often with the collusion of northern elites, established an extensive terrorist campaign against Reconstruction state governments and newly freed black southerners. A leading Confederate general, Nathan Bedford Forrest, was the first "Grand Dragon" of the new Ku Klux Klan, and even the famous General Robert E. Lee pledged his "invisible" support to the violent Klan. White terrorism destroyed the often progressive southern governments, and thousands of men, women, and children were severely beaten, killed, or raped by the Klan and similar white-supremacist groups. The Confederacy lost the four-year war, but fought on for "twelve more years—using every weapon at its disposal, including the ultimate one of mass terrorism—until the nation finally acceded to most of the Confederacy's modified war aims."[58]

After a few years of this white terrorism, northern interest in the South waned. Northern leaders were not interested in punishing those who led the rebellion. The Hayes Compromise of 1877 removed the few remaining federal troops and eliminated much federal protection of black southerners. The leaders of the old Confederacy had finally *won* most of their political–economic goals. This arch-conservative revolution ended most attempts to provide the newly freed slaves with substantial civil rights protection and economic help. Stetson Kennedy explains, black southerners were "sold back down the river into virtual enslavement, and all three of the new constitutional amendments—so far as blacks were concerned—were rendered dead letters for a century to come."[59] The Thirteenth, Fourteenth, and Fifteenth amendments officially gave African Americans citizenship rights, but most of these new rights were effectively denied by southern legislatures, federal courts, and presidential or congressional action until the civil rights revolution of the 1950s–1960s. Whites in the North and the South joined in solidarity on behalf of the white group interest in preserving systemic racism.

The Continuing Badges and Disabilities of Slavery

In a dissenting opinion to the important 1883 Civil Rights Cases, Justice John Marshall Harlan argued:

> That there are burdens and disabilities which constitute badges of slavery and servitude, and that the power to enforce by appropriate legislation the Thirteenth Amendment may be exerted by legislation of a direct and primary character, for the eradication, not simply of the institution, but of its badges and incidents, are propositions which ought to be deemed indisputable.[60]

Harlan was arguing that the federal government had a right to intervene and dismantle the lingering effects of slavery, not just slavery itself.

Yet the end of slavery did not bring an end to the badges, burdens, or disabilities of slavery. Comprehensive Jim Crow segregation became a social reality soon after Reconstruction, as extensive segregation laws and informal segregation practices kept African Americans from voting, attending good public schools, and using many public accommodations. By the 1880s and 1890s legal segregation was linked to the white elite's successful attempt to disenfranchise black voters and reassert the power of the Democratic Party against inroads made during Reconstruction by the Republican Party. New elite-controlled, authoritarian political regimes dominated all southern states, and these regimes worked with white planters and new southern industrialists to insure control of black workers in agriculture and the new industries. By the early 1900s, officially and informally enforced Jim Crow was the rule throughout southern and border states, and even to be found in some parts of northern and western states.[61]

A major Supreme Court decision, *Plessy* v. *Ferguson* (1896), involved segregation of Louisiana railroad cars, which was challenged by a man whose ancestry was one-eighth African and seven-eighths European. The court's decision delivered a major blow to the idea of civic equality by upholding the legality of so-called "separate but equal" facilities for white and black Americans. Following the tradition of white-supremacist thinking, this all-white Supreme Court reasoned, with one lone dissenter, that racism was natural and that

> legislation is powerless to eradicate racial instincts or to abolish distinctions based upon physical differences, and the attempt to do so can only result in accentuating the difficulties of the present situation.... If one race be inferior to the other socially, the Constitution of the United States cannot put them upon the same plane.

The racial privileges of whites as a group were maintained. Justice John Marshall Harlan, the dissenter, argued that

> the arbitrary separation of citizens, on the basis of race, while they are on a public highway, is a badge of servitude wholly inconsistent with the civil freedom and the equality before the law established by the Constitution. It cannot be justified upon any legal grounds.[62]

The long-term effect of this *Plessy* decision and similar federal court cases upholding segregation was to bar African Americans from fair access to major U.S. political, economic, and social institutions for decades.

By the early 1900s the police-state conditions in southern and border states shaped the lives of the more than 80 percent of African Americans who lived there. Most public facilities were segregated, including buses, water fountains, public toilets, parks, theaters, hospitals, colleges, churches, and even cemeteries. Black southerners were forcibly denied electoral influence.

Maintaining Segregation with Violence

White violence undergirded the growing edifice of Jim Crow segregation. A central aspect of these new arrangements was the omnipresent lynching, usually of a black man thought to have spoken against, organized against, committed a crime against, or insulted his white oppressors. The accusation was often fictional or greatly exaggerated. Some 3,513 lynchings of black men and 76 of black women were recorded for the years 1882 to 1927, but many more did not get recorded. In addition, many other lynchings took place before and after that period. Between the Civil War and the present, perhaps as many as 6,000 lynchings of black men and women have been perpetrated in the southern states and in certain areas of the northern and border states. Many thousands of other violent white attacks on African Americans have also gone unrecorded.[63]

Lynchings were savage events with a strongly ritualized character. Over the years from the late 1860s to recent times, thousands of whites have participated in them. One lynching account from the 1940s involved a black man accused of trying to rape a white woman. A participant told the story of a white mob's actions:

> I ain't tellin' nobody just what we done to that nigger but we used a broken bottle just where it'd do the most damage, and any time you want to see a nigger ear all you gotta do is go to see old man Smith and ast him for a peep at one.... Yes, ma'am, we done things I never knowed could be done and things I certainly ain't mentionin' to no lady.

After being cut, the black victim was doused in kerosene and burned, with the ending being that "the groanin' got lower and lower and finely it was just little gasps and then it wasn't nothin' a tall." After pulling him out of the fire, the white mob tied him to a tree, leaving him for his relatives to take down.[64]

In most lynching episodes there was no legal trial. At the heart of this ritualized barbarism was many whites' concern that white dominance must be maintained. These whites felt that antiblack violence would make local black residents afraid to challenge Jim Crow customs. Many lynchings involved large turnouts by white men, women, and children who cheered killings in local celebrations. In many cases black victims were brutally tortured, and pieces of bodies were gladly taken as souvenirs. The sexual mutilations of black victims, as well as the very emotional (and often unfounded) accusations of rape against them, signal once again the importance of the strong and irrational sexual thread in the history of white racism.

Segregation's Economic Impact

Legal segregation had a severe impact on the economic opportunities of black Americans. Once slavery was ended, black families were promised some productive land by certain federal officials. Those newly freed pressed for "forty acres and a mule" with which to begin a new life. Some federal generals initially gave confiscated Confederate lands to African

Americans. Yet most lost this land when the new president, Andrew Johnson, a white-supremacist southerner and slaveholder, overruled them. Property had to be protected, even if it belonged to slaveholders who fought against the United States. Yet again, the common interest of white southerners and northerners in protecting unjustly gained property and resources was stronger than stated commitments to social justice.[65]

Black southerners were not eligible for public land given away by the first Homestead Act (1862), and by the time the Southern Homestead Act came to be (1866), they were unable to take full advantage of it because of widespread white discrimination, intimidation, and violence against them. Those who were able to overcome these odds often found the land they secured to be poor for farming or lost it later on to white force or threats of force.[66] Black leaders like W.E.B. Du Bois argued that without new resources there was no possibility of real democracy: "To have given each one of the million Negro free families a forty-acre freehold would have made a basis of real democracy in the United States that might easily have transformed the modern world."[67]

After slavery came a period of renewed enrichment and capital accumulation by the larger white farmers and merchants in southern and border states. They made their fortunes from the labor of theoretically free black laborers, tenant farmers, and sharecroppers. Booker T. Washington described the conditions that free blacks faced on the large farms and plantations as "a kind of slavery that is in one sense as bad as the slavery of antebellum days."[68] In theory, tenant farmers and sharecroppers could sell their share of the crops, pay off debts, and buy their own land. Yet most were not able to make enough to escape the cycle of indebtedness to white landowners and merchants. When large-scale industrialization finally came to the South, black workers were virtually excluded, except for the lowest-wage positions.

Moreover, long before the Civil War, Jim Crow laws in the North had enforced racial segregation in employment, public transportation, hospitals, jails, schools, churches, and cemeteries. Indeed, the first Jim Crow railroad cars were established on Massachusetts railroads. In northern cities whites enforced housing segregation. Into the 1930s not only the 11 southern states had Jim Crow laws, but all the bordering states as well—from Delaware and Maryland to Missouri and Oklahoma. Some northern states like Kansas and Indiana had towns and cities with racial segregation statutes. Into the late 1940s numerous northern and western states, including Michigan, Colorado, Oregon, and California, had laws banning marriages between white and black Americans. Beyond these laws, white northerners openly enforced racial segregation in housing and employment by various informal means (de facto segregation).[69]

Persisting Patterns of Legal Segregation

Racist Barriers: 1910s to the 1930s

In 1910 more than 80 percent of black Americans, most the descendants of those recently enslaved, resided in the southern states. Most found themselves in agricultural areas with little access to productive farmland and facing segregation in most aspects of their lives. As a result, they began to migrate North in significant numbers. There, too, they met large-scale discrimination and exclusion.

In the North many southern migrants were concentrated in domestic and service positions; they were routinely excluded by employers and unions from better-paying jobs in expanding industrial settings. Black workers were often displaced by new immigrant workers from southern and eastern Europe. Like the Irish workers before them, these immigrants sometimes forced black workers out of good jobs into lower-paying ones.[70] Without the racist exclusion and discrimination, the black Harlems and South Chicagos "might have become solid working-class and middle-class communities with the economic and social resources to absorb and aid the incoming masses of Southerners."[71] This time the unjust impoverishment of black workers and enrichment of white workers stemmed from white control over access to better-paying jobs and jobs with the potential for mobility. Here we see how whites who actually arrived after the slavery period—and their many descendants—benefited greatly from legal and informal segregation in employment. Once again, whites had more or less exclusive access to the economic, housing, and political resources that enabled them and their children and grandchildren to move up the socioeconomic ladder.

Clashes with whites became frequent as southern black workers and their families moved into northern cities. Whites sometimes used violence to enforce traditional patterns of racial discrimination. During one white-generated riot in 1900 in New York, a mostly Irish American police force encouraged whites to attack black men, women, and children. One of the most serious riots occurred in 1917 in East St. Louis. There white workers, viewing black immigrants from the South as a job threat, violently attacked a black community. Thirty-nine black residents and nine white attackers were killed. This was followed in 1919 by a string of white riots from Chicago to Charleston. In the North and South, millions of white men, and at least half-a-million white women, belonged to the Ku Klux Klan or voted for its political candidates. During the years 1910 to 1930 numerous state and national politicians belonged to the Klan, and dozens of members of the Senate and House of Representatives were elected with the help of the Klan. Prior to becoming president, Warren G. Harding was closely tied to the Klan. And before he was a leading Supreme Court justice, Justice Hugo Black had been a member of the Klan. Klan activities included large-scale marches and thousands of cross burnings, assaults, and lynchings in towns and cities across the country—actions often seen as public-spirited and thus winked at by white government officials.[72]

Racist Barriers: The 1930s to the 1950s

During the 1930s most black men, women, and children still lived in the South's near-slavery of Jim Crow segregation, a subjugation that did not allow the build-up of significant economic or educational resources for most families. Segregation, with its extensive racist etiquette, was very much in place. Though the Supreme Court in 1915 had begun to invalidate a few restrictions on black voters, most were still not permitted to vote. In agricultural areas most worked as wage laborers, domestic workers, or sharecroppers. In the North black workers likewise remained mostly in low-wage jobs as unskilled workers, domestics, and laborers.[73]

During the Great Depression of the 1930s, unemployed whites frequently pushed black workers out of menial jobs. Whites in Atlanta organized a "Black Shirts" organization under the slogan of "No Jobs for Niggers Until Every White Man Has a Job." By 1932 half of black workers in cities were unemployed. Extreme hunger or starvation was often their lot.[74] Moreover, as federally funded employment programs began to put some black job-seekers back to work and provide some economic support, black voters shifted from a solidly Republican vote in 1932 to a solidly Democratic vote in 1936. Nonetheless, black workers continued to suffer much discrimination from the whites who administered New Deal agencies, especially in the South. In most federal relief programs black workers got lower wages than whites, were employed only as unskilled laborers, and were employed only after whites were. New Deal housing programs increased residential segregation of black families by restricting the new federally guaranteed home loans to homes in segregated areas and by locating public housing so that it would be racially segregated. President Franklin Roosevelt and most of his advisors were even unwilling to press for anti-lynching legislation to get rid of this violent means of subordinating African Americans, because they feared losing white votes. The U.S. government was still openly racist and segregationist in many of its own policies.[75]

During the long era of legal segregation from the 1880s to the 1960s African Americans, and numerous other Americans of color, endured many types of racial discrimination in employment, housing, medical care, education, and everyday etiquette. David Brown and Clive Webb have summarized much of the everyday reality. Segregated medical facilities meant that the provision of medical care for African Americans was far inferior to that for whites.... Low wages led to restrictive diets that lacked essential nutrients and rendered African Americans less immune to the diseases that spread through their neighborhoods as a result of poor sanitation.

Equally serious was extreme segregation of public schools. Fearing that education might encourage black resistance and operating out of the white-racist frame that viewed black Americans as unintelligent and undeserving, white-run southern and border state governments provided meager support for black public schools:

> In 1910, South Carolina, for instance, spent an average of $5.95 per black pupil, compared with $40.68 for the average white pupil.... Schools were forced to close during the harvest season so that every hand was available to work in the fields.[76]

Public schools thus reinforced a highly coercive employment system.

If this were not enough, extreme *deference rituals* were forced on black men, women, and children. They were required to show deference to whites by tipping hats, stepping off sidewalks, bowing their heads, or pretending ignorance. In everyday interactions most whites did not address black Americans with the normal "Mr.," "Mrs.," or "Miss" and insisted on using only their first names. Most whites also used such denigrating language as "nigger," "boy," "girl," and "uncle" for black Americans they knew.[77] These Jim Crow actions were implemented to insure that whites in all classes benefited from a strong sense of racial superiority—Du Bois's "public and psychological wage of whiteness."

Workers Become an Economic Surplus

Much black economic progress has come during wartime. During World War I white immigration from Europe to the United States subsided, but workers were still badly needed to produce U.S. war goods. Opportunities for employment in formerly all-white, male job sectors were opened up. During World War II the worker shortage again allowed black workers into some skilled blue-collar jobs for the first time. Similarly, the 1950s Korean War also permitted some expanded black employment in better-paying jobs. However, after the end of each war the employment situation for most black men and women changed for the worse. For example, white veterans and other white workers poured into many cities after World War II, usually taking the better-paying jobs. The jobs that remained for black workers were mostly menial and low-paying.[78]

During the 1960s Vietnam War there was again significant black mobility into better-paying jobs, with an assistance this time not only from that war and associated prosperity but also from the renewed civil rights movement. In spite of this, however, black workers were farther behind whites in income, occupation, and unemployment in the 1960s than they had been in 1945. Thus, in 1962 black workers in the prime working-age group still had an unemployment rate *three times* that of whites. While formal segregation laws were dismantled by the civil rights acts of the 1960s, large-scale informal discrimination persisted in most societal areas.[79]

Moreover, since the 1960s the United States has undergone very significant economic changes. Large-scale automation and massive corporate investments overseas have often created a harsh reality of substantial unemployment, under-employment, or lower real wages for many U.S. workers. By the 1960s substantial automation had created a situation where many of the country's black blue-collar workers were no longer needed by white employers in agriculture or numerous sectors of the industrial economy. Significantly, it was not until this labor surplus became a conspicuous economic reality in the 1960s that many white employers and other whites were finally willing to consider the abolition of the coercive arrangements of legal segregation. Many employers no longer sought out the large numbers of black workers upon whom they had formerly depended so heavily for necessary labor. A country that had built much of its prosperity off the backs of black workers was gradually abandoning many of them to a life of recurring unemployment or under-employment.[80]

Conclusion

The United States was originally built as a white republic. It was a principal part of the world racist order created by European colonialism and imperialism to enrich Europeans and impoverish indigenous peoples. The racist institutions established during the slavery period and undergirded by the U.S. Constitution have generated, enhanced, and reproduced the privileges and prosperity of most white Americans for many generations.

Today, there are many indirect and direct connections between the generation of white resources and wealth in the eras of slavery and legal segregation and the resources and prosperity of contemporary white individuals and families. The current U.S. racial situation is very much the legacy of black enslavement, and the badges and disabilities of slavery still lie heavily on black Americans. This reality is recognized, albeit only occasionally, at the highest levels of the justice system. For example, in a pioneering 1968 Supreme Court case, *Jones et ux.* v. *Alfred H. Mayer Co.*, the U.S. Supreme Court considered blatant housing discrimination and segregation in St. Louis. In that perceptive decision the majority of the court ruled that

> just as the Black Codes, enacted after the Civil War to restrict the free exercise of those rights, were substitutes for the slave system, so the exclusion of Negroes from white communities became a substitute for the Black Codes. And when racial discrimination herds men into ghettos and makes their ability to buy property turn on the color of their skin, then it too is a relic of slavery.[81]

For a brief period in the Supreme Court's long history, in the 1960s and early 1970s, a majority of the white justices recognized that persisting racial discrimination and informal racial segregation were relics of the old slavery system.

In a concurring opinion in this case, progressive white Justice William O. Douglas enumerated the ways in which persisting discrimination is connected in a direct line to slavery:

> Some badges of slavery remain today. While the institution has been outlawed, it has remained in the minds and hearts of many white men. Cases which have come to this Court depict a spectacle of slavery unwilling to die. We have seen contrivances by States designed to thwart Negro voting.... Negroes have been excluded over and again from juries solely on account of their race ... or have been forced to sit in segregated seats in courtrooms.... They have been made to attend segregated and inferior schools ... or been denied entrance to colleges or graduate schools because of their color.... Negroes have been prosecuted for marrying whites.... They have been forced to live in segregated residential districts ... and residents of white neighborhoods have denied them entrance.[82]

Few white justices have ever demonstrated such a deep understanding of systemic racism. Douglas recognized that legally or informally institutionalized segregation, like slavery, was a masterful machine designed to protect white privileges and unjust enrichment. Today, slavery's badges and disabilities persist because they are perpetuated by the racist framing and discriminatory practices of a great many whites.

3
The White Racial Frame
A Social Force

Our third president, the prominent theorist of liberty Thomas Jefferson, wrote in his only major book, *Notes on the State of Virginia,* that black Americans are racially inferior to whites in reasoning, imagination, and beauty. Furthermore, in his view blacks are more adventuresome than whites because they have a "want of forethought," are unreflective, and feel life's pain less than whites. In an extreme animalizing statement, Jefferson further asserted that even black Americans favor white beauty, "as uniformly as is the preference of the Oranootan [Orangutan] for the black women over those of his own species." Blacks are also alleged to have produced no important thinkers, musicians, or intellectuals. Improvement in black minds comes only when there is a "mixture with whites," which Jefferson argues "proves that their inferiority is not the effect merely of their condition of life."[1] As our first major secular intellectual and a major slaveholder, Thomas Jefferson played a central role in the development of racial rationalizations for the enslavement of black Americans, including the dominant white racial framing of this society.

Creating a White Racial Frame

The expansion of European countries from the 1400s to the early 1900s eventually brought colonial exploitation to more than 80 percent of the globe. The resulting exploitation and resource inequalities were global and stemmed, as W.E.B. Du Bois noted, from letting a "single tradition of culture suddenly have thrust into its hands the power to bleed the world of its brawn and wealth, and the willingness to do this."[2] For the colonizing Europeans it was not enough to bleed the world of labor and resources. Colonizers were not content to exploit indigenous American and African peoples and view that exploitation simply as "might makes right." Instead, they vigorously justified what they had done for themselves and their descendants. Gradually, a broad racial framing like that illustrated by Thomas Jefferson's commentaries early rationalized this extensive oppression and thereby reduced its conscious moral cost for Europeans and European Americans.

Much historical research demonstrates that there has long been in North America and elsewhere a dominant, white-created racial frame that provides an over-arching and generally destructive worldview, one extending across divisions of class, gender, and age. Since its full development over the seventeenth century, this powerful frame has provided the vantage point from which white Americans have constantly viewed North American society. Its centrality in white minds is what makes it a dominant frame throughout the country and, indeed, the Western world. Over time, this powerful frame has been elaborated by, and imposed on, the minds of most Americans, becoming thereby the country's dominant "frame of mind" and "frame of reference" in regard to racial matters.

Recall from Chapter 1 (pp. 25–26) that in this broad racial framing white Americans have combined at least these important features: racial stereotypes; racial narratives and interpretations; racial images and language accents; racialized emotions; and inclinations to discriminate. In this chapter we will touch on all these aspects, but focus especially on the first three dimensions. Typically, for a broad social frame like this, its deeply imbedded beliefs and attitudes are constantly reflected in the talk and actions of everyday life. One need not know or accept the entire frame for it to have a substantial impact on thought and action. Thus, each person may utilize just selected elements of the dominant racial frame.

The perpetuation of systemic racism in this country has required an intergenerational reproducing not only of racist institutions but also of the white-racist frame that buttresses them. The early exploitative relationships that whites developed in regard to African Americans and Native Americans were soon rationalized, and they became enduring racist relationships. From the beginning, white-imposed racism has been webbed into most arenas of North American life, including places of work and residence, and activities as diverse as eating, procreating, and child rearing. Racist practices in these everyday life worlds create, and are in turn shaped by, basic racist categories, stereotypes, images, and emotions in the minds of Americans, especially white Americans. The white racial frame is an over-arching umbrella frame that includes all such racist material, in regard to both African Americans and other Americans of color. In later sections of this chapter we will examine in detail the over-arching white racial framing of our past and present, with an emphasis on the role of white elites in framing and perpetuating antiblack and other elements of that broad and long-dominant racial frame. In Chapter 4 we will look at the present day, and focus on the array of specific antiblack stereotypes, images, emotions, and interpretations that persist in that frame, with an emphasis on the views of ordinary white Americans.

Major societal frames are typically created, codified, and maintained by those at the top of a society, although this construction and perpetuation takes place in routine and ongoing interaction with the views and practices of ordinary citizens. Those with the greater power typically have the greater ability to impose their social frames on others. As Karl Marx and Friedrich Engels long ago pointed out, "the ideas of the ruling class are in every epoch the ruling ideas: i.e. the class, which is the ruling material force of society, is at the same time its ruling intellectual force."[3] White elites have dominated the creation, discussion, and dissemination of a system-rationalizing racist frame in institutional arenas such as business, the media, politics, education, churches, and government. While there is indeed much popularly generated racist stereotyping, imagery, and interpretation, even this is usually codified and embellished by the elites.

As with most important societal frames, if the elites had been opposed to the development of the dominant racist framing, they would have actively combated it, and it would likely have declined in social importance. In a detailed analysis of the racist ideas and actions of presidents from George Washington to Bill Clinton, Kenneth O'Reilly has shown that conventional wisdom about presidents *following* a racist populace is wrongheaded. The historical evidence shows that most of these powerful white men who controlled U.S. political institutions at the top have worked hard "to nurture and support the nation's racism."[4] The dominant racist framing did not arise accidentally. It was, and still is, actively developed and aggressively propagated by whites in various social classes.

Eurocentric Framing: Early Views

For several centuries now, white religious leaders, business people, political leaders, academics, scientists, and media analysts have developed and disseminated to all people a complex and variegated white-racist framing that defends the theft of land and labor from people of color. The antiblack elements of the old white racial frame are perhaps the most developed and have long included various religious, scientific, and psychosexual rationalizations for racial oppression. Although the dominant racial frame has been elaborated and changed somewhat over time, in all its variations it has operated to rationalize, sustain, and script white power and privilege.

Negative Images of Colonized Peoples

By the mid-1400s the Portuguese were sailing regularly to Africa and exporting Africans in bloody chains. Views of European superiority were developed and fostered in the first imperialistic countries, Portugal and Spain, as they exploited the resources of many indigenous peoples. For a time, a few leading Catholic priests and theologians opposed the ruthless exploitation of indigenous populations, including the often genocidal operations of Spanish colonizers such as those led by Christopher Columbus against indigenous peoples in the Americas in the late fifteenth and early sixteenth centuries. However, in a 1550 debate Spanish theologian Gaines de Sepulveda argued that it was lawful to enslave indigenous populations because of their heathen, sinful, and uncivilized natures, which obligated the latter to serve those (the Spanish) with the superior culture. Gaines de Sepulveda represented the increasingly dominant European view and was perhaps the first European thinker to defend the barbarity of colonialism in comprehensive cultural terms.[5]

The English soon followed in the imperialistic ways of the Spanish. Prior to English colonization of North America and much of the globe, some negative ideas about non-English peoples overseas were already current in England, probably coming from other European explorers. For example, in 1611, a few years before English colonists brought Africans into the Jamestown colony, William Shakespeare's play *The Tempest*—set perhaps on the island of Bermuda—had featured the sinister figure of Caliban. Caliban is portrayed as the dark other, as a "savage and deformed slave." His mother is said to be from Africa. Caliban is portrayed as physically threatening to Prospero, a European man of intellect. Already, the English had some negative images of certain cultural others before their overseas conquests were well underway.[6]

"Christians" Versus the "Uncivilized Others"

From the 1600s to the 1800s the English and other European Protestants dominated the religious scene on the Atlantic coast of North America, and from the beginning their religious views incorporated notions of group superiority and inferiority. Early English Protestants regarded themselves as Christian and civilized, but those they exploited and conquered as unchristian and savage.

Very important to the emergence of European imperialism and colonialism was the early development of a strong acquisitive and predatory ethic, an ethic coupled with a missionary zeal convinced of the superiority of European civilization. At the center of European imperialism was a powerful drive to dominate the entire world, at whatever human cost, for economic and cultural gain. By the 1500s and 1600s the ever-spreading acquisitiveness and rapaciousness of the north European bourgeoisie was reinforced by the values of their Protestant religious groups. The individualistic Protestant ethic did not create their aggressive capitalism, but did foster certain values associated with capitalism, including a greedy individualism that contrasted with the more collectivistic values of the majority of the world's peoples.[7]

Most European colonists coming to the Americas saw themselves as Christian people of good virtue and advanced civilization. From the first century of colonization these Europeans portrayed themselves as, to use Ronald Takaki's phrase, "virtuous republicans." They did not, or should not, have the instinctual qualities of the "creatures of darkness," the black and red Calibans of the invaded countries that they saw in their stereotyped images. Europeans were rational, ascetic, self-governing, and sexually controlled, while the Native American and African others were irrational, uncivilized, instinctual, and uncontrolled.[8] The first non-Europeans with whom many European colonists came into contact were Native Americans. Rationalizing the often brutal destruction of indigenous societies, European colonists early developed some negative images of those they conquered. Native Americans were often viewed as "uncivilized savages" to be killed off or pushed well beyond the boundaries of European American society. Significantly, much white thinking about indigenous peoples in the first centuries alternated between great hostility, such as can be seen in the Declaration of Independence's complaint about "merciless Indian savages," and the paternalism seen in the image of a "noble savage" in some Western literature.[9]

In Europe and the Americas, a commonplace European or European American explanation for the exploitation and enslavement of other groups, especially people of African descent, drew on an old myth based on the biblical story of Noah and his sons (Genesis 9–10). This old story relates how a drunken Noah was encountered by three sons. Two of them, Shem and Japheth, did not look on him but covered his nakedness. Noah's son Ham looked but did not cover him. As a result, Ham's son Canaan was cursed by Noah and told that he would be the servant of his brethren. A later version of this myth views Ham as African and suffering the divine punishment of his descendants being made servants to other peoples, the descendants of Ham's brothers. However, in the Christian Bible there is nothing about Ham's African characteristics. It was later, in the Talmudic and Midrashic (Jewish) religious tradition, that Ham (or Canaan) was said to have "darkened the faces of mankind," and thus was asserted to be father to the African peoples. This Ham myth was picked up in Christian communities by the 1500s, and the story was used by European colonists to justify the subjugation and enslavement of Africans and African Americans.[10]

A religious theory of black subordination and separation remained strong throughout the slavery and legal segregation periods, and some of it can still be found today. For centuries religious myths about people of African descent have been retold as part of the dominant racial framing by members of white ruling elites, including ministers, business leaders, political officials, and judges, as well as by ordinary whites.[11]

Early Color Coding: The Link to Slavery

In the early seventeenth century English American colonists first used terms like "Christians" for themselves and "negroes" for African Americans. The latter term referred to African descent and was not yet a designation for a distinctive "race." Nonetheless, the conceptualization was gradually moving in the direction of a full-fledged biologized racism, for the colonists were paying increasing attention to skin color and the purity of their ancestry ("blood"). As early as 1614, Reverend Samuel Purchas spoke of the "black Negroe" and the "whiter European."[12] Moreover, many were arguing that there was a God-ordained hierarchy of human beings. It was thus part of the nature of being defined as "black" to suffer discrimination. One was only "black" in relationship to those self-defined as "white."

In the process of English colonialism and the African slave trade some of the world's lightest-skinned people came into contact with some of the world's darkest-skinned people. Gradually, color and other physical characteristics became central to a dominant racial framing that aggressively rationalized and sustained this intensive exploitation and oppression. In the prevailing European view, which was both verbalized and emotion-laden, the enslaved status of most African Americans was *natural*: African Americans were inferior because they were enslaved, and they were enslaved because they were inferior. The expansion of enslavement and color typing developed side-by-side, with one reinforcing the other. By the late 1600s colonial accounts refer to the unusual "complexion" of the slaves as making an impression on the "white" mind. The word "white" was increasingly used alongside "Christian" and "English" by the colonists to distinguish themselves from "negroes," who had no role in the naming process. By means of slavery European colonists had created a new group consisting of people from different African societies, one sharply differentiated from whites in rights and privileges. Enslaved Africans and their descendants became a major point of reference for the construction of the newly defined whiteness. In 1709 an English official noted in his diary that a Spaniard had petitioned the Massachusetts Council for his freedom and that a certain Captain Teat had alleged that "all of that [dark] Color were Slaves."[13] Darker skin color was early on taken by whites as the visible badge of enslavement.

The controlling language in the new nation was clearly that of the English colonists. They had power to shape all the everyday terminology used in interaction with one another and with those they oppressed. Increasingly, skin color was linked to older color meanings in English. In Old English, the word "black" meant sooted, while the word "white" meant to gleam brightly, as for a candle. In line with earlier Christian usage, the word "black" was used by the English colonists to describe sin, evil, and the devil. Old Christian images of darkness and blackness as sinister were transferred to the darker-skinned peoples exploited in the system of slavery. The European colonists, who were usually some shade of tan, brown, or pink in skin color, must also have seen that Africans varied greatly in skin color, with the majority being some shade of brown, not actually black. There was no obvious reason for the English to connect the longstanding religious images of evil and darkness with the skin color of Africans.[14]

In the first century of North American slavery the antiblack framing was becoming ever-more developed and comprehensive. The emerging racial framing increasingly focused not only on the negative blackness of the others but also on the virtuous whiteness of Europeans. Africans and African Americans were viewed as physically, aesthetically, morally, and mentally inferior to whites—differences that were regarded as more or less permanent. "Whiteness" was thus created by self-named whites in opposition to "blackness," in comparison to which it was not only different but quite superior. Significantly, the antiblack stereotyping and imagery was not "out there," but rather in the white mind and its deep racialized emotions. In their thinking and imaging, some whites went so far as to view the dark skin of Africans as a "natural infection" or as "pollution."[15]

Legal and Educational Underpinnings

At an early stage, the antiblack perspective of white Americans was imbedded in the new legal and political institutions undergirding slavery. By the 1670s slavery was firmly enshrined in colonial laws defining Africans as chattel property. From that time to the Civil War much law-making, North and South, strongly supported the barbaric institution. Consider the central colony in the first century and a half—Virginia. In that area could be found about 40 percent of all those enslaved, as well as many of the prominent whites who were speaking out on issues of equality and liberty. Thomas Jefferson published the cases of Virginia's General Court for the years 1730 to 1772. More than half involved legal matters of concern to slaveholders, "such as testamentary disposition of slaves, creditors' rights in a debtor's slaves, warranty in the sale of slaves, life estates in and mortgages of slaves, dower in slaves, and entailed slaves."[16] From the 1600s to the 1800s many state and federal court decisions revealed the *centrality* of slavery to the new nation.

As we have seen, the U.S. Constitution recognized the slavery economy and implicitly incorporated strong white-supremacist ideas in such provisions as the one that counted an African American as only "three-fifths" of a person. After the new nation was created, the unifying of ever-growing numbers of immigrants from various European countries was done in part through the legal and political doctrines buttressing white privilege and superiority. For example, in the first naturalization law in 1790, the new U.S. Congress made the earliest political statement on citizenship. Naturalization was restricted to "white persons." Whiteness thereby became an official government category; only European immigrants could qualify to become U.S. citizens. In contrast, African Americans who had ancestors going back several generations were not citizens.[17]

Moreover, from the colonial era to the present, educational institutions have also been critical to the transmission of the dominant antiblack framing. Elites have long maintained power in part by controlling processes of knowledge dissemination through public schooling. At an early point in colonial history, a New England minister, Samuel Hopkins, noted why whites see blacks negatively:

> We have been used to look on them in a mean, contemptible light; and *our education* has filled us with *strong prejudices* against them, and led us to consider them, not as our brethren, or in any degree on a level with us; but as quite another species of animals, made only to serve us and our children; and as happy in bondage, as in any other state.[18]

Historically, whites have learned much racial stereotyping and other racial framing at school, at home, and in church.

Emotional Underpinnings

From the seventeenth century to the present the white framing that justifies antiblack oppression, while overtly verbal-cognitive and legally enshrined, has had a very strong *emotional* character. Antiblack stereotyping, images, and actions have long been linked to such emotions as hate, fear, guilt, and repulsion.

For example, for generations many whites have been emotionally obsessed with what they term "racial mixing." Strong and irrational emotions are evident in taboos and laws against interracial sex and marriage, which have long been considered to be "unnatural" or "abominable" by many whites. In 1662 the colony of Virginia established the first explicit law against interracial sex, and in 1691 a law against interracial marriage was enforced by banishment.[19] Mixed-ancestry Americans were viewed not only as inferior but also as degrading what Benjamin Franklin called a "lovely" whiteness. As Franklin argued, white "amalgamation with the other color produces a degradation to which no lover of his country, no lover of excellence in the human character can innocently consent."[20] Like most whites of the eighteenth century, Franklin seems to have developed a substantial fear of black Americans. A slaveholder for several decades, then an abolitionist later in life, Franklin appeared to oppose slavery not so much because of its inhumanity, but because of its negative impact on the white population. Ironically and significantly, for most of U.S. history it was white men who were the most likely to cross the color line and force sexual relations on black women.

Strong emotions are also evident in the white violence that has long targeted black Americans. While most bloodthirsty lynchings of black Americans took place after the Civil War, they were preceded before that war by barbaric beatings, rape, torture, and mutilation of Africans and African Americans on slave ships, farms, and plantations. The early white framing of African Americans as "dangerous savages" and "degenerate beasts" played a role in rationalizing violence. To deserve such treatment "the black man presumably had to be as vicious as the racists claimed; otherwise many whites would have had to accept an intolerable burden of guilt for perpetrating or tolerating the most horrendous cruelties and injustices."[21] After slavery, the white-racist frame legitimated lynchings, whose sadistic character suggests deep and shared white emotions of guilt, hatred, or fear.

Fear is central to the white-racist framing woven through the system of antiblack oppression. Significantly, of the three large-scale systems of social oppression—racism, sexism, and classism—only racism involves the dominant group having a deeply rooted and often obsessively emotional fear of the subordinated group. The racist system of oppression is often deeply rooted in the identity of white men, women, and children.

Why do so many whites often react viscerally to the presence or image of the black body, especially that of black men? Joel Kovel has argued that many whites dislike black bodies because they project onto them their own psychological fears, which are often rooted in childhood fears. As they are socialized, young whites often learn, directly and indirectly, consciously and unconsciously, that the dark otherness of black Americans symbolizes degradation, danger, sinfulness, or the unknown—imagery dating back centuries and still present in many whites' imaginings. Over a lifetime many antiblack actions are strongly shaped by images in whites' unconscious minds. From this perspective, a primary reason for the intensely emotional character of the white-racist frame is that many whites project onto the black out-group their own deep-lying inclinations and forbidden desires, which cannot be openly acknowledged.[22]

Developing a More Explicit Framing of "Race"

A we/they **ethnocentrism** and Eurocentrism existed long before Europeans built colonial empires, but a well-developed exploitative, and soon to be fully racist, frame emerged only with European domination of peoples overseas. As Oliver Cox has noted, the modern racist perspective did not arise out of some "abstract, natural, immemorial feeling of mutual antipathy between groups," but rather grew out of the exploitative relationships of colonialism.[23] Indeed, there are significant variations across societies. Some do not develop the high level of xenophobia that others do. Historically, many indigenous societies showed a friendliness (xenophilia) toward Europeans when the latter first came into their areas. As it turned out, this friendly attitude was usually a serious mistake.

The racial framing that rationalized European exploitation did not develop all at once, but was elaborated as colonialism expanded around the globe. Initially, as we saw above, the "others" were primarily viewed as religiously and culturally inferior. This brought an early accent on a hierarchy of inferior and superior groups. A little later, those oppressed were seen as distinctive "races" that were inferior in physical, biological, and intellectual terms to Europeans. A fully developed concept of "race" as a pseudo-biological category was developed by Europeans and European Americans in the late 1600s and 1700s and was codified in the work of leading European and American intellectuals around the time of the American Revolution.

By the late-1700s these hierarchical relations were increasingly explained in overtly bio-racial terms. This biological determinism read existing European prejudices back into human biology; then it read that biology as rationalizing social hierarchy. Those at the bottom were less than human; they were alleged to have smaller and inferior brains. The concept of "race" in the dominant racial frame had at least these three important elements:

1. an accent on physically and biologically distinctive categories called "races";
2. an emphasis on "race" as the primary determinant of a group's essential personality and cultural traits; and
3. a hierarchy of superior and inferior racial groups.[24]

Early White Leaders and Intellectuals

Anthropologist Audrey Smedley has argued that "race was, from its inception, a folk classification, a product of popular beliefs about human differences that evolved from the sixteenth through the nineteenth centuries."[25] However, much of the effort to create a societal frame accenting a distinctive hierarchy of races has come from *white elites*. While most people tend to sort others into social categories, elites actively codify and propagate certain strong versions of social categorization. From the beginning, European and American elites worked hard to defend imperialism and its oppression. By the mid-to-late eighteenth century, white intellectuals and political leaders were arguing that "negroes" were a biologically different "race" from Europeans. In a lengthy book, *The History of Jamaica* (1774), prominent judge Edward Long, a slaveholder, argued that Africans were a "truly bestial" and different species. Long's book was published in the United States in 1788.[26]

Recall too that about this time our very important early theorist of equality and liberty, Thomas Jefferson, contended that black Americans were an inferior "race," a word he helped to make central to the racialized thinking of his day. In his influential book *Notes on the State of Virginia*, published in the late eighteenth century, Jefferson articulated the first well-honed and extensive arguments by a North American intellectual for black racial inferiority. As I noted previously, in his writings he views African Americans as inferior to whites in reasoning, imagination, beauty, and other important qualities.[27] Over his long lifetime Jefferson was a major slaveholder who owned hundreds of African Americans, even though he occasionally asserted that he disliked slavery. Among his famous words on the subject are those now inscribed on the Jefferson Memorial in Washington, D.C.: "Nothing is more certainly written in the book of fate than that these people are to be free." Significantly, his critical words that follow this quoted sentence are (probably intentionally) omitted on this monument: "Nor is it less certain that the two races, equally free, cannot live in the same government." For this reason, Jefferson was a supporter of exporting African Americans back to Africa, should they ever become free.[28]

During the eighteenth and nineteenth centuries white American leaders in business, politics, and the universities were greatly influenced by European intellectuals and writers, many of whom held openly antiblack views. The latter, in turn, were greatly influenced by reports from the European colonies in the Americas. The major Western philosopher of the late eighteenth century, Immanuel Kant, produced the first developed theory of race in modern terms. Many people have long viewed Kant as the leading moral philosopher of the West, a pure philosopher uncontaminated by racist thought. However, for decades Kant taught some of the first courses explicitly dealing with the geography and anthropology of race. At the heart of his influential thinking was an attempt to define humanity:

> If there is any science man really needs, it is the one I teach, of how to fulfill properly that position in creation which is assigned to man, and from which he is able to learn what one must be in order to be a man.

For Kant, one must be *white* to be fully human, for "humanity exists in its greatest perfection in the white race."[29]

During the 1770s Kant wrote of the hierarchy of "races of mankind," one of the early uses of the term "races" in the sense of biologically distinct, hierarchical categories. In one document Kant delineated a hierarchy, with whites at the top:

STEM GENUS, white brunette.
First race, very blond (northern Europe), of damp cold.
Second race, Copper-Red (America), of dry cold.
Third race, Black (Senegambia), of dry heat.
Fourth race, Olive-Yellow (Indians), of dry heat.[30]

At this point in Western history, even the most advanced European philosophy and philosophical anthropology were grounded in ideas about the supremacy of the white race and Western civilization.

Scientific Racism

From the mid-eighteenth century to the mid-twentieth century, the ever-expanding physical and social sciences were regularly and openly used to defend the oppression of Americans of color. Leading scientists developed a scientific view of black Americans and other peoples of color as innately inferior beings. Ideological racism is not something that comes only out of the margins of Western societies, but rather from their intellectual and cultural centers.

For example, between the 1770s and the 1790s the very prominent German anatomist and anthropologist Johann Blumenbach worked out a detailed racial classification that became very influential. At the top of his list of "races" were what Blumenbach called the "Caucasians" (Europeans), a term he coined because in his judgment the people of the Caucasus were the most beautiful of European peoples. Lower on the list were the Mongolians (Asians), the Ethiopians (Africans), the Americans (Native Americans), and the Malays (Polynesians). In this view "white" was viewed as the oldest color of mankind and had degenerated into darker skin colors.[31]

The new scientific racism firmly encompassed the notion of specific races with different physical characteristics, a belief that these characteristics were hereditary, and the notion of a natural hierarchy of inferior and superior races. In their broad sweep these racist ideas were not supported by careful scientific observations of all human societies but rather were buttressed with racially slanted reports gleaned by European missionaries, travelers, and sea captains from their experiences with selected non-European societies. Most scientists of the late eighteenth and nineteenth centuries, while presenting themselves as objective observers, tried to marshal evidence for human differences that the white imperialists' perspective had already decided were important to highlight.[32]

Celebrating and Expanding the Racist Frame: The 1830s to the 1930s

The International Industry of Racist Thinking

By the mid-nineteenth century the propagation of antiblack and other racist ideas and images had become a major industry in Europe and the United States. From then to now, literally thousands of articles and books have been written, as well as speeches given, as part of a racist framing machine that constantly defends white supremacy and racial oppression, most frequently antiblack oppression.

We should note too that this dominant racial framing is often challenged, when those who are oppressed fight back, such as in slave rebellions, abolitionist movements, and civil rights movements (see Chapter 8, pp. 268–277). However, when white interests have been seriously challenged, whites, especially those in the elite, have attempted to deflect or destroy those challenges. The elite must constantly combat counter-framed insights into the real nature of the oppressive racist reality that its members have fostered and maintained. For example, during the mid-decades of the nineteenth century the growing antislavery movement in Britain and the United States spurred an elite reaction that was quite extensive and combative. An even more developed and formalized racist frame was created in a vigorous attempt to defend slavery against abolitionism.[33]

Many U.S. and European intellectuals intensified arguments for white supremacy and African or African American inferiority. For example, in his 1830 lectures the leading German philosopher G.W.F. Hegel spoke about the "Negro" as "natural man in his wild and untamed nature" and argued that there is "nothing remotely humanized in the Negro's character." Black people were not human beings with a real history and human consciousness. Hegel based his racist judgments on the racist reports of numerous European travelers. Drawing on similar sources, leading authors as diverse as Thomas Carlyle, William Makepeace Thackeray, and Charles Dickens defended aggressively racist ideas and/or the enslavement of Africans.[34]

Count Joseph Arthur de Gobineau, a French diplomat and important racist thinker of the nineteenth century, argued that whites are

> gifted with reflective energy, or rather with an energetic intelligence.... They have a remarkable, even extreme love of liberty, and are openly hostile to the formalism under which the Chinese are glad to vegetate, as well as the strict despotism which is the only way of governing the Negro.[35]

In extensive writings Gobineau articulated a developed racist framing and, once translated, his writings became influential in the United States and numerous other countries. Later on, Gobineau's ideas would greatly influence some German Nazi thinkers and officials, indicating again how powerful the white-racist frame has been across the globe. Pre-eminent physical scientists also accepted notions of white supremacy. In the nineteenth century the leading French anatomist Paul Broca broke important new ground in understanding how the human brain works. Nonetheless, Broca was also a leading racist thinker who argued that variations in human head shape were linked to significant mental differences among racial groups. For him black skin and wooly hair were associated with inferior intelligence, while white skin and straight hair were the "equipment of the highest groups."[36] While Broca later retracted these views, many scientists and popular writers of the era aggressively spread his idea of head form being linked to "race" and character.

Political Elites

In the United States distinguished lawyers, judges, and political leaders promoted scientific racism and its white-supremacist assumptions. Recall that in the first half of the nineteenth century whites with an interest in slavery dominated the U.S. political and legal system. This influence was conspicuous in the previously mentioned *Dred Scott* v. *John F.A. Sandford* (1857) decision (see p. 33). Replying to the petition of an enslaved black American, a substantial majority of the Supreme Court ruled that Scott was *not* a citizen under the Constitution. Chief Justice Roger Taney, a slaveholder, argued that African Americans had, since long before the making of the U.S. Constitution,

> been regarded as beings of an inferior order, and altogether unfit to associate with the white race, either in social or political relations; and so far inferior, that they had no rights which the white man was bound to respect; and that the negro might justly and lawfully be reduced to slavery for his benefit. He was bought and sold, and treated as an ordinary article of merchandise and traffic, whenever a profit could be made by it. This opinion was at that time fixed and universal in the civilized portion of the white race.[37]

The *Dred Scott* decision showed that the dominant racial frame was well-established: all black Americans, whether slave or technically "free," were inferior beings with no rights, and white supremacy was the law of the land.

Senators and presidents played a role in spreading this dominant frame. President James Buchanan, a northerner, urged the country to support the racist thinking of *Dred Scott*. Before he became president, in a debate with Senator Stephen A. Douglas, Abraham Lincoln himself had argued that the physical difference between racial groups was insuperable, saying:

I am not nor ever have been in favor of the social and political equality of the white and black races: that I am not nor ever have been in favor of making voters of the free negroes, or jurors, or qualifying them to hold office or having them to marry with white people.... I as much as any other man am in favor of the superior position being assigned to the white man.[38]

Lincoln, soon to be called the "Great Emancipator," had made his white-supremacist views clear, views later cited by southern officials in their 1960s struggle to protect legal segregation. Indeed, today Lincoln's racist views are still quoted by white-supremacist groups in their literature and on a growing number of websites.

The end of slavery did not end the pervasiveness of the strong white-supremacist version of the dominant racial frame. Many whites pressed for a system of legal segregation. They had the support of President Andrew Johnson, who in 1867 commented on what he called the "naked savages," saying, "It is vain to deny that they [black Americans] are an inferior race—very far inferior to the European variety. They have learned in slavery all that they know in civilization."[39] Numerous white members of Congress also used the new racist science to argue for the subordination of black Americans.[40]

With the end of Reconstruction in 1877 came comprehensive Jim Crow segregation in the South and numerous other areas. Distinguished judges, including on the Supreme Court, played a key role in solidifying this legal segregation and in unifying white defenses of it. Recall that in *Plessy* v. *Ferguson* (1896) a nearly unanimous Supreme Court legitimated the fiction of "separate but equal" for white and black Americans in a case dealing with racially segregated railroad cars. This separate-but-equal fiction was legal for more than half a century, until the 1954 *Brown* v. *Board of Education of Topeka* decision desegregated some Jim Crow schools, and until broken down further by 1960s civil rights laws. Until then, there had been widespread agreement in the white elite and the white population about the desirability of thorough segregation for black men, women, and children.

Even whites opposed to official segregation articulated a belief in white superiority. Justice John Marshall Harlan, the lone dissenter in *Plessy* v. *Ferguson*, noted in his opinion that

the white race deems itself to be the dominant race in this country. And so it is, in prestige, in achievements, in education, in wealth and in power. So, I doubt not, it will continue to be for all time, if it remains true to its great heritage and holds fast to the principles of constitutional liberty.[41]

The white race, this opponent of government segregation noted, would probably dominate for all time. Two sentences later, Harlan added that "our Constitution is colorblind, and neither knows nor tolerates classes among citizens." Harlan was among the very first to publicly articulate the idealistic, and mythical, view that the U.S. Constitution was colorblind.

The open assertion of white-supremacist views was commonplace for government officials in the nineteenth and early twentieth centuries. Given increasing immigration in this period from non-European countries, these officials gave much attention to who was, or was not, "white." Between 1878 and 1923 a series of federal court cases decided that the following Americans were *not* white and thus were ineligible for citizenship: Chinese Americans, native Hawaiians, those half-Asian, those half-Indian, Burmese Americans, Japanese Americans, Filipino Americans, those three-quarters Filipino, and Korean Americans. They were placed, by white judges and other whites, toward the "black end" of the white-to-black racial desirability continuum that has long been common in white minds (see Chapter 7, pp. 209–222). Indeed, whiteness as an official criterion for immigrants to become U.S. citizens was not officially changed until the 1952 Immigration and Nationality Act.[42]

Social Darwinism

In his influential writings Charles Darwin applied the important evolutionary idea of natural selection not only to animal development but also to the development of human "races." In spite of his pathbreaking idea of human evolution, he too was unable to escape the racist framing common among scientists of his day. Thus, he saw this natural selection at work in the killing of indigenous peoples in Australia by the British, wrote of black people as a category between whites and gorillas, and spoke against social programs for the "weak" because they permitted the least desirable people to survive. In his view the "civilized races" would eventually replace "savage races throughout the world."[43]

During the late 1800s and early 1900s a perspective called "social Darwinism" argued aggressively that certain racially "inferior races" were less evolved, less human, and more ape-like than the "superior races." Prominent social scientists like Herbert Spencer and William Graham Sumner argued that social life was a life-and-death struggle in which the best individuals would win out over inferior individuals. Sumner argued that wealthy Americans, who were almost entirely white at the time, were products of natural selection and essential to the advance of human civilization. Black Americans were seen by many of these racist analysts as a "degenerate race" whose alleged "immorality" was a natural trait. Significantly, some consciously connected their racist doctrines with defenses of other societal oppression, particularly sexism and class oppression. For example, in the late nineteenth century one U.S. author, M.G. Delaney, vigorously argued that the races at the bottom of the ladder were inferior and female-dominated, while those at the top of the ladder were superior and male-dominated. From this perspective a strong patriarchal system was a clear sign of the "better races."[44]

By the late 1800s a eugenics movement was spreading among scientists and other intellectuals in Europe and the United States. Eugenicists accented the importance of breeding the "right" types of human groups. Britain's famous scientist Francis Galton argued for improving the superior race by human intervention. Like Galton, U.S. eugenicists opposed "racial mixing" because it destroyed racial purity. Allowing "unfit races" to survive would destroy the "superior race" of northern Europeans. Those from the lesser races, it was decided, should be sterilized or excluded from the country. Such views were not on the far-out fringe, but had the weight of established scientists, leading politicians, and major business leaders. For example, in 1893 Nathaniel S. Shaler, a prominent Harvard University dean, publicly argued that black Americans were inferior, uncivilized, and an "alien folk" with no place in the U.S. body politic and destined for eventual extinction under ongoing processes of natural law.[45]

In the first decades of the twentieth century most social scientists and intellectuals accepted some form of scientific racism. Thus, in 1923 Carl Brigham, a Princeton University psychologist who would later play a central role in developing college entrance tests, argued pugnaciously for the intellectual inferiority of various racial groups, using data from new psychometric tests given during World War I to draftees. Low psychometric test scores by Italian and Russian immigrants, as well as by black Americans, were explained in terms of their "inferior racial stocks."[46]

Madison Grant, another influential intellectual, developed racist ideas in *The Passing of the Great Race*. In this book's four editions between 1916 and 1923, Grant wrote that the new immigrant groups from southern and eastern Europe would interbreed and destroy the superior "Nordic race."[47] In 1920 Lothrop Stoddard, a Harvard-educated lawyer and historian, wrote, in another influential book, entitled *The Rising Tide of Color: Against White World-Supremacy*, of the "overwhelming preponderance of the white race in the ordering of the world's affairs ... the indisputable master of the planet."[48] Like many of his contemporaries, as well as many white commentators today (see below, pp. 93–95), Stoddard feared that in the future whites would be overwhelmed by large numbers of black Americans and other Americans of color. Grant and Stoddard were influential among white scientists and administrators at many colleges and universities, as well as among celebrated white politicians.

More Politicians and Presidents

Scientific racism was periodically used by white members of Congress to support passage of discriminatory legislation, including the openly racist 1924 immigration law, which excluded most immigrants other than northern Europeans. In this period overtly racist ideas were advocated by U.S. presidents. Former president Theodore Roosevelt liked scientific racism and praised Madison Grant's influential book for its "grasp of the facts our people need to realize."[49] President Woodrow Wilson was well-known as an advocate of the superiority of European civilization over all others, including those of Africa. As president, Wilson increased the racial segregation of the federal government. Significantly, no less a racist leader than Adolf Hitler would later report having been influenced by Wilson's racist writings.[50] (The first modern use of the term "racism" was apparently in a 1933 German book by Magnus Hirschfeld, who sought to counter the Nazis' and other European racists' notions of a biologically determined hierarchy of races.[51])

In 1921 President Warren G. Harding, who had been linked to the Ku Klux Klan, said he rejected any "suggestion of social equality" between whites and blacks, citing Stoddard's book as evidence that the "race problem" was global. Just before he became president, Calvin Coolidge wrote in *Good Housekeeping* magazine, "Biological laws tell us that certain divergent people will not mix or blend. The Nordics propagate themselves successfully. With other races, the outcome shows deterioration on both sides."[52] Ideas of white supremacy and rigid segregation were openly advocated by major white political leaders.

With the expansion of European and U.S. colonialism into Asia and Africa in the last half of the nineteenth century, new emphases were added to the prevailing racial frame. One relatively new emphasis was "teleological racism"—the view that non-European peoples, including Africans, had been created as inferior so that they could serve, and be civilized by, whites. A famous statement of this is Rudyard Kipling's 1899 poem, "The White Man's Burden" ("Take up the White Man's burden/ Send forth the best ye breed"). From Kipling's perspective whites had a missionary obligation to help "inferior races," termed in the poem as "half-devil, half-child."[53] These white-racist formulations explained not only the character and conditions of those oppressed but also celebrated whites as especially civilized, Christian, powerful, and generous toward those conquered. Variations on this old racist framing have long rationalized the oppressive policies directed by Western corporations and governments at peoples of color across the globe, to the present day.

Immigrants Becoming "White"

What the white elites have propagated as a white racial framing of society, the white majority has usually accepted, if often with their own adaptations. The transmission of the racist framing from one social group to the next is a critical mechanism in the social reproduction of racism. Most ordinary whites have come to look at their social worlds in white-racist terms and accepted the psychological wage of whiteness and racist ideas propagated by elites.

Thus, from the 1830s to the early 1900s millions of European immigrants accepted the dominant racial frame as a way to gain white privileges. Take the case of poor Irish immigrants who came in substantial numbers in the 1830s and 1840s. These Irish immigrants did not initially view themselves as "white," but identified with their home country. Once in the U.S., however, they were taught in overt and subtle ways that they were white by already established white ministers, priests, teachers, business people, newspaper editors, and political leaders with whom they interacted. They were pressured and manipulated by British American elites and their own leaders into accepting the dominant racial framing that privileged whiteness and denigrated blackness. Over the course of the nineteenth century most Irish immigrants and their children came to envision themselves as white and deserving of white privileges in regard to jobs and living conditions. Often coupled with this move to whiteness was active participation in efforts to drive black workers out of the better-paying jobs in numerous U.S. cities.[54]

Recent historical studies have shown how other European immigrant groups such as Italian and Jewish Americans also came to define themselves as white (see Chapter 7, p. 253). Many European immigrant groups accepted a comfortable place in a socially constructed "white race" whose privileges included such things as greater personal liberty, better-paying jobs, and the right to vote. They too often discriminated against black Americans and developed a strong antiblack perspective. Their general acceptance of the dominant racist frame—such as that reflected in popular performances at the blackface minstrel shows seen by many thousands in the decades just before and after 1900—created a "sense of popular whiteness among workers across lines of ethnicity, religion, and skill."[55]

Perpetuating the Racial Frame: The Contemporary United States

Periodically, the dominant racial framing developed in the first century of North American development has been added to, subtracted from, or rearranged in its emphases. Powerful whites have periodically dressed it up differently for changing social circumstances, although much of its racist reality has remained the same. New ideas and interpretations have been added to deal with pressures for change from those oppressed, particularly in regard to government remedial and antidiscrimination policies. After World War II, as we will see below, certain aspects of the dominant racial framing were altered a bit to fit the new circumstances of the 1950s and 1960s, during which era black Americans increasingly challenged the established patterns of compulsory Jim Crow segregation.

Continuing Elite Control: The Importance of the Media

In recent decades white elites have continued to dominate the construction and transmission of new or refurbished ideas, images, and narratives designed to buttress the system of racial inequality, and they have used ever-more-powerful means to accomplish their social ends. The U.S. mass media now include not only the radio, movies, and print media used in the past, but television, music videos, satellite transmissions, and the Internet.

Today, for the most part, the mass media are still controlled by whites. The overwhelming majority of full-time news reporters, supervisors, and editors at mainstream newspapers and magazines are white. On major television networks whites are over-represented in managerial jobs and as on-air reporters; they are greatly over-represented as "experts" in the mainstream media. In these media Americans of color have only a token presence in the choice and shaping of news reports and popular entertainment. The concentration of media control in a few corporations has increased dramatically in recent decades. In the twenty-first century fewer than two dozen corporations control much of the U.S. media. A recent study shows that nearly 97 percent of television stations are white-owned, with just 1.3 percent owned by African Americans (and an even smaller percentage by Latinos). More than 92 percent of full-power commercial radio stations are owned by whites. Less than 1 percent of the radio stations owned by whites have top executives who are black, Latino, or Asian American. Yet, Americans of color make up nearly one-third of the population and probably of users of the media. Such concentration usually means much less opinion diversity in social and political views in media programming.[56]

In addition, the mass media, especially television, are substantially supported by corporate advertisers. Directly or indirectly, advertisers have significant command over programming. Information about racial matters is usually filtered through a variety of elite-controlled organizations. This filtering is not coordinated, but reflects the choices of powerful whites socialized to the dominant value system in regard to racial issues. Looking for stories, reporters and journalists typically seek out established government, business, and think-tank experts. Historically, the right-wing of the elite, a large segment, has been committed to a more overtly stated racist perspective and has often pressed for curtailment or suppression of serious citizen protests against racial and other societal oppression. In contrast, historically the liberal wing of the white elite has been smaller and more attuned to popular movements. It has been willing to liberalize society to some degree and make some concessions to those protesting against racial oppression, for the sake of preserving societal order. The center of the elite has waffled between the two poles.

Recent decades have seen periodic shifts in the influence of these sectors of the white elite. During the late 1960s and 1970s many political and social science experts consulted by top executives in government and the media came from think tanks espousing views of those in the center or on the left of the elite. However, wealthy conservatives began in the 1970s to lavishly fund right-wing think tanks and press aggressively conservative views on universities, politicians, and media owners. In recent years right-wing think tanks—including the American Enterprise Institute, the Manhattan Institute, and the Heritage Foundation—have been successful in getting numerous right-wing experts into mainstream media. Working alongside a large group of other conservative intellectuals, media experts, and activists, right-wing think tanks continue to be successful in an indoctrination campaign aimed at conservatively shaping public views on racial issues and related social issues.[57]

Most Americans get their news from commercial television and radio programs, especially local programming. Using local and national media, elites have the capability to mobilize mass consensus on elite-generated ideas and views; this consensus often provides an illusion of democracy. These elites encourage collective ignorance by allowing little systematic, fully analyzed information deeply critical of the existing social and political system to be circulated through the media to the general population. Not surprisingly, omnipresent entertainment programs and incessant consumer advertising are dominant features of television and some other mainstream media.[58]

Given this dominance, and the generally weak history and other social science courses in our schools, most Americans are not well informed about many important aspects of U.S. society. The *Washington Post* published results of a survey of Americans on their political knowledge. Less than one-quarter knew the names of both of their U.S. senators; four in ten could not even name the Vice-President. Moreover, most Americans know little about U.S. history. In another survey, multiple-choice questions on U.S. history were given to respondents. Most could not choose 1775 as the year the Revolutionary War started, nor could they pick the area where that war ended (Virginia). Similarly, a Department of Education survey of high-school seniors found that six in ten lacked a knowledge of simple historical facts.[59] Even those Americans who think they know about U.S.

history often adhere to many myths and misconceptions taught in school. As one major research study has shown, current high-school textbooks communicate much in the way of inaccurate, distorted, and elliptical views of that history, particularly in regard to issues of U.S. racism and interracial conflicts.[60]

Because of this pervasive ignorance, white elites can easily persuade, create confusion in, or foster apathy in the general population. Television has often circulated racist stereotypes straight out of the dominant racial frame. These stereotypes create or reinforce negative racial images in many minds. A recent study found that television viewing had an important effect on white viewers' negative stereotypes of Latinos—when these viewers felt that they had learned important information about U.S. Latinos from watching television. In contrast, those whites who said that they had actually talked with, or had positive contacts with, Latinos were more likely to hold positive views of Latinos.[61]

Thus, with our national racial order firmly in place, most white Americans, from childhood on, have generally adopted the racially framed views, assumptions, and proclivities of previous generations, established white authorities, and/or the mainstream media. In this manner important aspects of systemic racism are routinely reproduced from one generation of whites to the next.

Increased Equality and Opportunity Rhetoric

Over the last half-century or so we have seen some significant changes in whites' discriminatory practices and in aspects of the rationalizing racial frame. Let us consider briefly some of this history. By the 1940s and 1950s black protests against Jim Crow were growing and having an impact on the U.S. image abroad. Legal segregation and protests against it were creating international problems for a U.S. government trying to fight a racist Nazi Germany and, after World War II, trying to contend with the Soviet Union for the allegiance of non-European nations. As early as 1952, U.S. Secretary of State Dean Acheson gave the U.S. Supreme Court a statement proclaiming that "the continuation of racial discrimination is a source of constant embarrassment to this government ... and it jeopardizes the effective maintenance of our moral leadership of the free and democratic nations of the world."[62] And a U.S. attorney general commented on the 1954 *Brown* school desegregation case (see below, p. 81) to the effect that racial segregation in schooling must be eradicated because it "furnishes grist for Communist propaganda mills." Thus, constitutional scholar Derrick Bell has suggested that, historically, white elites act to improve the conditions of black Americans only when whites themselves can benefit in the process.[63]

By the mid-1950s, and accelerating in the 1960s, the liberal wing of the ruling elite was pressing for a softening of blatantly racist prejudices and for modest new group-based remedies such as school desegregation and affirmative action, the latter aimed at integrating some men and women of color (and white women) into historically white-male-dominated employment settings. For a time, a more liberal approach rejecting Jim Crow segregation and accenting civil rights laws and affirmative action was successful in bringing some societal desegregation. From the 1950s to the 1970s federal courts ordered racial desegregation in various U.S. institutions. Reversing the earlier Supreme Court position in *Plessy* v. *Ferguson*, thus, a more liberal high court handed down *Brown* v. *Board of Education* in 1954—a unanimous ruling that "in the field of public education the doctrine of 'separate but equal' has no place."[64] Group-based remedies were increasingly used to implement school desegregation. In the face of black, Latino, and other protests in the streets—and sustained by substantial economic growth—some powerful white executives in multinational corporations decided not only to provide the civil rights movement with some funds but also to support certain political liberals in the Democratic Party in their efforts to expand government efforts against antidiscrimination and for social welfare programs. The liberal and centrist members of the elite were concerned with the U.S. image across the globe and with regaining social order in cities at home.[65]

From the 1960s onward the rhetoric of equality of opportunity grew in volume among members of the elite, including presidents and members of Congress. Black and other protests and rebellions of the 1950s and 1960s had an important effect in eradicating not only the system of the legal segregation but also most public defense of racial discrimination by many in the white leadership. Since the late 1960s most U.S. political and economic leaders have proclaimed at least the rhetoric of racial and ethnic equality. For example, a major advisor of leading business and political officials, the conservative Harvard professor Samuel Huntington, asserted in the influential policy journal *Foreign Affairs* that U.S. identity is centered in a widely accepted "set of universal ideas and principles articulated in the founding documents by American leaders: liberty, equality, democracy, constitutionalism, liberalism, limited government, private enterprise."[66]

By the late 1960s, moreover, a handful of white leaders and researchers were moved by the antiracist protests to reject current racist ideas and practices in stronger terms. An example of this race-critical perspective is the report of the 1968 Kerner Commission, established by President Lyndon B. Johnson to investigate black rioting in numerous cities. In a bold report this commission, most of whose members were white, concluded the United States was "moving toward two societies, one black, one white—separate and unequal." The report asserted that "white racism is essentially responsible for the explosive mixture which has been accumulating in our cities since the end of World War II."[67] However, this view, while accurate, was considered to be too radical by most white leaders, and the report and its realistic perspective were soon forgotten.

Clearly, the structural dismantling of a large-scale system of compulsory Jim Crow segregation from the 1950s to the 1970s both required and brought a renewed emphasis on equality and opportunity rhetoric in much public commentary by whites. However, while the everyday relationships and interactions of white and black Americans often changed somewhat, or significantly, with the demise of legal segregation, most whites in the elites and the general public were not interested in giving up most white power and privilege in historically white institutions. Societal equality was *not* even remotely on the agenda of societal change for most whites. As a result, even with an end to Jim Crow segregation, the dominant racial frame continued to incorporate many of its old antiblack and other racist features. It continued to rationalize persisting white power and privileges, but now under conditions of official desegregation.

The dominant racial frame was altered in some ways, especially by softening some racist imagery and re-emphasizing notions of fairness and opportunity that had actually been part of some versions of that frame for decades. Throughout the Jim Crow era, many whites felt that black Americans were usually treated fairly and/or had significant opportunities to succeed in society. Still, since the 1960s, accentuated notions of equality of opportunity and colorblindness have been moved to the forefront of common versions of the contemporary white racial frame, at least for a majority of whites. However, as I will demonstrate later, the more open professing by the white elite and public of the principles of **equal opportunity** and the official desegregation of public schools, workplaces, and public accommodations did *not* mean that black Americans now had true equality of access and opportunity. It also did not mean that most whites desired the federal government to implement large-scale racial integration of historically white-dominated institutions.

A Conservative Shift

As a result of this elite and public orientation, beginning around 1969 with the arrival of Richard Nixon's presidential administration, the rhetoric of fairness and equal opportunity was increasingly accompanied by a federal government that was backing off from many of its commitments to racial desegregation and the enforcement of the new civil rights laws. At the local level, there was increased police repression of aggressive dissent in the black community, such as the often illegal law-enforcement attacks on the Black Panthers and other militant groups by local police and FBI agents. The old racially framed images of "dangerous blacks" were dusted off and emphasized by prominent white leaders and media commentators who often proclaimed the rhetoric of equality of opportunity at the same time.[68]

Moreover, since the 1960s numerous conservative organizations have worked aggressively in pressing Congress, the courts, and the private sector to weaken or eliminate new antidiscrimination programs such as affirmative action, as well as an array of other government social programs designed to help the oppressed and impoverished (see Chapter 8, pp. 277–278). This organizational effort signaled the increasing influence on national policy of a conservative Republican Party that mainly represented the interests of white Americans. Even at the top of the Democratic Party there was some shift to the right, which could be seen in the relatively modest antidiscrimination policies of the 1970s Jimmy Carter administration and the 1990s Bill Clinton administration.

The federal courts provide another important example of this conservative shift. In the decades from the 1970s to the present numerous conservative, mostly white, judges have ruled that group-remedy programs for racial discrimination violate the U.S. Constitution, which they assert only recognizes the rights of individuals, not groups. For instance, in 1989 a conservative Supreme Court handed down a still-cited major decision, *City of Richmond, Virginia* v. *J.A. Croson Co.*, which knocked down a local Richmond program designed to remedy some past discrimination against black and other minority businesses with modest set-asides.[69] The high court ruled in favor of a white-run construction company, the plaintiff, which argued that the municipal government had unconstitutionally set aside some local contracts for small minority companies. The mostly white court ruled that the Richmond government had not made a compelling case for remedying antiblack discrimination, even though the government defendant's statistics showed that in a city whose population was one-half black, *less than 1 percent* of city government business went to black-owned firms. Similar philosophical and legal arguments against significant remedial action for systemic racism have been reiterated by the plaintiffs and justices in other federal court cases since this important case. Several subsequent cases have built on this precedent to weaken even modest affirmative action programs.

To this day, and in spite of common beliefs to the contrary, the appropriate government agencies, including the Supreme Court, have *never* pursued aggressive enforcement of civil rights laws in all major areas, including housing and employment, primarily because of white resistance. Over recent decades the conservative, mostly white and male, justices on the Supreme Court have intentionally and severely limited the reach of 1960s and later civil rights laws by rejecting the legal relevance of plaintiffs' arguments showing institutionalized racism and by narrowing the legal definition of discrimination to cover only discriminatory incidents where a defendant can prove that specific (usually white) actors discriminated because of intentional racial prejudice.[70]

Since the 1970s, in the major sectors of U.S. society, including the federal and state courts, we have seen a renewed accent by white officials on portraying major U.S. institutions as now "colorblind." Recall nineteenth-century Supreme Court Justice John Marshall Harlan's view that the "Constitution is colorblind, and neither knows nor tolerates classes among citizens." Harlan's strong colorblind view of the U.S. Constitution did not become commonplace among members of the white elite until the 1960s. Since then, white adherents of the colorblind perspective in the elite and general public have come to the forefront. They view racial discrimination at the hands of judges and other government officials as quite rare and see U.S. legal and political institutions as now operating in a colorblind fashion.

Still Arguing for Biological "Races"

For much of the nineteenth and twentieth centuries the standard view among whites, including scientists and others in the academic elite, of the difficult social and economic conditions faced by black Americans was that those conditions resulted from blacks' inferior biological and cultural heritages. However, by the 1940s numerous leading scientists were questioning conventional wisdom on biological racism, and by the 1960s many had rejected the old biological determinism.

Still, there were many physical scientists who accepted the idea of biological races. As late as the 1980s, one survey found that 50 percent of physical anthropologists and 73 percent of animal behaviorists believed there were biologically differentiated "races" within the species *Homo sapiens*. However, only 29 percent of cultural anthropologists and 34 percent of sociologists surveyed also agreed. By then, the majority of social scientists no longer accepted traditional biological determinism, with most evidently accepting the idea that "race" was actually a social construction.[71]

Nonetheless, in recent decades a few social and physical scientists at major universities, such as Arthur Jensen at the University of California and Richard Herrnstein at Harvard University, have continued to argue that racial-group differences in average scores on so-called IQ tests reveal genetic differences in intelligence between black and white Americans. In 1969 the *Harvard Educational Review* lent its prestige to an article by Jensen. His arguments there and over the next two decades received much national attention, including major stories in *Time, Newsweek, U.S. News and World Report*, and in major newspapers. Jensen argued that on average black Americans are born with less intelligence than whites, and that "IQ" test data support this contention.[72] Another widely read example of biological determinism was a 1990s book, *The Bell Curve*, which sold more than half-a-million copies. Well into the twenty-first century, this book is still being read and cited. Like Jensen, the authors of *The Bell Curve*—Harvard University professor Richard Herrnstein and prominent author Charles Murray—argued that the IQ test data show that black and Latino Americans are inferior in intelligence to whites. Though the authors had no training in genetics, they suggested that this supposed inferiority in intelligence results substantially from genetic differences.[73]

The fact that the book has sold many copies and was for a time widely discussed in the mass media—in spite of the overwhelming evidence against its arguments—strongly suggests that biologically oriented racist thinking remains commonplace among white Americans. Recently, the distinguished physical scientist James Watson, co-discoverer of the structure of DNA and Nobel prize winner, has again argued that the IQ test data indicate black people are less intelligent than whites: "All our social policies are based on the fact that their intelligence is the same as ours—whereas all the testing says not really."[74] It is significant that scholars and popular analysts who continue to make such ill-informed arguments do not recognize that they are thinking out of an uncritical white frame of reference. Thus, they write as though there is no other way to view the group data on these conventional skills tests (inaccurately termed "intelligence" tests) of children, other than their racist framing of the supposedly lesser intelligence of children of color. They do not critically analyze the fact that these tests were usually created by and normed on whites, and they do not acknowledge that much of the substance of these tests reflects the nuanced knowledge and culture of those (mostly white) analysts who make up these tests. Indeed, these IQ tests are actually skills tests that measure children's differential access to educational and economic resources, access clearly affected by institutional and everyday racism.

These racist arguments about contemporary intelligence levels are grounded in nearly 400 years of viewing black Americans and some other Americans of color as having an intelligence inferior to that of white Americans. Today, such views are much more than just an academic matter. Over recent decades versions of these racialized intelligence arguments have periodically been used by some members of Congress and other government officials to argue against antidiscrimination and other government programs that benefit Americans of color.

Today, new forms of biologically oriented racist thinking are appearing in yet other academic settings. For example, Jessie Daniels and Amy Schulz have recently pointed up the resurgence in biologically based racial thinking in human genome research. Some genome researchers are making use of old racist categorizations in researching group health and disease issues, their argument being that it is easier "to categorize people based on phenotypically based notions of 'race' rather than to look exclusively at individual genetic composition for prevention, diagnosis, and treatment of disease."[75] These biological researchers argue naively that their research on genetic links to human diseases confirms the old racial typology of Caucasian, African, Asian, Pacific Islander, and Native American, a typology first developed by the prominent racist thinkers Johann Blumenbach and Immanuel Kant in the eighteenth century.

Even though a century of physical and social science has shown how socially constructed and useless for assessing real biological ancestry and health issues these old racist categories actually are, their dominance in Western culture is so strong that some physical scientists cannot resist using them. Daniels and Schulz argue that one reason for this persisting racist conceptualization in genome research is that these researchers ignore voluminous social science research that shows the many ways that racial categories are socially variable and instead rely uncritically on the centuries-old racist typology of Blumenbach and Jefferson. Such racist interpretations of health inequalities enable these genetic researchers to avoid dealing with the systemic causes of the health inequalities they find between racial groups, and thus to blame such inequalities on something other than the societal racism that actually generates or reinforces them. Moreover, their use of discredited "biological race" categories actually helps to perpetuate the age-old racist framing of society.[76]

The Cultural Critique: More Stereotyping

Another aspect of older racist views that can be found in new dress today is what one might call the racial–cultural critique—the view that blacks have done less well than whites because of their allegedly deficient culture with its weak work ethic and family values. This is not a new stereotyped framing of African Americans. By the early seventeenth century, African Americans were seen by European Americans as quite inferior in civilization and morality. On a regular basis, these blame-the-victim views have been resuscitated among the white elites and passed along to ordinary whites and others as a way of explaining the often difficult economic and other social conditions faced by African Americans.

The common accent on inferior family and personal values among black Americans got a major boost in a 1960s government report called *The Negro Family*, which focused on social pathologies in black communities. Social scientist and later U.S. senator Daniel Patrick Moynihan there argued that "the deterioration of the fabric of Negro society" was mainly because of black family problems, and he emphasized what he called the "tangle of pathology" and crumbling social relations he saw in many black communities.[77]

Since this famous "Moynihan report," leading magazines and scholarly journals have periodically published articles accenting a strong version of this white-framed perspective on what some have called the "black underclass." This perspective accents the allegedly deficient morality and lifestyle of many black Americans. For example, an article in the *Chronicle of Higher Education* surveyed research on the black poor and underclass, noting that

> the lives of the ghetto poor are marked by a dense fabric of what experts call "social pathologies"—teenage pregnancies, out-of-wedlock births, single-parent families, poor educational achievement, chronic unemployment, welfare dependency, drug abuse, and crime—that, taken separately or together, seem impervious to change.[78]

To the present day, similar reports and stories designed to explain black problems in cultural terms regularly appear in the local and national mass media, as well as in an array of books on "what is wrong with black America."

Indeed, even recent books by a few relatively conservative African Americans—such as *Enough* (2007) by media commentator Juan Williams and *Come On People* (2007) by comedian Bill Cosby and psychiatrist Alvin Poussaint—have accented these perennial problems of impoverishment in many black communities and blamed them centrally on internal cultural issues. They call on poor black Americans to pick themselves up by their bootstraps and break out of these impoverished conditions. While these authors are operating from a sympathetic perspective and within the larger black community, even they adopt significant aspects of the old white racial framing of poor African Americans.[79] Conservative analysts, white or black, generally blame the victims for their plight, but usually without dealing in-depth with the systemic racism that is much more central to explaining well the difficult economic and family conditions faced by these impoverished Americans. They do not examine systematically the individual and institutional discrimination still faced by these and other black Americans in employment, housing, and numerous other societal arenas, discrimination that usually sets up prohibitive barriers to significant socioeconomic mobility. Clearly, too, they do not provide a thorough analysis of the aggressive government actions necessary to eradicate such structural racial barriers.

Moreover, much underclass theorizing and morals preaching by many whites barely disguise the racist fears, assumptions, and biases about black bodies and lives long held by many whites. The legal scholar Anthony Farley has argued that poor black communities in cities are often seen by whites as "urban Bantustans" that export a type of deviant pleasure by displaying themselves as the negation of white middle-class culture. Many whites can thus feel superior as "virtuous republicans" because of the negative view they hold of black culture and communities. At the same time, however, some whites (sometimes the same ones) also view these areas as dark seductive places where they can go for forbidden pleasures such as securing illegal drugs or prostitution.[80]

Denying Racism, Asserting Innocence

Most whites at all class levels have long held a fairly rosy view of U.S. history. Today, as in the past, there is a strong impulse to break the historical linkage between the genocidal and enslaving past and the conditions faced by Americans of color today. An important aspect of the contemporary racial frame buttressing systemic racism is the omnipresent notion of white innocence and virtue. Today, many whites deny the seriousness of antiblack racism in the past and present history of the United States. In interviews with powerful members of the white economic elite, my colleagues and I have found that many view white racism as having declined significantly in importance. For that reason they often argue that certain types of government action, such as affirmative action, are no longer needed as remedies for racial discrimination.[81] Optimistic views of an allegedly sharp decline in U.S. racism are also common among ordinary whites. For example, recent research involving white Californians has shown that their constructions of racial realities "are not a rational, unbiased reflection of available evidence, but instead reflect strong motivations to *deny* the impact of racism."[82] The whites in this study minimized racism except under conditions where their defensive motivations were reduced in the experiment, in which case they were more likely to see contemporary racism as a problem.

A certain defensiveness about racism is seen today in numerous assertions that the United States is a "post-racial" society. These assertions have become commonplace since Barack Obama was elected president. Recall that after this election the prominent business newspaper *The Wall Street Journal* offered a major editorial asserting that a "man of mixed race" being president was a "tribute to American opportunity, and it is something that has never happened in another Western democracy—notwithstanding European condescension about 'racist' America."[83] After this assertion of U.S. moral superiority, this white-framed piece continued: "One promise of his victory is that perhaps we can put to rest the myth of racism as a barrier to achievement in this splendid country."[84]

Recall too from Chapter 1 the comments made by then Republican presidential candidate Bob Dole about white innocence and lack of culpability today (p. 14). He argued that whites should not have to pay for the effects of past racial discrimination. Like many other whites, including those at *The Wall Street Journal*, Dole tried to break the connection between the racial past and the racial present, in his case temporizing on the question of compensatory **reparations** for damages inflicted by whites during the slavery and Jim Crow segregation. Powerful white men like Dole still control a majority of the major U.S. organizations and institutions as the twenty-first century unfolds, which is a major reason that this framing of contemporary white innocence in regard to past discrimination remains so strong.

A key factor in how the white racial frame operates today involves what Hernán Vera and I call whites' "social alexithymia," that is, the inability of a great many whites to understand where African Americans and other people of color are coming from and what their racialized experiences are like. This social alexithymia involves a significant lack of cross-racial empathy. As Jane Hill has suggested, this lack of white empathy often entails a line of mindful reasoning about white innocence something like this:

> I am a good and normal mainstream sort of White person. I am not a racist, because racists are bad and marginal people. Therefore, if you understood my words to be racist, you must be mistaken. I may have used language that would be racist in the mouth of a racist person, but if I did so, I was joking. If you understood my meaning to be racist, not only do you insult me, but you lack a sense of humor, and you are oversensitive.[85]

Hill adds that this "chain of reasoning makes the speaker the sole authority" over what her or his racist commentaries actually mean. Moreover, many whites are today unwilling even to listen to the views of those Americans who are regularly targeted by white racism—even to their views about the reality, character, harm, and pain of that everyday racism.

Sincere Fictions: Romanticizing the Past

Associated with a rosy view of U.S. society and the assertion of white innocence is a romanticizing of the racist past. This romanticizing can be seen in the long history of Hollywood movies dealing with U.S. history. Only rarely has a mainstream movie dealt honestly with slavery or Jim Crow segregation, and then almost never with much depth. Nonetheless, Hollywood movies dealing with racial matters have evolved in a positive direction since the early 1900s. In the famous 1915 movie *The Birth of a Nation*, film-maker D.W. Griffith used cinematic advances to spread a viciously racist, Klan-inspired image of black southerners during the Reconstruction period. In this epic movie, black Americans are portrayed as savages, corrupt legislators, and uneducated officials. In contrast, white southerners are shown as gracious, brave, and honest. There is no hint that in the Civil War white southerners were fighting for one of history's most brutal social systems. Then, if we move to the 1930s–1950s era, we see yet more racist images of black Americans in classic movies such as some Shirley Temple movies (for example, *The Littlest Rebel*) and *Gone with the Wind*, the latter still treasured by many people and periodically reissued in recent decades. The images of black Americans therein are not as vicious as in *The Birth of a Nation*, but they include highly stereotyped black figures such as a "mammy" and obsequious enslaved servants. Most whites are still gallant, gracious, or brave figures, and there is no hint of something being wrong with a society grounded in a bloody slavery system. Again we see the **sincere fictions** of the virtuous white self. *Gone with the Wind* is but one of many such portraits. Between the 1920s and the 1940s more than 75 films portrayed the Old South favorably and presented slavery as unproblematic and/or mostly benevolent. By the 1930s almost all the national mass media's accounts touching on the history of U.S. racism were romanticized and sanitized.[86]

Moreover, other movies made since the early decades of the twentieth century have often portrayed Africans as savages and whites as saviors, such as in the old Tarzan movies still shown in the United States and across the globe. The same is true for old cowboy-and-Indian movies, with indigenous Americans typically portrayed as savages. In addition, today on television and in documentaries, a "wild Africa" or "untamed" image is often portrayed by media producers as they accent Africa's distinctive animals and savannahs much more than its complex and critical history or diverse peoples.

More-recent movies dealing with U.S. racial history, such as *Glory* (1989) and *Amistad* (1997), have portrayed black Americans in a substantially less stereotyped and more humane light. While more-recent movies touching on racial issues have sometimes presented a white person as villainous, such images are usually more than balanced by those of whites who are honorable or heroic. In recent films we mostly see positive stereotypes of whites—as good, civilized, and the central heroes even in stories that are mostly about black people. As Hernán Vera and Andrew Gordon put it

> The portrayal of whites in *Birth of a Nation* is almost identical to their portrayal in *Glory* and in *Amistad*. What we have found in our analysis is a persistence across time in representations of the ideal white American self, which is constructed as powerful, brave, cordial, kind, firm, good-looking, and generous: a natural-born leader.[87]

In these movies there is no serious indication that the broader white-controlled society was ever deeply grounded in a pervasive system of institutionalized racism. A thorough and unromanticized movie on the deeper significance, venality, and human destruction of slavery or Jim Crow segregation has yet to be made by white directors at mainstream movie studios.

In recent years numerous writers and journalists have written accounts of U.S. history designed to preserve the white sense of innocence and of inculpability for the genocide, slavery, and segregation so central to that history. In a best-selling book one conservative journalist has argued not only that antiblack racism has come to an end but also that the historical background of white oppression of black Americans has been misperceived. In his view the enslavement of black Americans had good features. "Slavery proved to be the transmission belt that nevertheless brought Africans into the orbit of modern civilization and Western freedom."[88] Similarly, in a book attacking the idea of racial equality, the journalist William Henry, a Pulitzer Prize winner, argued that the European conquests were successful in dispersing superior cultures among inferior cultures, which were forced to accommodate.[89] Many defenders of slavery have articulated this Eurocentric view from the earliest days of colonialism in North America. Such arguments do not take seriously the bloody and barbaric character of slavery and the slave trade. There is no serious discussion here of the many millions of Africans who died in the European-controlled Atlantic slave trade nor of the severe destruction of African societies by that trade and later European imperialism (see Chapter 2, pp. 41–43).

The extreme oppressiveness of U.S. slavery is thus not taken seriously by many white Americans, and even by some recent immigrants who are not white. Not surprisingly perhaps, brochures circulated by southern local and state government officials still provide a distorted view of U.S. history. One South Carolina brochure provided to visitors at the state's travel centers has a two-page history of the state from the 1500s to the present, with no mention of slaves or slavery ever being there. Yet slavery was central to that state's economy for a long period. Moreover, a recent research study in North Carolina examined the way that slavery has been portrayed at 20 slave plantations that are tourist sites. Seven of the plantation websites do not even note the presence of slavery there, and only three of the 20 sites make serious efforts to present the oppressed experiences of those enslaved. The other 17 sites accent such things as house furnishings, gardens, and lives of the white families. Some try to play down the brutality of slavery and thus project images of "happy slaves." The lead researcher, Derek Alderman, accents the point that "plantations were not just about their white owners. As we come to terms with the legacy of racism in the United States, we have to recognize ... that there was brutality that happened in the Old South."[90]

A Whitewashed Worldview

Seen comprehensively, all the mental images, prejudiced attitudes, stereotypes, sincere fictions, emotions, racist explanations, and rationalizations that link to systemic racism make up a white racial frame, a racist worldview, one deeply imbedded in the dominant culture and institutions. The U.S. system of racism is not something that only affects Americans of color, for it is central to the lives of white Americans as well. It determines how whites think about themselves, about their ideals, and about their country.

We saw earlier how European immigrants to the United States in the early 1900s came to accept this worldview and its assumption that being "American" meant being white. Indeed, today the word "American" often means "white"—at least for many white Americans, and apparently for a great many others in the United States and across the globe. One can pick up newspapers or news magazines and find "American" or "Americans" used in a way that clearly accents *white* Americans. Take this sentence from a news writer in a Florida newspaper: "The American Public isn't giving government or police officers the blind trust it once did."[91] Clearly, "American" here means "white American," for a majority of black Americans have never blindly trusted the police.

One research analysis examined all articles in 65 major English-language newspapers for a six-month period and estimated that there were thousands of references to "black Americans" or "African Americans" in the articles. However, in the same newspapers there were only 46 mentions of "white Americans." In almost every case these mentions by newspaper writers occurred in connection with "black Americans," "blacks," or "African Americans." (The exceptions were three cases in which "white Americans" was used in connection with "Native Americans" or "Korean Americans.") A similar pattern was found for major magazines. Not once was the term "white Americans" used alone in an article; if used, it was always used in relation to another racial category. The same study examined how congressional candidates were described in news articles in the two weeks prior to a November election. In every case white congressional candidates were *not* described as "white," but black congressional candidates were always noted as being "black."[92] In the United States, blackness is usually salient and noted, while whiteness generally goes unmentioned, except when reference is specifically made to white connections to other racial groups.

Being American still means, in the minds of many, including editors and writers in the media, being white. This need not be conscious. For centuries most whites have probably not seen the routines of their everyday lives as framed in white. "Race" is often not visible when one is at the top of the racial hierarchy. Today, major social institutions, those originally created by whites centuries ago, are still dominated by whites. Yet from the white standpoint they are not white, just *normal* and *customary*. They are not seen for what they actually are—white-dominated institutions reflecting in many of their aspects the history, privileges, norms, values, and interests of white Americans. When whites live in these customary arrangements, they need not think in overtly racist terms. Nonetheless, when whites move into settings where they must confront people of color in the United States or elsewhere, they usually foreground their whiteness, whether consciously or unconsciously.

The sense of white entitlement is passed along in subtle ways. Edward Ball, a descendant of one of South Carolina's prominent slaveholding families, has underscored the sense of privilege and superiority passed along from slave plantation days to whites today. He notes that

> inwardly the plantations lived on. In childhood, I remember feeling an intangible sense of worth that might be linked to the old days. Part of the feeling came from the normal encouragements of parents who wanted their children to rise, an equal part came from an awareness that long ago our family had lived like lords, and that world could still be divided into the pedigreed and the rootless.[93]

Fear of a Multiracial Future

Recall the influential racist writers who in the 1910s and 1920s feared that whites were becoming a minority (p. 75). Today, many white media analysts, other commentators, and conservative political officials view "Western civilization" as under threat from groups that are not white or European. Racist thinking involves more than just rationalizing oppression, for it often represents a defensive response, a fear of losing power. In recent years many influential advocates of white superiority have directed their attacks at the values or cultures of new immigrants of color coming to the United States, such as those from Mexico, as well as at black Americans. In one interview study numerous elite white men expressed some fear of the growth of Americans of color in the United States, sometimes seeing Western civilization as under great threat.[94]

We observe examples of this fear among contemporary politicians, commentators, and intellectuals. For example, in speeches and articles, Patrick Buchanan, one-time candidate for the Republican presidential nomination, has argued that "our Judeo-Christian values are going to be preserved and our Western heritage is going to be handed down to future generations and not dumped on some landfill called multiculturalism."[95] Again we see the linkage between religion and a strong sense of European supremacy. We also see a concern for the reproduction of the white-dominated system

from current to future generations. In addition, Buchanan told one inter-
viewer that

> if we had to take a million immigrants in, say, Zulus next year or
> Englishmen, and put them in Virginia, what group would be easier to
> assimilate and would cause less problems for the people of Virginia?
> There is nothing wrong with us sitting down and arguing that issue
> that we are a European country, [an] English-speaking country.[96]

The Zulus, who are Africans, seem to represent in his mind the specter of
savage hordes who would not assimilate well into the country. Ironically,
Africans have been in the country longer than Buchanan's Irish ancestors,
and Virginia has been home to a great many African Americans for nearly
four centuries. During the 2008 presidential election, Buchanan continued
his accent on the centrality of whiteness with an article called "A Brief for
Whitey," in which he adopted a strong version of the old white-racist
frame that we have encountered before, one asserting that that African
Americans should be grateful for having been enslaved and Christianized
by Europeans. He aggressively criticized then-Senator Barack Obama in a
rather stereotyped way—for example, by only calling him "Barack," the
traditional segregationists' way of naming black Americans without using
last names. Buchanan agreed with Senator Obama on the need for a new
national conversation on race, but one that gives supposedly "silent" white
Americans "a voice." Considering that whites have long controlled most
major media outlets and other means of national communication, this is
an unreflective perspective on contemporary U.S. society.[97]

Similarly, *Forbes* editor Peter Brimelow lays out white fears for Western
civilization in a book, *Alien Nation*. For him, "the American nation has
always had a specific ethnic core. And that core has been white." Back in
the 1950s, he argues, most Americans "looked like me. That is, they were of
European stock. And in those days, they had another name for this thing
dismissed so contemptuously as 'the racial hegemony of white Americans.'
They called it 'America.'"[98] An immigrant from Britain himself, Brimelow
is a founder and funder of a far-right Internet website that has pressed to
sharply reduce contemporary immigration, a website that has published
openly racist analyses and discussions. In addition, influential Harvard
professor Samuel Huntington once argued that "[i]f multiculturalism
prevails and if the consensus on liberal democracy disintegrates, the
United States could join the Soviet Union on the ash heap of history."[99]
Today, great concern for white Western cultural supremacy is periodically
evident in the views of numerous white editors, scholars, and politicians.

Conclusion

The systemic racism that is still part of the base of U.S. society is interwoven with a strong racial framing that has been partially reworked at various points in U.S. history, but which has remained a well-institutionalized set of emotion-laden attitudes, concepts, images, and narratives defending the subordination of black Americans and other Americans of color. Until the late 1940s, U.S. commitment to a white-supremacist view was proud, openly held, and aggressive. Most whites in the U.S. and Europe, led by elites, took pride in forthrightly professing racist perspectives on others and racist rationalizations for imperialistic adventures. Brutal discrimination and overt exploitation were routinely advocated. Whites' global domination was "seen as proof of white racial superiority."[100]

Beginning in the 1940s, however, open expression of a white-supremacist perspective was made difficult by a growing U.S. awareness of actions of the racist regime in Nazi Germany. By the 1950s and 1960s growing civil rights protests against U.S. racism—with their counterframing of black freedom and justice—and the U.S. struggle with the (former) Soviet Union made the open expression of a white-supremacist ideology less acceptable, at least in public. The dominant racist framing changed slowly to reflect these conditions, with a renewed accent on equality of opportunity, and there was more white support for some moderate government programs to break down segregated institutions (see Chapter 4, pp. 122–124). Still, many important aspects of the old white-racist frame, sometimes dressed up in a new guise, have persisted to the present day. From the beginning, the age-old idea of the superiority of white (Western) culture and institutions has been a basic idea in the dominant frame that rationalizes continuing racial discrimination and related oppression.

Control over a society's ideas and discourse includes control over its central metaphors. The powerful in the elite usually decide what the dominant images and metaphors are, and thus what is or is not seen as true. Metaphors are integral to most conceptual frameworks.[101] Thus, for some time now, most elite whites and most other whites have viewed the last few centuries of societal development in terms of a broad imagery equating "human progress" with Western civilization. We hear phrases like "Western civilization is an engine generating great progress for the world" or "Africans have only seen real advancement because of their contacts with Western civilization." Western imperialism's bringing of "civilization" or "democracy" to other peoples is made to appear as an engine of great progress. However, this equating of "progress" with European civilization conceals the devastating consequences of European and U.S. imperialism and colonialism. Moreover, when whites speak of Western civilization as equivalent to great human progress, they are talking about the creation of social systems that do not take into serious consideration the interests and views of the indigenous or enslaved peoples whose resources and labor were ripped from them, whose societies were destroyed, and whose lives were cut short.

4

Contemporary Racial Framing
White Americans

Recently, researchers have found a strong association in some white minds of ape images with images of black Americans. In one social science study, white and other non-black college students who were exposed to black faces were quicker in recognizing hazy drawings of apes than those not exposed to black faces. A second study discovered that whites subliminally primed with ape images later paid more attention to black faces than to white faces, while those not thus primed paid more attention to white faces. Even more dramatic was the finding that white students' blacks-as-apes mental connections, primed by ape-related words, tended to shape their willingness to accept more police violence against a black criminal suspect than against a similar white suspect when these student subjects were shown videos of police violence. Such images of black Americans as apelike or ape-linked date back to the seventeenth and eighteenth centuries, including as we saw in an earlier chapter (p. 59) back to Thomas Jefferson. Such ape imagery seems to be yet another way of symbolizing black Americans as animalistic and threatening to whites.[1]

For most whites and many other non-black Americans, specific antiblack views are part of a broader racial framing of U.S. society. As we have already seen, this dominant white-created framing of society includes racial stereotypes, images, emotions, interpretations, and other important elements that legitimate discrimination. The elements of this broad racial framing have changed in some important ways over the centuries, but today they often bear a significant similarity to those of earlier eras. This pervasive, elite-fostered framing provides a racialized overview of the social world. It organizes and makes coherent the racial views of white elites and ordinary whites, and thus buttresses white power and privilege and generates discriminatory practices.

Persisting antiblack attitudes, images, and emotions today represent much more than a matter of a few scattered bigots; they are the pervasive and continuing legacy of the material exploitation and racist framing of slavery and segregation. The "everydayness" of contemporary racist framing among whites means that it operates in many situations of intergroup contact and regularly gets translated into alienated racist relations—that is, into relationships of white-on-black discrimination. Thus, we see yet another important aspect of the societal reproduction and transmission of the racist system. The perpetuation of systemic racism requires an intertemporal reproducing not only of racist institutions and structures but also of its rationalizing racial frame, which includes among other elements a racist ideology, racist attitudes, and racist images.

Racial Prejudice and Stereotyping: Specific Dimensions of the White Frame

Too often the realities of individual racial stereotyping and prejudice have been disconnected from the larger racial framing and from widespread discriminatory practices. Stereotyping and prejudice are part of a much larger social scaffolding. Antiblack stereotyping and prejudice are part of an expansive racial framing and are rooted in the everyday defense of white power and privilege. As Herbert Blumer put it, prejudice is "rooted in a sense of group position."[2] Racial prejudice has been defined as antipathy toward a racial other based on a faulty generalization. Such prejudice can be directed toward a group as a whole, or toward an individual as a member of that group. Typically, racial prejudice has both an emotional and a belief dimension. It usually includes a negative feeling about a racial out-group as well as a negative belief. The belief aspect is often termed a "stereotype." As false or exaggerated generalizations, stereotypes commonly serve as rationalizers of much discriminatory behavior.[3]

Today racist thinking and feeling attach great significance to *skin color*, which remains a badge of oppression for black Americans and many other Americans of color. This persistence is a clear example of the legacy of the past, of the marks and burdens of a "slavery unwilling to die." While many whites now reject, at least publicly or on a conscious level, a blatantly biologized racism, they still hold without misgiving many of the negative conceptions and images of black men and women that have been long associated with a biologized racism accenting certain "inferior races" and "superior races." Racist attitudes tend to distort the targeted group's origins, physical appearance, values, or culture. In the case of white views of black Americans, general principles and notions from the broad racial framing get imbedded in specific racist attitudes and stereotypes. In regard to ideas about group origin, for example, during the first two centuries of slave importation whites regarded Africans and African Americans as foreign, uncivilized, and unchristian. While some aspects of this older view have disappeared, other aspects can currently be found in a variety of white views and images that center on the alleged dangers ("savagery") of black men. Today, black men are often viewed by whites as deviant, dangerous, or violent. In regard to appearance, black men and women are still thought to have a distinctive and, for a great many whites, undesirable or ugly appearance. They are also often seen as lazy, criminal, or immoral.

Antiblack attitudes and images are revealed and reproduced constantly in the everyday discourse, commentaries, and writings of whites (and often other non-blacks) at all class levels. Seeing black Americans in negative terms and viewing whites in positive terms are perspectives shaped by elite indoctrination, such as through the media, but they also constitute the way a majority of ordinary whites regularly communicate with each other about racial matters. These racist views have been perpetuated over the generations by means of everyday communication. Racist attitudes and images are constantly available to virtually all whites, including the very young, by means of presentations in daily discourse, as well as in the media, through the writings of intellectuals, and in the speeches of politicians and business leaders. Such attitudes and images are adapted and used as the social situation warrants, and they vary in expression or impact depending on the situation and the persons involved. Over centuries now, these views have had a severely negative impact on their human targets (see Chapter 6, pp. 200–210). Racist ways of thinking and feeling can be conscious and directly stimulative of discriminatory action, or they can be unconscious and implicit in that action. Moreover, most racial stereotyping and prejudice not only portray the racial others negatively but also imbed a learned predisposition to act in a negative way toward the racialized others.

Racist Images and Attitudes, Past and Present: An Overview

Historical data on white images of and attitudes toward black Americans suggest that for centuries the overwhelming majority of whites have been openly and unapologetically racist. While there were no national opinion surveys before the 1930s, we can infer strongly antiblack attitudes from the omnipresent and unreservedly racist letters, speeches, actions, jokes, popular entertainments, and organizations of the slavery and legal segregation eras.

For example, in the decades before the Civil War there was an increase in popularly expressed racism, including racist images, attitudes, and invectives. One place this can be seen is in the growing popularity, especially among white workers, of whites-in-blackface minstrel shows. In front of large crowds, composed mostly of white working-class men, white performers made up in blackface did musical numbers and other comedy skits on stage. Extreme caricatures and mimicking of black Americans were centerpieces of these shows, which featured a vocabulary of racist epithets (such as "coon," "nigger," and "buck"), a mocking of black English speakers, and a portrayal of fantasies and fictions held in white heads (for example, the white-male fantasy of the oversexed black woman).

By presenting black people in such negative terms, the virtues of whites and whiteness were highlighted. Whites were seen as smart, courageous, and civilized, while blacks were presented as dumb, cowardly, deviant, oversexed, and uncivilized. The shows were very popular with white workers, including new European immigrants then seeking to be defined as "white." They were also eagerly attended by members of the elite, including presidents John Tyler (even at his inauguration) and Abraham Lincoln, as well as prominent novelists like Mark Twain. These highly racialized public entertainments continued well into the 1900s as a major form of mass entertainment.[4]

The Recent Past

National opinion surveys in the 1930s showed strong white support for overtly racist or segregationist views. A late 1930s Roper poll reported that eight in ten respondents thought that blacks should be kept out of white residential areas. In the late 1940s a Gallup poll found that 43 percent of those polled thought there should be racially segregated trains and buses. The majority opposed whites and blacks living and working together in the armed forces. (Ironically, this strong opposition was expressed just before President Harry Truman dramatically desegregated the U.S. armed forces.) A 1944 opinion survey found that half the respondents thought "white people should have the first chance at any kind of job." Just under half thought local restaurants should not serve both blacks and whites, and a similar proportion said they would not like having a black nurse in a hospital.[5] These national surveys probably included some Americans of color—the poll data are not reported by racial group—so it is likely that an even larger proportion of whites than of the total sample supported enforced racial segregation in restaurants, hospitals, housing, workplaces, and the armed forces.

By the 1960s publicly expressed support for legal segregation was waning, although whites' negative views of blacks were still strong. In a 1963 Harris poll a majority of whites nationwide admitted to a stranger, a pollster, that they agreed with negative statements about black Americans: they "tend to have less ambition," "smell different," and "have looser morals." Four in ten thought that blacks "have less native intelligence," and more than one-third thought that blacks "breed crime." In the 1960s, the era when some older white leaders today received their early racial socialization, a majority of whites still admitted openly to holding blatantly racist prejudices and stereotypes. Nonetheless, publicly expressed attitudes toward equal opportunity and public desegregation—at least in principle—were changing, for 57 percent of the white respondents said they approved of a federal voting rights law, and 62 percent said they approved of a fair employment practices law. Still, according to the 1963 survey white attitudes about certain personal contacts with blacks were often quite negative. Half said they would object to a black family moving next door, and 84 percent were opposed to a close friend or relative marrying a black person.[6]

The White Majority Today

In recent decades much has been made of the reduction among whites of certain racist attitudes. Some longitudinal data show that whites have indeed become less likely to give openly racist answers to pollsters and survey researchers than in earlier decades. For example, one 1942 survey found that only 47 percent of whites thought blacks were "as intelligent as white people," a proportion that had increased to 77 percent by 1968. In recent decades, thus, some journalists and other analysts have taken such findings to mean that a majority of the white population is today no longer significantly racist in attitudes, opinions, and images of black Americans. They argue the U.S. is now a post-racial society, or that there is an "end to racism." This is badly mistaken, and often naive or disingenuous. A significant decrease in overtly expressed segregationist or other blatantly racist attitudes does not necessarily mean that most whites are no longer substantially racist in some or much of their thinking about or imaging of black Americans and other Americans of color.[7]

A 2006 review by Lincoln Quillian of the extensive social science literature on whites' racial views and attitudes found that opinion surveys of whites indicate that most publicly support, when given abstract questions, equality of opportunity and equality of treatment and oppose racial discrimination. However, at the same time, the majority do not believe there is major racial discrimination widespread across this society, and they also do not think government should actively intervene to secure further racial equality. Quillian suggests that most contemporary whites, like earlier whites, reconcile the continuing reality of racial inequality with their beliefs about little discrimination by blaming people of color for their lack of effort. Thus, "even among persons who hold a sincere belief in race blindness, images and depictions of members of racial groups learned beginning in childhood are influential in their thinking."[8]

Indeed, responses to opinion surveys on racial matters can be misleading. Typical opinion surveys involve very brief questions and are seriously limited by the fact that many people give pollsters socially desirable answers, which in such cases often disguise their true racist views. Seen from this perspective, the apparent decrease in certain antiblack images, prejudices, and stereotypes among whites from the 1930s to the present likely reflects to a significant degree increased concern for social acceptability.[9] Clearly, it is less socially acceptable to publicly avow strong racist attitudes today, so many whites reserve many of their more blatantly racist comments for the private spheres of home, locker room, club, or bar. Indeed, social science researchers have found that many white respondents alter comments on racial issues in order to appear unprejudiced. And some researchers who probe deeply into the white mindset have found that indirect and subtle research measures (as well as in-depth interviewing) indicate that antiblack views and other negative racial subframes are still quite *common* among whites.[10]

This is true for whites across much of the age spectrum. For example, research on white students at three major college campuses found racial attitudes expressed on short-answer survey items were often different from those expressed in response to similar interview questions requiring more detailed commentary. On a brief survey item 80 percent of 451 white college students openly approved of marriages between blacks and whites. However, when a smaller group of comparable students were interviewed in-depth this figure dropped to about one-third. When given time to explain their views, the majority expressed reservations about marriage across the color line. A similar pattern was found for a question about affirmative action. Whites frequently used a variety of hedging phrases (for instance, "I agree and disagree"), some perhaps in order to play down their negative racist views. The in-depth interviews clearly indicated that a majority of these well-educated whites still held significantly negative racial attitudes on important issues like intermarriage.[11]

Social psychologists have found that, when given a test of subtle or unconscious racial stereotyping such as the implicit association test, most whites quickly associate black faces (photos) with *negative* words and traits (for instance, with evil character traits or failure). Most whites have more difficulty in linking black faces to pleasant words and positive traits than they do for white faces. Analyses of thousands of such facial-response tests at psychology websites have shown that the overwhelming majority of whites signal an antiblack, pro-white bias in such face-reaction tests.[12] Moreover, in research projects where whites have been shown black faces, even for milliseconds, key areas of their brains that respond to *perceived threats* have tended to light up automatically under brain scans. In these studies the more racial stereotyping that white subjects revealed on paper-and-pencil psychological tests, the greater their brains' threat responses were when they were shown black facial photos.[13] This type of research indicates that black photos and visages generate not only cognitive stereotyping in minds but also racialized emotions, such as fear and anxiety.

In addition, some of this implicit-attitudes research has demonstrated a social desirability effect. In another study using the implicit association test, researchers found that young white children showed a pro-white and antiblack bias in connecting white and black faces to good or bad words, but also that their self-reported racial attitudes showed a similar overt racial bias. However, in contrast, older white children and white adults who were similarly tested revealed a comparable implicit racial bias in matching white and black faces to good or bad words, yet showed less (or no) racial stereotyping on more overt psychological tests.[14]

Other contemporary research on white thought and behavior also shows the persistence of strong white-racist attitudes about black Americans and other Americans of color. In several research studies of white racial views that I and my colleagues have done over the last decade or so, we have found that whites often engage in racist commentaries and other performances, especially in backstage settings where only other whites, friends and relatives, are present. In one recent study 626 white students at more than two dozen colleges and universities kept journals for just a few weeks in one semester of racial events, discussions, and performances they encountered. They recorded a large number, nearly 7,000 instances, of clearly racist events—a number that, if calculated out for a whole year and for all white college students, might be in the hundreds of millions of such events per year. Many of these racist events were in backstage settings with white relatives or acquaintances, but others were in settings with a racially diverse group of people present. The diaries indicate that racist commentaries, joking, and actions are still commonplace among younger, better-educated whites. Moreover, examining these thousands of accounts, we find that African Americans are the non-European group that obsesses or preoccupies a large proportion of these whites. African Americans appear in a substantial majority of all the racist commentaries, racist jokes, and other racialized performances reported by these students from various regions. Other racial groups, such as Native Americans, Latinos, and Asian Americans, are periodically targeted, but verbal and other attacks on them make up only a minority of the events recorded by these students.[15] Clearly, much social science research shows that most whites have a more developed framing of black Americans than of other U.S. groups of color.

Antiblack Attitudes and Images: Key Examples

The specific attitudes that whites hold toward themselves and toward black Americans often take the form of, on the one hand, a model of white virtue, merit, and superior morality and, on the other, an "anti-model" of black deficiency, pathology, and threat. The positive model encompasses a range of sincere fictions about the white self, such as the images of white innocence and nobility discussed in Chapter 3 (pp. 88–89). The anti-model encompasses a range of images and attitudes, including the often inherited views of black men and women as lazy workers, criminals, dumb or violent athletes, or welfare cheaters. Such racist framing not only causes much daily pain and harm to black Americans but also corrupts the minds and understandings of white Americans.[16]

Attributions of Laziness

Specific negative representations of black Americans are critical parts of the contemporary racial framing. One particularly strong and age-old representation is that of black laziness. The Protestant ethic, with its accent on individual acquisitiveness, was important for early European colonists. Enslaved Africans who resisted in any way the very long hours of work typically imposed on them were judged by this ethic to be "lazy," even though these workers did much of the hard work that lay behind growing white prosperity. Similar white attitudes about black laziness persisted during the system of Jim Crow segregation, although again a disproportionate amount of the hardest work in the southern and border state economies was done by these much maligned black workers.

Descending through decades of U.S. history, the racist image of lazy men and women is still commonplace today. One national survey in the mid-1990s asked whites to evaluate on a scale just how work-oriented blacks are. Only a small percentage, 16 percent, ranked blacks at the hardworking end; just under half put blacks at the lazy end of the spectrum. A more recent study at a western university found that black employees, especially black men, were viewed as "lazy, irresponsible, and not serious about work"—characteristics that negatively influence white employers' employment and hiring decisions. Other recent studies have found similar patterns.[17] Moreover, such views of the black work ethic are also manifested in common white comments about lazy black welfare recipients. Notions of laziness are so strong as to overcome countering evidence. Researchers Justin Lewis and Sut Jhally had white subjects watch *The Cosby Show*, a popular television show from the 1980s and still seen in reruns across the globe. Whites generally liked the high-achieving black family (the Huxtables) portrayed on the show, yet many processed the images in a way that fit in with their pre-existing racial attitudes. Explicitly or implicitly viewing black Americans as a lazy group, these whites continued to view black Americans as inferior, and thus saw the success of the Huxtables as evidence that any black person could succeed if he or she would just work harder.[18]

Some socio-psychological research indicates that those with strong stereotypes of an out-group often attribute negative behavior by individual members of that out-group to its alleged group characteristics ("That's the way they are"). However, when they see positive actions or accomplishments by individuals in the out-group, they often attribute that to the uniqueness of the situation rather than to group characteristics. They will argue in the latter case that the person is an exception to the group, that they had a special advantage or luck, that anyone in the situation could have done well, or that it took exceptional motivation and effort to overcome the inherent weaknesses of the person's group. This is a common way that a great many whites respond to the actions of black Americans. They tend to view negative actions by individual black Americans as tied to the group, to its defective biology or culture, while positive achievements are frequently linked only to the individual or situational aspects of the case at hand—and not to the general values and perspectives of black families and communities.[19]

Negative Images of Black Women

African American women have been targets for racist stereotyping for centuries. Reviewing U.S. history, the pioneering scholar of black feminism Patricia Hill Collins has noted that "portraying African-American women as stereotypical mammies, matriarchs, welfare recipients, and hot mommas has been essential to the political economy of domination fostering Black women's oppression."[20] One chronic image, long reproduced on the packaging of some commercial products and in reissued movies like *Gone with the Wind*, is the Aunt Jemima image, that of the corpulent "mammy" borrowed from the racist past. In the dominant U.S. and European cultures images of black women are often intense and visual. For many decades highly stereotyped and caricatured negative images of black women (and men) were very common in popular art, ads, movies, television, and on postcards. Even today, "mammy" dolls and black female and male figurines with exaggerated physical features such as big lips, or in silly poses, can be found in numerous antique shops in the United States. Racist dolls and figurines are still popular with some white Americans. Indeed, they are still manufactured and can be found for sale in shops in several countries across the globe.[21]

A recurring white stereotype of black families is that of a large black *welfare* family with a woman in charge. This is a popular example of the underclass imagery of black Americans we examined as part of the contemporary black framing propagated by some intellectuals (see Chapter 3, pp. 86–87). A 1990s CBS News/*New York Times* poll found that the majority of those questioned thought that *most* poor people were black and that *most* welfare recipients were black. (In both cases, majorities were not black at the time, and still are not today.) Moreover, research in the twenty-first century continues to show a stereotyping pattern, with the common face of mothers getting public assistance still being that of a woman of color. Media and other popular images of black women and other women of color cheating off government assistance also remain commonplace.[22] The welfare reforms of the 1990s cut down significantly on the number of U.S. welfare recipients, but did not alter the racist images of them. Thus, one 2004 study found that whites' negative views of black Americans still hinder their willingness to spend money even on the strict and limited government welfare programs we still have, and that whites' "welfare attitudes are as strongly racialized in 2004, as they were a decade earlier."[23]

A major source of various welfare and poverty stereotypes is the mainstream media. Research has, for instance, shown that network television and news magazines exaggerate greatly the black presence among the country's poor, including in the photos they use. Another common stereotype found in the media and elsewhere is that of black Americans not wanting or caring about having intact, traditional two-parent families. Many white commentators seem to assume that black adults have quite different family values from white adults. However, in a recent survey 344 black adults were asked what their view of the ideal marriage partner was. These black respondents preferred "well-educated, financially stable, monogamous, and affluent partners who are spiritual, religious, self-confident, and reliable." This listing seems much like what a majority of white adults would probably list. Actually, the central difficulty for many black families lies not in their values but in the difficult socioeconomic circumstances this still-racist society constantly creates for them.[24]

Black women face yet other serious forms of gendered racism—the double burden of suffering racial prejudice and stereotyping because they are *black and female*. One example is the negative imaging of black women as "jungle bunnies." Since at least the seventeenth century, this white (especially white male) stereotype has accented black women's allegedly exotic sexuality. Researcher Diane Roberts has shown how white notions of blackness have frequently been loaded with sexuality. European books, beginning in the 1600s, portrayed black women and men naked and with exaggerated sexual organs. "The white world drew the black woman's body as excessively and flagrantly sexual, quite different from the emerging ideology of purity and modesty which defined the white woman's body," Roberts has explained.[25] This view has persisted now over the centuries. Thus, greatly influenced by and perpetuating such racist images, numerous white men during the days of slavery and Jim Crow segregation sought out, molested, and/or raped black women. Moreover, today, much social science research continues to show that some white men still image and seek out black women as exotic sex objects. In this manner, gendered racism is regularly inscribed in the bodies of black women.[26]

Even the dominant societal preferences for female body type are racialized in a manner that is usually biased against black women. From the seventeenth to the twenty-first century not only white politicians and missionaries, but also those whites developing the sciences of medicine, biology, and ethnography and those developing the media have set typical whites' skin, hair, and body type as the traditional standards for aesthetic superiority. For centuries white men have been the standard for male handsomeness, as well as masculinity and manly virtue. White women—in recent decades, especially those who are fair-haired and relatively slender—have long been the standard for female beauty. Not surprisingly, thus, whites have frequently described black women in terms that stereotype them as having "ugly" physical characteristics, including too-curly hair or dark skin color. Recently, a white female Louisiana state representative referred to a black female NAACP president as "buckwheat," an old white-racist term for black Americans that often accents "ugly" hair characteristics.[27] Not surprisingly, such negative images of black women create serious problems not only for women but also for young girls. As one young black woman put it in an interview:

> I went through a long, long time thinking I was like the ugliest thing on the earth.... It's so hard to get a sense of self in this country, in this society, where ... every role of femininity looks like a Barbie doll.[28]

Even so, this dominant gendered–racist imagery regularly generates resistance by black women. A 2008 study by Adia Harvey Wingfield of black beauty-salon owners found that such businesses are places where *black beauty* is routinely defined, honored, and enhanced, often in resistance to the dominant racial framing. While these are important places where black hair is often straightened to conform to a certain white-framed image of good hair, since the 1960s "black is beautiful" movements, many beauty shops have expanded hairstyling services to include more natural hair styles with African and Caribbean origins, such as braided cornrows, other braiding, afros, and dreadlocks. Adopting these natural styles is viewed by many black Americans as openly rejecting the dominant white-oriented images of beauty and style.[29]

Images of Black Men

Another common white stereotype in the dominant racial frame is that of the dangerous black man. This is a staple of much white thinking and imaging, including that of numerous white leaders and intellectuals speaking or writing about the black poor or "ghettos." Many whites, including numerous media commentators, seem to view the typical street criminal as a black man. During the first centuries of colonial development, whites constructed a view of enslaved black men as dangerous "beasts," a stereotyped view that has rationalized much racial oppression over the centuries. The beast-like image was then, as now, put into words, but it was also held at a deeper, more visceral and emotional level. As with black women, the bodies of black men are culturally stigmatized and routinely trigger antiblack stereotypes in white minds, which in turn often generate defensive or discriminatory actions.[30]

Racist images of and fears about black men can be found at all levels of white society. Members of the elite not only play a role in creating and maintaining common racist images, but also buy into some or all of these images. Take the example of Dwight D. Eisenhower, a leading U.S. general who served as president during the 1950s. While President Eisenhower did not publicly advocate the inferiority of black Americans, he did speak in racially stereotyped terms in private. Earl Warren, then chief justice of the Supreme Court, reported that Eisenhower told him at a 1954 dinner that white southerners opposed to school desegregation were "not bad people. All they are concerned about is to see that their sweet little girls are not required to sit in school alongside some big overgrown Negroes."[31] He meant of course black boys. White stereotyping of black boys and men often exaggerates their size or other physical characteristics. To describe ordinary school boys as "big overgrown Negroes" is reminiscent of the scary images of black men some white parents have used to discipline their children. Eisenhower did not mention the severe impact of the often violent white opposition to desegregation on the lives of black boys and girls, and their parents.

Today, this image of black people (especially men) as dangerous or criminal is still an important part of the racist framing in the minds of many whites, including those in the elite. Note, for example, the comments of William Bennett, a recent U.S. Secretary of Education. On a talk show he asserted that, "if you really wanted to reduce crime, you could—if that were your sole purpose—you could abort every black baby in this country and your crime rate would go down." Bennett then backed off, saying such actions would be "an impossibly ridiculous and morally reprehensible thing to do, but your crime rate would go down." Bennett insisted he had conjured up a hypothetical notion he did not agree with, but we see how firmly imbedded in some white minds this connection between African Americans and crime remains.[32]

As a result of these common images of criminality, many whites have fearful reactions to a black man encountered on streets, in public transport, and in elevators. In interview studies, numerous black men have reported aversive reactions taken by white women and men when they are walking the streets of U.S. towns and cities. Many whites frequently lock their car doors, cross streets, or take other defensive precautions when a black man is near. Some conservative commentators have asserted that this defensive action is "rational discrimination" because of the high black crime rate.[33] These commentators, like many ordinary whites, seem to assume that the majority of criminals who attack whites are black. However, most violent crime affecting whites is actually carried out by *white* criminals. Yet most whites do not routinely take similar defensive precautions when they are in the presence of white men, those who perpetrate the majority of violent crimes suffered by whites.

The emotionally freighted images of black men are often crafted in white minds in childhood. Many are gained in family settings. In the past and in the present, some white parents have threatened disobedient children with fearful images of black bogeymen coming to get them. In an interview conducted by one of my graduate students, a retired clerical worker described her mother's method of discipline:

> "The niggers would come in the night and steal us away and use us for their pleasure," that's what my mother told us. What an awful thing to do, don't you think, frightening little children like that.... She scared us to death. The first time I ever saw a colored person I just about had hysterics.[34]

This language of racism becomes what psychologist Lev Vygotsky called inner speech, the mind's language in considering and relating to racial issues. Racist words learned as children can carry many complex under- standings beyond their apparent meaning. Later on, such racialized lan- guage frequently triggers psychological linkages and understandings in minds, and thus can shape numerous actions we take in our social lives.[35]

Today, a major source of negative images of black men, as for black women, is the mainstream mass media. Many Americans watch local news several nights a week. These local news programs, now the major source of news information for a great many people, often accent violent crimes. One study of many cities found that crime was the subject of one-third or more of local news programming. In addition, a study of local news in Los Angeles found that while violent crimes got extensive coverage, nonviolent crimes such as fraud and embezzlement got very little. News stories about violent crime mentioning a suspect featured black suspects, usually men, in a much higher proportion than their arrest rate indicated would be accurate.[36]

Recently, other researchers have examined Los Angeles television news and also found that black residents were more likely to be portrayed as criminals and less likely to be portrayed as victims than white residents. Again black suspects were over-represented relative to their actual arrest rates, while the opposite was true for white suspects. The researchers suggested that this media imagery likely influenced the way many whites viewed their chances of being crime victims, as well as the way they might decide guilt or innocence if on juries in cases involving black defendants. In addition, a recent Los Angeles survey of 506 English-speaking respondents by Travis Dixon found that a person's time spent viewing local television news programs' over-representation of black criminals, as well as attention to crime news and trust of local news, predicted well the person's likelihood of holding traditional stereotypes of black people as criminals. (This was true after controls were applied for local neighborhood diversity and crime rates.) Those who paid the most attention to crime news were the most likely to be obsessed with local crime and to give harsher culpability ratings to hypothetical black suspects as compared to hypothetical white suspects. The amount of television exposure was also found to be directly related to racially stereotyped images of blacks as violent.[37]

The media theory called "cultivation theory" argues that heavy exposure to television content about the social world tends to influence how people see the outside society, even if that outside world is *not at all* like the television programming. Exposure to television images of crime tends to increase white exaggeration of actual black crime involvement, thereby reinforcing pre-existing black criminality images from the old white-racist frame.[38] From his studies, Dixon has concluded that "News viewing may be part of a process that makes the construct or cognitive linkage between Blacks and criminality frequently activated and therefore chronically accessible."[39] In this manner television viewing constantly reinforces antiblack stereotypes from the old white-racial frame.

Today, black men frequently face an array of other racist stereotypes. Historically and in the present, whites have often crafted images of black Americans, especially black men, as ape-like. This is a provocative way to symbolize them as threatening. Recall the recent research that has found a strong association in white minds of ape images with black images, including the one finding that ape–black stereotypes held by white college students shaped their willingness later on to accept police violence against a black criminal suspect. In addition to the studies mentioned previously, yet another study did a content analysis of hundreds of newspaper articles discussing death-eligible criminal defendants and found that words eliciting ape-like images in people's minds were more likely to have been used by newspaper writers for black than white defendants. Such animalistic imagery is part of the dominant white framing that likely helps to legitimate whites' targeting black Americans for discrimination, including discriminatory policing.[40]

When the mass media play up violent crime and mention black men in an unfair way, this affects not only ordinary whites' mental and emotional framing of black Americans but also their actions. Such negative imagery has numerous action consequences, as we just saw in the case of the newspaper writers. Another striking consequence can be seen in public reports by whites of black men attacking them, when in fact no such attack took place. One major study has documented dozens of these false reports by whites in various parts of the country in recent decades. Such racial hoaxes continue to the present day, often to cover up criminal or other socially deviant actions by those whites making such faked accusations.[41] In addition, researchers have found that showing white, Asian, and Latino research subjects (who were political liberals) local crime news videos increased their punitiveness in regard to criminals—but much more so when they were shown black perpetrators than when they were shown white perpetrators of crime. Such harsh predispositions may well affect various actions that whites and other non-blacks take in relation to black people while on the street, at the workplace, or as members of juries.[42]

Images of Drugs and Deviance

Many whites and some other non-black Americans seem to think that the majority of the poor, the homeless, drug-users, and drug-dealers are black Americans. As we have already seen, the mainstream media often exaggerate the role of black Americans in poverty. The same tends to be true for homelessness, drug use, and drug crime, and this biased media coverage contributes yet again to distorted racial images in many minds.

Actually, however, white youth are *more likely* than black youth to use marijuana or cocaine, to smoke cigarettes, or to drink alcohol. Recent surveys of high school students find that white students routinely indicate they are more likely to use drugs than black students. Research also shows that rates of drug abuse (also of child abuse) are higher for single-parent white families than for similar black families. Moreover, the general surveys of white and black adults indicate little difference in rates of drug use. Data on serious emergency room visits that are drug-related indicate that whites account for the lion's share, about 70 percent, of all such visits. The number of these drug-related emergency room visits has also grown much faster for whites than for blacks over the last decade or so.[43]

Thus, white and other non-black Americans account for seven out of eight illegal-drug-users, yet black Americans have become the national symbols of drug-users and dealers. This racially stereotyped framing affects white actions in serious ways. For instance, black drug-users are disproportionately targeted by the police (see Chapter 5, pp. 148–149). Blacks and Latinos make up most of those Americans put in jail for illegal drug use. In contrast, white drug-using and drug-dealing gets much less police surveillance and prosecution—even though a substantial majority of drug-dealers are white and there is much drug selling on predominantly white college campuses and in white suburban areas. This drug-using and drug-dealing reality clearly reveals the substantial racial bias in the U.S. policing and judicial systems. As we will see in the next chapter, numerous other aspects of our policing and judicial systems also reflect significant racial discrimination.[44]

Images of Black Athletes

A great many whites seem to assume that they are not racist because they cheer for black athletes on their favorite sports teams. They may feel that society is no longer racist because black players are common on college and professional football and basketball teams. However, research suggests that black male athletes are seen by whites as less intelligent and more animal-like than white male athletes. James Rada studied televised pro-football games on major television networks. In his sample of comments by on-air announcers, black athletes got most of the positive comments relating to physical talents. In regard to comments on cognitive abilities and intelligence, however, white athletes got most of the positive comments. All comments of sympathy were for white players. On-air commentaries also tended to portray white players in more friendly and intimate terms. Once again, black men were portrayed as less intelligent and more animal-like than white men, while the latter were shown as the "thinking men" on the field. The whites in this study were on-air media commentators, but their stereotyped views are probably shared by numerous whites who watch such sports programming.[45]

Moreover, even with increases in on-air sports commentators of color in the last decade, there is much evidence that white sports fans still view black athletes in terms of traditional stereotypes. A recent study by Abby Ferber compared the culture of white-supremacist groups and the general U.S. sports culture in their depictions of black men. Although one might expect great differences in these quite different cultures, she found remarkable similarities in the portrayals of black men as typically violent, hyper-aggressive, hypersexual, and inferior to white men. Today, black male athletes are viewed as acceptable, but only so long as they are "good" and under control of white owners or coaches. Many whites still frame black athletes in general as having an "inherently violent, aggressive nature lying just beneath the surface, threatening to spring forth at any time." In addition, by especially celebrating those black athletes who play by the white rules and fully accept white owners' or coaches' control, "Whites can tell themselves they are not racist, and they can blame African Americans for their own failures."[46] As long as they stay "good" and "well behaved," black male athletes can be viewed by whites as "exceptions to their race," an old strategy from the centuries-old white-racist framing of black men and women.

Exaggerating the Black Presence

The focus on black men and women as physically dominant, deviant, or dangerous in the media and in various other public and private discussions appears to create in many white minds the impression that there are more black Americans than there actually are. Thus, President Eisenhower's "big overgrown Negroes" image seems to extend to exaggerations about the black population. Over the last decade or two several surveys of whites, both college students and those in the general population, have shown that they substantially overestimate the size and proportion of the black population. Regularly, a majority of whites have estimated that black Americans make up at least 30 percent of the U.S. population, about two-and-a-half times their actual percentage.[47] This perhaps suggests an old emotion-laden conception, dating back to at least Thomas Jefferson, that there are too many African Americans, a demographic situation many whites view as threatening. Apparently, many white Americans periodically or habitually view their societal position in relation to the presence and number of black Americans.

Charles Gallagher has explored the reasons for these contemporary overestimations of the black population. In interviews with whites he found that a major source of exaggerated estimations is, yet again, the mainstream mass media. For example, whites who watched a lot of sports programs saw many black athletes and concluded the country has a high percentage of black Americans. Whites were also found to exaggerate the black presence because blacks seem so "vocal" about issues such as civil rights in the media. At least as important in shaping these overestimates, as we have already seen, is the impact of local crime news. The constant barrage of stories about black criminals in the local news gives most whites, as well as many others, the impression that the country has a much larger black population than it actually does. Once again, we see the profound impact of the media, and yet the media's exaggerated images and interpretations usually go unchallenged. In addition, most whites and other non-black Americans do not get information from other sources that counters these recurring media distortions.[48]

Mocking Black Americans

Today, many white Americans reveal their negative views and images in the ways they mock or joke about black Americans. Sometimes this mocking is quite overtly racist, such as in the many antiblack jokes told across the country on any given day. Among friends in the workplace, at a bar, on the Internet, or at home many whites tell stories and engage in racist conversations that mock alleged black mannerisms, morals, or speech. Moreover, in our recent research on white actions, in both private backstage and public frontstage settings, we have found that remarkably few whites object openly when white friends, relatives, acquaintances, or strangers engage in blatantly racist performances. This is true for well-educated whites as well as for other whites.[49]

Whites, including those in the elite, have crafted racist jokes about African Americans for centuries. Typical of elite and other white jokes is the one told back in the 1970s by Earl Butz, a former university dean and powerful secretary of agriculture. Joking about what the Republican party could offer to African Americans, he joked that all a black man really wants is loose shoes, warm toilet facilities, and sex. For many whites at all class levels, ridiculing black Americans or other Americans of color in joking commentaries is routine and commonplace, and apparently considered innocuous by most who do it.[50]

Associated with this racist joking is the mocking of certain black speech that many whites engage in when discussing black Americans. What whites believe to be a common black way of speaking is mocked through imitative language. This is done at all levels of white society. For example, in March 1970, President Richard Nixon and Vice President Spiro Agnew performed a piano duet at an elite Gridiron Club dinner. After a series of jokes about Nixon's "southern strategy" (the strategy to win politically by racist appeals to southern white voters) by luminaries on the program, Nixon and Agnew played two pianos. Nixon asked Agnew, "What about this 'southern strategy' we hear so often?" In counterpoint Agnew answered in mock black dialect, "Yes Suh, Mr. President, ah agree with you completely on yoah southern strategy." Nixon then played some favorite songs of certain Democratic presidents, while Agnew drowned him out with a vigorous rendition of "Dixie." The almost entirely white audience of the Washington, D.C., elite laughed loudly and enjoyed the racialized performances. In addition, we now know that President Nixon privately spoke of black Americans as genetically inferior to whites, according to a report of his advisor John Ehrlichman.[51]

Vicious mocking of black language and culture seems to be spreading, especially on the Internet. On the Internet, whites with Web literacy have developed many websites that feature crude, hostile, and racist parodies of what these whites consider black speech. For example, here is the opening of a mocking translation of a speech by Socrates: "How ya' gots felt, O dudes o' Athens, a hearin' de speeches o' mah accusers." Such mocking of black speech is linked on these sites to a broad range of racist stereotypes, jokes, and images. The site with the mocking Socrates speech listed events at a fictional "Ebonic Olympic Games": the "torching of the Olympic City" and the "Gang Colors Parade."[52] Antiblack websites spread racist images globally; indeed, there is at least one antiblack site in Russian. The Internet's anonymity and connectedness allow the spread of racist framing and opinions no longer acceptable to express in public settings to millions of people globally, particularly to the young who are most likely to surf the Internet unreflectively.

Less-severe mocking of black speech has become commonplace. For example, a white columnist for an Arizona newspaper wrote a satirical column on junk mail that promises "You have won 21 million dollars." The columnist wrote:

> From what I've seen on the TV about past winners, they prefer if you meet the camera crew fresh out of the shower and shouting, "Lawdy, Lawdy, Lawdy." Hey, no problem. We'll definitely be home, waiting behind the door in our bath towels and practicing our best Hattie McDaniel delivery.[53]

These "lawdy" comments make sense to readers because they draw on previous mocking of black speech by whites—in this case the exaggerated and white-contrived dialogue of the 1939 movie *Gone with the Wind*, one of the most racist movies ever made by Hollywood. (Hattie McDaniel was a black actor in that movie.) Whatever its intention, such mocking perpetuates stereotypes of blacks as odd, silly, or uncultured.

In movies, on television, and in newspaper and magazine columns, well-educated whites are often those who mock black language or behavior. In Hollywood films the "good guys" often speak prestige versions of the English language, while those portrayed as "bad guys," including black Americans, Latinos, and other Americans of color, often speak some negatively stigmatized version of English. Cartoon movies have made use of mock black English and other mock English accents, even for animals in these movies. In this manner language is mapped onto a particular group, as part of an aural stereotyping process, and old racist understandings are perpetuated in new forms. Anthropologist Jane Hill has studied this language mocking. Her special focus is on mock Spanish, which is common in the United States. Otherwise monolingual whites (and others) use made-up terms such as *no problemo, el cheapo*, and *hasty banana*, and phrases like *hasta la vista, baby*. Mock Spanish can be found on billboards and in movies, and gift shops. Such ridicule reveals underlying stereotyping of Latinos among whites who might reject more openly racist comments or practices. Mocking speech is seen as fun and justifiable. Hill also offers a probing analysis of whites' use of other mocking and racist language, such as the white insistence in Arizona on preserving the name of a mountain as "Squaw Peak," "squaw" being a derogatory term used by whites for Native American women. (It was originally a Native American term for woman, but long ago was taken over and made a very racist term by whites.) There is also much language mocking by whites in the media and in more private settings of the speech of Asian Americans.[54] While it may appear harmless to whites, language mocking supports traditional hierarchies of racial privilege and degradation without seeming to be racist in an old-fashioned, blatant sense. Indeed, many whites have denied that such mocking is racist or harmful, ignoring the many people of color who have pointed out the harm that such language mocking actually causes.

Such ridicule of language or speech is racist because it has significant meaning only if one knows the underlying racist framing, the racist stereotypes and images, of the groups of color that are targeted. Indeed, language mocking and subordination are not about standards for speaking as much as they are about determining that some people are not worth listening to and treating as social equals.[55]

The Language of Racism

Culture shapes language, and language fosters or facilitates many aspects of thought. The concepts and categories learned as children shape how we experience the world around us, and these concepts and categories—including racial stereotypes and images—are often delineated in sets of words and phrases. When racially coded language is embedded in minds, it and its associated concepts guide everyday thinking and behavior.

Today, antiblack racism is deeply imbedded in spoken and written English. Many whites still use epithets like "nigger," "coon," "spook," or "pickaninny" for African Americans, especially in private settings with friends and relatives and, increasingly, on white-oriented Internet sites. (One recent search for the word "nigger" on the Internet found 4.7 million sites listed.) Some whites still use terms like "boy" for a black man, as happened with President Barack Obama in the 2009 presidential campaign. Others persist in using other diminutive terms, such as replacing a black man's name that is William with "Willie." While in recent decades there has been a significant decline in white use of openly racist terms, at least in most public settings, an array of terms used in the media and in everyday, more public conversations of many whites has barely hidden racial meanings. For many whites, terms like *gangs, gangbangers, ghetto, inner city, the poor, the economically disadvantaged, welfare recipients, violent criminals, public housing,* and *drug pushers* symbolize black Americans or other dark-skinned Americans. Much white-racist commentary now uses such code words because they communicate (wink-wink) racist framing or inclinations without actually using more blatantly racist terms. A white person, including a media commentator, can use these terms to target or denigrate black Americans but still appear unprejudiced, at least to most other whites.[56]

Even in cases where color words and phrases were not crafted as intentionally racist, they can subtly reinforce antiblack framing. Thus, there are many phrases in English that use the words "black" and "white." Some may be racial in origin, but many seem linked to the old European tradition that associates negative concepts such as evil and the devil with darkness and blackness, and positive concepts such as purity and goodness with whiteness. The conceptual framework underlying these words and phrases accents black in negative ways and white in positive ways. In a standard dictionary the adjective "black" is listed as having these conventional meanings, in addition to color: dirty, soiled, wicked, sinister, connected with magic, gloomy, calamitous, marked with disaster, sullen, grim, and distorted. In contrast, the adjective "white" has these conventional meanings, in addition to color: marked by upright fairness, free of blemish, innocent, not intended to cause harm, fortunate, and favorable. In addition, the negative tone of many phrases using "black" can be seen in the following: to do a black deed; to be a black sheep; to tell a black lie; to indulge in the black arts (magic); to blacken one's name; to blackball someone; to be black-hearted; to have a black outlook; to be a blackguard (scoundrel); to have a Black Monday; to be on a black list; to give a black mark; to be blackmailed; and to be a black day. In contrast, we have the following: to be a white knight; to tell a white lie; to white list; to be the white hope; to be free, white, and twenty-one; and to say "That's very white of you."[57] While most such white–black distinctions in English are older than antiblack racism, they are commonplace in U.S. English conversations and thus can operate to subtly reinforce dichotomous, racial, or antiblack thinking.

Moreover, in numerous writings and presentations the positive achievements of whites may be put in the active tense, while those achievements of blacks may be put in the passive tense. Thus, Thomas Greenfield reports visiting Thomas Jefferson's Virginia slave plantation, where he was told by his guide, who was referring to large well-made doors that had operated since 1809 without need of repair, that "Mr. Jefferson designed these doors," and also that "the doors were installed in 1809." The enslaved African American workers who actually put up the well-crafted doors remained anonymous and in the passive tense.[58] As we noted previously, numerous slave plantations are now popular tourist sites that play down or ignore the enslaved workers who once labored there. Only recently have the public tours at, and written brochures about, a minority of slave plantations begun to give meaningful attention to the intelligence and agency of enslaved workers.

Moreover, today in many organizations a black man or woman who gets a very good job or position often is still said by whites to have gotten it through special consideration or affirmative action and not because of merit. In other cases, there is a *playing down* of black agency. Whites may recognize that blacks have achieved something, but run it down as flawed. For example, many whites have disparaged the innovative character of the music that has often come out of black communities, such as jazz in the early decades of the twentieth century or rap music in recent decades. There is also the strategy of viewing a black achievement as an *anomaly*. Success is something individual blacks do sometimes achieve, such as Bill Cosby's success as a comedian or President Barack Obama's successful election, but it is seen by a great many whites as an exception to the rule.[59]

The Nobel novelist Toni Morrison has suggested an even deeper point—that black Americans frequently function in important ways as a key metaphor and referent for white Americans in public discourse and in literature. Black Americans often seem to be an overt or hidden referent for much white thought and action.[60] We have seen previously how black Americans constitute a major reference point for whites—in crafting the Constitution, in the Civil War period, in creating wealth and prosperity, in law and politics, and in structuring residential areas in cities. In this and later chapters we observe black Americans as a key referent in many areas of contemporary life—in debates over schools, the criminal justice system, government welfare programs, housing and urban development, and political representation. Moreover, subtle use of the black referent even extends to the definition of what is "American."

White Emotions, White Rage

As we saw in the discussion of earlier American history in Chapter 3 (pp. 66–67), white ideas and understandings of racial matters are rooted in deep-lying emotions, which are central to the dominant white frame. For centuries many whites have been obsessed with blackness and have seen black people as fear-inspiring or dangerous. Whites have often been particularly emotional about such matters as interracial sex or marriage. However, the level of white emotional involvement in racist thinking and action varies considerably on an individual basis and in regard to a particular issue.

Consider, for example, the comments in this anonymous hate letter I received, apparently from a white man. The writer of the letter is familiar with extreme white-supremacist thinking and activities. The letter attacked a brief quote from me from a New Jersey newspaper article about current societal trends in regard to racial discrimination. Handwritten on a New Jersey city's superintendent of schools stationery, the letter read in part as follows:

> So we should give privileges to placate filthy dirty subhuman coons, your nuts. Never! Never! I'm telling you.... Whites such as myself are just itching to take to the streets and exterminate every dirty nigger ape as well as every white nigger loving commie dog (such as your self). [O.J.] Simpson is the catalyst that will finally awaken the latent, dormant nigger hatred extant in this county. There will be no compromise, no quarter given.... First we elect Buchanan types, next suspend habeus corpis [sic]. Third disenfranchise and resegregate niggers. Then either deportation or extermination. Sound familiar?

You white liberal swine are cancers even worse that filthy coons. When the reckoning comes, it will be curtains for them too. The only good nigger is a dead nigger.

[Signed] WHITE RAGE[61]

Judging from the letterhead and the vocabulary (if not the spelling), this letter seems to be from a well-educated white person. Note old white images of black people as dirty and subhuman. Note too the concern with "nigger-loving" whites. This type of racist venom extends beyond crude epithets and images to the goal of extermination. Perhaps most clear in this kind of racial diatribe is the high level of emotion.

While the letter is clearly extreme in its racist terminology, some of these racist themes have long been articulated, if in more restrained language, by many whites in the general public and in the elites. As I have shown earlier, racist images and attitudes are strongly held by influential and powerful whites. From time to time influential whites air their blatantly racist views openly. For instance, in the 1990s Marge Schott, then owner of the Cincinnati Reds baseball team, remarked to an employee, "I'd rather have a trained monkey working for me than a nigger." She was also reported to have called black baseball players "million-dollar niggers." She is not unusual in such behavior, some of it regularly bursting forth in public settings. Recall the earlier discussions of more recent racist ("nigger" and "nappy-headed hos") performances in public settings by major entertainment and media figures like Michael Richards and Don Imus.[62]

Denying Discrimination and Racism: The White Public

In Chapter 3 we examined briefly how elite whites, including media commentators and officials, have downplayed persisting racism and accented the image of a just society where equality of opportunity and colorblindness are actually the reality. These broad themes in some current incarnations of the dominant white framing provide the umbrella for much everyday discourse for white elites and the general white public. National surveys indicate that today a majority of ordinary white Americans see equality of opportunity as the societal reality. Included in this perspective is the idea that racial discrimination is no longer widespread and Americans of color who complain of it are paranoid, wrongheaded, or confused. Indeed, there is a common saying among many whites that a black person is "playing the race card," a phrase usually used to suggest that the black person is making an illegitimate demand because antiblack racism is no longer a serious obstacle. (Note too that this phrase is white-created.)

Soon after the 1960s civil rights movement declined in intensity, most whites were already moving toward the view that racial discrimination is no longer an important problem for the country. In a 1976 survey most whites (71 percent) agreed that "blacks and other minorities no longer face unfair employment conditions. In fact they are favored in many training and job programs." In addition, only a meager 12 percent of whites then agreed with the statement that "discrimination affects all black people. The only way to handle it is for blacks to organize together and demand rights for all." In surveys of this era, a substantial majority of black Americans had a quite different view, accenting the large-scale discrimination they actually faced.[63]

In more recent surveys, white and black Americans still differ dramatically in how they view contemporary discrimination. One recent Pew Research Center survey found that more than 80 percent of the black respondents reported widespread racial discrimination in at least one major societal area. Two-thirds reported that African Americans always or often face discrimination in jobs or in seeking housing; 50 percent said the same for shopping and restaurants. Also significant was the survey's finding that a majority of whites once again denied the black view of significant societal discrimination.[64] In addition, a CNN national survey on antiblack discrimination showed a similar pattern, with 87 percent of black respondents reporting that racial discrimination remains a serious national problem. Yet another CNN/ORC poll found that 61 percent of black respondents felt that antiblack discrimination was serious in their *local* area, compared to just 25 percent of whites.[65]

Moreover, a 2008 *Newsweek* opinion survey of white registered voters found that only 18 percent of whites thought that discrimination was the main reason why many black Americans cannot get ahead in the country. As whites have done in the past, most opted for blaming black Americans for their current socioeconomic conditions. Whites also tend to greatly overestimate the progress the African Americans have made in their socioeconomic conditions. One recent CNN/ORC survey found that nearly two-thirds of the white respondents agreed that the quality of life for black Americans had gotten significantly better over the last ten years, yet 61 percent of the black respondents disagreed, reporting that the quality of life had stayed the same or gotten worse. Interestingly, however, another recent ABC News/Post survey found that more than 84 percent of *both* black and white respondents reported having heard someone make an insulting or insensitive remark about African Americans.[66] Evidently, most whites know there are frequent racist commentaries being made by whites in everyday settings, yet do not want to see that as evidence of still serious racism in the society.

Today, as they have for decades, a majority of whites do not see the United States as a country with a problem of widespread racial discrimination. Most also do not view themselves as significantly racist in thought or action, often asserting, "I am not a racist." In recent years many have made such statements as "My family never owned slaves" or "My family did not segregate lunch counters." Many will say to black Americans something like, "Slavery happened hundreds of years ago—just get over it." They do not know, or pretend they do not know, that official slavery ended less than 150 years or so prior to their statements. In addition, whites making such historically oriented assertions usually do not admit that they and their families have benefited greatly from slavery, segregation, and/or present-day discrimination.

Many whites seem to mix negative views of black Americans with images of white innocence, thereby giving specific expression to elements of a broader racial framing. Take this example of a white college student's reply to a question about her first experience with black Americans, in this case black children:

> I switched from a private school which had no blacks to a public school, and I was thrown in the middle of a bunch of apes, no I'm just kidding.... And I don't know, my parents have always instilled in me that blacks aren't equal, because we are from [the Deep South].

In her interview she continues in this vein, making several negative comments about African Americans. Then at the end of her interview, she adds:

> I don't consider myself racist. I, when I think of the word racist, I think of KKK, people in white robes burning black people on crosses and stuff, or I think of the Skinheads or some exaggerated form of racism.[67]

We see here a strong imaging of a white self in positive terms. Research by Eduardo Bonilla-Silva and numerous others has demonstrated the array of rhetorical devices that a great many whites use in their everyday conversations and interactions, especially in public and with strangers, to try to portray themselves as "colorblind" and "not racist." Recently, researchers have found this to be true for whites at all educational levels, including those involved in counseling and other helping professions.[68]

It seems that many whites assert that they are not racist because they see racism as only something that *other* whites do, or have done in the past. Jerome Culp has summarized this:

> To many white people, not being racist means having less racial animosity than their parents (something almost all can at least claim); having less racial animosity than someone they know (something all can claim); or not belonging to a white supremacist group.... For many white people, unless they believe overwhelmingly

in the inferiority of black people, they are not collaborators with racism and are not racist.[69]

As we see in white views of some black athletes or black entertainment figures like Bill Cosby or Oprah Winfrey, many whites hold positive views of selected black men or women. However, these often superficial positive views reduce the ability of whites to see their own culpability in ongoing personal and institutional racism. It is possible to hold that black Americans can be good entertainers, musicians, or sports figures, yet also believe that black Americans are generally inferior to whites in character, morality, and/or intelligence.

Historical changes in racism have also been misperceived by most whites. When the legal segregation era came to an end with the passage of civil rights laws in the 1960s, most apparently concluded that serious racism was being rapidly extinguished. Today, most whites, like the woman interviewed above, seem to view what racism remains as a matter of isolated individual or Klan-type bigotry and not as a system of racism cutting across U.S. institutions. As a result, they do not see, or do not wish to admit, their own racism. Moreover, the level at which racist attitudes are held can vary in degree of consciousness. Thus, social psychologist Patricia Devine has suggested that those whites who reject overtly prejudiced views can still hold less conscious prejudices that exist because of prior racial socialization. For many this deep-lying attitudinal racism is a persisting bad habit that keeps breaking out into their everyday behavior. One reason is that human beings are characterized by automatic information processing, which can regularly involve unintentional activation of deep-lying racist images from the dominant white frame that the conscious mind may try to suppress.[70]

White Views on Government Action against Discrimination

If antiblack discrimination is no longer regarded as a major or well-institutionalized problem by the white majority, then it is not surprising that these whites see less need, or no need, for strong antidiscrimination efforts by local, state, and federal governments. From this perspective black Americans and others pressing for continuing or enhanced antidiscrimination programs, such as aggressive affirmative action, are making rather illegitimate demands.

Symbolic and Laissez-Faire Racism

Researchers like David Sears have described a contemporary white perspective called "symbolic racism." Whites often combine the notion of declining overt racism with the idea that blacks are now making illegitimate demands for societal changes. As these researchers see the current situation, a majority of whites have shifted away from old-fashioned, blatantly racist ideas and have accepted some modest desegregation while strongly resisting aggressive government action for large-scale desegregation. What they term "symbolic racism" or "modern racism" is grounded in white resistance to substantial changes in the racial status quo. Central to white concerns is a fear that whites have of losing status and power because of black attempts to bring more societal change. Deep-lying antiblack views—especially views of blacks violating traditional American work values—are still present, but white resentment of pressures for substantial change is central to the current racist framing. This symbolic racism perspective does capture some important elements of contemporary white perspectives, but it has been criticized for playing down old-fashioned blatant racism, when the latter still exists among many whites and is directly connected to negative views of substantial government programs to eradicate racial discrimination.[71]

Lawrence Bobo, James Kluegel, and Ryan Smith have suggested a more historical approach. Since the 1950s, and shaped by structural changes in the society, white attitudes have shifted from an accent on strict racial segregation and more overt bigotry to a "laissez-faire racism," by which Bobo, Kluegel, and Smith mean whites' continuing negative stereotyping of blacks and blaming of blacks for their problems. Roughly in line with, but probably lagging somewhat behind, the elite responses described in Chapter 3 (pp. 80–81), most ordinary whites have given up a commitment to aggressive government-imposed racial segregation (if they ever had such commitment). Also in line with the elite, they still strive to maintain white privilege and position in now informally segregated settings. Survey data since the 1960s, as we noted previously, indicate a substantial discrepancy between white views on the *principle* of desegregation versus white views on the *implementation* of desegregation by government. While surveys in the mid-1960s indicated that nearly two-thirds of whites accepted integrated schooling in principle, just 38 percent then accepted a role for government in pressing for more racial integration.[72]

Today this pattern persists. White support for the principle of school integration is well above 90 percent, while endorsement of aggressive government intervention to insure racial integration is far less. Recent survey data indicate similar discrepancies in white views of job and housing integration along racial lines. Recall the recent review by Quillian of opinion surveys of whites that show the majority publicly support equality of opportunity for Americans of color, yet also do not believe there is major discrimination in society and, thus, do not support major government intervention to secure further racial equality. Acceptance of the principle of racial integration does not mean that most whites wish to see government intervene aggressively to guarantee racial fairness or equality, or that they wish to personally have significantly more contact with black Americans. Most whites thus maintain a positive sense of self and insist on greater social privileges and resources, while fending off what they see as illegitimate black demands for a fair share of those privileges and resources.[73]

Negative Views on Affirmative Action

Affirmative action is a major example of a remedial program designed to deal with contemporary racial discrimination. Most whites, including most white leaders, have *always* been opposed to aggressive affirmative action since it was first proposed in the 1960s. For example, in a 1970s survey of mostly white local and national leaders in business, farming, unions, the media, and academia, most were overwhelmingly opposed to affirmative action for black Americans in school admissions and jobs. A substantial majority thought that equality of opportunity, not equality of results, was the best way to eradicate racial inequality. In surveys in this era the white public agreed with these white leaders.[74]

Today, most whites continue to be unsupportive of substantial affirmative action. Recent surveys reveal that far more than half of whites do not believe that government and private agencies should be making aggressive remedial efforts on behalf of Americans of color, although milder remedial programs are sometimes viewed as acceptable. One recent *Newsweek* opinion survey of white voters found that 72 percent disapproved of giving "preferences to blacks and other minorities ... [in] hirings, promotions, and college admissions." Three-quarters also felt that such preferences had resulted in less-qualified people being hired, promoted, or admitted. Moreover, 39 percent also indicated that they thought the United States had gone too far in "pushing equal rights."[75] Indeed, today many whites believe that they are likely to be victims of government affirmative action policies. One Pennsylvania survey asked a question as to how likely it would be that a white worker might lose a job or a promotion to a less-qualified black worker. Most black respondents thought this was unlikely, while most whites thought it was likely. National polls using such a question have gotten similar responses: the majority of whites seem convinced that antiwhite discrimination is now significant. In contrast to these white views, interestingly, the most recent surveys of African Americans show that they still overwhelmingly support affirmative action programs, with 72 percent expressing such a view in a recent Gallup poll.[76]

As in the past, many whites still comment on the socioeconomic and other problems of black Americans with such statements as, "Why can't they be like us?" One common notion is that if "they" will just work harder, then normal societal processes will enable them to have greater economic mobility. One survey asked whether respondents agreed with this statement: "The Irish, Italians, and many other groups overcame prejudice and worked their way up, African-Americans and other minorities should do the same without any special help from the government." Most whites agreed.[77] Moreover, many whites argue that they oppose affirmative action only because of the principle of fairness; that is, they oppose affirmative action only because such programs unfairly benefit some at the expense of others. Yet, firmly racist views appear to lie beneath the surface of such anti-affirmative-action arguments for many whites. One recent experimental study examined why white conservatives were opposed to affirmative action for African Americans and found that the intensity of their racist framing of African Americans predicted the character of their opposition to remedial programs for discrimination.[78]

Imaging the White Self

As we have seen in previous chapters, the dominant racist framing of white Americans encompasses much more than antiblack views. Among the important elements are positive views of white superiority, virtue, and merit. The broad white racial frame views the white-dominated history of the United States as mostly meritorious and unproblematic for the present. Today, as in the past, group merit and individual merit are judged by standards created by the white majority. In Chapter 3 we noted the common images of white superiority and virtue that recur in Hollywood films (pp. 89–90). From the first years of movie-making to the present, when racial matters have been portrayed, whites as a group have almost always been portrayed as morally superior, intellectually superior, or otherwise meritorious. In these movies—including recent television movies—there may be a few white individuals who are bigots, but white society as a whole is not portrayed as institutionally racist. Some white person is usually a central hero, even in movies substantially or mostly about Americans of color (for example, *Glory* or *Gran Torino*).

Among the elites and in the general public, whites have developed numerous sincere fictions about whites and whiteness that reproduce aspects of the dominant racial frame at an everyday level. Such sincere fictions frequently describe whites as "not racist" and as "good people" even as the same whites take part in discriminatory actions or express racist views. This moral privileging of whiteness may be conscious, or it can be half-conscious or unconscious. One older California study found evidence of this unconsciousness in research on white women; whiteness was difficult for most of the white Californians to even name. More recent research by Karyn McKinney using white student biographies has found a similarly unreflective response to questions of whiteness for most whites.[79] Most whites do not think much about being white, or about the society's white-created racial hierarchy. And when they do, that thinking is often in response to the strong presence of black Americans or other people of color. Being white, one might say, means rarely or never having to think about it. Whiteness is of course the national norm, and thus just "normal" for most whites.

Moreover, one survey found that nearly two-thirds of white respondents did *not* think that whites as a group had benefited from past and present discrimination against black Americans.[80] As we have seen, many whites have asserted their innocence with a torrent of comments such as "My family never owned slaves" and "My family never segregated any lunch counters." This white guiltlessness is professed at all class levels, including by presidential candidates like Bob Dole and Pat Buchanan.

Fostering and Learning Racist Attitudes

In Chapter 3 we examined how white elites have insistently fostered a racial framing that rationalizes the everyday realities of unjust impoverishment and enrichment across the color line. This effort is a major source of the racist framing held in minds of the non-elite population. Through various means elites have regularly pressured and manipulated ordinary white Americans to accept the dominant racist framing and its component elements. After the major elements of an era's white racial framing and structural arrangements are in place, ordinary whites need less pressuring, for they generally understand what is in their group interest. Indeed, ordinary whites often generate new permutations on the old racist ideas, innovations that in their turn reinforce or enhance the old racist framing.

The often hidden power of the elite works through propagating the dominant racial frame by means of the mass media and the educational system, as well as in workplaces and churches. For centuries newspapers, magazines, advertisements, and, more recently, media like television and the Internet have played a central part not only in generating the dominant racial frame, but also in creating specific racist images that are the implemented features of that frame.

For example, in the century after the Civil War many racially stereotyped images of black Americans were aggressively circulated in what was the relatively new means of commercial advertising. "Black faces were used to sell everything from tooth paste to pancakes. Distorted images appeared on boxes and tubes, and even on vaudeville stages, to make white people laugh."[81] By the early twentieth century the great expansion of the mass media—especially newspapers, magazines, and radio—provided many more avenues for the circulation of antiblack and other racist images. In addition, the emergence of Hollywood movie-making on a large scale, and then television, in the middle decades of the twentieth century, created or reinforced many negative images of Americans of color in many millions of American minds. We have noted previously the impact of racist movies like *Gone with the Wind*, as well as the impact of racial stereotyping in more recent movies that are less obviously racist.

Today, many negative racial images of black Americans and other Americans of color are still generated and circulated rapidly in the U.S. media, especially on television and cable networks, on radio talk shows, and on many Internet websites. Old-fashioned antiblack images are still found on some consumer goods, like candy bars and toothpaste, sold in various countries across the globe. However, in the United States almost all the old blatantly racist images on mainstream consumer goods have disappeared, or images like those of Aunt Jemima and Uncle Ben have gradually been altered to appear much less stereotypical.

In capitalistic societies like the United States consumerism is based not only on the consumption of material goods but also on the consumption of important beliefs, images, and narratives, which have long included substantial racist elements. In marketing these goods and attracting consumers, the corporate executives in media corporations and related corporations generally do not confront, but rather reinforce and recreate, pre-existing racist beliefs, imagery, and narratives from the dominant racial frame.

The Role of Conformity

Some analysts have viewed racial prejudice as a sort of demon in an individual, indeed often as a type of psychological abnormality. Frustration–aggression and authoritarian–personality theories of prejudice focus on the externalization function of prejudice—the transfer of a person's internal psychological problems to an external object, such as a racial other, as an attempted personal solution for a serious and internal psychological problem. From this psychological viewpoint, those who are racially prejudiced are seriously "sick" individuals. There are certainly whites who fit this interpretation, some of whom belong to the racist-extremist groups. However, much social science research indicates that social *conformity* is a much more important factor in shaping the racial views and prejudices of a majority of people, including a majority of whites. Most whites accept the social contexts in which they are socialized and usually hold to many of the racial prejudices taught at home and school or through the mainstream media.[82]

In this society the white self is typically shaped through interaction with other people. Much learning about the superiority of whites and inferiority of racialized others comes from informal lessons learned as children at home and school and as adults socializing with relatives and friends. White images of people of color are typically passed along family lines of communication. Conformity to views of important relatives and friends is a central source of routinized racist framing. Most racial views are not the result of individual pathologies but reflect shared social definitions and narratives. In this way racial prejudices and other elements from the dominant racial frame function as a means of social adjustment to the views of an important in-group. In general, as several scholars have noted, "our most private thoughts and feelings arise out of a constant feedback and flow-through of the thoughts and feelings of others who have influenced us. Our individuality is decidedly a part of a collective movement."[83] Thus, sociologist Maurice Halbwachs suggested that our personal understandings about society are not just in some nook of our minds to which only we have access. Our racial understandings, and the dominant racial framing we use, are regularly reinforced and recalled to us externally within the social groups of which we are part. In this way a particular person's understandings, images, knowledge, and framing hang together because they are part of the "totality of thoughts common to a group."[84] Negative images of people of color are old and deeply imbedded in white communities; they become part of the evolving white self, but one emerging in important collective contexts.

Some psychological research indicates that people often do not think through what they are doing in everyday behavior but proceed as if they are on automatic pilot; they tend to operate in line with the routinized scripts they have learned from their important socialization settings. Given that racist images, attitudes, and inclinations are generally well-learned elements imbedded in individual and collective memories, much racist behavior on the part of whites thus has an automatic and routinized character.[85]

For most whites the earliest socialization in racist attitudes begins in the family. A CBS poll of high school students found that half of those whose parents made overtly racist comments admitted that they too had made such comments. Consider this interview with a white father, who responds to a hypothetical question about an adult child dating a black person thus:

> I'd be sick to my stomach. I would feel like, that I failed along the way.... I'd feel like I probably failed as a father, if that was to happen. And it's something that I could never accept.... It would truly be a problem in my family because I could never handle that, and I don't know what would happen because I couldn't handle that, ever.[86]

This man's comments signal more than negative attitudes toward and images of the black out-group; they point to his emotion-laden view of his white self and to how he sees being a white father. The comments highlight the family context of such ideas. Quite evident too is the substantial emotion being expressed. While perhaps more strongly stated than some, his views are in line with the interracial dating and marriage views still expressed in research studies by a great many whites.[87]

Mainstream theories of the cognitive development of children have often suggested that most do not form clear ideas on racial matters until they are at least five or six years old. Until that time, egocentricity is said to be the child's natural state. However, recent research using photos of white and black faces and good/bad word associations has found that even white preschoolers already tend "to categorize racially ambiguous angry faces as black rather than white; they did not do so for happy faces."[88] In addition, one major ethnographic study of numerous white children in a preschool setting found that three-, four-, and five-year-olds periodically interacted with children of other racial groups using sophisticated understandings of racist ideas and epithets. One example in this study was the use by young white children of the word "nigger" for black Americans, and the white children's indicating that they had some understanding of the racist meanings associated with that vicious epithet. They were not just unreflectively imitating what they had heard white adults say. White children there regularly used a racial framing and its terms to define themselves as white and to exclude or exert power over children of color. Recall too the socio-psychological research discussed earlier that showed that, as children age, they usually learn to hide their racist views from strangers (pp. 102–103).[89]

We should note too that while most children are initially socialized into racist thinking in family groups, they also learn subtle and blatant racist ideas and images from their neighborhood and school peer groups, from children's books and school books, and from the media.

Group Isolation and its Consequences

Recent research continues to show U.S. neighborhoods are still highly segregated. One survey found that 86 percent of white respondents reported many whites living in their area, while 66 percent of black respondents and 61 percent of Latino respondents said the same about the dominance of their own groups in their residential areas. While this question was stated in rather vague terms, the survey results do confirm what demographic analyses routinely show—that Americans still live in racially segregated communities and that whites are the most racially segregated of the major groups.[90]

Residential segregation is a basic part of the societal process whereby systemic racism is reproduced from one generation to the next. Residential segregation breeds significant social and mental isolation; the absence of equal-status experiences with black families in neighborhoods contributes materially to white unfamiliarity with and stereotyping of black Americans. This is also true for many other families of color. In Chicago, several *New York Times* journalists did important field research on the impact of residential segregation in regard to cross-racial attitudes. They interviewed Chicagoans in two adjacent working-class suburbs, one predominantly white and one predominantly black. Whites were found to be very isolated and mostly living out their lives "without ever getting to know a black person." In both communities there were fears and suspicions of the other group. However, the source of these fears varied significantly. The black suburbanites were "fearful because much of their contact with white people was negative," while "whites were fearful because they had little or no contact" with similar black Chicagoans.[91]

Because of the racial demography and spatial ecology of everyday life, the majority of blacks spend much more time interacting with whites than the majority of whites spend interacting with blacks. Most black Americans work or shop with large numbers of whites, whereas relatively few whites do the same with large numbers of blacks. The racial views of most white Americans are not likely to be shaped by numerous equal-status contacts with black Americans. The sense of white superiority is reinforced by the continuing process in which most whites live separated from black Americans or other Americans of color.

Children living in isolation can be significantly affected. One recent study of intergroup attitudes examined white first- and fourth-graders attending heavily white schools where they had very little contact with African Americans. In contrast to studies of white children at more racially diverse schools, these white children revealed much more racial bias in rating hypothetical interracial encounters. These white children were asked to rate white and black children in ambiguous situations on picture cards where interactions between the children could be interpreted as one child having, or not having, negative intentions toward the other child. ("Either a child meant to push the other off the swing or the child fell on his own.") These very segregated white children were more likely to attribute negative intentions in ambiguous situations to blacks than to whites. The tested children also indicated that they felt that wrongdoing by a black child was likely to prevent interracial friendships, whereas similar wrongdoing by a white child was less likely to affect such friendships. The racial bias of the white children in the very homogeneous schools was shown to be significant as measured in terms of hypothetical interracial interactions.[92]

Psychological studies also show that whites who are asked to describe a black person often see fewer descriptive aspects of that person than when they are asked to describe a white person. Members of an in-group tend to see the people in their group in more complex and differentiated terms than they see people in an out-group. Isolation increases bonding and conformity to the norms of the in-group, and the stronger one's attachment to the in-group, the greater the likelihood of prejudice and stereotyping directed at out-groups. This general phenomenon is especially serious when members of a particular group, like white Americans, have great privilege and power over other groups in society.[93]

Activating Antiblack Prejudices and Stereotypes

Racist prejudices, stereotypes, and emotions are serious not just in themselves, but because they motivate actions implementing and reinforcing the dominant racial hierarchy. White Americans vary in how important their racist views and emotions are in their everyday understandings and practices. Some are so overtly racist in their thinking and emotions that they are completely taken over by their internalized racism. They may join openly white-supremacist groups and target African Americans and other people of color for assault and other violence. In significant contrast, other whites recognize their own racist upbringing and proclivities and join groups openly working against white racism.

Social science research reveals, as one might expect, a significant link between racial attitudes and discriminatory actions. One recent review of 57 research studies found a consistent but moderate relationship between measured attitudes and discrimination. The researchers also found that measures of emotional prejudices were more strongly related to measures of discrimination than were measures of racial stereotypes and beliefs. Especially revealing was that the measures of emotional prejudices were significantly related to "both observed and self-reported discrimination," while the racial stereotype and belief measures were "related only to self-reported discrimination." These data thus suggest that some people are hiding their true racial views on the explicit measures of stereotypes and prejudice and that "we now know that what they do is substantially related to how they feel, and somewhat related to how they think."[94]

Other recent research has found that people who show an implicit racial bias on measures like the implicit association test (associating white and black faces with positive and negative words) are more likely to engage in overtly racist actions. Researchers at Rutgers University found that white and other non-black subjects who revealed greater implicit bias toward black Americans were more likely than other subjects to report engaging in racial discrimination, such as hurling racist slurs, excluding black people, and threatening physical harm to black people. Moreover, in assessing hypothetical university situations, white students with strong racial biases were also more likely than other whites to recommend budget cuts for black, Asian, and Jewish student organizations (that is, potential economic discrimination).[95]

Racist thought or action is often precipitated by some type of visual or verbal cue. Perhaps the most common cue is the black body itself. When whites perceive someone to fit their internalized criteria for blackness— which can be skin color, other physical characteristics, and/or speech— their minds may generate negative attitudes or images, and they may act according to those attitudes or images. Psychologists have suggested that there are several possible responses to a racial cue. Some whites do not automatically activate an antiblack stereotype when they encounter a black person. They activate a positive image and generally act in antiracist ways. Another group of whites react routinely and consciously to such racial cues with an overtly negative evaluation and actively express their negative views in discriminatory action. For a third group of whites, their negative evaluations are also activated in response to racial cues, but they are not clearly aware of these negative reactions. They act on racist views but only unconsciously. Yet another group of whites is like the previous one, but they are aware of the negative evaluations and will try to counter them, albeit to varying degrees. Sometimes this countering is because of a personal distaste for the racist reaction, but in other cases it may be only a desire to be seen as socially acceptable to other people.[96]

These four types of responses overlap in many lives. Depending on the time in a person's life, or the social situation, an individual may react to particular racial cues in different ways. Under certain circumstances, many whites who hold strong racist prejudices and stereotypes will not act on them out of concern for social acceptability. In contrast, many whites with strong racist views will express their negative views in settings, such as in backstage settings with only white friends and relatives, where they do not feel social pressures to act in non-racist ways. Thus, location and context are often quite important in the expression of racist thought and actions.[97]

Conclusion

Racist stereotypes, images, emotions, and interpretations—all part of the dominant white racial frame—are central to the operation of systemic racism in the contemporary United States. This framing lies behind most discriminatory action taken by whites against black Americans and other Americans of color. Among whites this framing is reinforced and perpetuated by millions of taken-for-granted comments, stories, and actions that target Americans of color every day in both public and private settings.

White-racist images and attitudes do not stop at U.S. borders. At any given moment, white Americans working overseas are telling antiblack jokes and making other racist comments to people around the globe, or television stations across the globe are playing racist U.S. television programs and movies, such as *Gone With the Wind*, old Tarzan and cowboy-and-Indian classics, or more recent movies like *Glory* or *Gran Torino* with their more subtle racist notions or imagery. U.S. media corporations have long played a major role in circulating the white racial frame's negative images overseas. Increasing numbers of people around the world now get much information and entertainment from U.S. movies, syndicated television programs, and videos, as well as directly from such sources as U.S. armed forces radio and television broadcasts.[98]

Currently, all but one of the eight or so international corporations that dominate the world's global media market are U.S.-based. These include General Electric, AT&T/Liberty Media, Disney, Time Warner, Sony, News Corporation, Viacom, and Seagram. These corporations not only control the production of media products such as movies and television shows, but also control many media outlets such as major television networks and publishing facilities. A few other corporations—just below these dominant companies in size, and from the United States, Europe, and Japan—assist in this concentrated corporate dominance of the world's mass media. These large international corporations have often invested in local mass media, thereby reshaping local popular cultures and traditional music and art. Several times in recent years, representatives of countries such as Brazil, Mexico, Sweden, and the Ivory Coast have held conferences to try to stop the Western media from destroying local popular cultures. However, in spite of such efforts to keep local control, the trend over recent decades has been more corporate mergers building very large media companies and to Western (and Japanese) control of the mass media in many countries on the planet. This process of increasing Western control over local media products and cultures is not new, but has been going on since the nineteenth-century spread of European and U.S. imperialism.[99]

As a result of contemporary globalization, U.S. media corporations are perhaps the most important force shaping the white-racist framing, including racist stereotyping and imaging, that is spreading around the world. For example, one study of the impact of U.S. media on educated groups in Turkey has shown that powerful images of whiteness and blackness are brought to that country by U.S. movies and new magazines.[100] Antiblack images are now common in many countries. Recently, researchers in rural Japan gave implicit and explicit attitudinal tests to children and adults who had little or no contact with Americans and found significantly negative views of black Americans. In addition, a survey of Japanese international students in the United States found that they too often held very negative views of African Americans, views influenced by whether they had seen positive or negative portrayals of African Americans in the U.S. media.[101]

A study of 15 rural Taiwanese found that the respondents sometimes realized that U.S. media engaged in racist stereotyping, yet most still held negative views of black Americans. They generally thought black Americans were self-destructive, dirty, lazy, unintelligent, criminal, violent, or ugly. Negative images were usually gleaned from U.S. television shows, movies, and music videos the respondents had seen in Taiwan.[102] More recently, a survey of 345 mainland Chinese high school students found that, the greater their use of U.S. print media, television, and movies, the more negative were their stereotypes of African Americans, such as stereotypes of black violence and hedonism. In contrast, the greater their use of Chinese television and print media, the more likely they were to have positive images of African Americans, although this relationship was not as strong as for negative effects of the U.S. media. The researchers interpreted their findings as reflecting the reality of the U.S. media still portraying African Americans in disproportionately negative terms, while the Chinese media do not have this generally negative portrayal. The Chinese media mostly portray African Americans as impoverished citizens, as protesting for their rights, and as attractive sports figures. Especially popular in China at the time of this research was the Houston Rockets NBA basketball team and its star Chinese player, Yao Ming. Ming's association with predominantly black NBA teams apparently had a positive impact on how black Americans were viewed by these Chinese students.[103]

Drawing on informal interviews with Latino immigrants from Central America, sociologist Nestor Rodriguez has concluded that the U.S. mass media are creating negative views of black Americans there. "I have traveled to Guatemala and seen theaters showing the same violent, racist movies we show here," he says. "When I asked one migrant in Houston why some migrants have antiblack attitudes, he responded that they first learn about blacks from U.S. movies."[104] As a result of the globalizing U.S. media, antiblack images and attitudes are often carried by Asian, Latino, and other immigrants coming into the United States. This negative racial framing frequently becomes the basis for negative attitudes toward, and negative interactions with, black Americans, from the earliest days of interpersonal contact. From this experience, black Americans in their turn may develop negative views of certain immigrants. Thus, the negative attitudes of Asian or Latino immigrants toward African Americans— and the negative attitudes of African Americans toward Asian or Latino Americans—are often part of the much larger system of white-generated racial framing and other white-managed racism, which these particular groups had no role in initiating.

5
Racial Oppression Today
Everyday Practice

Recently, researchers at the Massachusetts Institute of Technology sent applications to an array of job ads made by Chicago and Boston employers. Using made-up names that sound (especially to whites) like typically white or typically black names, they found that applicants with "white-sounding" names were 50 percent more likely to be contacted by employers than those with "black-sounding" names. Moreover, when the researchers increased the job credentials of the tester-applicants, this was far more likely to get whites a callback from employers than blacks. Being black with eight years of job experience was necessary to get the same treatment as a white applicant *with no experience.*[1]

To many white observers racial discrimination and other racial oppression no longer seem important because they are no longer matters of official discrimination and legal segregation. Racism is often asserted by whites to be gone or declining in this "post-racial society" because there are at least a few African Americans or other people of color in numerous professional or managerial positions in many historically white organizations. Yet, one can recognize the periodic social changes in whites' racial domination in the United States without downplaying the still-strong relationship between being a black person or other person of color and being a target of serious racial discrimination, as from the employers in this study. In one way or another, virtually all Americans of color continue to suffer some discrimination today because white racial framing and domination of Americans of color remain major organizing features of our group life. The enduring racial hierarchy is still well-supported by a range of dominant-group prejudices and stereotypes, and it is perpetuated most centrally by the racial discrimination still carried out by a great many whites on a recurring basis in most areas of this society.

The Heart of Racism: Discriminatory Practices

Mainstream social scientists have often examined the paired ideas of racial prejudice and racial discrimination. As we noted previously, a common perspective has been one of individual bigots acting out racial attitudes in discriminatory ways. In recent decades, however, some scholars have argued for a different emphasis in looking at racial prejudice and discrimination. They prefer to accent the *institutional* and *systemic* racism that undergirds individual acts of discrimination. In its origin, this institutional racism viewpoint mostly stems from a long line of African American scholars and activists, going back centuries. As I underscored in Chapter 1, thinker-activists like Douglass and Du Bois long ago put white society and its societal institutions at the center of serious critical analysis of U.S. racism. The 1960s civil rights movement brought a renewed emphasis among black intellectuals and activists on the institutional contexts of individual acts of discrimination.[2]

While in recent years numerous mainstream scholars have rejected a critical institutional-racism perspective, it remains the most important approach to understanding the depths of the U.S. system of racial hostility and discrimination. Today, black Americans and other Americans of color generally experience discrimination not just as the actions of individual white bigots in one social arena, but rather as everyday, recurring actions of white actors across many of life's arenas—actions that are backed by a multifaceted and powerful system of white power and privilege. While all racial discrimination is carried out by individuals, the social context is very important, for that is where the framing, norms, and proclivities perpetuating racial discrimination are institutionalized. Individual acts of discrimination activate the underlying hierarchical relations of power in which whites generally dominate Americans of color.[3]

Over recent decades the international attack on all racial and ethnic discrimination has accelerated. The United Nations International Convention on the Elimination of All Forms of Racial Discrimination, implemented in 1969, defines discrimination as:

> any distinction, exclusion, restriction or preference based on race, colour, descent or national or ethnic origin which has the purpose or effect of nullifying or impairing the recognition, enjoyment or exercise, on an equal footing, of human rights and fundamental freedoms.

This broad view accents not only distinctions on the basis of racial grouping, but also institutionalized restrictions, preferences, and exclusion aimed at impairing human rights. It underscores the costs associated with being the target of discrimination. In another passage, the Convention adds that the "existence of racial barriers is repugnant to the ideals of any human society."[4] In addition, since the early 2000s the United Nations has had two important world conferences dealing explicitly with international racism issues, including issues of reparations for U.S. slavery and colonialism. The U.S. government declined to participate in either conference.

The Social Context of Racist Practices

Contemporary patterns of discrimination are grounded in the benefits that whites have historically secured from four centuries of racial oppression in North America. Most forms of racial discrimination transmit the legacy of this oppressive past of slavery and Jim Crow. Today discriminatory practices reproduce and reinforce the unjust impoverishment and enrichment of the past. Discrimination reflects and perpetuates the age-old racist frame, with its associated array of antiblack attitudes, images, and emotions. When blacks encounter whites in many contemporary settings, they often meet negative beliefs about and interpretations of their abilities, values, and orientations. Many racial barriers persist today because a substantial majority of whites still harbor some antiblack stereotypes, prejudices, images, and interpretations, and because a large minority are very negative in their perspectives on black Americans. When most whites interact with black Americans at work, in restaurants, on the street, at school, or in the media they tend to think about the latter, either consciously or unconsciously, in terms of racist stereotypes or other racist framing inherited from the past and constantly reiterated and reinforced in the present.

As we observed previously, the translation of antiblack attitudes into actual discrimination is shaped not only by these views and attitudes but also by social norms, such as by what other people might think, and by perceived behavioral controls, such as what the other's responses to one's discrimination might be. Routinized discrimination in housing, employment, politics, and public accommodations is carried out by whites acting alone or in groups. The social norms guiding discrimination can be formal or legal, but most today are unwritten and informal. Moreover, much antiblack action is not sporadic but is carried out repeatedly and routinely by numerous dominant-group members influenced by the important norms of their key social networks. Whites have the power to discriminate as individuals, but much of their power to harm comes from membership in traditionally white networks and organizations.

Everyday Racism: Subtle, Covert, and Blatant

Clearly, the character of everyday discrimination varies significantly. Whites may actively persecute people of color, or they may engage in an array of avoidance behaviors. Discrimination can be self-consciously motivated, or it can be half-conscious or unconscious and deeply imbedded in an actor's core beliefs. At the level of everyday interaction with black Americans and other Americans of color, most whites can create racial tensions and barriers even without conscious awareness they are doing so. Examples of this include when white men lock their car doors as a black man walks by on the street or when white women step out or pull their purses close to them when a black man comes into an elevator they are on. Stereotyped images of black men as criminals probably motivate this and similar types of defensive action.

Experiencing white racism is not about one or two incidents, but rather it is a lifetime experience from which one cannot ordinarily escape. It involves discrimination in all areas of life, in most weeks, over lifetimes. In one 2009 California study researchers conducted six focus groups (group interviews) with 40 black working-class and middle-class women of childbearing age. Echoing reports of previous studies, these women described numerous instances of racial discrimination from the time they were children to the present day. They noted interpersonal and institutional racism: "Racism was experienced in various social settings: examples included work and school settings, in everyday social interactions such as shopping and in other settings defined by public space, and when interacting with health care, justice, and housing systems." The women also discussed the impact whites' racism had on them, the stress that it caused, as well as the ways in which they dealt with it on a daily basis:

> The women maintained a pervasive sense of vigilance in anticipation of future racism events for themselves and their children, preparing themselves behaviorally, cognitively, and emotionally for potential racism encounters: "It's the skin you're in," verbalized by one woman, seemed to capture the inescapable sense of pervasive awareness and vigilance that women in all the focus groups described experiencing on a chronic basis.[5]

Today, as in the past, our system of racial oppression is sustained by many thousands of everyday acts of mistreatment of Americans of color by white Americans, incidents that range from the subtle and hard to observe to the blatant and easy to notice. These acts of mistreatment can be nonverbal or verbal, nonviolent or violent. Moreover, many racist actions that crash in on everyday life are, from the victim's viewpoint, unpredictable and sporadic. Such actions are commonplace, recurring, and cumulative in their negative impact. They are, as one retired black teacher in her eighties put it, "little murders" that happen every day.[6]

In a specific setting, such as an employment setting, a white person in authority may select another white person over an equally or better-qualified black person because of a preconceived notion that whites are more competent or just because of discomfort with people perceived from the old white-racist frame as different. This latter type of subtle discrimination includes, in John Calmore's words, "the unconscious failure to extend to a minority the same recognition of humanity, and hence the same sympathy and care, given as a matter of course to one's own group." The selectivity results "often unconsciously—from our tendency to sympathize most readily with those who seem most like ourselves."[7]

The racist system is made even more complex by its reinforcement in many other aspects of the everyday behavior of white Americans. When whites make racist comments to other whites, or when they think or say racist things when watching television by themselves or with their families, they also reinforce and maintain the white-racist system, even though no people of color are present.

Who Does the Discriminating?

Discrimination targeting African Americans and other Americans of color comes from all levels and categories of white Americans. Most whites are involved in some subtle, covert, or blatant way in creating, reinforcing, or maintaining the racist reality of U.S. society. Depending on the situation and opportunity to discriminate, large numbers of whites do actively discriminate. Judging from housing audit studies, perhaps half of all whites are inclined to discriminate in some fashion, whether subtly or blatantly, in situations where they have housing to rent or sell to black individuals or families. It may well be that whites discriminate at similarly high levels in other major institutional arenas, although this is an area where much more research is needed.

There are of course actively antiracist whites, who regularly speak out against white racism, even to the point of risking injury, friendships, and jobs. However, in regard to discriminatory practices, most whites seem to fall into three other categories of action. One large group of whites regularly engage in overtly discriminatory and other racist behavior. Some of these whites are greatly consumed by racist hatred, as can be seen in the many serious **hate crimes**. A second, much larger, group of whites discriminate against black Americans and other Americans of color in a variety of ways, as the occasion arises, but frequently discriminate in less overt or more subtle ways and may often not be consciously aware of their discrimination. A third group of whites are consistently bystanders, engaging in less direct discrimination but knowingly providing support for those who do. Whites in the latter two groups commonly reject the blatant discrimination in which some whites in the first group engage, even as they themselves engage in more subtle or covert racial discrimination. In addition, most whites in these three latter groups routinely think in white-oriented terms when choosing mates, neighborhoods, schools, or business partners. The racist system is thereby reinforced in daily interactions. Research studies also suggest that a sense of white superiority, however dim, is part of the consciousness of most whites, including those who are relatively liberal on many racial matters.

In addition, research suggests that a substantial majority of whites, including those who are racially liberal, typically do not see the overtly racist actions of other whites as serious enough for them to intervene, or as serious enough to deter their relationships with those who engage in overtly racist behavior. One recent study examined how 120 college-educated whites reacted to a racist act. Recruited for a psychology study, the students faced an experimental set-up that, unknown to them, had a black actor and a white actor playing out a scenario in which the black person gently bumped the white person on leaving the room. The experimenters varied what the white actor said after the bump: (1) nothing; (2) blurted out, "I hate when black people do that"; (3) said "nigger." After the incident the researcher came in to start the "study" and asked each white student to pick the white person or the black person as a partner. The fact that the white person had made racist comments did not upset most of the white students or deter most from picking the white actor as a partner.[8] These researchers made an educated guess that such white reactions in choosing a white-racist partner over a black partner may have reflected unconscious racial biases. Yet, many whites still do react the way numerous white students did because they in fact think in consciously and blatantly racist terms about black people, or because they do not find the racist actions of other whites to be serious enough for them to intervene in or to risk losing a friend or acquaintance.

Recall too our recent research that involved gathering brief semester journals from 626 white students at various colleges and universities. Recording racial events observed in their daily lives, these students reported thousands of clearly racist events. In these many accounts there is not one describing whites, including the diarists, aggressively and assertively protesting a racist commentary or other racist action by whites in a frontstage setting, one with a diversity of strangers. Only rarely in the journal accounts (about 1–2 percent) do we even see white students or other whites engaging in assertive dissent to racist commentaries and actions by white friends, acquaintances, and relatives in backstage settings. This lack of assertive confrontation was true for the journal writers, even when they later said in their diaries that they should have intervened. Numerous students commented in their diaries that they recognized their friends and relatives were doing racist stuff, but added that they were still "nice people" to be with. These diaries indicate that even those whites who make extremely racist comments or engage in highly racist actions are typically viewed by other whites as doing something relatively harmless.[9]

Interestingly, when issues of racism are discussed in the mass media, it is often working-class whites (sometimes stereotyped as "rednecks") who get tagged as the most serious racists by mainstream media commentators or analyses. Blue-collar violence against black Americans or other Americans of color often does get significant news attention. Yet elite and middle-class whites are less frequently the focus of serious attention in media discussions of racial problems, and media discussions of discrimination that do involve a few middle-class or elite discriminators usually avoid making connections to broader issues of systemic racism. The portrait of discriminatory practice that emerges from much social science research is different. Judging from the diaries noted above and the many interviews that I and my colleagues have conducted with white Americans and Americans of color over the last decade or so, as well as from numerous other recent field studies of discrimination in housing, employment, and public accommodations cited in this and other chapters, the majority of whites who do the serious discriminating in this society are those with significant power to bring harm, such as white employers, managers, teachers, social workers, real-estate agents, lenders, landlords and apartment managers, and police officers.[10]

Middle-income and upper-income whites are heavily implicated in contemporary racial discrimination, although it is likely that in most major institutional areas, such as corporate promotions and urban policing, white men account for the lion's share of the discriminatory actions. Generally speaking, these middle-income and upper-income whites are the ones in a position to most significantly affect the lives of a great many black Americans and other Americans of color. Nonetheless, given the right circumstances, most whites in all income groups have the ability to put Americans of color "in their place," to frustrate or sabotage their lives for racist reasons.

Lifetimes of Racial Discrimination

Whether subtle, covert, or blatant, discriminatory practices are commonplace and recurring in a great variety of social settings, ranging from public accommodations to educational facilities, business arenas, workplaces, and neighborhoods. How frequent is the discrimination faced by its targets? What forms does this discrimination take? As we have seen, whites often play down these realities.

As we have seen previously, national opinion surveys reveal that black Americans face much discrimination, in the present and over their lives. For example, a recent Gallup poll on how black residents are treated in local communities found that the majority of black respondents said that blacks were not treated equally. In contrast, three-quarters of the whites polled said that blacks were treated the same as whites in their community. More detailed questions also revealed significant differences in how black and white respondents viewed blacks' treatment by local police, employers, and store clerks. Another Gallup survey asked black respondents if they had experienced discrimination at work, dining out, shopping, with the police, or in public transportation just during the last month. Nearly half (47 percent) said that they had suffered discrimination in one or more of these areas in this short period.[11] Surveys in particular cities reveal a similar pattern. A survey of 202 black Bostonians found that 80 percent viewed racial discrimination there as a significant problem. The overwhelming majority felt that black Americans lose out on good housing in the area because of their fear of how they will be received in historically white communities. Substantial percentages reported personally facing discrimination from the police or in workplaces, and nearly half felt they were unwelcome in shopping areas or restaurants in the metropolitan area.[12]

Even these substantial data are likely underestimates of the frequency of such racial discrimination. Such survey questions are usually brief and customarily deal with only a few of the many types of racial mistreatment black Americans and other Americans of color face in this society. Indeed, survey researchers themselves have suggested that more detailed questioning would likely reveal a more substantial portrait of racial discrimination.[13] There are yet other reasons why the existing survey data do not adequately describe the reality of everyday racism. Most Americans are taught by their parents, peers, teachers, and clergy to focus on individual reasons for personal barriers or failures. The reasoning behind such socialization seems to be that a system–blame orientation makes a person seem weak to those she or he respects. Thus, some black Americans and other Americans of color who suffer from much discrimination may feel that talking too much about discriminatory barriers suggests that they are not capable of dealing with these everyday difficulties.

In addition, the terminology used in most surveys likely leads to many underestimates. We have found in our research interviews with African Americans that the term "discrimination" itself is reserved by some only for very serious abuse by whites. Lesser forms of mistreatment, because they are so commonplace, may not be characterized as discrimination. For example, a black college professor explained to me that he does not ordinarily think of certain everyday examples of differential treatment— such as white cashiers not putting money in his hand because they do not want to touch a black person—as "racial discrimination." It is only the more serious incidents that he would recall if asked a question by a pollster about having encountered racial discrimination recently. Racial obstacles are so much a part of black lives that they generally become a part of the societal woodwork. This everydayness of racist barriers means that for many black Americans a researcher's brief question about discrimination will bring quickly to mind primarily the more serious incidents that stay at the front of the mind—and sometimes not the many intrusions of more subtle racism that occur in one's life. Yet, not recalling some discriminatory incidents when questioned briefly does not mean these encounters are of little consequence. In order to survive in a racist society, black Americans and other Americans of color cannot attend consciously to all the racist incidents that intrude on their lives. The personal and family cost of too-close attention to much discrimination is too great.

To my knowledge, there is no research on the frequency of the incidents and events of discrimination faced by individual black Americans over their entire lifetimes. In a few exploratory interviews with black respondents, I have asked a question about frequency and gotten large estimates. I asked a retired printer from New York City how often he faced discrimination over his eight decades of life. After careful reflection, he estimated that he confronts at least 250 significant incidents of discrimination from whites each year, if he only includes the incidents he consciously notices. Blatant and subtle mistreatment by white clerks in stores and restaurants are examples he had in mind. Judging from my own field studies using in-depth interviews with black Americans, this man's experience seems representative. Over the course of a normal lifetime, a typical black man or woman likely faces *thousands* of instances of blatant, covert, or subtle discrimination at the hands of whites.

Patterns of Discrimination: Political and Legal Institutions

For centuries now, local, state, and federal governments have been proactive in protecting or expanding the system of racial discrimination. White government officials and programs have often favored the racial and political-economic interests of white Americans. Government programs historically provided much access to homesteading land and numerous other valuable resources exclusively to white Americans. Coupled with this age-old "affirmative action" for whites, governments created and reinforced extensive patterns of racial exclusion targeting Americans of color. Over centuries, white-dominated legislative, executive, and judicial branches of local, state, and federal governments routinely upheld slavery and Jim Crow segregation.

Discrimination in Voting and Representation

In 1915 the U.S. Supreme Court finally began to knock down a few state Jim Crow laws that severely discriminated against black voters. Over the decades since, black voters have been allowed into the southern political system. Yet, increases in political representation in the South and North came slowly. Finally, in the 1960s the civil rights movement forced major legislative changes, including passage of the 1965 Voting Rights Act. By the 1970s, in part because of enforcement of this act, millions of black citizens were finally voting in the South. As a result, the number of black elected officials has increased from a few dozen in the 1960s to several thousand today.

Nonetheless, in many areas black voters are still unable to elect black officials in representative numbers. Moreover, where they are able to elect some representatives, the latter are often unable to make their voices heeded in the still white-dominated legislative bodies. Researchers have identified an array of blocking strategies still used by white officials to reduce black representation or voting: gerrymandering political districts, changing elective offices into appointive offices, adding new qualifications for office, purging voter-registration rolls, suddenly changing the location of polling places, creating difficult registration procedures, and using numerous other strategies to dilute the black vote. One dilution strategy consists of intentionally setting up or continuing at-large electoral systems, instead of utilizing elections by smaller electoral districts. The purpose is to enable white voters, who dominate the larger political unit, to determine who will be all the political representatives in that unit.[14]

Until the 1960s most political efforts aimed at reducing the number of black and Latino voters were headed up by people associated with the Democratic Party. However, in the mid-1960s Barry Goldwater and Richard Nixon campaigns, voter-restriction activities were increasingly undertaken by Republican Party operatives. In recent decades these voter-restriction activities have continued to be part of presidential campaigns. Among the most common of these efforts today are the "ballot security" programs of local Republican operatives. One recent research report explains that these security programs focus almost entirely on *minority* voting precincts, usually with very weak evidence of voter fraud to justify them. They have recently involved "intimidating Republican poll watchers or challengers who may slow down voting lines and embarrass potential voters by asking them humiliating questions," "people in official-looking uniforms with badges and side arms who question voters about their citizenship or their registration," "warning signs … posted near the polls," and "radio ads … targeted to minority listeners containing dire threats of prison terms for people who are not properly registered—messages that seem designed to put minority voters on the defensive." Some Republican operatives have even mailed false voter information about voting qualifications to confuse and deter black and Latino voters.[15]

Since the nineteenth century many U.S. political campaigns at the local, state, and federal levels have been riddled with racial issues. In recent decades numerous campaigns by members of the Republican and Democratic parties have made use of racial appeals, blatant or subtle, to white voters. Recall Richard Nixon's so-called southern strategy, which used racist appeals to attract white southerners from the Democratic Party to the Republican Party. In recent years, indeed, it appears that key members of the Republican Party (see Chapter 8, p. 265) have decided that the Party should become primarily one for white Americans, with mostly token appeals to the political interests of black Americans and most other Americans of color. Since the 1960s the Republican Party has shown little interest in the civil rights issues of great concern to many voters of color. While the Democratic Party has seen far more participation by Americans of color in its deliberations, elections, and stated policies, since the 1980s its majority-white elected officials have also failed to increase the input of Americans of color into most state and national policymaking to a truly representative level. Today, some 140 years after African Americans officially gained access to the political process through the post-Civil War amendments to the Constitution, historic promises of equal political representation remain yet unfulfilled in most of this society's political institutions. The election of an African American president in 2008 has not changed that general picture.

Racism and the Supreme Court

We saw earlier the critical role of the U.S. Supreme Court in maintaining white dominance in such cases as *Dred Scott* v. *Sandford*, which upheld slavery and the degradation of black Americans, and *Plessy* v. *Ferguson*, which legitimated Jim Crow segregation after the Civil War. This is the historical legacy. Today, whites as a group still benefit greatly from a legal system of their own making, one that favors the broad group interests of whites. It is not sufficient, as the white founders made very clear in their harsh criticisms of authoritarian British rule, for there only to be equality in access to the law. There must also be fair representation in the creation of the laws. This is not yet a reality for all Americans. At the top of the U.S. legal system black Americans constitute a very small percentage of state attorney generals, district attorneys, leading civil and criminal lawyers, and judges in major state and federal courts. Other Americans of color are also greatly underrepresented in such positions. Given the fact that a greatly disproportionate share of decisionmakers at the top of the U.S. judicial and political system are white, it is not surprising that white assumptions and interests generally predominate. The assumptions of most whites in control of these institutions include:

1. the idea that racial inequality is no longer a serious societal problem needing significant government intervention; and
2. the notion that the legal system currently operates in a generally fair and nonracist fashion.

Recall the Supreme Court case discussed in Chapter 3, *City of Richmond, Virginia* v. *J.A. Croson Co.* (1989). In that case a white-run construction company argued that a Richmond program setting aside a little business for formerly excluded minority companies was unconstitutional. Knocking down the modest set-aside program, a majority of the Supreme Court ruled the city officials had not made a compelling case for the remedial program and had not demonstrated the continuing reality of racial discrimination there. However, the city officials had shown that, in a city whose population was half black, less than 1 percent of city business went to black-owned firms. The high court dismissed these data and the testimony of city officials that legal segregation had for decades been the rule in the city and that discrimination in construction contracting was still commonplace. Arguments that large-scale racial discrepancies in business development indicated a high probability of discriminatory practices by white businesses in the present were rejected by the high court's white majority.[16]

Justice Sandra Day O'Connor, writing for the plurality, did note "the sorry history of both private and public discrimination in this country" and recognized the reality of "past societal discrimination." Yet she accented the "past," not the present, in her weak analysis and described societal discrimination as "amorphous" and having no clear link to the present-day reality of black business conditions in contemporary Richmond. As one critic put it, the use of "amorphous" here means that for the court's white majority societal discrimination is "something sporadic, erratic, and diffuse—something that leaves no clearly demarcated traces and produces no readily ascertainable direct effects."[17] Yet the impacts of past discrimination in any U.S. city, as the data in this book repeatedly demonstrate, are typically major, evident, systemic, and *anything but* sporadic.

In addition, the white majority in the *Croson* case once again bought into the old white-racist framing that the problems of black Americans are the result of their own values and choices: "There are numerous explanations for this dearth of minority participation [in construction businesses], including … black and white career and entrepreneurial choices. Blacks may be disproportionately attracted to industries other than construction."[18] Here the majority suggests that black Americans—who have much experience as construction workers—do not go into construction contracting businesses just because of personal preferences. In making such an unreflective argument the judges provided *no* evidence of such black inclinations. Indeed, they made the racist assumption that black Americans do not like to prosper economically. Such a notion of disparate rationality is overtly "racist and without any evidentiary basis."[19]

In a stinging dissent, the court's only black justice up to that point in U.S. history, Justice Thurgood Marshall, concluded that a

> majority of this Court signals that it regards racial discrimination as largely a phenomenon of the past, and that government bodies need

no longer preoccupy themselves with rectifying racial injustice. I, however, do not believe this Nation is anywhere close to eradicating racial discrimination or its vestiges.[20]

The idea of eradication, he noted, represents "wishful thinking" on the part of naive or prejudiced white justices.

Prominent legal scholar Jerome Culp has described the white justices' assumptions in cases like this as "white supremacist," in that "the interests of black Americans are not considered important enough to be examined or put into the constitutional calculus—the interest blindness assumption." White group interests once again took precedence over black group interests. The interests and concerns of black Americans in cities like Richmond are indeed not hard to discover. Most black Americans there and elsewhere report substantial racial discrimination in many areas of their lives, including the employment and business arenas, and seek to end that discrimination with antidiscrimination and related remedial programs.[21]

Police Malpractice

The U.S. racial hierarchy is routinely reproduced by the actions of a broad array of government agents. White police officers have historically played, and many still often play, a major role in the subordination of black Americans, including those who seek to protest societal racism. Data on police violence in U.S. history are chilling. For example, in the years 1920–1932 substantially *more than half* of all African Americans killed by whites were killed by white police officers. In addition, police were often implicated in the estimated 6,000 bloody lynchings of black men and women from the 1870s to the 1960s. In recent decades, police harassment and violence have been openly resisted by black Americans. For example, analysis of black community riots for the years 1943 to 1972 indicates that the immediate precipitating event of many of these community uprisings was the killing or harassment of black urbanites by white officers. Rioters openly protested this police action. This reaction to police harassment or killings has also been seen in major rioting by black citizens in Los Angeles and Miami in the 1980s and 1990s, and in a few other cities since then.[22]

In spite of improvements in U.S. policing since the 1970s, police violence and mistreatment have continued to oppress black Americans and their communities. A recent Gallup poll found that one-fifth of the black respondents reported that they had suffered discrimination at the hands of police officers, a proportion that has increased a little in surveys over recent years. Another Gallup poll found that 42 percent of black respondents (and three-quarters of young black men) indicated that they had experienced some type of racial profiling by police over their lifetimes.[23]

Since 1994 the U.S. government has been legally required to collect data on police brutality. However, the Congresses in power after that date have failed to appropriate money to collect these important data. One social science study analyzed 130 police-brutality accounts in several cities. In these cases the targets of police malpractice were almost always black or Latino. The latter made up 97 percent of the victims of police brutality. Yet the overwhelming majority (93 percent) of officers involved in these incidents were white.[24] Police brutality still usually involves white-on-black or white-on-Latino violence. Moreover, some police harassment and brutality targeting Americans of color seem to be linked to maintaining de facto housing segregation. Even today, if black men have to be in historically white residential areas, they often run the risk of harassment by the public or private police officers there.

In recent years many law-enforcement agencies have used a policy of screening and stopping motorists just because of their racial characteristics—what black Americans call the offense of "driving while black" (DWB). A recent ACLU report summarized racial-profiling studies involving numerous police departments as showing "large differences in the rate of stops and searches for African Americans and Latinos, and often, Indians (Native Americans) and Asians, even though these groups are less likely to have contraband."[25] For example, black rappers and other black musicians have been explicitly targeted for special surveillance, stopping, and searching without reasonable suspicion by police departments in New York, Miami, and Miami Beach. In addition, in numerous states, police officers have been documented stopping motorists of color on vague notions that they might possibly have drugs.[26] State judges in California, Rhode Island, New Jersey, and Minnesota have periodically issued orders against such racial profiling, in some cases as a result of studies showing significant racial disparities. For example, one California study showed that Latinos and African Americans were far more likely to be searched by highway patrol officers for no obvious reason than were whites. And a Rhode Island study showed that a majority of Rhode Island police departments had significant racial differentials in such groundless searches.[27]

Significantly, in 2008 the ACLU and other plaintiffs settled a class action lawsuit on racial profiling by Maryland State Police (MSP) officers in the Interstate 95 corridor. Studies over a long period showed that motorists of color were disproportionately targeted and stopped and searched without good reason. An ACLU report notes that the settlement

> agreement provides substantial damages to the individual plaintiffs, a requirement that the MSP retain an independent consultant to assess its progress towards eliminating the practice of racial profiling, and a joint statement by all parties involved in the lawsuit

condemning racial profiling and highlighting the importance of taking preventative action against this practice in the future.[28]

Since many whites are predisposed to see blacks and Latinos as inherently criminal, an old idea in the white racial frame, the stop-and-search policing pattern that looks for illegal drugs is not surprising and has engendered little protest from most whites. In spite of the popularity of drug-courier profiling, no government agency has yet shown that drug profiles accenting people of color are valid. Such racialized policing is sometimes defended as statistical, or rational, discrimination. But this is just another erroneous rationalization for police discrimination. Recall from Chapter 4 that black youth use drugs less often than white youth, and that black drug-users of all ages make up about one-eighth of illegal drug-users. Whites make up some 70 percent of illegal drug-users. These proportions are roughly in line with white and black population proportions. Quite clearly, discrimination is evident in the fact that black Americans account for 37 percent of those arrested by the police for drug use. In addition, the majority of drug couriers are likely to be white, as are the overwhelming majority of drug pushers.[29] As we noted in Chapter 4, the extensive white drug-using and drug-dealing in this country gets much less police surveillance and prosecution, yet more evidence of discrimination in the policing and judicial systems.

For several years, U.S. House member John Conyers and U.S. Senator Russ Feingold have introduced the End Racial Profiling Act, which prohibits racial profiling and requires law-enforcement departments to collect stop-and-search data, to have effective complaint procedures, and to insure that those abused by police departments have a right to sue. This legislation has yet to be passed. Moreover, in May 2008 the United Nations Special Rapporteur on racism officially spoke out against continuing racial inequality in the U.S. justice system and called on the U.S. Congress to pass the End Racial Profiling Act, as well as to set up an investigative commission to examine continuing racial discrimination in areas such as public education and housing.[30]

More Discrimination: The Criminal Justice System

Racial discrimination extends beyond policing to the numerous aspects of the criminal justice system. Few judges are black, and many white judges appear to have little understanding of the lives of the black Americans— mostly working-class or poor people—that they often face. These judges generally do not come from the same community backgrounds as black defendants in their courtrooms, and as a result some discriminate in subtle or blatant ways against those in their courtrooms. For example, in the 1990s one New Haven study of more than 1,000 arrests did a statistical analysis of bail-related variables and found that "after controlling for eleven variables relating to the severity of the alleged offense, bail amounts set for black male defendants [by judges] were 35 percent higher than those set for their white male counterparts." In contrast, these researchers found that local bond dealers, operating more realistically, charged significantly lower bonding rates for black defendants than for white defendants.[31]

There is much recent evidence of discrimination in the criminal justice system. In spite of congressional concern and minor tinkering with drug laws, there is still significant differential punishment for two types of cocaine use. One lawyer has explained:

> Powder cocaine is a drug of the affluent suburbs, while crack is used and sold in the inner cities. Since 1986, people convicted in federal court of possessing just five grams of crack cocaine … face a mandatory sentence of at least five years in prison—and when you get five years of federal time, you do almost all of it. But those caught with powder cocaine must be in possession of 500 grams to get the same five-year sentence.… And day after day, black men are moved out of their homes and communities to serve stiffer sentences than their white, powder-using counterparts.[32]

There has been no significant change in these harsh mandatory sentencing laws in spite of evidence they are very discriminatory. (Pressures from the U.S. Sentencing Commission have gotten Congress to reduce possible sentences, but not to eliminate the cause of this huge racial differential.) The Barack Obama administration has pressed for elimination of discrimination in the sentencing guidelines, but they have not yet been changed. Note that recent data show that only 9 percent of those arrested for crack cocaine use are white, while 82 percent are black. Whites account for a majority of those arrested for using powder cocaine. While illegal drug-use is about as common among white men as among black men, black men are far more likely than white men to be arrested for such drug crimes. This is one major reason why there are disproportionately large numbers of black men in U.S. prisons.[33]

In the United States institutional racism has long been evident in the application of the death penalty, both in the distant past and the present. Consider some historical data. Between 1908 and 1962 *all* those put to death for rape in the state of Virginia were black, even though 45 percent of those convicted for rape were white. Between 1930 and 1967 black men made up 89 percent of all those executed for rape across the country. Moreover, for decades now it has been the case that, although white victims and black victims of murder are about equal in number, it is disproportionately those who kill whites who actually get sentenced to death. About 80 percent of those executed since the 1970s have been executed for killing whites. A recent review of death penalty cases involving homicides in California once again found that those who had killed whites were much more likely to get the death penalty than those whose victims were not white. In this regard, apparently, those in control of the criminal justice system often value the lives of white Americans more highly than the lives of other Americans.[34]

In addition, one Philadelphia study found that black defendants were four-times as likely as white defendants to get the death penalty for murder, even when the severity of the crimes was taken into account. And a recent study of 500 capital punishment trials in Texas's largest county, that surrounding Houston, found black defendants in capital cases were more likely to get the death penalty than similar white defendants, indeed even more so than whites who had committed much more heinous murders.[35] In recent years, moreover, many people convicted of murder, often people of color, have been shown by DNA and related evidence to be innocent of the crimes for which they were convicted. Since the 1970s more than 100 people sentenced to death have thus been freed.[36] The white racial framing of certain people of color as especially criminal is not just a problem in the minds of many whites. It can result in differential policing, unfair but deadly punishments for similar crimes, and false convictions of the innocent.

Significantly, those who decide on pursuing the death penalty in our criminal justice system, the district attorneys and similar state officials, are overwhelmingly white. In one study a very small percentage of the nearly 1,900 such government officials in the United States were found to be black. These mostly white officials overwhelmingly control who gets tried, what the charge is, how the trial will proceed, and what the punishment will be. For example, in many areas of the country black jurors are knocked out of jury pools by the racialized use of peremptory challenges by prosecutors, in clear violation of a Supreme Court decision requiring race-neutral reasons for such exclusion. White district attorneys desire this exclusion for racial reasons, as one training video for Philadelphia prosecutors makes clear. "Let's face it," the video says, "the blacks from low-income areas are less likely to convict. There's a resentment to law enforcement."[37] Moreover, recent surveys of public defenders and metropolitan judges in Minnesota, generally known as a liberal state, found that about half of each group thought that the (mostly white) prosecutors in Minnesota still discriminate against potential jurors of color in the use of their peremptory challenges.[38] In this manner—and in spite of a weak Supreme Court decision (*Batson* v. *Kentucky* 1986) attempting to restrict such practices—potential jurors of color who might disagree with the interpretations of white authorities or who bring a generally unrepresented real-life perspective to many court cases are often excluded from fair participation in the workings of the justice system.

Violence against African Americans

The Long History

For several centuries whites used extraordinarily levels of violence—from chains and whippings to lynchings and other mob violence—to keep African Americans racially subordinated. From the 1620s to the 1960s, violent acts by whites acting individually and collectively were a recurring part of this enslavement and Jim Crow subordination. Violent practices were perpetrated by ordinary whites and members of the elite, including the famous founders Thomas Jefferson, George Washington, and James Madison. After the Civil War, whites were fearful of freed black Americans and engaged in large-scale violence to create official segregation. The emerging system of legal segregation was enforced with private and police violence. Well into the 1990s some southerners serving proudly in the U.S. Congress had earlier been outspoken advocates of violence-enforced Jim Crow segregation.

Today, many whites exhibit naiveté or willing ignorance about this brutal history of enforced segregation and violence. One white caller to a radio show assessing public reaction to a jury's decision that black athlete O.J. Simpson was not guilty of murder suggested half-jokingly that whites should riot. The talk-show host and other callers concluded that "white people don't riot."[39] However, these whites showed an ignorance of U.S. history. Virtually all U.S. racial riots from the 1840s to the 1930s—and there were many—were characterized by whites attacking black Americans. In 1863, during the Civil War, many white workers in New York City rioted for days over draft laws and the use of black workers to break a strike. In that rioting more than 100 people, including numerous black Americans, were killed—the largest for any riot in U.S. history. The decades after the Civil War saw many killings of black men, women, and children by white mobs, including lynchings.

In the early 1900s there were many more riots by whites targeting African Americans. There were several major riots by whites just in 1919— in Longview, Texas; Phillips County, Arkansas; Washington, D.C.; Chicago, Illinois; Knoxville, Tennessee; and Omaha, Nebraska. The growing competition between black and white workers was often an underlying factor in this white rioting, and all-white police forces usually did nothing or took the side of white rioters. As late as the 1960s, white mob violence against nonviolent civil rights demonstrators could be seen regularly on U.S. television networks, a bloody visual reality that helped bring the end of legal segregation.[40]

Recent Violence and Other Hate Crimes

White attacks and other hate crimes against black Americans and numerous other Americans of color are still part of the U.S. landscape. The most recent (2008) FBI report on hate-based crimes noted that 4,956 people had been victims of racially motivated crimes in the previous year. Seven in ten of those victimized (3,434) were targeted because of an apparent antiblack bias—with 76 Native Americans, 234 Asian Americans (and Pacific Islanders), and 830 Latinos also being victims of racialized crimes.[41] These numbers are certainly serious underestimates, because most (nearly 15,500) of the 17,500 U.S. police jurisdictions do not report their hate crimes, or report zero hate crimes. Indeed, a 2009 report by the Southern Poverty Law Center (SPLC) calculated from various data that at least "210,000 people a year are victimized by hate crimes, the vast majority of them motivated by race or ethnicity."[42] Although African Americans are still major targets, according to the SPLC report much of the recent increase in hate-based crimes has involved immigrants of color, especially those from Latin America. In addition, the number of racist hate groups, such as Klan and neo-Nazi groups, has grown dramatically in recent years—by nearly 50 percent over the last decade (up to 926).

Some hate incidents have ranged from the placement of threatening nooses on doors and the scrawling of racist graffiti on homes and cars, to aggressive verbal harassment of pedestrians and co-workers, to more violent attacks including killings. In the late 1990s, a black man, James Byrd, Jr., was walking down a Jasper, Texas, road. Three white men, with tattoos suggesting ties to white-supremacist groups, beat him savagely, tied him to a pickup, and dragged him until his head was severed. One reportedly said to the others, "We're starting *The Turner Diaries* early," referring to large-scale violence against the U.S. government by white supremacists in that very racist novel. The Jasper lynching triggered copycat crimes in several other cities. While incidents like this lynching are often carried out by working-class whites, the responses of some elite and middle-class whites sometimes reveal an indifference to hate-based crimes. For example, the first *New York Times* article on the Jasper lynching was actually buried on page 16.[43]

Numerous violent hate crimes are still regularly reported. One 2007 hate crime took place in West Virginia, where a black woman was reportedly raped and tortured for days by six white men and women. According to press reports, these whites made her eat feces, raped her, and constantly called her "nigger." One who assaulted her said, "That's what we do to niggers around here." Yet this coordinated attack by whites against a black woman was not even recorded by local authorities as a hate crime.[44]

In addition, in recent decades many whites have engaged in using hangman's nooses as a threat against Americans of color. For example, a series of noose incidents were reported in 2008 in Hempstead, New York, including a noose drawn on the locker of a black sanitation employee and several nooses placed around the Hempstead police department. Black town employees filed complaints against the government for allowing "intolerable work conditions."[45] In addition, the *New York Times* reported a rash of noose incidents a few months before the Hempstead events. Hangman's nooses were "anonymously tossed over pipes or hung on doorknobs in the New York metropolitan area—four times here on Long Island, twice in New York City, once at a Home Depot store in Passaic, N.J." This *Times* story also noted that an interracial couple in Suffolk County, New York, had a Klan-type cross burning on their lawn. Hanging nooses and burning crosses are serious events because they conjure up images of white mobs' engaged in brutal lynchings, especially in the minds of many black Americans who themselves, or whose immediate ancestors, have suffered such incidents under Jim Crow segregation.[46]

Periodically, some whites in the now-growing number of white-supremacist and racial-nationalist groups have threatened large-scale violence against black Americans, other Americans of color, or government agencies viewed as supporting people of color. For example, the 1995 bombing of the Oklahoma City federal building by anti-government terrorists, who were white supremacists, killed 169 people. Somewhat later, several other bomb plots were uncovered, one targeting the Southern Poverty Law Center in Montgomery, Alabama, and others targeting federal buildings in Spokane and Austin. In recent years, moreover, some members of white militia and supremacy groups have stockpiled weapons and explosives and prepared bombing ventures. Today, there are hundreds of Klan, neo-Nazi, skinhead, and other white-supremacist groups, with at least 300,000 whites as active or passive supporters.[47]

The Spatial Basis of Systemic Racism: Housing Segregation

The Persistence of Segregated Neighborhoods

If we view the layout and activities of a typical city from a few hundred feet above the streets, the spatial structure of modern residential segregation can be clearly seen. For the most part, black Americans live separately from white Americans, and the latter are often significantly separated from other Americans of color as well. If we look closely, we see whites and blacks moving about daily routines, but find that black urbanites are more likely to cross the racial–territorial boundaries of our towns and cities than are white urbanites. Proportionately, blacks spend much more time interacting with whites than whites spend interacting with blacks. There is a strong racial topography to U.S. towns and cities.

Metropolitan areas in the North and South continue to have a high degree of residential segregation. The most recent census (2000) revealed that U.S. cities remain very segregated, especially between whites and blacks. One common statistical measure of segregation, the index of dissimilarity, has decreased slowly for black–white segregation, although not for other groups. Calculations from 2000 census data indicate this dissimilarity index for black–white housing segregation averaged 64.9 for central cities of metropolitan areas, compared to 56.6 for suburban areas. Both figures indicate high levels of residential segregation. Between 1990 and 2000 these figures decreased by 4.9 in central cities but only 2.1 in the suburbs, in both cases a slower rate of decline than for the years 1980–1990. At the current rate of decline, it will take at least 130 more years for white–black residential segregation to disappear from U.S. cities. Comparable census figures for Latino segregation from whites are somewhat lower—52.7 for central cities and 46.5 for suburbs. Census figures for Asian American segregation from whites are substantially lower but still significant—39.9 for central cities and 40.5 for suburbs.[48]

There are increasing numbers and percentages of Americans of color in the suburbs, yet a disturbing segregated pattern has emerged there. Black Americans are almost as segregated in suburban areas now as in 1990, and Latino and Asian American populations are actually more segregated now than they were in 1990. Racial enclaves are becoming rather commonplace in suburban areas. The only figure indicating a significant decline in segregation of Americans of color from white Americans is for white–black segregation in central cities, although this rate of decline may be decreasing compared to earlier decades. In addition, the census data for the two decades between 1980 and 2000 also show that this decline in white–black segregation is mostly in cities with relatively small black percentages of the total city population. Those metropolitan areas where African Americans are at least 20 percent of the population saw a decline in housing segregation in 1980–2000 period that was *only half* that that of metropolitan areas where African Americans were less than 5 percent of the population. Yet, nearly half the African American population lives in these larger metropolitan areas where residential desegregation has proceeded at a slow pace.[49]

Recent research also shows that middle-class black Americans still suffer significantly from racial and class segregation. Even when middle-class black Americans have some white residents in their neighborhoods, these whites tend to be less well-off than the middle-class blacks there. In addition, their middle-class neighborhoods tend to be more economically troubled and have weaker public services than typical white middle-class neighborhoods. Even middle-class black Americans, thus, have not achieved real equality with white middle-class Americans when it comes to their housing settings, as well as in regard to other important economic and political conditions.[50]

Segregation as Slavery Unwilling to Die

Systemic racism has long involved white control of much space and territory. Since the 1600s, being defined as "black" has meant limitations on where one can work, live, and travel. During slavery, most African Americans were separated in slave quarters, and their spatial movements were greatly controlled by law and institutionalized violence. After slavery, southern and border state elites created an extensive system of segregation, following the lead of northern elites. Before the Civil War, the Jim Crow laws in the North enforced separate housing areas at a time when southern cities had no comparable segregation. (Those enslaved often lived near slavemasters.) Firmly in place by the early 1900s, the rigid segregation by white law or custom of blacks from whites in housing and other institutional areas could be seen in all parts of the country.[51]

Today, housing segregation provides empirical evidence of the impact of past and present racial oppression. In residential segregation we observe what the U.S. Supreme Court, in a pathbreaking 1968 decision, *Jones* v. *Alfred H. Mayer Co.*, called "a relic of slavery." Ruling on a housing discrimination in St. Louis, the majority argued that current discrimination is actually a long-term consequence of slavery:

> This Court recognized long ago that, whatever else they may have encompassed, the badges and incidents of slavery—its "burdens and disabilities"—included restraints upon "those fundamental rights which are the essence of civil freedom, namely, the same right ... to inherit, purchase, lease, sell and convey property, as is enjoyed by white citizens."[52]

In a concurring opinion, Justice William O. Douglas used stronger language, concluding that

> the true curse of slavery is not what it did to the black man, but what it has done to the white man. For the existence of the institution produced the notion that the white man was of superior character, intelligence, and morality.... Some badges of slavery remain today. While the institution has been outlawed, it has remained in the minds and hearts of many white men. Cases which have come to this Court depict a spectacle of slavery unwilling to die.[53]

Justice Douglas then listed the many kinds of racial discrimination faced by African Americans.

As we have seen numerous times in this book, systemic racism is maintained by social-inheritance mechanisms that transmit resources and privilege over generations. Each generation of whites inherits an array of racialized privileges, including the ability to enter residential areas and job settings reserved more or less for whites—and thereby the ability to build up family wealth in the form of access to buying a nice house, and thus a housing equity. In parallel with the social transmission of white privileges is the transmission of discriminatory barriers for black Americans. Whites tend to ignore or downplay these persisting barriers and instead stereotype African Americans as being likely to run down neighborhoods where they live.

Certainly, many areas that African Americans have moved into have had deteriorating housing and neighborhoods. Yet few whites are aware of the racial and other political-economic factors involved in such housing decay. Most have had to rent where the rents are relatively low, and thus where numerous public services are usually inadequate. And those who have bought houses often have faced similarly serious spatial, economic, and public-services limitations. Most white critics of black housing situations and communities have thus routinely ignored the

> fact that discrimination in employment, in money lending, and in choice of neighborhood often ensured that the only houses African Americans could afford would be older properties in already declining areas. Whites failed to understand that the higher finance costs that blacks were forced to pay often left them unable to pay for the upkeep of a dwelling.[54]

Access to significant economic and other social resources over several centuries of systemic racism has long meant unjust enrichment for a majority of whites and unjust impoverishment for a majority of African Americans, generation after generation.

Patterns of Housing Discrimination Today

For the first 350 years of colonial and U.S. development, residential segregation was often legally imposed. After the 1968 Civil Rights Act went into effect, residential segregation across the color line became more informal, as it remains today. One factor maintaining this racial segregation is the array of racist attitudes, images, and emotions still in many white minds. Negative views of African Americans as neighbors are usually grounded in age-old racist stereotypes, such as notions of black men being dangerous and black families being likely to be into drugs or on public welfare. Many whites get fearful when the black percentage of their local neighborhood or community reaches a certain modest level.

Research has shown that, when a predominantly white residential area becomes more than about 8 percent black, some whites will consider moving out. As the percentage reaches about 20 percent in what was once an all-white or nearly all-white residential neighborhood, many whites will not even consider moving into such an area. Today, still, very few neighborhoods are both racially diverse and stable. The rest are racially segregated, or are diverse but in the process of becoming more segregated. Segregation is mostly enforced by the hostility of white homeowners, occasional violence against families of color, and whites quietly deciding not to move into already integrated areas, as well as by the racial steering and other discriminatory practices of many in the real-estate industry.[55]

Today, housing discrimination cuts across a variety of institutions and includes a range of white discriminators—landlords, homeowners, bankers, realtors, and government officials. Numerous research studies indicate that many whites in each group will discriminate under certain circumstances. One major reason for racially segregated housing is the continuing discrimination by rental housing owners, managers, and real-estate salespeople. In the mid- to late-1990s a number of housing audit studies, using white and black testers (and sometimes Asian and Latino testers), demonstrated that racial barriers in regard to rental housing and purchased housing were commonplace in two-dozen metropolitan areas.[56] More recently, field studies of rental housing continue to confirm that these racial barriers persist. One study after hurricane Katrina (2005) using black and white testers in several southern states discovered much racial discrimination in rental housing. As one National Fair Housing Alliance official put it, we

> measured what the apartment seekers were told about unit availability,... security deposit, rental rates, discounts for evacuees, and other terms and conditions of apartment leasing. In 66 percent of these tests—43 of 65 instances—White callers were favored over African-American callers. This is an extremely high rate of discrimination.[57]

In addition, a recent research project in Los Angeles also found substantial discrimination in initial responses of landlords to housing rental inquiries. The researchers sent out 1,115 email messages inquiring about vacant rental housing. To each message they randomly assigned a distinctive African American, Arab American, or white American name. The phone inquiries using African American and Arab American names got significantly fewer positive responses than the white names, with African American names getting the worst overall response, for both corporate-owned and privately owned rental units. Los Angeles landlords were discriminating against African Americans and Arab Americans even before they had gained important information about the potential renters' incomes, credit, or references.[58]

Yet another recent research study of rental and homebuying discrimination examined 2,176 cases of racial discrimination filed with the Ohio Civil Rights Commission. Some 80 percent of these involved African Americans, even though they made up only 18 percent of the Ohio population. Black women were the most likely to report housing discrimination, with half of the racial mistreatment occurring up front as exclusionary discrimination and half coming later after black individuals or families had moved into the housing. The exclusionary cases mostly cited landlords and owners as the antiblack discriminators. These cases usually involved a direct refusal to rent or sell (including the overt use of racist slurs) or more covert discrimination in the form of lying about housing availability or of using racially differential standards for renter or buyer qualification. Real-estate agents, bankers, and insurance companies also played a discriminatory role in some cases. Once housed, some African American renters and homebuyers then faced racially differential treatment in regard to pets or rental conditions, or they faced racial harassment or intimidation by whites. Most of this racial discrimination was perpetrated by white landlords and owners, but some was done by white agents at banks and insurance agencies or by their white neighbors. These researchers note the pain and energy loss that the human targets of housing discrimination regularly face, as they "go through a series of steps to try to counter the inequality they are experiencing, including negotiation, avoidance, confrontation, and in the case of filing a discrimination suit, politically and legally fighting what is unjust."[59]

As we see in the Ohio study, white homeowners still play a very important role in housing discrimination. Indeed, a significant percentage of whites will openly assert that they should still be *allowed* to discriminate on racial grounds. One housing survey found that 27 percent of white respondents were willing to publicly admit that they still felt there should be a law that allows a (white) homeowner to discriminate against African Americans in the sale of a house. Possibly many others felt the same way, but were unwilling to say so to a pollster.[60]

Many whites and some others argue that African Americans are racially segregated because *they choose* to be thus segregated, that is, "blacks prefer to live with their kind."[61] Yet, black families often do try to improve housing situations and neighborhood services by seeking an apartment or home in predominantly white or racially integrated areas, yet they frequently run into entrenched white opposition. Research by Maria Krysan and Reynolds Farley examined the responses of 2,000 black respondents in several cities to questions about neighborhood-mix preferences. The average black respondent was quite open to living in a diverse neighborhood, indeed preferring a 50–50 black–white mix, but willing to consider any residential mix with a visible black presence. Most did not prefer living in mostly black communities. In addition, another survey of black, white, Latino, and Asian groups in Los Angeles found that the black respondents were the most open to living in racially integrated neighborhoods and usually did not express opposition to the significant presence of other racial groups. For a majority of whites, however, Asian and Latino Americans were considered more desirable as neighbors than black Americans.[62]

It is true that many African Americans do not wish to be among the first families in a predominantly white area. This is not, however, a result of a preference to be segregated. Because of continuing white acts of antiblack violence—with hundreds of violent acts against black homeowners and renters, including cross-burnings, recorded in the last decade—and because of threatened violence against those who move into white areas, black Americans are often unwilling to be *pioneers* in moving into historically white areas.[63] Not surprisingly, one social science study found that just one in three black respondents said they were willing to move into an overwhelmingly white residential area. The reasons given by those who were unwilling to move into such an area were much more likely to be fear of white hostility than a dislike of whites or a commitment to living with other black residents as a matter of solidarity. "Blacks are certainly not averse to living with whites as long as they can be sure they will not be treated with [racial] hostility."[64] This view contrasts greatly with why a great many whites do not wish to move into diverse urban neighborhoods that have substantial numbers of black residents.

Insurance Agents and Lenders

For many years federal government regulations intentionally and openly fostered racial discrimination in lending. Only since the 1960s have federal regulations sought to ban such lending discrimination. The 1968 Civil Rights Act and the Equal Credit Opportunity Act officially prohibit mortgage discrimination. Nonetheless, research shows continuing and widespread discrimination by banking and other lending institutions against black Americans and other Americans of color who seek housing mortgages and loans. Many white-run insurance companies also create subtle or blatant housing barriers for Americans of color. One study used black, Latino, and white testers, who presented themselves as homeowners seeking insurance to three major insurance companies' offices in nine cities. The researchers found the overall rate of racial discrimination to be 53 percent in regard to such things as insurance coverage and price. They found that being white increased insurance options and saved money.[65]

Some lending discrimination appears to be motivated by a concern for what are termed "sound business practices," and thus does not appear to be intentionally discriminatory. Thus, numerous lenders and property insurers frequently refuse to provide services, or do provide services but on unfavorable terms, for people seeking to buy older homes in residential areas where the home valuations are lower. Such lending practices can have a very negative impact on homebuyers from groups with long histories of facing institutional racism. As housing expert Gregory Squires has noted:

> many of those underwriters and sales agents who follow these rules really do believe they are acting on the basis of sound business practice.... Obviously, racism went into the formulation of such rules, and these industries no doubt have as many racists as any other. But such institutionalized practices, with severely discriminatory effects, are often carried out by people who simply are not thinking about race.[66]

Thus, the routinization of racially oriented decisions in the housing industry is such that some whites who practice it may not be aware of it. Indeed, black Americans and other Americans of color have seldom been consulted by white-run insurance companies and banking organizations that determine the rules generally favoring white homeseekers.

A significant aspect of the major recession of 2008–2010 involved white lending officials' discriminatory lending practices. One of these practices was to aggressively channel black and Latino homeowners into subprime (high-interest) home loans when they would have qualified for regular-interest, less risky loans. Federal Home Mortgage Disclosure Act reports indicate black and Latino homebuyers were more than twice as likely as white homebuyers to receive expensive subprime mortgages from lenders—even after loan amounts and household incomes were taken into account. This was also true when residential areas were otherwise economically similar. One study of a 97-percent-white working-class suburb and a 97-percent-black working-class suburb in the Detroit area, with similar family income distributions, found that a substantial majority of home loans in the black suburb had the high interest rates, compared to just 17 percent in the otherwise comparable white suburb.[67]

One investigative report has described how mostly white bankers, who were not at the time making much money on conventional home loans, worked with officials in the George W. Bush administration to expand loans to families of color whom the lenders knew would have trouble repaying them, and in the process making substantial profits for the lenders. Although the official government rationale was that these subprime mortgages would "increase homeownership," most of these high-interest loans were not for first mortgages, but rather for second mortgages aggressively peddled by lenders to unsuspecting customers with the argument the latter could use their existing home equities for important family needs such as paying medical bills. However, a *majority* of those families of color conned into these problematical home loans had credit scores that should have enabled them to get loans with more favorable interest rates and conditions, which they did not receive from the mostly white lenders. There seems to have been significant racialized thinking behind many such discriminatory loans. As one investigative reporter put it:

> working-class Black and Latino families, over half of whom were eligible for conventional loans, and burdened by several years of stagnant and falling wages during a jobless recovery, were led by mortgage companies into clear and blatant cases of predatory racially-inspired lending.[68]

As a result, the NAACP filed a lawsuit against several major firms that had made these discriminatory loans.

The results of these discriminatory loan offers and decisions have been catastrophic for many families and communities. Because of the loss of jobs and other economic impacts of the major 2008–2010 recession, many black and Latino homeowners lost their homes to foreclosures. That meant a significant loss in family assets—estimated as of 2009 at more than $164 billion just for loans taken out after 2001. Note that most families of color have their modest assets, if any, in home equities, so this economic loss has been devastating for many communities of color.[69]

Numerous other local, state, and federal government programs have long had a racially discriminatory impact. One Dallas report found that homes in African American residential areas were much more likely to be torn down by the city's Urban Rehabilitation Standards Board than similar homes in predominantly white areas. A city audit found that the board had often failed to notify black property owners of impending demolitions.[70] For decades, using a variety of urban redevelopment approaches, white politicians and business leaders across the country have tried to rebuild their central cities, and in the process have often further segregated black families and destroyed older black communities. Urban redevelopment projects have frequently taken neighborhoods inhabited by working-class or poor African Americans and other Americans of color and converted them into business districts or gentrified residential areas mostly for affluent whites.[71]

Today in the United States there is no national watchdog organization that proactively and aggressively seeks out and punishes the omnipresent housing discrimination. When individual complaints are brought by victims of housing discrimination, they often get no redress, for there is currently mostly weak government enforcement of state and federal antidiscrimination laws. In most residential areas white landlords and real-estate salespeople can discriminate more or less with impunity. A 2008 report of the National Commission on Fair Housing thus found that federal and state laws banning racial discrimination in rental and sales housing are either weakly enforced or unenforced in most areas, even as this country remains substantially segregated in terms of its housing patterns. Indeed, one housing expert has estimated that less than one-third of the many housing-discrimination complaints filed each year in the United States are resolved in a way that is satisfactory for the complainant. Even these resolutions usually do not involve stiff penalties for the discriminators, penalties that might act to discourage future discrimination. Moreover, if one considers the millions of housing-discrimination incidents that are estimated by housing experts to occur each year in the United States, *very few* are resolved to the satisfaction of the targets of that discrimination. In this case, as in numerous others, the United States does not live up to its often proclaimed "post-racial society" rhetoric.[72]

Discrimination in Employment

Residential segregation makes possible, or strongly reinforces, numerous other types of racial exclusion, discrimination, and subordination. When residential segregation is extensive, job segregation tends to follow. Over the decades since World War II, racial polarization across the broad geographical expanse of metropolitan areas has often increased with the movement of many white middle-income families to the suburbs, typically leaving behind a mostly working-class and poor population of color in central cities. This suburban migration has generally been stimulated by the investment decisions of large corporations, banks, and developers, and has been aggressively assisted by federal subsidies for home mortgages and public services such as roads. Much employment has decentralized, and many suburbs have had growing numbers of jobs for their often predominantly white populations. The creation of better-paying jobs away from central cities has frequently made it difficult for many Americans of color to have reasonable access to such good-paying employment.[73]

Today, significant discrimination in employment—subtle, covert, and blatant discrimination—remains an important aspect of everyday reality for African Americans and other Americans of color. Thus, many still experience differential treatment in their attempts to secure their families' everyday needs. Derrick Bell has concluded that a major function of antiblack discrimination today is "to facilitate the exploitation of black labor, to deny us access to benefits and opportunities that otherwise would be available, and to blame all the manifestations of exclusion-bred despair on the asserted inferiority of the victims."[74]

Each year numerous lawsuits are filed charging racial discrimination against white employers, and tens of thousands of employment discrimination complaints are filed annually with state agencies and the federal Equal Employment Opportunity Commission (EEOC). As we have seen, recent surveys of black Americans have found that they report significant levels of personal and group discrimination in employment. One major study of more than a thousand black employees found that about 60 percent reported racist barriers in their workplaces in the last year.[75]

Discrimination in Hiring: Recent Research

Some discriminatory treatment occurs at the point of hiring, while other racial mistreatment is encountered later on in the workplace. Many corporate executives and their subordinate managers make little serious effort to recruit and hire black employees or other employees of color, especially in higher-level positions. Indeed, there is significant variability across U.S. firms. Studies using government records have found that many U.S. companies hire far fewer workers of color than yet other comparable companies drawing from the *same* labor pools, a result strongly suggesting routinized discrimination in the former companies.[76]

Numerous studies have examined racial discrimination in the hiring process, from several different angles. Recall the MIT study in which applicants with "white-sounding" names were much more likely to be contacted by employers than those with "black-sounding" names (see p. 135). In addition, an important Milwaukee study matched pairs of black and white male applicants, with similar job credentials and self-presentations, and had them apply for 350 less-skilled jobs. Some 34 percent of the white applicants were called back, but just 14 percent of the equally qualified black applicants. Strikingly, a subgroup of the white applicants who indicated to employers they had been in prison were *more likely* to be called back than the black applicants with no criminal record. Employers likely drew on racial stereotypes of black men in screening them out of their hiring pools. Significantly, a survey of these discriminating employers a few months later on found them saying that they would *not* discriminate between white and black ex-offenders, leading researchers to conclude that these employer surveys are probably not good ways to research or assess racial discrimination.[77]

Researcher Marc Bendick, Jr., recently reviewed 16 of these situational-testing studies involving racial and national-origin discrimination in employment. In research using white testers and testers of color, white applicants have been found to be favored over applicants of color

(African Americans or Latinos) at net rates of discrimination averaging about 20 percent of the time. In these studies racial discrimination has been found in various stages of the hiring process. Critics of this testing research who suggest that these discrimination rates are "low" ignore the reality that black and Latino employees face this type of discrimination not just once, but repeatedly over years and decades of work. There is typically a significant cumulative racial differential over time, as whites use their earlier job advantages to build on and move up later on. In addition, employees of color, unlike their white peers, usually face much discrimination in other areas of their lives, which makes dealing with employment discrimination more difficult and painful.[78]

The research shows that in the hiring process black workers are less likely to obtain jobs than whites with equivalent credentials. This has been found to be true for other cross-racial competitions in certain job categories. For example, one study of 40 Los Angeles hotel employers found that almost all preferred immigrant Latino workers to native-born black workers for maid jobs. These mostly white employers, accenting what many call "soft skills," insisted that the immigrant workers had a better work ethic, attitude, and communication skills. However, the researchers found that these code words covered up the real reason for the employers' preference for immigrant workers—they were less likely to protest exploitative work conditions and thus were more controllable. The employers provided little evidence for their contentions about the need for soft skills, and indeed did not mention English-language skills (on which native-born workers were likely better skilled) as an example of communication skills that are useful in housekeeping jobs.[79]

In addition, discrimination has been found for an array of better-paying jobs. For example, a recent study of hiring at upscale restaurants in New York City found a relatively high rate of discrimination against applicants. Using pairs of applicants involving a white tester and a black, Asian American, or Latino tester—who were matched for age, appearance, gender, and mannerisms—the researchers sent them to more than 100 restaurants offering jobs. The applicants of color were less likely than their white partners to be interviewed for the open position, and were a little more than half as likely to get an offer of employment as the white tester. In addition, employers did not examine the previous employment experience of white testers as carefully as they did for the testers of color.[80]

This research shows clearly that many white employers view certain groups of workers as much more acceptable than others, and individual applicants are often judged by their racial group characteristics. Yet white employers often argue that they choose white over black workers because they know whites as a group are better qualified, and they may defend such choices by recourse to the notion that it is "rational" discrimination.

However, the workers they deem unacceptable, such as black workers, are often just as qualified as, or better qualified than, those whites who are actually chosen, as we observe in the numerous employment test studies.

Where jobs are located interacts with changing urban spatial realities and also with intentional discrimination. One major study examined the situation of black workers and other workers of color in the large cities of Atlanta, Boston, Detroit, and Los Angeles. Like some previous urban researchers, they found that the movement of jobs from central cities to suburban areas by employers had a serious impact on black employment in cities. Some employers seemed to intentionally choose workplace locations inaccessible to black workers. In Boston and Los Angeles the researchers' surveys found that employers were more likely to express a desire to move their businesses away from neighborhoods with increasing numbers of black families than from other urban neighborhoods. The spatial mismatch of jobs in many cities often appears to be linked, at least in part, to this intentional movement away from black workers and populations. Moreover, numerous employers admitted to these researchers that their hiring decisions involved racist stereotypes about the personality traits, attitudes, and behaviors of black workers and other workers of color.[81]

Hiring: More Racial Barriers

An array of racial barriers face black workers and other workers of color as they seek employment. Private employment agencies today control much of the applicant flow into white-collar jobs. One study found that "screening out 'undesirable' applicants is one of the services many employment agencies provide to their client firms." In this study black testers posing as job applicants faced discrimination at private employment agencies about two-thirds of the time.[82] Yet other racial barriers involve the country's job information networks. These are generally segregated along racial lines, and this segregation has a serious impact on workers of color. Sociologist Deirdre Royster examined white and black students at a technical college and found that, even though on average they worked harder and did better in their training, the black graduates of the program had much more difficulty in finding jobs than did the white students. Pre-existing white networks usually gave white students much better job opportunities than the black students.[83] Lack of access to important white social and employment networks typically has a very negative impact when it comes to finding jobs. One recent statistical study demonstrated that, compared to comparable white male workers, black male workers must spend significantly more time and effort looking for work. As a result, black workers frequently have less work-experience and less secure and stable employment careers. Even new white immigrants to the United

States generally get the significant privileges of whiteness, which include access to the white-oriented employment networks.[84]

As we saw in the case of upscale restaurants, barriers in hiring and other workplace areas affect black Americans at all class levels. Those who are well-educated are at least as likely as the less well-educated to report hiring and other workplace discrimination. One Los Angeles study of 1,000 black workers found that about 80 percent of those with a college degree and almost all of those with a graduate-level education reported workplace discrimination, compared to just under half of those with less than a high school education. A majority of highly educated Asian and Latino workers also reported workplace discrimination.[85]

Hiring problems often mean underrepresentation in numerous important workplaces. For a few days early in April 2007, Media Matters did a count of the racial and gender characteristics of hosts and guests on the prime-time news programs of cable channels CNN, Fox News, and MSNBC. They found that all of the 35 hosts and co-hosts were white, and all but six were white men. On six major programs some 85–97 percent of the guests were also white.[86] In addition, recent research on advertising agencies, many of them being part of very large global firms, found that African Americans made up just 5.3 percent of all advertising managers and professionals. Yet, the relevant Census Bureau and EEOC data suggest this percentage should be in the neighborhood of 9.6 percent. As researchers Marc Bendick, Jr. and Mary Lou Egan point out, eliminating this employment gap would necessitate a significant increase in the industry's number of black managers and professionals.[87] Their research also found that black employees tended to be hired for certain segregated advertising positions—such as those mainly dealing with customers of color—with less influence and pay than white employees with comparable credentials. In addition, black college graduates currently holding jobs in advertising were found to be paid about one-fifth less on average than their otherwise comparable white colleagues.

One very important finding from this study of black white-collar employees in advertising agencies applies to numerous other employers. Many U.S. employers, in both the private and the public sectors, complain they cannot find enough "qualified" employees of color. If they take any remedial action in this regard, they tend to emphasize educational or training strategies to improve future job situations for workers of color. However, as Bendick and Egan point out in their study, this is not the main reason for low percentages of black employees in advertising and many other employment settings. The more important reason is "persistent unwillingness by mainstream advertising agencies to hire, assign, advance, and retain already-available Black talent."[88] This unwillingness, and its associated practices, are usually rooted in a racist framing of black

Americans in general and as employees, as well as in the positive preferences of white employers for employees who look like they do. One lawyer who knows the advertising industry described this employment arena as one where "favoritism rules and merit is cast aside."[89] Not just in the advertising industry, but in many other employment sectors, the central problem is the common practice of white managers operating out of the traditional white racial frame and using predominantly white networks to hire or advance white managers and professionals like themselves. In this process they frequently "ignore the availability of *tens of thousands* of African Americans with educational and experience backgrounds comparable to whites routinely hired in their industry."[90]

Wage Loss, Job Tracking, and Job Flight

Racial discrimination in employment also involves the exploitative relationship that often enables the mostly white major employers to take more of the value of the labor of workers of color than of comparable white workers. Today, as in the past, some employers pay black workers less because they are black. They do this directly, or they do it by segregating black workers into certain job categories and setting the pay for these categories lower than for predominantly white job classifications. The Marxist tradition has accented the way in which capitalist employers take part of the value of workers' labor for their own purposes—thus not paying workers for the full value of their work. Similarly, in numerous situations white employers have the power, because of subtly or blatantly institutionalized discrimination, to take additional value from the labor of black workers and other workers of color, especially in the form of paying lower wages.

Researchers at the Urban Institute have estimated that black workers today lose more than *$120 billion* in wages each year because of the various kinds of overt and subtle employment discrimination they face, dollars that generally remain in white employers' hands.[91] Employers benefit from lower wages they sometimes pay to black workers for the same work as white workers, as well as from the job divisions they have created between workers that reduce cross-racial worker organization. These divisions include job tracking and job segregation. Thus, today a majority of black men still are employed in unskilled, semi-skilled, service, or other relatively low-paid blue-collar jobs or in professional and managerial jobs disproportionately servicing black clients or consumers; or they are unemployed or in part-time employment. Recent Bureau of Labor Statistics data indicate that substantially fewer black men than white men aged 20 and older have jobs (62 percent versus 72 percent), with a black male unemployment rate more than twice that for white men.[92] In addition, black women tend to be concentrated in service jobs, other unskilled blue-collar jobs, professional and managerial jobs oriented to black clients and consumers, or moderate-wage clerical jobs. They too face serious unemployment and underemployment problems.

As noted previously, a problem facing many black workers and other workers of color is their abandonment by U.S. employers who restructure their businesses to meet certain profit goals. Many jobs, especially the less-skilled, are moved overseas by capitalist employers seeking lower-wage labor and less government regulation. By their overseas and related investment strategies they have created high unemployment and underemployment for many black workers and other workers of color in the United States. One recent study examined outsourcing of U.S. blue-collar and white-collar jobs overseas and found that black workers were especially hard hit by the loss of blue-collar jobs, even more so than white or Latino workers. More than five million U.S. manufacturing jobs have been lost since 1979, about half of these so far in the twenty-first century. Black workers were more concentrated in these lost jobs, and these losses help to explain why in recent years the unemployment rate for black men has often risen faster than for whites and some other groups. Today, moreover, some lower-paying white-collar (for example, clerical) jobs disproportionately held by black female and male workers also are endangered by the increasing export of jobs by U.S. employers.[93]

Even when U.S. politicians and media analysts describe the U.S. economy as "very good," a great many workers are unemployed or are underemployed in low-wage or part-time jobs. If the U.S. economy turns sour, as it periodically does, black workers typically face even worse conditions than white workers. When they are no longer needed, many less-skilled black workers are kept as a sort of "reserve army" of workers—in a condition of painful poverty and unemployment, or in the prison–industrial complex—until they may be needed again.

Job Mobility and Hostile Workplace Climates

Today, employees of color also face significant racial discrimination when seeking promotions and job mobility within many private and public workplaces. Thus, the overwhelming majority of employment complaints made to the Equal Employment Opportunity Commission (EEOC) on racial–ethnic grounds are for barriers beyond the hiring stage. In some cases, white male workers are simply given better access than black workers or other workers of color to job assignments and training programs that enable them to climb the employment ladder.[94] In other cases white employees get better mentoring and continued access to important white networking.

One major Pentagon survey of 40,000 U.S. military personnel—including enlisted members and officers—found that 18 percent of the black personnel had faced racial discrimination in regard to their assignments or careers during the last year. (The proportion would likely have been much larger if they had reported on their entire careers.) Another survey of black officers found that many reported not getting the same quality of mentoring as white officers. Like students in the technical college study noted previously (p. 166), officers of color were less likely to be brought into the informal white-dominated networks that often provide critical information necessary for doing well on the military promotion ladder. For many black officers this lack of mentoring and lesser access to networks have restricted their ability to take advantage of career-enhancing assignments, and this in turn has reduced their ability to be competitive with whites for promotions up the military job ladder.[95]

Lack of mentoring and related advancement problems face black employees in many historically white organizations in the public and private sectors. Recent research on corporate advancement shows that women of color have not done well in the upper ranks of corporate executives. One large-scale study found that barely 1 percent of senior corporate executives were black women, compared to about 3 percent for black men and 77 percent for white men. Interviews with 150 senior executives by the Executive Leadership Council found that they said they valued having racial diversity among the managers of their companies. However, when asked for reasons for this serious underrepresentation of black women among senior managers, they cited poor networking on the part of the women, a perception gap, and some other vague factors. Only 15 percent cited discrimination. Most tended to blame the black employees themselves and suggested that the latter take on more challenging assignments, plan careers better, and take better advantage of critical feedback.[96] Apparently, they rarely blamed higher-level white executives in their companies for poor mentoring and other types of subtle or overt discrimination.

This result is not surprising. Black managerial employees, female and male, in U.S. corporations frequently find promotion avenues barred or restricted. One recent review of the literature by Benjamin Bowser summed up the contemporary employment situation this way:

> In the corporate and academic worlds, whites are promoted in due course, sometimes—because of extenuating circumstances—even when they do not fully meet the standard. Blacks must be twice as qualified to demonstrate that they are only as qualified as whites for the same promotion.[97]

Other types of discrimination also make U.S. workplaces racially difficult or hostile. The aforementioned survey of 40,000 military personnel found that three-quarters of the black personnel had faced offensive racial encounters during the last year. In addition, 52 percent had been told offensive racist jokes or stories; 49 percent had suffered unwelcome attempts to draw them into offensive racial discussions; 46 percent had endured acts of racial condescension; 37 percent had encountered hostile racial stares; 28 percent had endured racist comments; 23 percent had been excluded from activities because of race; and 20 percent had been confronted with racist periodicals or other materials. Some 9 percent had been threatened with retaliation if they did not go along with racially offensive actions against them, and 6 percent had been physically threatened because of their race.[98]

A number of recent reports also indicate a hostile work climate at many U.S. corporations. A group of black employees at Microsoft, the large software company, filed a discrimination lawsuit charging top corporate executives with having a "plantation mentality," by which they apparently meant a hostile racial climate in regard to such things as everyday interactions, promotions, or pay for black employees.[99] In a great many corporate workplaces, the white executives and managers who do much hiring and promotion often harbor the conventional stereotypes (for example, "blacks are not hardworking") noted previously, racist views that make these white executives and managers less comfortable with, and less likely to promote, their black employees. Moreover, in many employment settings white executives, managers, and other employees often make use of overtly marginalizing and categorizing looks and language for black employees. For example, black employees may periodically or routinely be categorized and marginalized as "you people" or "one of them."[100] One veteran diversity consultant, Michele Synegal, has reported on the frequency of difficult corporate racial climates in her experience. Among managers and employees of color, depending on the particular workplace, 18 to 36 percent reported blatant discrimination, such as a denial of promotion, and 40 to 49 percent cited other discrimination such as lack of mentoring and exclusion from networks. Some 30 to 50 percent of the black employees had encountered racist jokes and slurs in their workplaces.[101]

Even in professional sports, where in recent decades there have been many black players, there is still subtle and blatant discrimination in recruitment and workplace conditions. Recently, *The New York Times* sports columnist William Rhoden has done significant research on discriminatory patterns in the recruitment or treatment of black football, baseball, and basketball athletes, those in the big-time sports. He has provided much evidence of black athletes being mistreated by the white owners of sports teams, even to the point of their becoming "million dollar slaves" whose lives in their sports are dominated in numerous problematical ways by white owners. Rhoden demonstrates how a national conveyor belt brings talented black youngsters "from inner cities and small towns to big-time programs, where they're cut off from their roots and exploited by team owners, sports agents, and the media."[102]

Racial Barriers in Business

In recent years some mainstream media and economic analysts have suggested that the solution to employment problems for troubled black workers is more "black capitalism" and "black enterprise," that is, the development of more small businesses in the so-called free market system. This often uninformed approach has typically ignored the important structural barriers faced by black Americans in creating such new businesses.

Building a successful business requires access to the necessary economic resources. Unjust impoverishment of black Americans in the past continues as unjust impoverishment for their descendants in the present. Recent research by Melvin Oliver and Thomas Shapiro has shown how difficult it has been for African Americans to build up much in the way of family assets and resources because of centuries of far-reaching slavery, legal segregation, and informal discrimination in the present day. Until the late 1960s, government-sanctioned slavery and Jim Crow segregation kept black Americans out of business sectors serving white consumers and communities. This extensive racial oppression has kept their descendants today from inheriting the economic resources necessary (such as substantial home equities) to develop a significant share of business in the economy under present-day conditions of official desegregation. Until relatively recently in this country's 400-year history, African Americans were forced by blatant discrimination and overt segregation into a major economic detour away from the more lucrative business opportunities outside their own communities.[103]

Today, how well black businesspeople succeed in business depends substantially on certain distinctive business costs, some of which are linked to past discrimination they or their ancestors have suffered. Not only are members of a racially subordinated group like African Americans likely to have less education or business experience because of past and present racial discrimination, but they often lack access to the important social networks or to the business knowledge necessary to compete effectively with more privileged whites. An average black businessperson will not have the same socioeconomic resources, experiences, and opportunities of her or his advantaged white competitors. There is the generational transmission of privilege and wealth that we have raised previously. Comparing a black (B) and a white (W) businessperson, Martin Katz has emphasized the persisting cost structure of discrimination:

Financial advantage—and hence disadvantage—is transferable across generations. If B's heirs and W's heirs each inherit their mothers' businesses, they will likely face cost curves similar to those of their parents. B's daughter will thus face a higher cost curve than W's daughter.... Cost structure analysis thus suggests that discrimination is likely to result in racial cost disparities which can persist long after the discrimination has ceased.[104]

With a less-developed or more segregated work or business history, because of past or present racial hostility and discrimination, black businesspeople will have more trouble starting a new business venture. Even less-prejudiced white lenders will be less willing to loan to black entrepreneurs with fewer resources or a less-developed work or business history. The abolition of some blatant discrimination, which was attempted through the 1960s civil rights movement and laws, has not dramatically restructured the economic resources and business inheritances that have favored whites for centuries, and still persist today. Institutionalized racism remains a continuing reality.

If a black entrepreneur manages to start a business, he or she is likely to face an array of racial hurdles. One review of many studies found that black contractors and other contractors of color face problems getting government contracts and that, if they get contracts, they may often face much white hostility, such as sabotage at work sites. They may also endure racist comments in carrying out business contracts, and many often face racial barriers in securing financing for their business. Much recent research has demonstrated that firms owned by black Americans and many other Americans of color typically have less access to significant financing than similar firms owned by whites. Restricted access to financing, including venture capital, clearly reduces the viability and potential of new businesses.[105]

Very important too is the problem of being excluded from important, pre-existing business networks. Most U.S. business sectors have critical networks of interrelated white businesses, often termed "good old boy networks." This term signals that many white businesspeople are aware of this *non-meritocratic* way in which the vested interests of whites are commonly protected and extended, to the disadvantage of businesspeople who are not white. Without fair access to important local business networks it is hard to get a viable share of local business contracts, in both the private and public business sectors. One Urban Institute report examined 58 racial disparity studies for major state and city governments and found that the share that black construction, goods, and services firms received of government contract dollars was much less than expected based on the black percentage of all firms.[106] Doing business is a daily struggle with elements of white racism for most black businesspeople, especially those operating in historically white markets and areas.

Even those operating with mostly black customers frequently encounter serious difficulties with elements of systemic racism. Recall the recent study by Adia Harvey Wingfield of black entrepreneurs who had started beauty salons (p. 107). She found that, like their predecessors under Jim Crow, they faced very significant discriminatory barriers. "Because of lenders' discriminatory practices, owners' limited social networks, and white patrons' unwillingness to patronize some of these establishments, black entrepreneurs find themselves limited in the types of business ventures they are able to develop." These women have had to work aggressively "to develop viable businesses in part by capitalizing on the beauty concerns that have their origins in the gendered racist ideals which abound in the larger society."[107] Indeed, Wingfield suggests the concept of systemic gendered racism for the complexity of societal pressures and discriminatory conditions that black female entrepreneurs routinely face.

Racial Barriers in Education

Segregation and Resegregation in the Public Schools

Recent opinion polls indicate that the overwhelming majority of whites (80 percent) think that black Americans have as good a chance to get a good education as do white Americans. This contrasts with less than half of black Americans who feel the same way. As we will see in this section, social science data show that this majority-white view is misinformed. One reason for continuing racial inequalities and racial segregation in U.S. education lies in housing patterns. As we already have seen, racial segregation in housing remains pervasive in the United States. Whether in a city, in the suburbs, or in rural areas, such housing segregation sets significant limits on the amount of school desegregation that is possible without some substantial form of pupil transportation.[108]

Today, the separation of white schoolchildren from schoolchildren of color remains very substantial, and is clear evidence against premature "post-racial America" arguments. Government data indicate that segregation of white from black children in metropolitan schools is very high and has increased a little over the last decade. This increased school segregation is particularly significant given that residential segregation has decreased a bit in this period.[109] Today, more than 44 percent of U.S. schoolchildren are black, Latino, Asian American, and other children of color, a percentage rising to over half in southern and western regions. Black and Latino children are today likely to be very segregated. About 40 percent of these are now in schools that are 90–100 percent children of color, an increase from less than one-third in the 1980s. Typically, these highly segregated schools have more children from low-income families and far fewer educational and economic resources, as is seen in the relatively fewer dollars spent for each pupil and their less-experienced teachers. Millions of children of color, as well as poor white children, remain "locked into 'dropout factory' high schools, where huge percentages do not graduate, have little future in the American economy, and almost none are well prepared for college."[110] Moreover, although they too are supported by federal money, public charter schools are on average even *more* racially segregated than other public schools, and thus most do not provide a way out of extensive racial segregation in U.S. schools.

In the late 1960s and early 1970s, much federal government action was directed at school desegregation. However, backtracking actions designed to limit racial desegregation or to resegregate had begun by the early 1970s at the highest levels of the U.S. government. Early in his Republican presidency, Richard Nixon made it clear to his advisors that he was committed to reducing pressures on historically white school systems to desegregate. Nixon's most important appointment to the Supreme Court, the conservative William Rehnquist, was at the time well-known for his opposition to government efforts at breaking down school segregation.[111]

At least since the 1970s the executive and judicial branches of the federal government have often allowed, and sometimes even encouraged, the racial resegregation of public school systems that had in the 1950s and 1960s been under pressure or court orders to desegregate. By the mid-1970s conservative appointments to the Supreme Court presaged a long-term movement, lasting to the present day, away from eradicating the burdens of "slavery still unwilling to die" in public schools, as well as other important institutions. In the very important Supreme Court case *Milliken* v. *Bradley* (1974), a majority conservative Court, in a close decision, firmly blocked local school officials' attempts at a metropolitan-wide school desegregation plan combining the city of Detroit and its suburbs. Dissenting in this case, the first African American ever to serve on the high court, Thurgood Marshall (joined by three other justices), noted that after decades of government steps toward racial desegregation the conservative members of the Court were now seriously backtracking.[112] By the 1990s, moreover, various federal courts were allowing public school systems to abandon racial desegregation altogether, even if they had never had a meaningful desegregation program to get rid of Jim Crow segregation. In the cases *Board of Education of Oklahoma* v. *Dowell* (1991) and *Freeman* v. *Pitts* (1992), a conservative Supreme Court made it clear that they viewed the large-scale resegregation of public schools to be permissible and constitutional if it did not involve active government enforcement of racial segregation.[113]

Contemporary research shows that public schools are resegregating across the country, substantially because of decisions of conservative judges and other government officials. During the George W. Bush era (2001–2009), numerous federal judges and other officials worked with local governments to end even voluntary school desegregation, as well as other antidiscrimination programs, thereby signaling that racial inequality could often be ignored by local governments. In 2007, for example, a conservative Supreme Court majority knocked down voluntary school desegregation programs in Seattle and Louisville. In addition, the Bush administration's "No Child Left Behind" (NCLB) law put increased pressure for change in pupil achievements on the segregated public schools and teachers in low-income communities, yet did not provide the necessary economic and human resources to bring such changes in the educational achievements for many low-income students, especially as compared to resources available to white middle-class students. As education scholar Zeus Leonardo has recently pointed out, this NCLB approach represents a type of colorblind racist thinking that "names the symptoms, rather than the causes, of racial inequality."[114]

Research shows that the lack of educational achievement for many children of color is not because their parents are not supportive of education, a view often argued by whites to explain persisting racial differences in educational outcomes. One recent Department of Education report showed that 94 percent of black parents checked on their children having completed homework, as compared to 82 percent of white parents. In surveys and other studies the overwhelming majority of parents of color reveal themselves to be strongly committed to better educations for their children.[115] Indeed, today most students of color have themselves strongly internalized the value of getting more education, including a high school education and going to college.

The continuing racial segregation of public schools is not accidental, nor is it the fault of communities of color. Over decades now, many white parents, politicians, and school officials have worked hard to keep their public schools as white as possible. There are various mechanisms to implement such goals. For example, one research report on New York City schools found widespread racial channeling and steering of students. Trained testers, posing as parents, were sent to 28 elementary schools. Of the 99 visits made by parent testers, half were by whites and half by people of color. White-parent testers were able to speak with an educator, such as the principal, much more often than their black and Latino counterparts. Whites were two-and-one-half times more likely to get a school tour and were, on average, given much more information. The school staff members were more likely to mention programs for gifted children to the white testers than to the black and Latino testers. The system's personnel tended to channel white students disproportionately into certain schools and programs, and students of color disproportionately into other schools and programs. The report describes this differential treatment as a type of institutional racism that is rooted in conscious prejudices, malign neglect by officials, and a lack of representation in decisionmaking by the families of color that are served by the public schools.[116]

Moreover, once they are inside public schools, students of color periodically face discrimination by some teachers and administrators. A Florida study by David Figlio examined records for 55,000 students from families with two or more children in a major district's schools and found that black students with distinctive black-sounding names (like "LaQuisha") averaged lower scores on reading and math tests, and got fewer recommendations for gifted classes, than their own brothers or sisters without such names. "The estimated relationship between names and test scores suggests that a reasonably large fraction of the Black–White test score gap can be explained by children's naming patterns."[117] According to this study, black children with exotic-to-whites names probably get less attention from white teachers who assume their names indicate they will not do well in school. Because many whites are privately and publicly critical of black naming patterns for children, such a racialized view might well negatively affect their interactions with black children.

Racial Barriers at Colleges and Universities

In spite of the numerous obstacles that many black children and other children of color face in getting equal and first-rate K-12 educational opportunities in this society, their educational achievements have been significant in recent decades. For example, younger black Americans are now only a little less likely to have completed high school than comparable whites. Among those aged 25–29 in 2007, nearly 94 percent of whites had completed high school, compared to nearly 88 percent of similar African Americans.[118] Most young African Americans have gotten at least a high school diploma, albeit often one from a high school that did not have the educational resources and college-oriented programs available to a majority of white students. Still, their personal achievements have closed much of the racial gap in educational attainment from earlier decades. However, this closing of the educational gap has not translated into an end of discrimination in education or in job markets.

African Americans and other Americans of color still face many difficulties in getting a good college education, which is increasingly necessary for decent-paying jobs in this society. Discrimination, whether blatant, covert, or subtle, is still commonplace at most stages of education at historically white colleges and universities. For example, subtle discrimination persists in some of the standard screening measures used for admissions at undergraduate and graduate levels. How merit is measured, usually by standardized tests, has largely been determined by white educators. Historically, college entrance tests and related screening devices have been designed by whites from upper-middle-class backgrounds. Indeed, some leading social scientists of the 1910s and 1920s who helped to develop the forerunners or early versions of today's college entrance tests, such as Princeton University's Carl Brigham, were outspoken white supremacists. By means of psychometric testing and statistical analyses numerous social scientists then sought to demonstrate the intellectual superiority of the "Nordic race" over other racial groups. Indeed, sociologists Tukufu Zuberi and Eduardo Bonilla-Silva have recently demonstrated that numerous psychometric and other statistical approaches developed by the various social sciences in the last century have roots in early attempts to demonstrate white racial superiority.[119]

College entrance tests and similar diagnostic tests have usually been designed, consciously or unconsciously, to measure the things that white middle-class people know or do well. For example, college entrance tests have used questions about such things as toboggans and polo, items more familiar to middle- and upper-class whites than to most working-class people, including most people of color. In addition, most tests are written in the variant of the English language most accessible to white middle-class people.[120] In addition, white middle-class youth often do better than those from other racial groups on such tests because they mostly come from families with substantial economic and cultural resources (such as numerous computers, substantial libraries, and test tutoring), resources often linked to the unjust enrichment of their white ancestors during the slavery or Jim Crow eras, as well as to racial privileges they and their parents have in society today.

Students of color are less likely to have families that can support their college attendance, substantially because of the negative socioeconomic impacts on their families of past and present racial barriers. One recent Department of Education study showed that the percentage of all black students who started college coming from families with yearly incomes less than $32,000 was nearly half (49.1 percent), which compared to only 16.1 percent of white beginning students.[121] Better incomes typically mean access to better housing, to better-resourced high schools, and to colleges and universities. Thus, white middle-class students tend to have a better pre-college education, which gives them an edge in scoring well on entrance tests and completing college degree programs. Their typically better background resources also mean advantages in financing a college education and, later on, in competing for jobs and other societal rewards.

Negative Campus Climates

If they get past the college entrance barriers, black students and many other students of color commonly confront a range of discriminatory barriers on historically white college campuses. Discrimination by whites on and off campus is usually a recurring problem. One research study questioned 153 black students, faculty, and staff at a major university, and nearly all reported facing racial discrimination in the last year. In addition, other research at the historically white campus of a major state university in the 1990s found that most black students there reported serious discrimination on or near campus. Negative encounters with white students included being called "nigger," encountering racist graffiti, various defensive reactions by white students, and whites often assuming black students had to be athletes or affirmative-action students. Black students reported significant differential treatment by faculty members, including being treated as the spokesperson for the race, graded down for writing on African American topics, and subjected to subtle racist joking. Students also reported hasty treatment by academic advisors who gave more time to white students, a lack of interest by administrators in black students, racial biases in the educational curricula, fewer campus activities for black students, over-policing of some black events, and weak efforts at student retention. Many students considered dropping out because of the negative racial climate.[122]

Moreover, recent research that I and other colleagues have done continues to reveal that these patterns remain commonplace at historically white colleges. Recently, Leslie Houts Picca and I had 308 students of color at more than two-dozen colleges and universities keep diaries of racial events and commentaries they encountered for a few weeks during one college semester. One all-too-typical example of blatant discrimination still found on a college campus can be seen in this recent diary account from a black college student attending a historically white college. He notes a recurring problem with racism there:

> This is one of those sad and angry nights for me. Tonight marks the third time since the beginning of the school year that I've been called a nigger by a bunch of white students on a ... weekend.... At first I used to wonder where they actually take the time in their heads to separate me from everyone else by the color of my skin. I used to just blame alcohol consumption for their obvious ignorance and racist attitudes, but I have since stopped trying to make excuses for them. I have to admit that at times like this ... I don't understand how such a system of hate could exist.... Sometimes it seems that if I am around all white people, then I become nothing more than a token Black "exhibit" for their amusement. I guess that even I have to

be careful not to judge all based on a few bad examples, which more often than not is the fate of many in the black community today. The saddest thing however, is that these people, these college students are supposed to be the supposed crème de la crème, the future business and political leaders.[123]

This savvy student discusses racist attacks and commentaries he has endured in diverse campus area settings. He has faced barbed epithets hurled by presumably well-educated whites. He observes too that he is encountering the racist actions of "future business and political leaders." These are not isolated incidents affecting one student, for the 308 student diarists recorded hundreds of racist events, most involving whites targeting people of color.

In recent years students of color at numerous historically white colleges have had to face racist commentaries and attacks. Thus, in a recent one-week period the University of Virginia—a campus designed by Thomas Jefferson and built by enslaved labor—experienced six racialized events including racist slurs yelled at black students, a birthday card with racist slurs put on a black student's door, and a "nigger" message put on another's dorm door.[124] White students at various universities have held parties mocking Martin Luther King, Jr. and the civil rights movement. Students at University of Connecticut law school recently had a Martin Luther King, Jr. "Bullets and Bubbly" party. Whites wore baggy clothes and fake gold teeth and held machine guns. Clemson University students recently mocked the King holiday with a "ghetto-fabulous" party. Researchers C. Richard King and David Leonard report that white students there dressed up "in blackface, drank 40s, wore fake teeth grills, flashed gang signs and, in some cases, padded their posteriors to conform to their stereotypes of the Black female body." They also report that, a few weeks later, white students at Santa Clara University had a "Latino-themed party" at which "young women feigned pregnancy, the young men played at being cholo and everyone reveled in the symbols and spectacle they associate with Latinos."[125]

A great array of similar racist events—including a variety of "ghetto" and blackface parties, bake sales, and skits—have taken place at many other colleges and universities, including Washington University, New College, University of Tennessee, University of Texas, Trinity College, Whitman College, Willamette College, Texas A&M University, University of Connecticut, Emory University, University of Mississippi, Stetson University, University of Chicago, Cornell University, Swarthmore College, Tufts University, Massachusetts Institute of Technology, Macalester College, Johns Hopkins University, Dartmouth College, Syracuse University, Tarleton State University, University of Colorado, University of Arizona, University of Alabama, University of Illinois, University of Delaware, and several University of California campuses.[126]

One recent study of Halloween events drew on 663 observation journals by college students in several regions. Students recorded many examples of white students engaging in ritual costuming—that is, dressing in costumes mocking and stereotyping Americans of color. The authors concluded that Halloween provides a convenient context in which whites can "trivialize and reproduce racial stereotypes while supporting the racial hierarchy."[127]

Developing classroom exercises in connection with this research, Jennifer Mueller and Rosalind Chou, instructors at a southwestern university, asked students in two courses to recount what they saw at Halloween, especially costumes and events at parties or while trick-or-treating. In both cases the number of racist costumes reported was large, given the small classes. In Mueller's case her 32 students reported seeing 20 Indian costumes, four Middle Eastern (for example, terrorist) costumes, 19 Mexican/Latino costumes, nineteen blackface costumes, and 40 other costumed portrayals of African Americans. In Chou's class the 33 students reported seeing five Indian costumes, six Middle Eastern/Asian–Indian (for example, terrorist) costumes, eight Mexican (for example, migrant worker) costumes, ten blackface costumes, and 22 other costumed portrayals of black Americans. The latter included "ghetto fabulous" images, gangsters, pimps, prostitutes, crack babies, crack mothers, rappers, athletes, large-bottomed women, jungle tribesmen, and welfare mothers. In both classes almost all of the costumed events involved whites donning the costumes, and almost all were negative and mocking portrayals of people of color, with African Americans getting the majority of such attacks. The students observed these racialized costumes at many different settings, including student parties, restaurants, bars, neighborhoods, and church parties. These extensive racist performances by mostly well-educated whites at Halloween reveal the deep realities of a still-racist society: "Whites contemporarily engage Halloween as a sort of 'ritual of rebellion' in response to the seemingly restrictive social context of the post-Civil Rights era, and in a way that ultimately reinforces white dominance."[128]

In addition, several campuses have seen local conservative weeklies, daily Internet newsletters, or other student publications mount openly hostile attacks on affirmative action programs, on faculty and students of color, or on administrators of color. For instance, one such incident took place recently at Dartmouth College, where a new Asian American college president was openly mocked with racist commentary and stereotyping in a campus Internet newsletter.[129]

Part of the problem in these many cases of racist incidents likely lies in the fact that many white high school students come to historically white colleges and universities, with their now diversifying college populations, unprepared for this new diverse reality. Their high schools, as we have seen, are often overwhelmingly white and their neighborhoods are isolated from populations of color. Interestingly, a few recent research studies have examined white first-year college students who were randomly paired with non-white roommates and found that these interracial relationships were different from those between randomly paired white first-year students. The interracial roommate pairs resulted in less extensive joint activities and more breakups than the all-white pairs. One study found that unobtrusively measured racial attitudes of white first-year students predicted the longevity of these interracial roommate relationships. Those who expressed the most negative attitudes were the most likely to have difficulty in relating to roommates who were not white.[130]

Moreover, today as in the past, campus cultures at most historically white institutions are still strongly white-oriented and resistant to changes in their practices that involve a conventional white framing. At most such institutions the majority of white trustees, administrators, advisors, faculty members, and students have shown little desire to remake their campuses to fully integrate the interests, history, and concerns of students of color into the mainstream of campus life and culture.

Discrimination in Public Places

Racial discrimination has a distinctive spatial dimension, and its character can vary as a person of color travels from their home space to various public spaces. Much discrimination targeting Americans of color still occurs outside social contexts where the presence of family or friends significantly reduces its likelihood. In a recent conversation I had with a black professional with a Ph.D. degree, he quickly listed an array of everyday discrimination he faces today in public places, including the unwillingness of white clerks to touch his hand, probably out of some stereotype of "dirtiness" or "danger." He also reported white clerks treating him with substantial discourtesy in comparison with nearby white shoppers and the obsession white clerks have with the possibility of him being a shoplifter. He has recently faced whites who stereotyped him as unintelligent at his gym and in his workplace, and whites who stared when he was walking with a white woman on the street. Much racist action still takes place in public places and public accommodations.[131]

Recall the survey in which nearly half the black respondents said they had experienced discrimination while dining out, shopping, in public transportation, in encounters with police, or at work in just the last month (p. 142). Restaurants are often reported to be a problem for black diners. Discrimination there often includes poor service that seems racially motivated and being seated at an undesirable table, such as at the back of the restaurant near the kitchen. Another survey of 131 African Americans found three-quarters had encountered some racial discrimination—ranging from rejection to verbal or physical harassment—in a hotel, motel, or fast-food restaurant.[132]

Significant discrimination still occurs in retail stores, in spite of the high and growing use of such stores by customers of color. One Gallup poll found that 46 percent of black shoppers felt they were not treated as well as whites in downtown or mall stores. A number of recent lawsuits have charged major retailers with discrimination against black customers needing to write checks and with discriminatory overcharging.[133] A report by the New Jersey Citizen Action (NJCA) group cited data for New Jersey, and nationally, that showed a pattern of black and Latino car buyers being quoted substantially higher financing rates than comparable white car buyers. Financing mark-up charges for black buyers averaged as much as 60–70 percent higher than for white buyers.[134] Moreover, a field audit study examined the treatment of black and white customers in retail establishments and found black customers were often not served as quickly as comparable whites. Additional discrimination takes the form of extra surveillance from white sales clerks. One term used for this latter type of discrimination is "consumer racial profiling," which includes "slow or rude service, required pre-payment, surveillance, searches of belongings, and neglect, such as refusing to serve African-American customers."[135]

Law professor Anne-Marie Harris has described the numerous costs of what has been termed "shopping while black" in this way:

> Most of the time, white consumers can run errands, shop, dine out, and take in a show with the expectation of at least minimally appropriate service in the establishments where they spend their money. However, African-American consumers' patronage and money are somehow regarded as less valuable than that of the white consumer.[136]

We observe in numerous retail settings the high cost of shopping for many black customers, as well as many other customers of color, especially the time lost and the less-than-equal shopping opportunities. There are also significant actual and potential costs for the white-run stores, for in some retail categories customers of color now make up more than 30 percent of shoppers. Clearly, much retail discrimination today is still irrational in conventional economists' terms.

Discrimination in Health Care

We have previously noted the health inequalities faced by black adults, including their significantly lower life expectancy than whites (p. 21).

Data on infant mortality is one of the most dramatic indicators of the severe impact of accumulating and systemic racism on black Americans. The black infant mortality rate of 13.6 deaths per 1,000 live births is very high for Western countries and more than twice the white infant mortality rate (5.7). Recent research makes clear that this serious health inequality is substantially the result of the multi-dimensional impacts of systemic racism. For black mothers these immediate and cumulative impacts include having substantially fewer economic resources on the average than white mothers, as well as having less adequate access to pre-natal and post-natal health care in a country that rations much health care according to racial or class characteristics. These impacts also include having to face direct and indirect discrimination by white health professionals. All these factors affect not only the available health care options but also the psychosocial stress on black women. Not surprisingly, such ongoing stress has been found by researchers to be associated with negative effects on health, including on the birth weights of babies delivered from stressed black mothers. Even when researchers do statistical controls for education and income, they find that black women are still more likely to give birth to lower-birth-weight babies than their white counterparts. Such a negative outcome, researchers suggest, can be attributed in substantial part to the stresses of everyday racism.[137]

Black women, men, and children often face recurring discrimination when they try to make use of professional services, such as in the area of health care. Black patients being treated for physical or mental illness are, depending on the illness, less likely or far less likely than otherwise comparable white patients to get standard and adequate care. One recent survey of research on health care institutions listed numerous studies showing racial discrimination:

> Quality of care was lower for black Medicare beneficiaries than for others hospitalized for congestive heart failure or pneumonia.... older African American women receive mammography less often than socioeconomically and demographically matched European American women ... nonwhite (mostly African American) pneumonia patients were less frequently admitted to intensive care units than similarly ill and similarly insured European American patients.[138]

In these studies statistical controls for contextual factors like income do not eliminate the pattern of racial inequality and discrimination in the provision of health care.

One significant issue is the negative framing, the negative stereotypes, held by many white medical personnel. In one study innovative researchers used actors to portray black and white patients with coronary disease symptoms. Some 720 physicians were asked to look at these recorded interviews and other patient data, assess the probability of coronary disease, and suggest treatment. Researchers found differences in proposed treatment: blacks, especially black women, were less likely to be recommended for cardiac catheterization, compared to whites with the same dress, occupations, and medical histories. Another recent study reported in the *New England Journal of Medicine* found that black patients with lung cancer were less likely to receive the best surgical treatment than white patients.[139]

One research study of racial attitudes using the online implicit association test examined the responses of 2,500 people who self-identified as physicians. Some 70 percent of these physicians showed that they implicitly preferred whites to blacks, with men having a stronger preference than women.[140] Moreover, a recent Harvard Medical School study examined the connection between the explicit and unconscious racial bias of 287 Boston and Atlanta physicians and their thrombolysis recommendations for white and black patients. These mostly white physicians showed no overt bias for white or black patients on explicit questions about racial matters that were asked of them, yet they did show a pro-white, antiblack bias on the implicit association tests also given to them. In addition, as their pro-white bias increased, so did their likelihood of treating white and black patients differently in regard to medical procedures. "Results suggest that physicians' unconscious biases may contribute to racial/ethnic disparities in use of medical procedures such as thrombolysis for myocardial infarction."[141]

The reasons for these patterns of differential medical treatment along racial lines are yet to be fully explored and documented, but they probably include not only the general antiblack stereotypes of the white racial frame but also specific stereotypes shared by some white medical practitioners, such as the notion that black patients who get special or expensive treatments are not as likely as whites to take proper care of themselves after treatment. More research remains to be done, but there is no reason to expect that the racism of the larger society does not extend into everyday thinking and decisions in the health care professions. Yet again, the current research data suggest that whites' racist framing can lead to actions that seriously harm black Americans.

One likely problem in many such professional settings, as well as other settings with interracial interactions, is the lack of cross-racial empathy that many whites demonstrate, the social alexithymia noted previously (p. 89). Psychological researchers have staged situations of people needing help in public places and discovered that white bystanders will often not respond to a black person's call for help in a staged emergency situation. Whites are much more likely to respond to calls for help from a white person. The racial identity of the person needing help strongly affects white responses. While overt dislike of black people is one likely reason, yet another possible reason has been suggested by researchers: the more whites see of black people suffering, such as in the mass media, the more they come to see that condition as normal, and the less sympathy or empathy they have for blacks in difficulty.[142]

Health and Environmental Racism

Another area of racial discrimination faced by African Americans and other Americans of color today involves issues that are also linked closely to health concerns. Extensive research by sociologist Robert Bullard and his associates continues to demonstrate widespread problems with toxic wastes for many communities of color across the country, from San Francisco to Houston to New York City. In many rural areas, towns, and cities, toxic waste dumps and other garbage dumps have been disproportionately located, usually by white officials, in or near communities of color. This has meant that citizens of color disproportionately bear the social and health costs of these waste facilities. For example, one family in Tennessee filed a personal injury lawsuit against local government officials after discovering that the white officials had known for a decade that well water in their area was seriously contaminated, but had not fully informed them of the dangers. Although the lead plaintiff is very physically fit, she got breast cancer, as did her mother. Her father died of cancer, and three other relatives have also had cancers. Research into county records revealed that the nearby landfill had allowed dumping of toxic wastes for years, with toxins getting into nearby water sources for a community of color. Bullard, who assisted the family in its lawsuit, has noted that this is yet another example of institutionalized environmental racism: "Governments target communities of color that don't have money, lawyers or power in office."[143]

Current research using geographical information system (GIS) techniques has also shown that the distribution of hazardous waste treatment and storage facilities in various towns and cities across the country likely reflects extensive racial discrimination. Using such GIS techniques, one recent study examined racial disparities in the location of this country's hazardous waste facilities, comparing what they found with findings in previous studies that did not use these more advanced techniques. They found that the "magnitude of racial disparities around hazardous waste facilities is much greater than what previous national studies have reported." This was true even when they controlled for various economic and political variables that might have affected the location of waste facilities. According to these social scientists, their data strongly suggested "that factors uniquely associated with race, such as racial targeting, housing discrimination, or other race-related factors are associated with the location of the nation's hazardous waste facilities."[144] Clearly, research studies regularly demonstrate major racial disparities in the location of toxic waste facilities, with populations of color paying a disproportionately heavy health cost for these inequalities.

Conclusion

Being black in U.S. society means always having to be prepared for antiblack actions by whites—in most places and at many times of the day, week, month, or year. Being black means living with various types of racial discrimination from cradle to grave. This lifetime reality is also true for most other Americans of color. Until whites quit thinking, feeling, imaging, and acting in racist ways—and thereby maintaining their racial privilege and power—the centuries-old system of racial oppression will persist.

In a June 1963 address to the nation, President John F. Kennedy explained why he had recently called out the Alabama National Guard—against the wishes of the governor of Alabama, George Wallace—in order to enforce a federal court order allowing two black students to enroll at the all-white University of Alabama. He said:

> This nation was founded by men of many nations and backgrounds. It was founded on the principle that all men are created equal, and that the rights of every man are diminished when the rights of one man are threatened.... One hundred years of delay have passed since President Lincoln freed the slaves, yet their heirs, their grandsons, are not fully free. They are not yet freed from the bonds of injustice; they are not yet freed from social and economic oppression.[145]

After accenting this important theme of slavery unwilling to die, Kennedy continued by positioning the issue of racial equality as a moral question that the country must face. After the speech Kennedy sent to the U.S. Congress proposals that would soon became the 1964 Civil Rights Act. This important new law officially prohibited much overt racial discrimination and officially abolished legal segregation in employment, schools, federally assisted programs, and public accommodations (see Chapter 8). Over the next few years, the 1965 Voting Rights Act and the 1968 Civil Rights Act would prohibit discrimination in voting practices and in housing. However, as we have already seen, these important laws banning racial discrimination are often weakly enforced or unenforced, and black Americans and other Americans of color still do not have the full and equal opportunities promised in the official rhetoric of the 1960s. Indeed, more decades of delay have passed since President Kennedy's famous speech, and the heirs of those who endured slavery and Jim Crow have not yet become "fully free" from the "bonds of injustice," from "social and economic oppression."

6
White Privileges and Black Burdens
Still Systemic Racism

In an interview project that I conducted, a distinguished black professor who taught for many years at a historically white university explained the cost of dealing with racism:

> If you can think of the mind as having one hundred ergs of energy, and the average man uses 50 percent of his energy dealing with the everyday problems of the world … then he has 50 percent more to do creative kinds of things that he wants to do. Now that's a white person. Now a black person also has one hundred ergs; he uses fifty percent the same way a white man does, dealing with what the white man has [to deal with], so he has 50 percent left. But he uses 25 percent fighting being black, [with] all the problems being black and what it means.[1]

By virtue of an accident of birth, African Americans must typically expend an enormous amount of energy defending themselves and their families from the assaults of racism on a regular basis. In contrast, over their lifetimes, white Americans on average have a major life-energy advantage, for they do not waste large amounts of time dealing with the impositions of antiwhite discrimination. This is one important example of *white privilege.*

More generally, white privilege includes the large set of advantages and benefits inherited by each generation of those routinely defined as "white" in the social structure and processes of U.S. society. The actual white privileges, and the sense that one is entitled to them, are inseparable parts of a greater societal whole. These advantages are material, symbolic, and psychological. They infiltrate and encompass many thousands of interactions and other events played out in an individual white American's experiences over the course of a lifetime.

Whiteness is so commonplace, so habitual, and so imbedded that it exists even where and when most whites cannot see it. Stated or unstated, it is a fundamental given of this society, as well as other Western societies. White prerogatives stem from the fact that society has, from the beginning, been structured in terms of white enrichment, white gains, and white group interests. The active or passive acceptance of this racialized system as normal has long conferred advantages for whites, even including antiracist whites seeking to eradicate racism. Today, most whites of all political persuasions will say they are opposed to racism, although a majority continue to overtly, covertly, or subtly support racist framing, practices, and institutions.

Privileging White Experiences and Interpretations

Much research indicates that a majority of whites still have an uncritical habit of mind that accepts the existing racial order with little questioning. In this research most whites, including white students, tend to explain persisting racial inequalities without connecting them to the larger system of white power and privilege. A majority even deny that they as a group have benefited significantly from past or present racial discrimination (see Chapter 4, pp. 125–126).[2]

As we noted in Chapter 4, sociologist Karyn McKinney recently collected the racial autobiographies of white college students. These autobiographies reveal that most of these well-educated whites do not understand their white privilege, largely because they do not face racial discrimination and because they do not have significant equal-status contacts with people of color. Most have never assessed the racial worlds in which they live critically. Still, this and similar research has revealed that some whites, albeit a modest number, have come to better understand their racial privileges. At a certain turning point, whites who have had significant and sustained contacts with people of color often come to understand more about how everyday racism operates and about their own privileged racial place in society. Today, as in the past, a central difficulty in bringing more racial change to society lies in the fact that most white Americans do *not* have close and equal-status relationships with black Americans or other Americans of color. Indeed, most whites have the option to stay relatively isolated in socio-racial terms and thus to avoid encountering the critical views and often painful experiences of Americans of color.[3]

White privilege also includes an entitlement to decipher a black person's everyday reality. For example, the mother of one newborn reported a white nurse's comment on seeing her infant: "Oh, this one's a militant, a little Black Panther!"[4] The newborn was immediately constructed as "black" (in this case, the mother was white, the father black), and downgraded, humorously, in white eyes as an alien and potentially dangerous racial other. Whites often take it for granted that they are entitled to their interpretation of black conditions without consulting black Americans.

In addition, most whites tend to be defensive when reminded of their white privilege and their position in society's racial hierarchy. In one recent study researchers asked groups of white college students to write an essay about the ways in which they had been privileged or had been disadvantaged because they were white. Those who were asked to write about their racial privileges later scored higher on a modern racism scale with antiblack items (for example, "Blacks are getting too demanding in their push for equal rights") than did those white students who had been asked to write about the disadvantages of being white or about a race-irrelevant topic. Thus, when these educated whites had to consider racial privilege and inequality, most "justified their privileged status by denying the existence of discrimination" and accenting antiblack stereotypes. Like much other research, this study suggests whites' racial understandings typically involve a strong sense of their position on the racial ladder and a need to defend that position.[5]

Social Transmission of White Privilege

From the beginning, the North American system of racial oppression was designed to bring many benefits for white Americans. Slavery, and subsequent Jim Crow segregation and contemporary racial discrimination, have all provided whites with many social, economic, and political advantages. For that reason whites, as individuals and as a group, have a vested interest in actively maintaining this system. Systemic racism ensures whites "greater resources, a wider range of personal choice, more power, and more self-esteem than they would have if they were ... forced to share the above with people of color."[6]

Today, most white Americans underestimate not only the level of their privileges but the degree to which these privileges exist because they have been passed down from their ancestors. Consider again the principle of unjust enrichment. The coercive taking of one's personal possessions by an individual criminal has some similarities to the coercive taking of one's labor or just due by a white slaveholder or, today, by an array of white discriminators.[7] And such unjustly gained advantages often have a strong societal inertia. When large groups of whites gained jobs, income, property, status, or wealth unjustly under slavery and Jim Crow segregation, and then passed these advantages and wealth to later generations, that did *not* make the advantages and wealth inherited (and enhanced today) by their white descendants to be justly held. Moreover, each white generation's discriminatory actions not only create new opportunities for unjust enrichment but also provide social processes of transmission that pass earlier unjustly gained economic and cultural capital to later white generations. For centuries, the system of oppression has created severe inequalities in life chances between whites and blacks (as well as between whites and other Americans of color), and the societal transmission of these inequalities remains critical to the continuing reproduction of that racial oppression.

Racial Consciousness: Elites and Ordinary Whites

Periodically over the course of our history, white elites have intentionally tried to divide ordinary white and black Americans in order to reduce or eliminate the possibility of joint protests over working conditions and other political–economic conditions. They have generally been successful. While there have been historical periods when some white farmers and workers have joined with their black counterparts, for most of North American history the overwhelming majority of white farmers and workers have been active players in maintaining systemic racism.[8]

Over the last century, thus, most white workers have been more likely to join racially with their class oppressors than to join with their brothers and sisters of the same socioeconomic class across the racial line. One likely reason there has been much less social class struggle in the United States than in Europe is because white workers have historically been more interested in struggling against their potential class allies—black workers and other workers of color—than they have been in struggling against class enemies, the capitalist employers. Historically, a majority of white workers have usually rejected social class solidarity with black workers, and thus have regularly weakened or destroyed their own consciousness of class and of themselves as exploited workers under capitalism.

Today, as in the past, white workers who are living in modest circumstances may not feel privileged, especially relative to elite whites. They certainly sense the need for significant economic improvements in their lives. However, because most also accept the white racial frame and its racial myths and misconceptions about society, they seem unable to see deeply into the real sources of their class oppression under modern capitalism. Their racial framing likely makes it hard for most to understand not only the situation of the racially oppressed, but also their own situation of class oppression. Nonetheless, this lack of understanding does not mean that class oppression is not still a major part of this country's social fabric. In the U.S. today, as in the past, racial structure and class structure constantly co-exist, overlap, and interrelate. Being white includes not only a higher racial status in society no matter what one's social class is, but also *on average* having a higher social class position and greater income and resources than if one were black. More often than not, a somewhat higher or much higher position in the social class system comes with birth into the top rank in the system of racial categorization. The systems of racial oppression and of class oppression routinely co-reproduce each other.

Benefits of Whiteness: A Brief Overview

Privileged Access to Societal Resources

From at least the mid-1600s to the 1960s this country's economy was openly, often imperiously, run as a racist system often using black labor and indigenous lands to create resources and prosperity for whites. Historically, whites have also been direct beneficiaries of much government assistance intended to create white prosperity and upward mobility. An array of aggressive "affirmative action" programs for whites only have long provided a substantial basis for prosperity and mobility. For example, in the 1600s several colonies provided land grants to white colonists, land unavailable to those enslaved. Moreover, from its passage in the 1860s to the 1930s, the federal government, operating under the Homestead Act, gave away millions of acres of government (originally Native American) land for little or no cost to white families homesteading midwestern and western areas. African Americans were generally excluded from access to this land because they were then enslaved (in the 1860s) or, later during the Jim Crow era, because they were locked into the near-slavery of debt peonage in southern agriculture. Overt violence was used by Klan-type groups to drive out black families that did manage to gain some land on their own. The federal homestead program created many billions of dollars of wealth for white homesteaders and their descendants, with the latter often benefiting to the present day.[9]

As we have seen in previous chapters, numerous large-scale preferential programs for whites were legitimate and openly implemented for more than 300 years. Even later white entrants into the U.S., such as millions of immigrants from southern and eastern Europe, benefited greatly from antiblack laws and practices during the late nineteenth and early twentieth centuries (see Chapter 2). Some conservative scholars have tried to argue that the societal situation of African Americans since desegregation in the 1960s is essentially similar to the harsh societal conditions faced by the hardworking white European immigrants in the decades just before and after 1900. So, black Americans must reform themselves culturally and work harder like these European immigrants.[10]

However, this historically naive view ignores the huge advantages that white immigrant groups generally had over the black Americans who were already in the cities into which immigrants settled. The European newcomers were able to move up the economic ladder because most arrived when the economy was expanding greatly and jobs were relatively abundant; because many of them had some skills or modest money resources; because most faced far less job and other discrimination than black urbanites; because they were not excluded from residential areas near workplaces as black urbanites often were; and because cities were then increasingly under control of political machines oriented to the immigrant group voters. European immigrants and their children joined important whites-only unions and secured better-paying blue-collar or government jobs from which black Americans were barred. As a result, the immigrants and their descendants were generally able to do much better economically, politically, and residentially than the black Americans who had already resided in the country for centuries before these European immigrants arrived.[11]

Since the nineteenth century, indeed, many white workers have tried to keep black workers out of better-paying jobs. Until the 1960s most unions discriminated more or less openly against black workers, reinforcing the strong racial segregation in the labor market and increasing white workers' incomes relative to those of black workers.[12] Not surprisingly, thus, this long history of white workers' racial privilege is the backdrop for present-day racial privilege. For example, in recent years many black workers have confronted informal job tracking favoring white workers, as well as informal discrimination in unionized and other blue-collar workplaces created or collaborated in by white workers. In examining such workplaces, numerous researchers have found that these discriminatory practices range from subtle to blatant harassment—such as putting hangman's nooses, hoods, or racist effigies at black workers' job positions—and that white managers often ignore these actions. By means of everyday discrimination, white workers often maintain their dominance of certain more desirable jobs in many work settings. As a result, black workers and other workers of color are frequently kept in a state of stress that may in turn keep them from performing as well as they might otherwise, or that forces them to quit—both of which responses mean more job opportunities, promotions, or other employment benefits for white workers.[13]

More Government Handouts for Whites

In the first decades of the twentieth century yet other major government-controlled resources were given away, or made available on reasonable terms, almost exclusively to white Americans. For example, the Air Commerce Act gave U.S. air routes to new companies, mainly those started by aviators who had been trained during World War I. During that war African Americans were not allowed into the segregated Army Air Corps, and thus had no opportunity to participate in this giveaway of major resources that over time also generated significant white wealth. Numerous other important economic resources and opportunities, such as access to government-controlled mineral resources and the radio and television airwaves, were similarly kept from African Americans, especially in the early twentieth century, by means of very overt racial discrimination.[14]

Similarly, during the 1930s and 1940s, numerous federal New Deal programs provided very discriminatory access to yet more important resources. As noted in Chapter 2, key government programs heavily favored white Americans. One of the most important subsidy programs was the Federal Housing Administration's (FHA's) loan insurance and related programs, later buttressed by veterans' housing programs. These enabled millions of whites to buy their first homes. Many of these whites accumulated enough home equity to use later on for start-up capital for businesses or funding advanced education for children and grandchildren. For many years the FHA worked with the white-dominated real-estate industry and white homeowners to make sure that black Americans and other Americans of color not only got much less government and private housing assistance than whites, but also had to reside in rigidly segregated communities. Other 1930s New Deal programs provided much important aid to white farmers, bankers, and business executives, enabling them to survive the Great Depression and, soon thereafter, to thrive during World War II and the post-war years. Their white descendants have greatly benefited, to the present day, from the great array of New Deal and post-war programs.[15]

Several historians have recently examined numerous New Deal and post-war programs, such as the FHA and veterans' housing programs, and have shown in detail how they were typically set up and administered in a highly discriminatory fashion. While many relief laws and government programs of the Great Depression and most of the post-war housing and veterans' programs looked non-discriminatory on their face, and sometimes African Americans did benefit from them, their routine administration was usually left in the hands of local white officials—a reality that the all-white southern contingent in Congress insisted upon. These local officials generally privileged white individuals and families in need, often to an extreme degree, and black individuals and families got far less government assistance under these programs than they deserved. In addition, some programs such as Social Security intentionally excluded certain lower-paid categories of workers, such as household workers and farm workers, job categories where a great many black Americans and other Americans of color worked. As Ira Katznelson has put it, the era of aggressive new public assistance programs from the 1930s to the 1960s was one when government "affirmative action was white." Even more dramatic is the fact that these government affirmative-action programs played the central role in creating the new post-war reality of a large white middle class.[16]

In addition, the growing number of federal government contracting programs after 1940 made contracts available more or less exclusively to white businesses. Firms owned by Americans of color were not allowed significant access to these contracts until the 1970s. In the decades just before and after World War II many government programs helped white builders, contractors, and other businesspeople to get a start and often to thrive. These included privileged access to building permits, licenses, and government franchises. Over the decades since, these and other multi-billion-dollar federal aid programs have helped to build up prosperity for many white businesses. This pattern of racial favoritism for white firms set up the framework for their domination of major business sectors in most U.S. counties and cities to the present day. Recall the research studies cited in Chapter 5 (pp. 173–174) that have shown that whites still dominate most business networks and get a much greater share of construction, goods, and services contracts from state and local governments than one might expect based just on the white percentage of all business firms.[17]

Cultural, Legal, and Political Advantages for Whites

Whites have profited not only economically but also educationally, politically, legally, and aesthetically from systemic racism. Whites have generally had privileged access to critical cultural and networking capital over the generations. As we have seen, white Americans have, on the whole, had much greater access to good educational programs than have black Americans for centuries. Until the 1960s, most colleges and universities—except historically black colleges—were all-white or nearly so. Today, white students' access to good college programs is still significantly greater than for black students—and unencumbered by the racist barriers black students currently face. For most of the years since public elementary and secondary schools were first created on a significant scale in the nineteenth century, they have been overtly segregated along racial lines. The period of active school desegregation was relatively brief, and increasing de facto segregation is increasingly the societal trend in the United States (see Chapter 5, pp. 174–176). Typically, all-white or mostly white public schools have better educational resources and facilities than schools composed predominantly of students of color. Moreover, once a family's children have access to good educational capital, they are more likely to be successful in securing good jobs and housing, and thus are more likely to be able to pass along substantial economic and cultural benefits to their descendants.

Generally speaking, much contemporary U.S. culture is still substantially shaped by the white population's European heritage. White views and values, especially those of Anglo-Protestant groups, have been determinative in U.S. political–economic and legal development. From the 1600s forward, European-origin whiteness has been the normative standard for much of what is valued in society. The dominant language has long been English, with the most privileged variant and accent being that of middle-class whites. (All people speak English with an accent.)

Those not from Europe, including Africans forced into the new country, have had to adopt the language of the dominant group. In addition, the core legal system is rooted substantially in the English legal system, and the country's capitalistic economy is heavily European in origin and values. The U.S. political system was also originally crafted using European (often English) political ideas about republicanism, branches of government, and limited democracy. Moreover, today this political system often does little to implement real democracy in its operations at state, local, and federal levels. Indeed, from the beginning the U.S. political system has allowed those with substantial money, usually well-off whites, to generally control the major political institutions.

In some recent analyses of U.S. society, there is a tendency to play down this white-European dominance in favor of a "melting pot" perspective that sees the central U.S. culture as a grand mixture with substantial input from many and diverse immigrant groups over several centuries, including Africans and other immigrants of color. However, apart from a few matters such as popular entertainment, music, certain sports, and, to some degree, religion, most of the U.S. culture and political economy is still heavily shaped by white Anglo-European values, practices, and arrangements.

Controlling U.S. Institutions: The Role of White Men

Not only have whites dominated the economic, political, legal, and educational values of this society, they have also been in firm control of the key roles and top positions in all the powerful institutions for centuries. In earlier chapters we have seen how this dominance was established, and then transmitted over generations. Today, all major large-scale institutions remain white-normed and white-framed in their internal sociocultural structures, and white individuals are mostly in command at and near the top.

Even after a few decades of affirmative action for Americans of color and white women, the overwhelming majority of those who run most of the powerful political, economic, and legal organizations in society are still white men. *One* major exception is the current U.S. president, the first American of color ever to hold that position. Recent research shows that there is a concrete ceiling that generally blocks black Americans, other Americans of color, and white women from many of the higher-level positions in the society. White men disproportionately control most powerful U.S. institutions—from an overwhelming majority of Fortune 1000 companies and elite universities, to the military branches, to federal and state legislatures. In most of these sectors they make up 75 to 100 percent of those in the very top positions, percentages greatly disproportionate considering that white men today make up less than one-third of the adult population.

Most higher-level executives in various business sectors are white men. We previously noted a large-scale study that found barely 1 percent of senior corporate executives were black women and about 3 percent were black men, while more than three-quarters were white men. Clear evidence of the corporate world's failure to promote meritorious black employees is the fact that so few Fortune 500 companies have ever had a black executive as the very top. In 2008 there were only five black CEOs. (There were seven Latino CEOs.) Indeed, only ten Fortune 500 companies have *ever* had a black CEO. In addition, recent studies of Fortune 500 corporate boards have found that about 8 percent of the boards' directors were African Americans. Note too that these studies have not reported on the power of these directors; many people are put on the boards for cosmetic reasons and have little influence on day-to-day operations.[18]

Interestingly, one recent psychological study has shown that those few black executives who do make it to the top of the most successful corporations tend to have disarming appearances and mannerisms. This study measured what researchers termed "babyface looks" (defined as rounded face, full cheeks, large forehead, small nose) and concluded that black top executives "who rated high on the babyface scale worked for companies that ranked higher in the Fortune 500 and had higher annual revenues than blacks with more mature faces." The opposite was true for the white executives studied. The more "mature," older, and assertive the whites looked, the more likely they were to head the highest-ranked companies. Once again, the white frame's stereotypes of the black man evidently come into play.[19]

In recent years numerous white commentators have made much of the idea they call "reverse discrimination," which is a white-created term. Some surveys indicate that many whites now believe that discrimination against people of color has declined dramatically and that whites, especially men, are now major victims of discrimination. While some white men in historically white institutions do occasionally lose a few opportunities for hiring or advancement because of modest remedial programs—usually to well-qualified white women or people of color—the available societal statistics refute the common notion of widespread reverse discrimination. We have examined numerous data on white male dominance previously, and we can recall here the striking reality of white men still making up nearly 90 percent of the CEO positions at Fortune 500 companies, a much greater proportion than one would expect given their percentage of the population. Indeed, the most successful "quota" program in U.S. history appears to be the one that sees to it that white men continue to dominate very disproportionately most powerful U.S. institutions. Over more than four decades now, all government and private antidiscrimination programs put together have brought rather modest changes in executive composition and decisionmaking in most of these powerful institutions, where there is still heavy white-male dominance.

White men also dominate among those Americans with the greatest amounts of wealth. A 2008 *Forbes* study of the wealthiest 400 Americans found that very few were not white. Only one (Oprah Winfrey) was black, and women of all backgrounds made up just 10.5 percent. The overwhelming majority were white men, the wealthiest of whom was still Microsoft's Bill Gates, worth $57 billion. Most had inherited substantial money capital and/or significant cultural capital, such as access to a very good education and important social networks, that enabled them to move up economically over their lifetimes. The majority of wealthy whites do not now, and did not in the past, pull themselves up just by hard work. Some significant portion of these whites' inherited economic and cultural wealth likely originated from various mechanisms of undeserved enrichment secured by earlier white generations during the periods of slavery and/or legal segregation, as well as during the contemporary era of still prevalent racial discrimination.[20]

White Women: Second-Class Citizens in White America

White women are significantly more common than Americans of color at the top of major corporations and many other powerful organizations, as we see in the recent count of about 40 white women as Fortune 500 CEOs. (This compares with about 19 Fortune 500 CEOs who were in that same count black, Latino, or Asian American women and men.) Yet these modest numbers make it quite clear that white women have not penetrated these decisionmaking heights in anything akin to proportionate numbers. Gender discrimination remains central to this society, and changes have come slowly. As we have seen previously, white women have historically played a much less central role than white men in creating and maintaining our ongoing system of racial oppression. No women were among the prominent founders of this nation. While white women were not explicitly singled out for gender oppression in the new U.S. Constitution, they were seen by most male founders as quite unequal by nature and thus in need of male control. State and federal laws made sure that they were second-class citizens under a father's or other male's control. In the colonies, and later the United States, white women had certain legal rights, in contrast to the situations of black men and women. Constitutionally, they were "free persons" and thus had limited rights, albeit those allowed by white men who made the laws. In contrast, as the *Dred Scott* case (1857) made clear, black Americans "had *no rights* that the white man were bound to respect."[21]

Moreover, from the late 1600s to the 1860s white women in the upper-income group sometimes inherited significant resources, including on occasion enslaved African Americans gained under inheritance laws. In subsequent decades, many white women at various class levels have directly benefited from the labor of exploited black servants (usually women) working in their homes. Over several generations, many white women have also benefited to some degree from the undeserved enrichment of their families through the discriminatory arrangements of slavery, legal segregation, and contemporary racial discrimination. For centuries white women's access to economic and cultural resources, privileges, and opportunities—though significantly restricted by patriarchy and sexism—has on the average been significantly greater than that of black women or men. Still, we should keep in mind that it is white men who have played the most central role, to the present day, in creating, shaping, and maintaining the ongoing system of racial oppression.[22]

The Many Costs of Racial Oppression

Unjust impoverishment and the struggle against everyday racism for black Americans and numerous other Americans of color are the other side of the unjust enrichment and enhanced opportunities for white Americans. In earlier discussions we have examined many of the burdens and barriers that constitute racial oppression, particularly the discriminatory barriers in employment, housing, education, law, politics, and public accommodations. For African Americans this recurring and widespread discrimination has many costs and consequences—not only economic costs but also psychological, physical, family, and community costs.

Substantial Economic Costs

In recent decades, U.S. government census data have shown the median family income of black families to be consistently in the range of 55 to 62 percent of the median family income of white families. During the late 1980s and into the 1990s this percentage declined. In the late 1990s black median income was still about 60 percent of white median income, and today it is only about 62 percent. Current data indicate that black households still have a much lower median household income ($33,916) than white households ($54,920). Consider too the cumulative impact of such family inequality. Examining data for the generation of Americans now entering retirement years, researchers have estimated that the average white baby-boom family will earn $450,000 *more* than the average black baby-boom family over their respective lifetimes of work, assuming about 45-year work lives. This is one major economic cost of being black in the United States.[23]

In addition, the percentage of Americans in poverty remains high in the United States, nearly 12 percent in the most recent data. And this percentage is much higher for black (and Latino) Americans than for whites. Black families face poverty at a much greater rate (24.5 percent) than white families (8.2 percent), and also an unemployment rate much higher than for whites. Black workers are often among the first laid off during economic downturns and among the last to be recalled. Coupled with a high unemployment rate is a depression-like underemployment rate. In recent decades this rate has been one-third or more of black workers in many areas, much greater than for whites. Underemployment includes workers without jobs and those who can only find part-time work or who make very low wages.[24]

One dramatic indicator of generations of privileged white access to material and educational resources is seen in measures of family wealth. Recall the Federal Reserve data from Chapter 1 (p. 20) that showed very large differentials in wealth between white and black families. In the 2007 data the median net worth for white families was $170,400, compared with a median net worth of just $17,000 for black families and just $27,800 for all families of color. These data indicated increased wealth inequality compared to a few years earlier. The wealth of white families is about ten-times that of black families, with much of that wealth consisting of housing equities built up over generations of discrimination severely limiting black access to housing and other socioeconomic resources.[25] In addition, white families are far more likely than black families and many other families of color to have significant wealth in such important things as interest-bearing bank accounts and stock in companies. Even white families in the lowest income fifth of white families have greater wealth (net worth) than black families with substantially higher incomes— because of the white wealth advantages that have accumulated over many generations. Thomas Shapiro has summarized the great impact of this accumulating wealth: "Wealth is critical to a family's class standing, social status, whether they own or rent housing, the kind of community they live in, and the quality of their children's schools."[26]

A National Urban League *State of Black America* report has summarized the current state of the socioeconomic conditions faced by black Americans: they are "twice as likely as whites to be unemployed, three times more likely to live in poverty and more than six times as likely to be incarcerated." This report uses an Equality Index, a statistical summary measure of white–black inequalities in the economy, education, health, community engagement, and the justice system. Their 2009 summary index shows a little decline in the overall socioeconomic position of African Americans, relative to whites—71.5 percent in 2008 to 71.1 percent in 2009. The trend line over the previous five years shows an even greater relative decline. In their data the economic area is the one "with the greatest degree of inequality (from 57.6% in 2008 to 57.4% in 2009), followed by social justice (from 62.1% to 60.4%), health (from 73.3% to

74.4%), education (from 78.6% to 78.5%) and civic engagement (from 100.3% to 96.3%)."[27]

Some of these income and wealth-inequality data do briefly appear in the mass media, but there is usually no attempt to understand the role of centuries of systemic racism in creating much of this racial inequality. Instead, many public commentators once again argue that black workers and their families are mostly to blame. They suggest that black Americans and certain other Americans of color are not working hard enough, are culturally handicapped, or do not have the intelligence to do better.

The Value of Stolen Labor

Gaining an adequate explanation for such large racial inequalities requires much deeper probing. As we saw previously, undeserved impoverishment for blacks and undeserved advantages for whites began at an early point in this country's history. Much of the economic advantages and prosperity of whites in earlier centuries came directly or indirectly from the labor of enslaved Africans and African Americans, or from the country's general economic development spurred by profits from slave farms, slave plantations, and the slave trade.

James Marketti once estimated the dollar value of the labor taken from enslaved African Americans from 1790 to 1860 at, depending on the historical assumptions, from at least $0.7 billion to as much as $40 billion (in 1983 dollars). This is what black individuals and their families lost in income because they did not have control of their own labor under slavery. Taking into account the lost interest on this stolen wealth from then to the present day, the economic loss for black Americans is then put at from $2.1 to $4.7 trillion (in 1983 dollars). Extending this calculation for the entire period from the beginning of enslavement in the 1600s, and calculating it in terms of current-year dollars, would certainly increase the dollar value of this lost wealth to a much higher figure.[28]

After the Civil War, newly freed black Americans faced continuing economic oppression. There were proposals in Congress to give those recently freed some land—the famous "forty acres and a mule"—to begin new lives. Yet relatively few black families got access to the land promised, and inequality in agricultural land was a major cause of persisting racial inequalities after the Civil War. Using antiblack violence, as well as Jim Crow laws, whites in southern and border states generally denied black individuals and families access to good land, fair credit arrangements, political power, and educational and other cultural capital. The costs of Jim Crow segregation for black workers included not only little access to economic capital over the next several generations—even in the form of small businesses or farms—but also the lower wages stemming from widespread discrimination. White planters extracted much profit from the highly exploited labor of their black tenant farmers and sharecroppers. Under the burden of Jim Crow, economic losses were again high. Researchers have estimated the costs of the labor market discrimination against black Americans for the years 1929 to 1969 (in 1983 dollars) at $1.6 trillion.[29] Calculating the cost of racial discrimination for a longer period, from the end of slavery in 1865 to 1968, the end of legal segregation, and putting it into current-year dollars would likely increase the cost estimate to far more. Moreover, since the end of official segregation black Americans have suffered additional economic losses. For the year 1979 alone, one estimate of the cost of continuing racial discrimination in employment was put at $123 billion for black workers. Recall too the recent Urban Institute estimate that black workers today still lose more than $120 billion annually because of employment discrimination.[30]

A simple total of the current economic worth of all black labor stolen by whites through the means of slavery, segregation, and contemporary discrimination is huge—perhaps six to ten trillion dollars. This latter figure is staggeringly high, indeed about 70 percent of the Gross Domestic Product (GDP) generated in the United States in a recent year. In addition, these monetary figures do not include other major costs—the great pain and suffering inflicted, the physical abuse, or the many untimely deaths. Consideration of this massive non-economic damage needs to be figured into the ultimate social cost accounting for this country's racial oppression targeting African Americans. In addition, adding in the economic and non-economic costs inflicted on other Americans of color would raise the total social cost of systemic racism to an even higher figure.

Economic Consequences of Racial Barriers

In order to build up successful families and provide for children, parents need access to significant economic, educational, and other social resources. Exclusion from even one major opportunity to secure resources can have both immediate and long-term consequences for the families involved. Stephen DeCanio has developed an economic model that suggests that African Americans who had no significant material property because of slavery and who were emancipated without the promised arable land were as a group fated to endure major long-term economic inequality compared to whites even if they had experienced favorable employment conditions, which they did not. The initial and significant gap in this land access "would have produced by itself most of the gap in income between blacks and white Americans throughout the late nineteenth and early twentieth centuries."[31] This huge racial disparity has passed along to subsequent generations, to the present day. The long-term impact of initial racial inequality in agricultural resources would, as David Swinton has noted, "prevent attainment of racial equality even if current discrimination ended and blacks and whites had identical tastes and preferences."[32] Not only were black families substantially excluded from homestead lands by law or white violence, they were also forced into racially segregated schools, workplaces, and residential areas. Legal segregation in the South and de facto segregation in the North generally kept black families from generating the socioeconomic resources necessary to compete effectively with whites over many lifetimes.

The impact continues into the present. Consider a black person and a white person trying to set up a new business today. Often such entrepreneurs must draw on family savings, such as a house equity, or borrow from relatives and local banks. The black entrepreneur is much less likely than a white entrepreneur to have significant personal or family resources to draw on because his or her family has been unable to build up economic resources due to generations of systemic racism. A black entrepreneur is more likely to face discrimination in getting bank loans today. (Recall the discussion of discrimination in lending in Chapter 5, pp. 160–173.) Once white families garner some economic resources, they may invest those assets and profit from what might be called the "money value of time." Having significant economic and other family resources, often unjustly gained because of systemic racism, over some period of time allows for the further enhancement of these family resources. In the past, however, the black businessperson's parents and grandparents likely faced harsh segregation, which cut down sharply on what they could earn, save, and pass on to the later generations.

Even if the black entrepreneur's predecessors had been able to start a small business, they would very likely have been limited to black customers and would have been located in a black community. Such a business would probably have had no name recognition outside the black community. Jim Crow discrimination and segregation thus reduced business visibility, especially with non-black customers, and the effects would persist into later generations of business operation. This has not been a problem confronting most white businesses. Lack of capital or name recognition stemming from past racial discrimination means that today the black business may well have much more trouble than an otherwise comparable white firm in getting new customers and employees. The removal of legal segregation in the 1960s thus did not get rid of its substantial and lasting impact in the current economy.[33]

Today there is relatively little monetary inheritance across the generations for most black families. The majority of those securely in the middle class today are first generation, so they have not had the time to accumulate substantial assets for two or more generations like the majority of white middle-class families. Historically, a great many whites have gotten some material advantages in terms of the transmission of material assets in the form of homes, savings, land, securities, or small businesses. Many have also gotten other significant advantages, such as access to quality education, that can translate into material advantages. Centuries of discrimination in employment and housing mean that today black families are significantly less likely to own their homes than whites. Discriminatory practices in home sales, loans, and insurance have long limited the ability of black Americans to build up housing equities that whites have often used to start a business or help the next generation in their families to get a better education.[34]

Recent research has shown that the current white–black differential in wealth is *not* the result of differences in savings rates, but exists because black individuals generally inherit little or nothing from their families. Whites are much more likely to inherit significant wealth from parents, and much of this is again in home equities, which stem from the ability of previous generations to purchase homes because they had better jobs and incomes and generally did not face discrimination by white real-estate agents and banking officials. Melvin Oliver and Thomas Shapiro summarize the impact of various affirmative-action programs for whites, some of which we have noted previously:

> There is a long and rich history that includes the homestead act of 1862 and the land-grant colleges of the 19th century, Federal Housing Administration loans, Social Security, and the GI Bill, as well as the continuous benefits of tax codes that subsidize homeownership, property, and wealth. America's broad middle class accumulates two thirds of its wealth through homeownership enabled more by federal actions than private thrift, savings, and investments. The reach of these social-investment actions, however, by both intent and omission, has not been extended to low and moderate-income families, and only barely to Hispanics and African Americans.[35]

Interestingly, in recent opinion polls whites often say that black Americans are now roughly equal with them, as though these whites do not or cannot see the many barriers and costs of racism faced today by black Americans (see Chapter 4). However, at some level or in some settings, most whites seem to be aware that being black in America involves major personal, family, and economic costs. For example, political scientist Andrew Hacker reports on asking white college students how much they would seek in compensation if they were suddenly changed from white to black. Most white students indicated that "it would not be out of place to ask for $50 million, or $1 million for each coming black year."[36]

Additional Cultural Costs

From the first years of the colonial period to the present day, African Americans have taken much strength from their social and cultural heritage, one strongly rooted in extended families and friendship networks. The knowledge carried in these networks includes positive values and perspectives on life, as well as portraits of role models that buttress identity and self-respect. Black Americans have had to be like experienced anthropologists and know white society well in order to survive or thrive; they have had to be experts on how to respond to hostile white actions. Black American culture did not arise freely but under conditions of oppressive slavery, segregation, and contemporary discrimination. It thus has important elements of cultural resistance. While this home culture has many strengths, and draws on its African heritage, it also reflects the past and present exclusion of black Americans from the many privileges and resources available to whites, as well as the **forced assimilation** into Anglo-American ways often pressed on black Americans. Reflecting on earlier centuries, legal scholar Patricia Williams has concluded that black enslavement "was that of lost languages, cultures, tribal ties, kinship bonds, and even of the power to procreate in the image of oneself and not that of an alien master."[37] Because of this and the impact of later segregation and discrimination, full cultural decolonization is a major step yet to be taken for most Americans of African descent—a key argument made by many Afrocentric analysts.

In recent years some analysts have tried to counter arguments that racism is still systemic with the contention that the U.S. now has very much of a "rainbow culture." The suggestion is that many whites accept much of the music (for example, jazz and rap) and some other entertainment that has emerged from black communities. However, whites in decisionmaking positions, such as at the head of powerful media corporations, generally control the way in which black music and entertainment elements move into the white-dominated society and culture. For example, in its early stages after the 1960s civil rights movement rap (hip-hop) emerged as a type of urban protest music and commentary, as a type of resistance against a white-racist society, yet under the control of these media corporations much of this black cultural assertiveness has been significantly channeled, weakened, or watered down. As Ellis Cashmore put it, whites have converted much of black culture "into a commodity, usually in the interests of white-owned corporations" and "blacks have been permitted to excel in entertainment only on the condition that they conform to whites' images of blacks." Thus, many whites can feel good by accepting black achievements in music, entertainment, or sports. "Aspects of the black experience can be integrated into the mainstream and, with the advent of the mass media, consumed without even going near black people," Cashmore tells us. "Hit a button and summon the sounds and images of the ghetto."[38] This apparently respectful acknowledgment by whites of black cultural achievements usually conceals, just below the surface, old white-framed stereotypes of black Americans as entertaining, hypersexualized, thug-like, or marginal to the U.S. mainstream. In addition, much of what was once a protest music form, rap and hip-hop, is substantially altered, and no longer has the power of antiracist resistance that it once had.

The absorption of a few elements of a subordinated culture into the dominant culture does not mean much if there is little change in the fundamental aspects of the dominant culture and society, such as in its prevailing legal practices, discriminatory ways of employment, and discriminatory political and business practices. Under the contemporary regime of racism, African Americans are still pressured to assimilate and adapt in a more or less one-way fashion to the dominant white-controlled culture and institutions.[39]

The Broad Psychological Impact

Writing as Jim Crow desegregation was starting to decline, in the year before he was killed, Dr. Martin Luther King, Jr. contended that, if white racism is to be eradicated, then whites "must begin to walk in the pathways of his black brothers and feel some of the pain and hurt that throb without letup in their daily lives."[40] In much recent research many black Americans have indicated that they still feel like "outsiders" in the United States. The omnipresent reality of racial hostility and discrimination generates this distressed feeling. Racism is constructed not just in the framing in white minds, but also in the ways that whites regularly interact with black men, women, and children. Thus, when a black person enters an organization that is predominantly white or walks down a street where whites are numerous, "race" is seen and created in those specific places by recurring white animosities and actions. In interactions with whites, blacks are often excluded from full human recognition, important social positions, and significant societal rewards.[41]

Recurring racial discrimination can bring a significant psychological toll. For instance, few whites reflect on the impact of the defensive actions they often take when they are near black men. As mentioned earlier, frequently when a black man is near, white women will tightly clutch their purses and white women and men will take such defensive actions as getting out of elevators, crossing the street, or locking car doors. If such actions come to whites' attention, they tend to view them as "minimal slights." Yet these actions can have a negative and lasting impact, for the targeted black man will probably feel like an outcast or alien. At a minimum, every black person has to develop strategies to counter this daily psychological warfare by whites.[42] Contemporary social science has documented the severe negative effects that marginalization and dehumanization have on the physical and emotional health of human beings. Under slavery, segregation, and contemporary racism, recurring discrimination and degradation have brought onerous psychological and physical health burdens to many black Americans.

Recurring Challenges to Self-Confidence and Identity

The impact of everyday racism includes a range of psychological reactions—from anxiety and worry to depression, anger, and rage. In interviews with many African Americans, my colleagues and I have found that they often speak poignantly about the recurring impact of blatant and subtle racial discrimination on the self-esteem and self-confidence not only of themselves but also of friends and relatives. In recent research we have found that a great many African Americans, especially older women and men who had significant experience with Jim Crow, today suffer from something like the post-traumatic stress syndrome—with its pain, depression, and anxiety—that has been documented for military veterans of some U.S. wars.[43]

Many African Americans are especially concerned about the negative impact of racism on the youth. Psychologists have extensively examined the impact of racial stereotypes on student performance. In numerous studies by Claude Steele and his colleagues, black and white students have been given skills tests similar to the Graduate Record Examination (GRE). When this examination was presented to black students as a test of their "intellectual ability," they did less well on the tests than white students of comparable ability. In contrast, when the test was presented to the black students without the suggestion that it was a type of intelligence testing, they performed at a level similar to that of the white students. This is a situation of "stereotype threat," one where commonplace stereotypes are brought to the front of black students' minds. Stereotype threat can distract and create anxiety and self-consciousness that hurts test performance. If black students come to think that they are not as intelligent as whites, they may not perform as well as otherwise comparable white students. Stereotype threat has been found to be the most damaging to the performance of black students who strongly identified with the area of performance being tested. As Steele has noted, the stereotype threat in research settings has a short-run impact on test performance, yet in the longer term, recurring stereotype threats in society can seriously "undermine the identity" of those affected.[44]

Ours is still a society where the lack-of-intelligence stereotype is regularly pressed on black Americans and some other Americans of color in schools and through the media. Indeed, discussion of white–black "IQ" differentials reappears every few years, usually resurrected by conservative or uninformed whites like Nobel laureate James Watson, whose recent views we noted in Chapter 3 (p. 85). Spoken or written stereotypes, when repeated enough times, can have a negative impact, perhaps reducing a person's effort to achieve certain important personal or family goals. From cradle to grave, whites force black Americans to live out their lives under a constant bombardment of stereotype threats and, as a result, to create an important repertoire of psyche-saving measures to counter them.

Numerous neo-Marxist and feminist analyses have explained how those who are oppressed sometimes help to create or reproduce their own oppression. Caught in the vise of an oppressive society, those who are subjugated often internalize the negative views and stereotypes of their own group, an internalizing that can lead to low self-esteem and self-hatred.[45] This is true for class, gender, and racial oppression. Over time, many who are racially colonized come to accept, to some degree, the racist framing and rationalizations put out by the white colonizers. For example, one recent research study examined how black men and women were portrayed in various advertisements featured in two black-oriented magazines, *Jet* and *Essence.* The researchers found that both black men and women were portrayed positively and negatively in the magazines' advertisements. Most surprising perhaps was the extent to which numerous ads used negative black stereotypes from the white racial frame.[46] In order to survive, black Americans and other Americans of color must constantly battle not only the everyday discrimination of whites but also the racist imagery and questioning routinely placed in their own minds by long years of living in a racist system.

Rage and Energy Loss

Some time ago, psychiatrists William Grier and Price Cobbs examined the extent to which anger and rage among black Americans are created by the pervasiveness and complexities of everyday discrimination. Drawing on their own clinical interviews, they concluded that successful psychological counseling with black Americans must deal directly with this omnipresent discrimination. They concluded that black Americans

> bear all they can and, if required, bear even more. But if they are black in present-day America they have been asked to shoulder too much. They have had all they can stand. They will be harried no more. Turning from their tormentors, they are filled with rage.[47]

Today, anger and rage over white racism are still commonplace among black Americans. Overtly expressed or silent, this rage can lead to inner turmoil, emotional withdrawal, and serious physical problems.

The seriousness of black anger over discrimination is made clear in the following comments from an interview with the distinguished black professor whose quote opened this chapter. Replying to a question about the level of his anger (on a scale from one to ten) toward white racism, he answered:

> Ten! I think that there are many blacks whose anger is at that level. Mine has had time to grow over the years more and more and more until now I feel that my grasp on handling myself is tenuous. I think that now I would strike out to the point of killing, and not think anything about it. I really wouldn't care. Like many blacks you get tired, and you don't know which straw would break the camel's back.[48]

In his interview he made it clear that he gets most angry from observing the discrimination that white Americans of all ages constantly inflict on black young people.

Dealing with racism regularly entails an array of other psychological costs as well. For example, a rather vigilant, cautious, and defensive approach to life is usually necessary. Some psychologists have pointed out that to survive everyday racism a black person has to view every white person as "a potential enemy unless he personally finds out differently."[49] Recall too the opening chapter quote from the black professor that noted the energy loss imposed on black Americans. The latter must expend an enormous amount of energy defending themselves and their families from the assaults of blatant and subtle racism on a more or less daily basis.

Note too that the energy thus drained from black Americans can have major benefits for whites even beyond the immediate benefits of racial discrimination. Over their lifetimes white Americans on average have a major life-energy advantage, for they do not waste large amounts of time dealing with the impositions of antiwhite discrimination. As a consequence of the energy waste, black men, women, and children may not be able to achieve what they might otherwise have achieved; they may not have enough energy left after dealing with everyday racism to develop to their full human potential. This energy drain may also mean they do not have as much energy to put into their families, organizations, and communities as they might otherwise have had. In this way the negative impact of racism on an individual often has major societal consequences.

The Negative Impact on Physical Health

The stress, anger, and rage created by everyday racism can generate serious physical health consequences. When asked in interview studies about the costs of the discrimination they face, black respondents frequently cite a broad range of health problems—from hypertension and stress diabetes to stress-related heart and stomach conditions. Several studies have examined the relationship between experiences with discrimination and various diseases, especially stress-related diseases. For example, one recent study of a large sample of black women found modest statistical associations between breast cancer incidence and level of reported experience with racial discrimination. This relationship between cancer incidence and discrimination experience held true when other factors affecting cancer risk were controlled for, and the relationship was strongest for black women under age 50.[50]

One qualitative field study that my colleagues and I conducted involved focus group interviews with middle-class African Americans. Several participants gave details on how high blood pressure and other health problems were linked, at least in part, to everyday discrimination. One nurse in the Midwest commented on her body's reactions to a workplace with a hostile racial climate, saying:

> That's when I got high blood pressure. And my doctor.... I told him what my reaction, my body's reaction would be when I would go to this place of employment ... which was a nursing home. When I turned into the drive-way I got a major headache. I had this headache eight hours until I walked out that door leaving there. I went to the doctor because the headaches had been so continuously. And he said ... "You need to find a job because you do not like where you work." And within myself I knew that was true. But also within myself I knew I had to have a job because I had children to take care of. But going through what I was going through wasn't really worth it because I was breaking my own self down ... it was constant intimidation. Constant racism, but in a subtle way. You know, but enough whereas you were never comfortable.... And then I finally ended up on high blood pressure pills because for the longest, I tried to keep low. I tried not to make waves. It didn't work. I hurt me.[51]

Contemporary racism literally makes people sick. Like other research studies using in-depth interviews with black Americans, we found that they often associate the racial discrimination they encounter over a lifetime with such physical problems as chronic fatigue, back pain, insomnia, and recurring stomach problems and headaches. Discrimination has both physical and psychological impacts.

Much health research has focused on high blood pressure. In these contemporary studies most black respondents report significant problems with discrimination. However, the statistical relationship between reported discrimination and high blood pressure has varied, with some studies reporting a clear relationship between level of discrimination and high blood pressure, while others have not. One reason for the variability may be the way in which African Americans, especially of different ages, deal personally with and recall everyday discrimination. For example, one recent study found the highest blood pressure levels in older black adults who verbally reported the least discrimination. These researchers suggested that in this reporting of less discrimination there may be some internalized oppression going on—that is, some older respondents may be blaming themselves and view unfair treatment by whites as deserved or they may use denial of the discrimination they have faced as a personal coping strategy.[52]

Numerous studies are documenting the often severe impact of everyday racism on various other diseases for African Americans and, in a few cases, other Americans of color.[53] For example, one recent review article examined the various links between racial discrimination and the disparity in rates of heart disease for black and white Americans, with the former having substantially more heart problems, especially at younger ages, than the latter. The researchers suggest three kinds of impacts on heart disease from U.S. racism. They first note that institutionalized racism "can lead to limited opportunities for socioeconomic mobility, differential access to goods and resources, and poor living conditions," all of which have negative impacts on cardiovascular health. A second type of impact comes because of the stress that societal racism causes, which "can induce psycho-physiological reactions that negatively affect cardiovascular health." A third impact lies in the "negative self-evaluations of accepting negative cultural stereotypes as true (internalized racism)."[54] This study might also have added a note on the impact of the frequent discrimination that African Americans and other Americans of color face in dealing with white medical personnel (see Chapter 5, pp. 184–185).

Demographic data on longevity indicate the physical harshness of racism in cold statistical terms. As I noted previously, African Americans average significantly shorter lives than white Americans, which has been true for centuries. Historical studies indicate that most enslaved black Americans died by the age of 40, while on average white slaveholders lived more than 40 years. By 1900 the life expectancy for an average black person was still only about 32–35 years, about 16 years less than that for the average white person. Today, this black/white gap has closed significantly but is still rather large. The average black person has a life expectancy four to six years (varying by gender) less than the average white person. Among all major U.S. racial groups today, African Americans have the lowest life expectancy and highest death rates in numerous death categories. For many deceased African Americans, everyday racism could indeed be listed on their death certificates as a major cause of death.[55]

A Complex and Accumulating Burden

Thinking in terms of the complex and cumulative impacts, Rodney Coates describes everyday racism as a cage:

> To the casual observer, each wire does not appear to be sufficient in and of itself to retain the bird. But when viewed from either within or as a whole we see a finely constructed cage. The problem, from a pedagogical, policy, research, or activist perspective, is that we tend to concentrate on only one wire or phenomenon, removal of which leads to great anticipation that the war has been won. Unfortunately, while even more insidious wires are being constructed, the others are left intact.[56]

Repeated encounters with white-racist framing and racial mistreatment accumulate across many institutional arenas and over long periods of time. The lifetime number of such encounters for the average black adult is undoubtedly in the thousands. Moreover, the impact on an individual is usually much greater than what a simple summing of her or his experiences might suggest. The cumulative impact of psychological and physical problems directly or indirectly linked to everyday racism can likely be seen in the significant differentials in health and in life expectancy noted previously. The steady "acid rain" of racist encounters with whites can significantly affect not only one's psychological and physical health but also one's general perspective. Thus, research by Tyrone Forman indicates that African Americans locked into traditional "black jobs" report a weaker sense of efficacy and less satisfaction with the quality of their lives than those not thus segregated in these traditional jobs. Of course, most black Americans, even those not in traditional job categories, face recurring discrimination of a blatant, covert, or subtle type in various areas of life. Thus, a black American's life perspective must of necessity embed a repertoire of responses designed to counter the discriminatory actions of many whites.[57]

For many white commentators, the relatively little discrimination that remains in society is only a problem of individual bigots and localized impacts, which should only be dealt with on an individual basis. This view of contemporary racism is way off the mark. The assaults of blatant, covert, and subtle racism have strong effects not only on individual African Americans (and other Americans of color), but also on their larger social circles, for the reality and pain of discriminatory acts are usually shared with relatives and friends as a way of coping with such inhumanity. Over time the long-term pain and memory of one individual becomes part of the pain and collective memories of larger networks, extended families, and communities. This negative impact requires the expenditure of much individual, family, and community energy to endure the oppression and to develop strategies for fighting back.

The Price Whites Pay for Racism

Writing in a 1960s Supreme Court decision, Justice William O. Douglas argued that

> the true curse of slavery is not what it did to the black man, but what it has done to the white man. For the existence of the institution produced the notion that the white man was of superior character, intelligence, and morality.[58]

Thus, such white-supremacist thinking entails living a lie, for whites are not in fact superior in character, intelligence, or morality. This commonplace self-deception generally takes a corrupting toll on the souls of white Americans.

According to surveys cited previously, a majority of whites do not have much empathy for the suffering of those who face racial discrimination. For a great many whites, participation in racial discrimination, or winking at its practice by other whites, feeds a distancing of the racial others. This distancing in turn feeds further discrimination, alexithymia, or insensitivity. Thus, some analyses of corporate workplaces have concluded that discrimination by white male executives and managers often lies in their inability to deal well with any group—be it black or female—that is quite different socially from themselves. As a result of this social difference, there is an often unconscious failure to extend to the racialized others the same recognition of humanity they enjoy themselves.[59]

Living a Hypocritical Ethic

Traditionally optimistic approaches to racial matters have accented the egalitarian values supposedly held by the majority of white Americans. Some decades back, Gunnar Myrdal, a Swedish social scientist, and his U.S. colleagues conducted a major study of Jim Crow segregation, reported in the influential 1944 book, *An American Dilemma*. Representing the small liberal wing of the U.S. elite—the majority in that elite then supported Jim Crow—these progressive researchers argued that whites were under the spell of the American creed. This creed encompassed the "ideals of the essential dignity of the individual human being, of the fundamental equality of all men, and of certain inalienable rights to freedom, justice, and a fair opportunity."[60] As they saw it, this abstract equality ethic was in great tension with the society's Jim Crow segregation and other racist practices—thus the phrase "an American dilemma." Myrdal and associates saw the U.S. racial problem as solvable in principle because it was situated in whites' failure to live up to the American creed of equality. However, as sociologist Oliver C. Cox pointed out in a critical review at the time, these social scientists failed to understand that the problem of U.S. racism is not at base a problem of failed ideals, but rather of the social, economic, and political interests of whites as a racially privileged group. The vested interests of whites orient them to keeping a system of racial privilege and hierarchy that works to their advantage, and for most this outweighs their rhetorical commitments to equality and justice values.[61]

Myrdal and his associates were right that the reality of white racism has kept the United States from realizing the grand rhetorical ideals that for centuries whites have proclaimed to be important: equality, fairness, and justice. Today, as in the past, the majority of whites have at best a limited commitment to these equality and justice ideals in their everyday practices. They seem to wish these ideals to be implemented mainly for themselves, but not aggressively for the racialized others. The evidence presented in this book strongly suggests that most whites do not yet wish to see such principles actively incorporated into a thoroughly reconstructed U.S. society.[62]

Suffering for the Racist System

Some of the price that systemic racism has demanded from whites can be calculated in lives. For example, the slavery system not only cost millions of African and African American lives over the course of its bloody existence, but it also took some white lives. Being a white sailor on slave ships or a white overseer on slave plantations was often a dangerous job, as those enslaved sometimes lashed out at or killed their immediate oppressors. Slaveholders sometimes lost their lives as well, or their plantation houses and fields were burned to the ground by those enslaved. The Civil War, the "war over slavery," took 620,000 lives on both sides, more than all other U.S. wars taken together. African American soldiers died in significant numbers fighting against slavery and for the Union, but most of those soldiers killed and maimed were ordinary white farmers and workers.[63]

Moreover, white farmers and workers who have long accepted the psychological wage of white superiority are much less likely to organize effectively with farmers and workers of color. For centuries, this lack of united organization has meant less desirable working and living conditions for ordinary Americans, including white Americans. Today, the impact of historical Jim Crow segregation can still be seen in continuing tensions and divisions between many white workers and workers of color. In various areas of the country many white workers are still slow to organize aggressively with black workers and other workers of color. Indeed, many whites still do not have a strong class consciousness that might enable them to better understand their own economic difficulties in this capitalistic society. Even in the twenty-first century, racial consciousness and acceptance of the psychological wage of whiteness are still dominant for the majority of white workers. When white workers have refused to organize aggressively with workers of color against exploitative employers, they have often received less in the way of wage and workplace improvements than they might otherwise have secured.

Recall too that, before and after the 1860s Civil War, ordinary whites continued to pay a heavy political price for structural racism. In creating an undemocratic society where barbaric violence against black Americans was enshrined in laws, such as fugitive slave laws, or legitimated by informal practice, such as thousands of brutal lynchings, whites lost some liberty as well. This was especially true for southern and border states with large numbers of enslaved black Americans—where the system of social control for enslaved blacks spilled over into greater political inequality for less-powerful whites than in the North. In these states the dominant political arrangements, for whites as well as blacks, were authoritarian—with elite-dominated, one-party political systems the general rule. The autocratic white elites dominating local and state governments were typically uninterested in providing adequate social-welfare institutions, such as public health programs, public schools, and public colleges, for ordinary whites or blacks.

Today, southern states still reflect this racist heritage in many ways. As a group, these states not only have larger proportions of poverty-stricken citizens but also generally weaker public schools and universities, public health programs, and other important public programs providing for the general welfare of citizens than do the northern states as a group. Inferiority in public services affects the white, black, and other citizens of these states in very significant ways. The weak public sector is one of the continuing legacies of the authoritarian eras of racialized slavery and Jim Crow segregation—and of the openly racist, one-party governments in place in most southern states until the 1970s. In addition, the intense political conservatism of the majority of southern white voters today is in substantial part a lingering consequence of the South's racist past (see Chapter 8, pp. 264–265).[64]

The Costs of Social Isolation

Today white and black Americans are, as we have documented previously, largely segregated in terms of residence and neighborhood, a de facto segregation largely maintained by whites. This racial segregation has had severe consequences for black Americans, limiting access to jobs and services. It has also had some negative consequences for whites who have fled the central cities and moved to distant suburbs, frequently for clearly racist reasons. In the process white families have generally paid a price in terms of higher housing costs, long-distance commuting, pollution from automobiles, and problems associated with metropolitan growth and central city decline. This growth is costly in terms of infrastructural costs—for transportation, water, and sewage systems—that increase greatly with sprawling suburban and exurban development. When the economic health of central cities declines significantly, this can have a significantly negative impact on inner-ring white suburbs, which often lose jobs and businesses as well.

Whites also pay for continuing racism in elevated levels of racialized fear and ignorance. Recall the Chicago study of two adjacent suburbs, one white and one black (Chapter 4, p. 130). Whites there were found to reside in an isolated bubble where they were generally able to live out their lives with few experiences that enabled them to get to know black Chicagoans. They were often fearful of their black counterparts because they had had few contacts with them. Such social isolation is serious because it means that whites with greater privileges and power do not have the experience necessary to view other Americans with accuracy and sensitivity. Most do not understand, nor wish to understand, the oppressive reality and experiences of black Americans and other Americans of color. Given this lack of understanding, it is easy for whites to see black Americans as quite different. Gary Orfield suggests that whites growing up in suburban enclaves have "no skills in relating to or communicating with minorities."[65] In the future, as the country becomes ever-more diverse and multiracial, this white orientation will become a major disadvantage for social interaction. In addition, such white isolation will be ever-more of a handicap as the United States becomes more involved in international trade and diplomacy in a world where the leadership is becoming much more diverse and where non-European nations are becoming ever-more powerful economically and politically.

Denying Deep Interracial Realities

There is a deep secret about the nature of the so-called "whites" that few so named wish to confront. The secret is that many "whites" are *black*, and that most "blacks" are *white*. That is, many white and black Americans have *both* European and African ancestry. Indeed, many black Americans have as much European ancestry as they do African ancestry. One major source of this mixed heritage is the many thousands of instances of white men coercing and raping black women during centuries of slavery and segregation. Indeed, if one reverses the infamous one-drop-of-blood rule, which has long categorized any American with a little African ancestry as "black," then those with *any* European ancestry should by the same rule be "white." Sally Hemings, the famous enslaved servant of Thomas Jefferson, was at least three-quarters European in her ancestry (see Chapter 2, p. 41). It is likely that many of her (and Jefferson's) descendants have passed in society as white. Many of her descendants who have been taken as black have had white cousins. At least three-quarters of African Americans, it has been roughly estimated, have at least one European ancestor somewhere back in time. By an inverted one-drop-of-blood rule, they too are "white."[66]

In addition, estimates are that at least 5 percent (perhaps 20 percent) of white Americans have some African or African American ancestry gained now over many generations. In addition to those whites whose ancestors were African but who were able to pass into the white community, there were some European immigrants who came to the United States with African ancestry—especially immigrants from Spain and Portugal and other parts of southern Europe. Whites with African ancestry have included prominent Americans. Among them is Jacqueline Kennedy Onassis, who has been celebrated in the media as a paramount symbol of white womanhood. Another is the actor Humphrey Bogart, who is regularly treated as a paramount example of white masculinity.[67]

Several recent books and a documentary by white and black researchers have shown that today many white families, especially in the South, have black ancestors and relatives. However, many of these white families do not recognize, or have intentionally rejected, their black ancestors and contemporary black relatives. These books report that some whites with whom the authors have talked were quick to deny the documented cross-racial linkages of their ancestors. Once again, collective forgetting and denying are crucial ways in which whites have resolved the internal tension between the ideals of social justice and equality and the reality of racist oppression, including that tension present in their own ancestry and kinship networks.[68]

Once the fact that most black Americans have some European ancestry and many white Americans have some African ancestry is made clear, one can perceive how profound the pathology of racism is for white Americans. Systemic racism inclines whites to see what is *not* there— that is, white racial purity—and to not see what *is* there—that is, white multiraciality. This failure to see what is there afflicts not only whites with black ancestry but also many other whites. Examples of the latter include the white historians and other intellectuals who long denied Thomas Jefferson's multiracial descendants because they believed Jefferson was "too moral" to have transgressed the racial–sexual boundary in the case of the young enslaved teenager Sally Hemings.

One can push the argument about the African linkages of white Americans farther back into human history. Archaeological research indicates that the earliest members of *Homo sapiens* evolved in Africa. If one goes back far enough, *all people* now living have African ancestors. Indeed, all living humans are distant cousins. However, this point about common African origins and ancestry is rarely noted by white Americans. It would appear that by negatively framing or attacking black people, many of those who see themselves as "white" are thereby negatively framing or attacking themselves, their own kin, and their own family tree.[69]

Conclusion

Systemic racism has had, and currently has, profound human consequences. This is regularly recognized by international agencies. United Nations reports calculate a Human Development Index (HDI). The HDI is an evaluation of quality of life and incorporates data on income, health, and education indicators for various countries and for subgroups within these countries. For 177 countries examined in the most recent (2008) index, the United States ranked only fifteenth in terms of its overall quality of life. One reason for this is the condition of certain Americans of color in the United States. A similar index, the American Human Development Index, recently rated quality-of-life statistics for black Americans, Latinos, Native Americans, Asian Americans, and whites. White Americans and Asian Americans ranked at the top on this quality-of-life index, while African Americans, Native Americans, and Latinos ranked much lower. The quality of life for black Americans as a group remains relatively low, and that of white Americans quite high, by national and international standards.[70] As we have seen previously, black families today average about 62 percent of what white families earn and survive on about 10 percent of the wealth of average white families. As individuals, they can expect to live four to six years less than whites. These are the severe long-term costs of systemic racism.

Even these damning data tell only part of the story. To these statistics must be added centuries of uncounted pain, suffering, health damage, and rage over injustice. Only by adding all these important factors together can one assess accurately the long-term impact of slavery, segregation, and continuing racism. The total cost of nearly four centuries of systemic racism has been extraordinarily high—one likely reason the majority of white Americans spend much effort in denying the reality and/or causes of current racial inequality in the United States.

While whites as a group do pay some price for the centuries-old system of U.S. racism, that price pales when put up against that paid by African Americans and numerous other groups of color. They typically pay a direct, overt, heavy, immediately painful, and ever accumulating price for white racism, while white Americans pay a more indirect, usually unseen, and long-term price. Moreover, most whites get very substantial advantages and privileges from the operation of systemic racism.

7
Systemic Racism
Other Americans of Color

Recently, Southern Poverty Law Center (SPLC) researchers interviewed 500 working-class Latino Americans in several towns and cities in Tennessee, North Carolina, Louisiana, Georgia, and Alabama. These Latinos reported much mistreatment, mostly from whites:

> In Tennessee, a young mother is arrested and jailed when she asks to be paid for her work in a cheese factory. In Alabama, a migrant bean picker sees his life savings confiscated by police during a traffic stop. In Georgia, a rapist goes unpunished because his 13-year-old victim is undocumented.

Anti-Latino hostility and discrimination were perpetrated by numerous other whites as well:

> [Latinos] are routinely cheated out of their earnings and denied basic health and safety protections. They are regularly subjected to racial profiling and harassment by law enforcement.... And they are frequently forced to prove themselves innocent of immigration violations, regardless of their legal status. This treatment—which many Latinos liken to the oppressive climate of racial subordination that blacks endured during the Jim Crow era—is encouraged by politicians and media figures who scapegoat immigrants and spread false propaganda. And as a result of relentless vilification in the media, Latinos are targeted for harassment by racist extremist groups, some of which are directly descended from the old guardians of white supremacy.[1]

While the West and Southwest have traditionally been the home for most Latinos, the Latino population in the South has grown rapidly in recent years. As we move well into the twenty-first century, the Latino residents of a supposedly liberalized South still face much racial hostility and discrimination, most it from whites thinking and acting out of an anti-Latino subframe of the white racial frame. That centuries-old white frame, central to antiblack thinking from the days of slavery to the present, has been expanded by whites since the mid-nineteenth century to cover Latino immigrants and other immigrants of color, as well as their numerous descendants.

Foundational and Systemic Racism: A Brief Review

In recent years some scholars and other analysts have argued that social science researchers, government agencies, and the media give (1) far too little attention to the racial histories and discriminatory situations of groups such as Latino, Asian, and Native Americans and (2) too much attention to the racial history and current situation of African Americans.[2] On the first point, they are correct, for a review of current research and policy literatures reveals that these Americans of color have not received nearly the research or public policy analysis and attention that they deserve, especially given their often long struggles with white racism in this society.

However, on the second point, they are generally incorrect. Much more in-depth attention needs to be given by researchers and policymakers to the history and contemporary situation of African Americans. As we have seen in previous chapters, a comprehensive understanding of the racial situations of all Americans of color, those who are black and those who are not, requires digging deeply into U.S. history to uncover the system of racial oppression in the very foundation of the nation created by Europeans and European Americans in the seventeenth and eighteenth centuries. White elites and the white rank-and-file were central to an extensive land theft and enslavement process from the first decades of European colonization. By the middle of the seventeenth century those enslaved, mostly African Americans, were firmly positioned and viewed by European Americans and their new legal system as chattel property. This bloody white-on-black enslavement, coupled with the genocidal seizure of Native American lands, was well-institutionalized and early rationalized in an evolving and increasingly extensive white racial framing of society. Thus, white-on-black oppression has been a central reality of this society from its first century. This system of antiblack oppression, now for centuries, has penetrated every major area of this society, and thus has shaped the lives of Americans of all racial backgrounds.

African Americans have played no role in creating the dominant system of racial oppression, except to be its constant targets and resisters. And they have had no role in creating the dominant racial frame rationalizing this oppression, although they had regularly resisted and protested that framing and the systemic racism of which it is part. Today, as in the past, how most of these racial patterns are implemented, named, and discussed is largely controlled by white elites, including those in the U.S. media and in higher education. The U.S. reality is a centuries-old system of racial oppression that is rationalized by what is best termed a "white racial paradigm" or a "white racial frame." As I have shown previously, this centuries-old white frame includes not only racist ideas and stereotypes, but also racist images, emotions, and narratives involving both white Americans and various Americans of color.

This longstanding structure of white-on-black oppression has regularly been extended by whites for each new non-European group, such as the Latinos noted in the opening of this chapter, those who have mostly come into the U.S. sphere of direct domination since the nineteenth century. Thus, U.S. society is not a multiplicity of disconnected racisms directed at peoples of color. The structure of racial domination initially developed for enslaving African Americans and killing off or driving away Native Americans was later extended by descendants of the U.S. founders for the oppression of other non-European groups. From the mid-nineteenth century to the present day, numerous other groups of non-Europeans—such as Chinese, Japanese, Mexican, and Puerto Rican Americans—have been brought into this highly racialized U.S. system, often to be exploited for their labor. White elites and the white public have long dominated and evaluated later non-European entrants coming into the United States from within the previously established and highly imbedded system of antiblack oppression and its centuries-old white racial framing.[3]

The Scope of White-on-Black Oppression

Let us review very briefly a few important aspects of this white-on-black oppression in order to recall why it is so central to the experiences of all Americans, including those entering in later centuries. The whites who crafted the system of racial oppression were most concerned with the "black race within our bosom," to use founder James Madison's phrase. African Americans were the only group brought in large numbers to North America in chains and were the only group explicitly singled out several times in the U.S. Constitution for coercive control and subordination. They were the main group incorporated into the economic and social center of the new society as chattel property from the first century of colonial development. They were placed in a position at the economic center because their labor was used to create much of the economic development and prosperity of the new North American nation. They were the first group explicitly viewed by colonial and U.S. legal systems as having no rights whatsoever, as the 1857 *Dred Scott* decision made clear.

White-on-black oppression extended beyond the economy. It destroyed cultures, families, and heritages. During slavery and Jim Crow segregation many black women were sexually assaulted by white men. The children that resulted, and most of their descendants, were classified as black under the white-racist rule of descent. African Americans are the largest racial or ethnic group in North American history to involuntarily lose substantial control even over their own procreation—the largest group whose actual physical makeup was significantly determined over time by the coercive control and sexual assaults of many white men. No group has lost so much of its home country ties and cultural heritage (see Chapter 6, p. 206). In their pioneering analysis, Michael Omi and Howard Winant have argued that the U.S. social system has seen multiple and overlapping "racial formations" that have evolved historically.[4] While this is an important insight, these multiple racial formations are *not* all of equal significance in the past or present development of this society. The system of white-on-black oppression is very old, deeper in its structure, and more foundational, while other racist arrangements, structures, and interpretations have been greatly shaped by that system and are thus linked in many ways to it.

Timing and Size

The time of entry, size, distribution, and economic importance of non-European groups have made a difference in the character of their racist incorporation by whites into the society. Note the extent, scale, and location of the oppression of Africans and African Americans over several centuries. Because of their early centrality to the North American economic system, African Americans have been more at the core of the white-dominated society than smaller or more regionalized groups. Today, as in the past, sizeable numbers of African Americans are found in more areas of the United States than any other large non-European group.

Viewed historically, black Americans have been oppressed much longer by whites than any other group except Native Americans. Over nearly four centuries whites have routinely stolen much of the value of black labor under slavery, segregation, and contemporary racial discrimination. Moreover, the extremely large number of black Americans who were, and are, oppressed underscores the central significance of white-on-black oppression. Between 1619 and 1865 approximately six to seven million black Americans lived under conditions of slavery in North America.[5] Moreover, between 1619 and today several tens of millions of black Americans have lived in this country—and thus have had their labor taken and their lives burdened and truncated by slavery, segregation, and contemporary discrimination. The total number historically is larger than for any of the other groups that have suffered racialized oppression in this country.[6]

Another sign of the centrality of white-on-black oppression is the high level of white effort and energy put into maintaining it. From the first decades of colonialism, black Americans have been at the core of the racist system because they are the group whose subjugation has been given the greatest attention. Over four centuries now, white Americans have devoted enormous amounts of energy to oppressing black Americans—initially for labor reasons and later for a range of economic, social, and ideological reasons. Indeed, in the U.S. Civil War many thousands of southern whites gave their lives to maintain the slavery system. In contrast, whites as a group have, to this point in U.S. history, put less time and physical and mental energy into exploiting and oppressing groups such as Asian and Latino Americans, if only because the latter have been in this country in very large numbers for shorter periods of time.[7]

Once systemic racism was established, substantial individual and collective resistance by black Americans forced whites to put even more effort into maintaining and periodically reshaping white-on-black oppression. Thus, African Americans were central to the two largest and most successful antiracist movements in U.S. history—that of the abolitionists from the 1830s to the 1860s, and that of the civil rights movements in the 1950s and 1960s. As noted, the oppression of African Americans was crucial to the development of this country's bloodiest war, and the course of that Civil War was affected by the participation of thousands of formerly enslaved black men as Union soldiers, without whose dedicated participation it might have been a stalemate. Moreover, from the first century to the most recent year, white-on-black oppression, and black resistance to it, have regularly shaped the trajectory of local and national politics in this country in fundamental ways.

For the first 200 years of colonial development, the only other non-European groups of significant concern to European Americans were Native American societies, which were mostly seen as enemies to be destroyed or driven far from white borders. Until the 1870s these indigenous societies rimmed the western boundaries of white expansion on the continent. Over several centuries Indian societies were generally able to confront whites on their own turf and draw on strong indigenous resources. Whites were intent on the destruction or displacement of the indigenous societies by whatever means were necessary. By the 1870s Native Americans had lost the ability to make treaties as separate nations and were usually forced into isolated reservations, where they have periodically been targets of private and government intervention intending to steal more land or other resources, destroy community solidarity, or force acculturation to white culture.[8]

While they have been the recurring targets of extreme white brutality and recurring genocide, Native Americans have not played as a central role in the *internal* socio-racial reality of the colonies or the United States as have African Americans. Native American labor never became integral to the booming eighteenth- and nineteenth-century economy of the new white-controlled country, nor were Native Americans integrated as a group into the new country's core socioeconomic institutions. Still, the ideological notions of white supremacy and superiority over those viewed as "inferior" peoples were early honed by white colonizers in regard to both Native Americans and African Americans. Native Americans were seen as people who were not making "proper" use of the land, and thus as available targets for whites' theft of much land. Whites mostly viewed Native Americans as uncivilized "savages" to be driven away or killed off in genocidal invasions. Much attention was given to rationalizing this bloody land theft in racist terms by leading European and European American intellectuals and political leaders, as well as by the white public. Early on, anti-Indian ideas and imagery became part of the developing white racial frame. Nonetheless, whites have historically put much more effort into developing the broad-ranging and persisting antiblack subframe of that broad white racial frame.

Rationalizing White-on-Black Oppression: The White Racial Frame: Focusing on Black Americans

As we have previously seen, a broad white racial frame, with its many stereotypes and other elements explicitly targeting African Americans, was created early in this country's history and was elaborated in subsequent centuries. By the last decades of the eighteenth century most whites agreed on a white-supremacist framing with two key features: (1) white Europeans have a God-given right to exploit the labor of Africans and African Americans; and (2) the savage and un-Christian "black race" is far inferior to the civilized and Christian "white race." This framing was not just tacked onto this nation's new institutions; it was an intimate part of the nation's foundation. Since that time, whites have developed and extensively utilized this racial framing, ranging from those whites in corner taverns to white members of the U.S. Supreme Court. For the first two-plus centuries, numerous laws, including state and federal court decisions, adopted this perspective in insuring the enslaved subordination of black Americans. Moreover, from George Washington in the 1790s to Richard Nixon in the 1970s, most U.S. presidents openly expressed antiblack views and took significant antiblack actions based on these views.[9]

Since the eighteenth century the lion's share of racist discussions by whites, inside and outside the halls of great political and economic power, have likely centered on the relationship of white and black Americans. Over this long period white popular commentators, white scholars, and white politicians—those who mostly dominate public discussions of racial matters—have written literally thousands of articles and books trying to rationalize slavery, segregation, and contemporary racism. The overwhelming majority of articles and books articulating a racist framing of this society have focused centrally, often exclusively, on rationalizing and assessing the racial subordination of black Americans. While the literature of white extremist groups such as the Ku Klux Klan, today as in the past, does sometimes attack Native Americans, Asian Americans, and, increasingly now, Latino Americans, such racist attacks tend to be less common than those against black Americans (and, in some white-supremacist circles, Jewish Americans). In the last decade or two, numerous white writers have published racially framed arguments against new immigrants of color in various media, but even in this period the majority of racist books, articles, and Internet commentaries have been focused on African Americans.[10]

Today, as over the last century, whites regularly extend this old racial framing of white superiority to numerous other Americans of color, including Native Americans, Latinos, and Asian Americans. As we will see below, hostile actions generated by this racial framing periodically move well beyond verbal attacks—to the stark reality that can be seen in many hate-based crimes, including numerous violent crimes, targeting Americans in numerous groups over recent decades.

White Identity and Emotions

During the first century of development a sense of white identity was brought about both in regard to the Native Americans on the borders of white territory and in regard to African Americans within the midst of the white colonists. By the late 1700s, however, this sense of whiteness was increasingly asserted mostly in terms of white views of a contrasting and undesirable blackness. This orientation has persisted. For centuries now, a majority of whites have viewed the country in substantially white–black terms. Moreover, judging from field interviews that my associates and I have done with whites in recent decades, the racialized "other" most central to white identity and framing—and the only such group that seems to obsess a large number—is black Americans. This research and other interview studies of whites suggest that the racist socialization of whites in regard to Americans of color other than black Americans is usually less systematic and basic to white identity, emotions, and practices. For example, interviewing in the racially diverse state of California, Ruth Frankenberg found that white women there accorded a hyper-visibility to black Americans and a "relative invisibility to Asian Americans and Native Americans; Latinos are also relatively less visible than African Americans in discursive terms."[11]

The antiblack orientation is much more than verbal-cognitive. As we saw in earlier chapters, strong emotions, such as fear and loathing, and visual images often undergird antiblack attitudes of many whites. The racist emotions of these whites seem weaker in regard to other

Americans of color. For example, whites seem to be much less likely to go into defensive maneuvers when an Asian or Latino man is nearby than when a black man is nearby. Whites are also less emotional about interracial marriage when it does not involve whites and blacks (see below, p. 242).

In some areas this heavy or exclusive focus by whites on black Americans may now be affected by the increasing size and impact of the Latino population. For example, numerous areas of the United States, from the Northeast to the South and Southwest, have seen whites mounting racist attacks, verbal and physical, on Latino immigrants and their families. These attacks involve racial discrimination, and that in turn has meant the expansion of the anti-Latino subframe of the dominant racial frame, a rationalizing subframe that may eventually rival in its racist details and extent the subframe developed by whites for black Americans.

Implementing the Racial Status Continuum: Immigrants of Color

The highly developed system of racial oppression originally created for African Americans has regularly influenced the way most whites have reacted to, oppressed, or accepted other people of color. Since the 1850s, one by one, most other non-European groups have been recruited by white employers and politicians as cheap labor. Some others have come as political refugees. Many of these immigrants have originated in countries linked to overseas economic imperialism on the part of U.S. corporations or to U.S. military operations. Examples are China, Japan, and the Philippines in the nineteenth century, and Korea, Taiwan, Vietnam, Cuba, and Iraq in the twentieth and twenty-first centuries.

Each new immigrant group is placed, principally by dominant whites, somewhere on a *white-to-black status continuum*, the commonplace measuring stick of social acceptability. This socio-racial continuum has long been imbedded in white minds and practices, as well as in the developing consciousness of Americans of color, including immigrants. Generally, the white-imposed **racial continuum** runs from white to black, from "civilized" whites to "uncivilized" blacks, from high intelligence to low intelligence, from privilege and desirability to lack of privilege and undesirability. Since the seventeenth century, blackness has been conceptualized as the opposite of whiteness and Europeanness. Philosopher Lewis Gordon has summarized this reality: "One is black the extent to which one is most distant from white. And one is white the extent to which one is most distant from black."[12] Central to U.S. society is a comprehensive white-superiority framing imbedded in an underlying social-structural reality. "White" and "black" are socially constructed categories riveted to a white-dominated structure of racial oppression, and it is those with the greatest power, white Americans, who mostly control who gets placed where in the continuum's various racial categories. This longstanding continuum accents physical characteristics and color coding in which European features and cultural norms are highly privileged.

On occasion, some Americans of color are placed by whites toward the privileged white end of the racial spectrum. Thus, some Latinos and Asian Americans have from time to time been classified as "honorary whites" or "near whites," such as in white-led, anti-affirmative-action efforts where Asian Americans are praised as being the equals of whites who supposedly need no antidiscrimination protection or affirmative action. In addition, legal scholar Frank Wu has accented the opposite phenomenon in which some people of color are defined as "constructive blacks," as being near or at the black end of the racist continuum.[13]

Of course, all racially defined groups do not share the same fate or have the same experiences in the United States. As we saw earlier, the treatment of Americans of color has varied according to their time of entry, size, culture, physical characteristics, and economic resources. In the case of Asian and Latino groups, as we will see below, whites added a new dimension to the placement equation, that of "foreignness." Yet in *every* case it is the dominant white group that has set the major terms for their incorporation, framing, and continuing treatment. For instance, one important study of early California history shows that Mexican, Asian, Native, and African American groups did not develop in the same way, yet each was shaped by the pre-existing framework of white supremacy, the central organizing principle of society brought there by white migrants from eastern states. The latter whites brought a well-developed white-racist frame rationalizing black subordination and applied their racist ideas, with some new embellishments, to other groups seen as biologically, intellectually, and culturally inferior.[14]

For later groups of non-European immigrants, whites' racist framing and practices targeting them have been tailored to the particular entry or mobility conditions of these immigrants. When, for instance, Asian or Latino groups have become important for white employers seeking their labor or brought into the country for other reasons, whites have ranked and categorized them along the light-to-dark (and close/not close to European American culture) continuum used for previous groups. Often the lighter a group is, and the more Anglicized it seems to whites, the better it will be treated and viewed. Thus, if light-skinned Cuban Americans are defined by whites as "nearer to white," they will typically have a different societal experience than darker-skinned immigrants of color, including the darker-skinned Latinos whom many whites place toward the "black end" of the old socio-racial continuum.

Later Entrants into the Racist System: Chinese and Mexican Immigrants

By the early decades of the nineteenth century white adventurers and entrepreneurs were moving rapidly into western North America. Over the nineteenth century yet more non-European groups were brought into the ever-expanding, white-controlled land area of the United States. The racist system developed for African Americans was easily extended to Asian, Native American, and Mexican groups. Each set of relations between European Americans and a non-European group has historical specificity, and this means different experiences and, often, distinctive long-term outcomes. Historical circumstances, particularly timing and mode of entry into the sphere of white domination and the group's size and prior resources, have usually meant a significant difference in experiences with whites. Let us examine briefly the experiences of two important immigrant groups from China and Mexico.

Chinese Immigrants

In the 1850s Commodore Matthew Perry sailed U.S. warships into Tokyo Bay, and by this show of military might forced a treaty granting trading rights with Japan to the United States. By the late nineteenth century the United States was involved in major imperialistic pursuits in Asia and elsewhere around the globe. U.S. and European missionaries and business people moved across the world, invading numerous Asian countries. Western incursions disrupted the Asian economies and sometimes stimulated out-migration. For example, in the mid-nineteenth century various enterprises in Hawaii and on the Pacific Coast were seeking low-wage workers. U.S. labor recruiters secured 200,000 Chinese workers between 1848 and 1882 to work on railroads, in mines, and in personal service jobs. The Chinese immigrants were sought as workers who would work at low wages and set a model of hard work for other workers. When Chinese labor was imported in the 1850s, whites across the country already had in place a well-developed system of antiblack racism. This white-supremacist system was adapted, embellished, and expanded to encompass these new Asian immigrants. Anti-Chinese images and stereotypes took root not only in the views of the white elites seeking to justify exploitation of Chinese laborers, but also in the views of white workers who faced significant competition from these hardworking immigrants.[15]

As historian Ronald Takaki has pointed out, at an early point in time the Chinese immigrants were often associated "with blacks in the racial imagination of white society."[16] They were "Africanized" and grouped with African Americans, with both groups being seen as dangerous to the health of U.S. politics and society by many whites who framed the society in white-supremacist terms. Even into the late 1920s, the U.S. Supreme Court upheld state laws placing Chinese Americans in racially segregated black (not white) schools. Early on, the *San Francisco Chronicle* compared Chinese workers to African slaves: "When the coolie arrives here he is as rigidly under the control of the contractor who brought him as an African slave was under his master in South Carolina or Louisiana."[17] These Asian immigrants were seen as racially subordinated workers with very few rights.

Over several decades many whites came to frame these Chinese immigrants as yet another threat to whites' racial purity. In 1880, for example, the California legislature passed a law prohibiting whites from marrying a "negro, mulatto, or Mongolian." "Mulatto" referred to someone with black and white ancestors, while "Mongolian" meant Asian. Both terms were, and still are, derogatory. Earlier, in 1854, the California Supreme Court overturned a lower court's ruling convicting a white man of murder on the basis of testimony by Chinese Americans. A California law declaring that "no black or mulatto person, or Indian, shall be permitted to give evidence" against a white person was said by this court to include the Chinese because they fell under the term "black person." The court *explicitly* said that the term "black" includes "all races other than Caucasian."[18] Moreover, in areas of the southern United States, where some Chinese laborers were also imported, they were initially assigned a black or near-black position, although they were sometimes allowed in certain business situations to operate precariously as a sort of middle group between whites and blacks. Even modest variations from the white-on-black system of oppression were routinely controlled by powerful whites.[19]

In the 1840s, many thousands of white workers and adventurers began to migrate to California. Chinese and other Asian workers were intentionally used by white employers to displace better-paid white workers. With increasing competition between white and Chinese laborers came the adaptation and application by these white workers and their allies of negative racist stereotypes, images, and epithets already used to defame black Americans. Like black Americans, Chinese immigrants were often called "niggers" or similar epithets and described in vicious racist imagery as savage, deviant, criminal, or child-like. The physical appearance of the Chinese was viewed by whites as only slightly different from that of African Americans. In cartoons Chinese Americans were portrayed as having what were thought of as African features such as darker skin and big lips. Once again, whites portrayed themselves as the physically superior, aesthetically incomparable, and highly civilized group. Instead of working to build organizational alliances with Asian American workers against exploitative practices of white employers, white workers persisted in their commitment to a strong white-racial consciousness, and white unions frequently led the growing anti-Asian agitation.[20]

Together with other leading newspapers, the *New York Times* compared "millions of degraded negroes in the South" with a similar "flood-tide of Chinese … with all the social vices."[21] The country's mass media spread the racist imagery of an inassimilable and foreign "flood" of Asian immigrants—a theme still common in some anti-Asian (and anti-Latino) framing today. This white fear of being overwhelmed by those who are not white and who do not fit well into established white culture is an old theme that began in eighteenth-century antiblack racism—in, for example, the intellectualized racism of founder Thomas Jefferson (see Chapter 3).

Over time whites did distinguish the Chinese immigrants more clearly from African Americans. While both groups were often seen as lazy, devious, or criminal, the Chinese were additionally stereotyped as culturally alien and undesirable immigrants. A racist immigration law *excluding* "undesirable" Chinese immigrants was passed in 1882 by the U.S. Congress. Only in World War II, when China was a U.S. military ally, were Chinese immigrants—and only 105 immigrants a year—again allowed to come into the United States legally. In the intervening decades, the overwhelming majority of whites viewed Chinese Americans not as Americans but rather as an alien and excludable "race." For example, in 1896, even as he defended some rights for blacks as the lone dissenter in the *Plessy* v. *Ferguson* case, the U.S. Supreme Court Justice John Marshall Harlan added this gratuitous negative comment on the Chinese:

> There is a race so different from our own that we do not permit those belonging to it to become citizens of the United States. Persons belonging to it are, with few exceptions, absolutely excluded from our country. I allude to the Chinese race.[22]

At the end of the nineteenth century the view of the white leadership was that Asian Americans should not be U.S. citizens and should mostly be excluded. This accented dimension of Chinese foreignness is an amplification of earlier European views of all non-Europeans. Enslaved Africans and Indians were early viewed as alien and uncivilized. Even some early European immigrants, such as the French in the early 1800s, were initially seen as alien by native-born British Americans, and harsh legislation was crafted against them. However, it was with the immigration of significant numbers of Asians and Mexicans that whites greatly amplified their old racial framing in regard to the dimension of "foreignness" for certain peoples of color. Thus, sociologist Claire Jean Kim has argued that Asian immigrants have long been triangulated between whites and blacks, with a negative evaluation on the two axes of superior/inferior and insider/foreigner. Initially, the white view of Chinese immigrants stressed their similarity to African Americans in inferior racial status and inferiority, but over time the dimension of foreignness was given ever-greater emphasis.[23]

The established U.S. system of white supremacy, with its ingrained coding of racist framing and discriminatory practices in all major institutions, was once again extended and adapted, this time for Chinese Americans. As Gary Okihiro has put it, "insofar as Asians and Africans share a subordinate position to the master class, yellow is a shade of black, and black, a shade of yellow." The two groups are kindred peoples "forged in the fire of white supremacy."[24]

Other Asian Immigrants

After the Chinese were excluded, there was a division within the white community regarding the possibility of more Asian immigration. Needing labor, some West Coast employers pressed hard for new workers from other Asian countries. Soon, modest numbers of Japanese and Filipino workers were imported to fill low-wage jobs in Hawaii and on the West Coast. However, many whites—including some powerful members of the elite—were still opposed to the presence of more Asian immigrants, typically on racist grounds.

Initially, Japanese and Filipino immigrants had to endure white-supremacist attacks that characterized them, like African and Chinese Americans, as unintelligent, physically ugly, lazy, or unmanageable. In chorus with other white-supremacists of his day, for example, James Phelan, U.S. senator from California, claimed that Japanese immigrants were a threat to the "future of the white race, American institutions, and Western civilization."[25] Aspects of antiblack imagery were applied by whites to these new Asian immigrants, but whites especially emphasized the "foreign" character of these immigrants. Like the Chinese, the Japanese faced the anti-foreign stereotypes portraying them as unassimilable and very threatening to the dominance of the "white race." Eventually opposition to Japanese immigration led to the infamous "Gentleman's Agreement" between the United States and Japan, whereby under U.S. government pressure the Japanese government agreed to cut off most immigration to the United States. Similarly, the modest numbers of Filipino immigrants permitted in the 1900 to 1930 period were cut sharply to just 50 a year by the 1930s.

Interestingly, in the late nineteenth and early twentieth centuries, some whites were opposed to overseas imperialism by the United States in Asia and Latin America because they feared such involvement would bring more immigrants of "inferior" or "mixed" blood into the U.S. mix. However, yet other white-supremacists lauded U.S. and European imperialism because it meant that whites brought "civilization" to their "little brown brothers" overseas. Many whites shared the sentiments in British poet Rudyard Kipling's poem of the time: "Take up the White Man's burden/Send forth the best ye breed." In this view superior whites had a missionary obligation to civilize the world's peoples of color. Indeed, this latter view won out in the United States. When the U.S. military defeated Spain in the 1890s Spanish–American War, the Philippines and Cuba became major colonies in the growing U.S. empire.[26]

Realizing that classification as near black on the white-to-black status continuum means consignment to extreme oppression, Asian immigrants and their descendants have often tried to break out of this white-determined racial classification. The Naturalization Act of 1790 explicitly limited the privilege of naturalized citizenship to "white" immigrants. This designation of white was created in opposition to black, and for some decades being non-European meant being classified politically and legally as more or less black in the minds and practices of whites in power. Between 1878 and the 1920s numerous U.S. courts were forced to examine applications for naturalization from members of various Asian groups. In an 1878 case, *In re Ah Yup*, a federal judge decided that a Chinese American could not become a naturalized citizen because he was *not white*. This decision explicitly cited the classification of races by the European racist thinker Johann Blumenbach in arguing that the meaning of "white person" was generally agreed upon and did not include Asians. Consistently, these court cases decided that those who were partially or totally Asian were not white and were thus ineligible for citizenship. The white judges mostly made it clear that being white meant not having any known non-European ancestry. Significantly, this explicitly racist criterion for U.S. citizenship was not eliminated from U.S. law until the 1952 Immigration and Nationality Act.[27]

The Incorporation of Mexican Immigrants

The first Mexican residents of the United States did not immigrate, but were brought into the United States by violent conquest as a result of the Mexican–American War of the 1840s. Mexicans were incorporated into the ever-expanding U.S. empire by whites determined to spread European dominance across the North American continent. Significantly, many whites who invaded northern Mexico in the early decades of the nineteenth century were from the slaveholding South, and some brought enslaved African Americans.

Whites who migrated to these southwestern areas usually carried the system of U.S. racism in their minds, propensities, and practices. Not surprisingly, they applied their white-supremacist, antiblack framing to local Mexicans, who were seen as intellectually, physically, morally, and culturally inferior. Indeed, at the time of Anglo-American settlement of Texas and California a significant number of Mexicans, including those in leading families, had some African ancestry. (The early Spanish conquerors of Mexico had brought in enslaved Africans.) This multiracial heritage undoubtedly fueled racist reactions to Mexicans by whites immigrating there. Indeed, whites often called Mexicans "niggers" or epithets with similar meaning and treated Mexicans in the same racist ways they did black and Native Americans. Stephen F. Austin, a white adventurer who founded new communities in Texas, viewed Mexicans as a "mongrel Spanish-Indian and negro race."[28] In the congressional debate over annexing Mexico, a leading U.S. senator, John C. Calhoun, opposed such annexation. The United States had never

> incorporated into the Union any but the Caucasian race.... Ours is a government of the white man ... in the whole history of man ... there is no instance whatever of any civilized colored race, of any shade, being found equal to the establishment and maintenance of free government.[29]

Nonetheless, the annexation took place. Most whites had no trouble moving from malevolent conceptualizations of the "black race" to similarly venomous views of other "colored races." Such views all became part of the ever-expanding white-racist frame.

By the early 1900s, agricultural and industrial expansion created an increased demand for low-wage labor in the Southwest. White employers there moved to secure immigrant workers from Mexico; large numbers were recruited for farms and factories, with federal government assistance. After a decline in Mexican labor importation during the 1930s depression, during World War II white employers again sought Mexican workers for low-wage jobs, especially in agriculture. Periodically since World War II, employers and their allies in government have sought Mexican workers to do low-wage agricultural and manufacturing jobs, even as growing numbers of U.S. political and nativist groups have agitated against such immigration, especially in recent decades. By bringing in large numbers of Mexican workers, U.S. employers have helped to change the demographic and political landscape in very significant ways.

Like black Americans, Mexican Americans have been recurring targets of white-supremacist actions. Indeed, the first extensive discrimination targeting U.S. Latinos was aimed at Mexican Americans, in the mid-nineteenth century. After the Mexican–American War, many Mexican families lost their lands by force or chicanery to white Anglo newcomers. Those who lost their lands often became landless laborers or sharecroppers on land formerly owned by Mexicans or Mexican Americans.[30]

In the century after the Mexican–American War there was little official racial segregation in the Southwest, but much informal discrimination by whites targeting Mexican Americans, especially those who had substantial Indian or African ancestry. In numerous areas Mexican Americans faced blatant discrimination and overt segregation in employment, housing, schools, and public accommodations. This blatant discrimination lasted well into the 1960s—with some instances continuing to the present day. As Joan Moore explained in a 1970s book: "for decades the Texas Rangers terrorized the Mexican Americans of the Rio Grande Valley, and even today, although they are reduced in numbers, *los rinches* are still used to 'handle' Mexicans."[31] In the Sunbelt states this informal discrimination was a logical extension of, and often patterned on, that developed for black Americans, but whites added new embellishments—such as aggressive hostility to the Spanish language—to their racist framing and discriminatory practices. For decades Mexican children, to take just one important example, were punished for speaking Spanish in public schools and their names were often Anglicized.[32]

In 1897 a federal court ruled that a Mexican American petitioner could become a naturalized citizen only because of special treaty agreements. The white judge declared that if a "strict scientific classification of the anthropologist should be adopted, he would probably not be classed as white."[33] Periodically, other Latinos have faced this type of racist categorization. For example, in the last census of Cuba conducted by the Spanish colonial government before the U.S. conquest of the island, the Mexican and Chinese residents there were listed as "white." However, in the 1907 U.S. census, after the U.S. takeover of that island, both these groups were listed as "colored." Racial classification is often a matter of government action. Well into the middle of the twentieth century prominent whites, including some in state legislatures and the U.S. Congress, openly described Mexican Americans as mixed-race "mongrels" or "inferior coloreds"—often with specific reference to their "inferior" Indian or African "blood." In contrast to the white framing and treatment of Asian immigrants, in the case of Mexican Americans many whites have given much more attention to their "mixed blood," indeed to the present day. Once again, we observe the operation of the socio-racial continuum so well imbedded in white minds and practices.[34]

Anti-Mexican stereotypes and rationalizations of discrimination developed among white workers as well as in the white elites. The situation was comparable to that of Asian immigrant workers. Because of competition with Mexican workers—especially after the large-scale immigration beginning in the 1910s—white workers and union organizations often participated in verbal and physical attacks on Mexican immigrants, including periodic lynchings.

In some settings, in the past and the present, Mexican Americans have been able to fight racial discrimination better than African Americans. One reason is that the white discrimination faced by Mexican Americans has usually been more informal. Another is that as a group Mexican Americans have historically had somewhat greater resources to draw upon, including being close to their home country. Mexican, other Latino, and Asian immigrants who have come to the United States in the last century have usually had the ability to maintain strong links to their home country. These ties have provided family and moral support, and sometimes monetary aid, in the face of racist barriers established by white Americans. For these immigrants and descendants home ties have generally not been destroyed by centuries of oppression, as they have been for most African Americans. In addition, from the 1850s to the 1920s Mexicans on both sides of the U.S.–Mexico border had a history of armed struggles against oppressive whites, struggles that have inspired some in later generations to openly fight anti-Mexican discrimination. Given their social and political resources, Mexican Americans were even able to gain modest political power in a few areas of the Southwest at an early point in time.[35]

When Chinese, other Asian, and Mexican immigrants were brought into the United States by employers seeking to exploit their labor, most whites automatically placed them in a racialized status much inferior to that of native-born whites. They were initially categorized at or near the "black end" of the white-to-black racial continuum. This placement has not meant that Mexican Americans or other Americans of color have shared exactly the same treatment from whites as black Americans, but history shows that whites, especially elites, set the terms for each group's incorporation into society, for their level of economic and political development, and for the character of the racial oppression they face.

Intermediate Placement and Status

From the first stages of the development of systemic racism in the seventeenth century, African Americans were placed at the bottom of the racial hierarchy, with the only other non-European groups—the Indian societies—usually being destroyed or forced beyond white-controlled territory. As new non-European groups entered the country from the 1840s to the early 1900s, they were initially placed near the black end of the racist continuum in terms of the white racial framing and oppressive practices. Over time, as we noted previously, powerful whites have moved some people to an intermediate position on this white-to-black racial continuum.

Some Americans with ancestral roots in Asia or Latin America have been able to alter their racialized status within the white-dominated society, but only because whites have come to see them as "better" in racial, physical, and/or cultural terms than African Americans. Writing in the 1940s, sociologist Oliver Cox emphasized the determinative importance of this white-controlled ranking, saying:

> Whenever there are two or more races in the same racial situation with whites, the whites will implicitly or explicitly influence the relationship between these subordinate races.... The race against whom the whites are least prejudiced tends to become second in rank, while the race that they despise most will ordinarily be at the bottom.[36]

Certain lighter-skinned, more white-looking, more acculturated—as defined by whites—subgroups among Asian and Latino Americans have sometimes been viewed and framed by whites as more acceptable than the darker-skinned, less white-looking, less acculturated members of these same groups. At various times in history, some Asian and Latino Americans have been accepted by whites in an intermediate racial status, especially if they are a small part of a local population or intermediate placement is of benefit to whites. Thus, in the early decades of Anglo-American settlement in the Southwest, a few lighter-skinned Mexican Americans in Texas, New Mexico, and California, especially those with land and money, were treated more or less as "honorary whites." After World War II, to take another example, Japanese Americans, including some who had been in U.S. concentration ("detention") camps, were more likely to be hired than African Americans in certain better-paying job categories in California. Their educational attainments were one reason, but so was their placement by whites in a more **intermediate status** on the racial continuum.[37]

More recently, a few groups among Latinos, such as lighter-skinned, middle-class Cuban Americans and South Americans, and certain groups among Asian Americans, such as middle-class Japanese, Chinese, and Asian-Indian Americans, have periodically been accepted by whites as closer to the white than the black end of the old racial continuum. Nonetheless, this near-white placement can be unstable and fluctuating. And it is not ordinarily extended by whites to the majorities of certain racialized groups, such as Mexican Americans and Puerto Ricans.

Whites make much use of placement in the intermediate status to keep the racist system flexible but intact. For example, when media or other analysts say positive things about the success of certain Asian or Latino American groups, they tend to single out those who are lighter skinned or especially "white-acting." They point to achievements of selected middle-class Japanese Americans, Asian-Indian Americans, or Cuban Americans to suggest that these Americans are working harder and conforming better to the white-determined core culture than African Americans. Whites and others operating out of the dominant racial frame often cite some in these groups as examples of achievement "who do not need affirmative action." In this way the dominant racial frame and hierarchy are protected, as one group of color is often placed or played off against another, usually to white advantage.[38]

Since the 1960s certain Asian American groups, such as Japanese or Asian-Indian Americans, have periodically also been cited by white opinion makers as "**model minorities**." Whites, especially elites, again have determined how groups of color are to be viewed. At earlier points in history, as we have seen, these and other Asian Americans were often typed negatively as "black" or "near-black" on the country's racial continuum, but now certain people within that Asian umbrella category are publicly constructed by whites as nearer to white. Somehow, their "non-whiteness" and their foreignness are not as much of a problem in the white mind as they once were. Not surprisingly, the stereotyped "model minority" term and framing were originally created and circulated starting in the 1960s by white social scientists, media commentators, and politicians who sought to condemn African Americans for their recurring protests against discrimination. Certain Asian Americans were said by many whites to be moving up the economic ladder unhindered by discrimination and without such protests. Today, as in the past, these Asian Americans are still said to be models of success because of their commitment to the "Protestant work ethic" and other values of importance to such white analysts and commentators.[39]

Thus, the model minority stereotype remains very much a part of the contemporary white racial frame. It not only misrepresents the condition of Asian Americans, many of whom are poor and most of whom still suffer significant discrimination at the hands of whites, but it also creates resentment among non-Asian Americans of color because it is widely used to assert that the United States is now a just society. The ability of whites, especially the powerful, to control the placement of peoples of color on the white-to-black continuum and to define their social position in U.S. society is yet another valuable tool used for the reproduction of systemic racism.

The Position of Immigrants and their Children

Until the increased immigration that began in the 1960s, there were modest numbers of Asian and Latino Americans in the United States. Today, their numbers are growing significantly. Majorities of the larger Asian American groups, except for Japanese Americans, and majorities of the larger Latino groups are immigrants or their children. These important groups tend to be concentrated in metropolitan areas in western and southwestern states and in a few other large metropolitan areas like New York, Chicago, and Miami. In the last few decades we have seen an increase in some of these areas in anti-immigrant groups and agitation targeting these groups. However, as yet, the image of them as threatening "foreigners," which was once very strong for early immigrants from these areas, does not seem to be prevalent in the general population. Indeed, recent national opinion polls continue to show that most Americans do not see immigration, including Asian and Latino immigration, as a major U.S. problem or a national priority for government action.[40]

In certain areas with substantial numbers of Asian and Latino immigrants, such as in Texas and California, the Asian and Latino American communities are much larger and play a more significant role in interracial relations than in other U.S. regions. There immigrants of color, especially Latinos, have periodically been targeted in aggressively racist terms by certain white-run groups, such as the far-right "Minuteman" groups. For them and similar nativist whites the foreignness imagery is very strong. In these areas, moreover, a great many whites have shown greater antagonism than people in other regions toward such things as the Spanish language, bilingual programs, and assisting immigrants with public services. For example, the Proposition 187 campaign in California in the mid-1990s tried to seriously restrict hospital and other government services for undocumented immigrants, but the proposition that passed was eventually voided by the courts. And in 2004 Arizona voters passed a similar measure, which also faced legal challenges. A Proposition 209 campaign in California successfully implemented a law eliminating affirmative action programs for college students of color, which especially hurt Latino and black students. And a late-1990s Proposition 227 campaign successfully put limits on the use of bilingual education in California, thereby destroying some of the most effective learning programs for immigrant children.

Interestingly, some recent research suggests that a pre-existing conservative framing of society is more important in shaping these increases in states' anti-immigrant legislation than the actual numbers of Latino immigrants. For example, after studying the anti-immigrant legislation passed by state legislatures, two researchers concluded that

> ideological framing is the most consistently important factor determining legislative responses to newcomers.... The current rush to legislation is a made-up crisis.... These immigrants have become part of a larger political dynamic and positioning based on racialized fears and misperceptions about the impact of immigration.[41]

Note too that this contemporary opposition to immigrants of color, as intense as it is, has been somewhat more muted than it probably would have been a century ago. Indeed, today even many whites active in opposing immigrants of color frequently speak in the language of civil rights. The black-led civil rights movement of the 1960s forced the passage of important civil rights laws and brought some significant changes in the U.S. racial climate and structure. Since that time, Asian and Latino immigrants and their children have benefited to a degree from these changes. Thus, they have not had to face the official segregation imposed on African Americans and other Americans of color in the recent U.S. past.

Gradually Blending In?

Some social commentators and analysts today actually see the children and grandchildren of recent Asian and Latino immigrants, as well as the descendants of earlier immigrants in these groups, as progressively blending into the dominant white group and thus becoming "white." Sociologist Nathan Glazer has described Asian and Latino Americans as becoming significantly less different from whites in residence, income, and attitudes. As he sees it, eventually the "two nations" making up the United States will "become the black and the others."[42] Similarly, political scientist Andrew Hacker has argued that Asian and Latino American groups should be viewed as having "been allowed to put a visible distance between themselves and black Americans. Put most simply, none of the presumptions of inferiority associated with Africa and slavery are imposed on these other ethnicities."[43] As he sees it, second and later generations of these groups are gradually merging into the white category through conformity to white ways and movement into the middle class. Other commentators have gone farther and argued that certain groups, such as Mexican Americans, already are viewed and accepted by whites and others as "whites," and thus no longer need the protection of antidiscrimination laws and affirmative-action programs.

However, arguments that Latino or Asian Americans are gradually or rapidly blending into the dominant white group are problematical for a number of reasons. For one thing, some commentators seem to accent such a blending into whiteness because it enables them to distance themselves, and white society, farther from African Americans, whom they view as the most troubling and deviant racial group.[44] Perhaps most problematical for the progressive blending arguments is the reality of continuing and substantial discrimination by whites against Latinos and Asian Americans, including those who are middle class. We will examine some evidence in later sections of this chapter.

The research data do indicate that whites are more willing to accept Latinos and Asian Americans into their neighborhoods and other social arenas than they are African Americans. Thus, one sign of the partial acceptance of Latino and Asian Americans as intermediate groups on the racial continuum can be seen in white attitudes toward intermarriage. In one early-2000s survey 37 percent of whites said they would be opposed to a close relative marrying a black person, and only 23 percent said they would approve such an intermarriage. This contrasted with the greater positive support among these white respondents for white–Asian intermarriages (31 percent approving and 22 percent opposed) and for white–Latino intermarriages (32 percent approving and 22 percent opposed) in their families.[45] In these three examples the rest mostly said they would not oppose or favor such intermarriages.

According to Census reports, racial intermarriages now make up only a little more than 7 percent of all marriages. The overwhelming majority of all marriages are still within groups. And a substantial majority of intermarriages involving whites are between whites and groups other than blacks. For example, one recent census survey estimated that among white husbands some 50,224,000 had white wives, but only 117,000 had black wives. In contrast, 530,000 of these white husbands had Asian American wives and 489,000 had wives from other non-black groups. Many analysts view these latter intermarriages as important indicators of Asian Americans and other non-black groups progressively blending into the dominant white society and, often, as signals of the end to a racist society.[46]

In several ways, however, intermarriage figures are ambiguous measures of the pace and character of such societal change. Many intermarriages may represent two people relating to one other for reasons that do not indicate broad societal changes in adaptation patterns between groups. For example, historically many white–Asian marriages have been between white men and Asian war brides from areas where the U.S. government was involved militarily. These relationships account for a significant number of current intermarriages. There is also a growing international trade in Asian and Latino brides for white men. In these cases the patterns of intermarriage disproportionately reflect certain distinctive choices of individuals, including white men who are seeking "traditionally submissive" mates, rather than a broad and mutual adaptation between members of two different racial groups. There is certainly need for more research on a number of these intermarriage issues. For example, we do not yet have much data on how the increasing numbers of multiracial families are treated by their relatives or neighbors in this society. A few scattered studies suggest that white–black families are often not treated well by their white relatives and neighbors. We have even less information on the experiences of other types of multiracial families.[47]

Who is White Today?

Today, many analysts who are especially hostile toward or critical of the large numbers of Latino and Asian immigrants in the United States tend to accent certain groups within these broad umbrella categories, such as Mexican Americans or Southeast Asians (for example, the Vietnamese), respectively. The latter groups, it seems, look and act less like middle-class whites, at least as seen by many whites. In this manner anti-immigration analysts and activists pick among the groups in the umbrella Latino and Asian categories to suit their particular ideological purposes. As these groups have grown, intense opposition has emerged from some sectors of white America. We noted previously the former *Forbes* editor Peter Brimelow's assertion that the American nation "has always had a specific ethnic core. And that core has been white."[48] Arch-conservative analysts like Brimelow and media commentator Patrick Buchanan seem particularly worried about the large numbers of immigrants of color threatening "Western culture" by watering it down or replacing it. Less-strident views making the same point on the supposedly deteriorating "white core" of U.S. society can be found in such prestigious journals as *Foreign Affairs*. These nativistic analysts certainly do not view Latino and Asian immigrants and their children as white or as blending easily into a white-dominated society.[49]

Moreover, being categorized as nearer the white than the black end of the old racist continuum does not mean that a group, or member of a group, is viewed as being truly "white" by whites. According to some pioneering research, most whites do *not* see the larger groups of Latino and Asian Americans as white. Thus, we gave a questionnaire to 151 white college students asking for them to place a long list of U.S. racial–ethnic groups into "white" or "not white" categories. Very large majorities (86–100 percent) indicated groups like the following were clearly "white": Irish Americans, English Americans, German Americans, and Italian Americans. In contrast, not one listed African Americans as white, and substantial majorities classified all Asian American groups (such as Japanese Americans and Chinese Americans) as not white and all Latino groups (such as Mexican Americans and Puerto Ricans) as not white. This group of well-educated whites had no trouble placing these various groups on a racial–color continuum, which is still central to their thinking. These data strongly suggest that very substantial majorities of white Americans are, contrary to the blending arguments noted above, not yet incorporating groups of color into a white, or even near-white, category in their minds.[50]

Moreover, some surveys have found that the majority of Latino Americans do not see themselves as white, especially when they are given a full array of possible options. In one 1990s Houston survey, the majority of Hispanic respondents, including the majority of those born in the United States, said that they did not think Hispanics were members of the "white race." Moreover, in a recent Pew Hispanic Center/Kaiser Foundation survey of nearly 3,000 Latinos, only small or modest percentages of the numerous Latino groups in their sample identified their racial group as "white," with one exception. Just 17 percent of the Mexican American respondents identified as white, compared to 19 percent of Puerto Ricans, 14 percent of those from Central America, and 29 percent of those from South America. The only exception to this pattern was Cuban Americans, some 55 percent of whom chose white as their racial group. Majorities of the Mexican American and Puerto Rican respondents, those from the two largest U.S. Latino groups, chose Latino/Hispanic as their racial group, as did the sample as a whole.[51] In addition, some recent interview research on Asian Americans suggests that most do not see themselves as white, although many try to conform aggressively to the ways of whiteness. Clearly, having an intermediate status on the prevailing racial spectrum does not mean that one is seen, or sees oneself, as fully white.[52]

Some analysts have argued that the growing population of "multiracials," that is, Americans who identify as from more than one racial group, will eventually weaken or force a replacement of the conventional racial categories, and thus the racial continuum, of U.S. society. In the 2000 census nearly 98 percent of the population identified as being from just one racial group, but 2.4 percent identified as being from two or more racial groups. This very small population of those who identify as multiracial is growing, but knowing its actual size is complicated because of societal pressures not to identify as multiracial. We have a little recent research on some of these pressures. One study examined whether Californians with black–white or other mixed-racial heritage could successfully assert a multiracial or white identity. Interviewing 46 Californians with multiracial ancestry, the researchers found that those who were Asian–white or Latino–white in parentage were usually able to self-identify successfully as either multiracial or white, or as both. However, those who had black–white parentage mostly identified as black because that is the way others viewed them in their everyday lives. These researchers speculated as to whether the multiracials who did not have some black parentage might eventually become part of an expanded "white" racial category.[53]

Continuing Racial Discrimination: Asian Americans

As we have seen previously, an intermediate status on the established white-to-black racial continuum does not mean equality in rights or privileges. Today, there is still much racist framing and discrimination, including violent attacks, directed at intermediate groups, with a disproportionate number of these directed at darker-skinned members. We only have space here to briefly sketch the contours of this serious discrimination (see chapter notes for additional research, pp. 345–346).[54]

Recently, one large survey of Asian, Latino, and African Americans found substantial majorities of all three groups felt there is still much racial discrimination against their particular group, that all three groups face similar racial problems and should develop coalitions to deal with them, and that the country would be in better shape if there were more Asian, Latino, and African Americans in positions of authority in major U.S. institutions.[55]

Numerous recent studies show that, even though many Asian Americans are moving into the economic mainstream and suburban neighborhoods, they still face significant discrimination. Many Asian Americans—including managers, administrators, and professionals with good-paying jobs in historically white institutions—report ingrained patterns of anti-Asian discrimination in numerous societal areas. For example, one recent study involved interviews with 43 mostly middle-class Asian Americans, who often described in detail facing discrimination by whites in schooling, policing, business, and employment settings. In this field interview study and others like it, Asian Americans have recounted racial discrimination ranging from blatant and obvious, to rather subtle, to quite covert. Commonly cited examples include the omnipresent "glass ceilings" that keep most Asian American employees from moving up to higher-level white-collar positions in historically white employment settings.[56]

Asian Americans report discrimination in an array of other areas, including public accommodations, policing, and government service and politics. For example, in one incident several Asian American students were excluded from service at a Syracuse restaurant, then were beaten by hostile whites as they left. Recall too the recent FBI hate crime report that listed 234 hate-based crimes that targeted Asian Americans and Pacific Islanders, a figure probably much lower than the actual number because nearly 90 percent of police jurisdictions do not make an effort to report on local hate-based crimes. Indeed, U.S. Civil Rights Commission reports have indicated that in numerous communities the usually white-controlled police agencies are slow to offer adequate protection to Asian Americans from likely hate-based crimes, crimes that seem to be on the increase.[57]

Political discrimination remains a problem in other areas as well. For example, one California study of the redevelopment of a shopping center showed how the white minority in a substantially Asian American urban area forced that redevelopment project to be done just their way. "Rather than reflecting the city's current and future position as a major node for Asian-themed businesses, the shopping center was remodeled to provide a place where whites could shop and 'feel at home.'"[58]

In addition, recent research on Asian Americans has found very significant health problems stemming from the racial discrimination they face, as well as from the often intense pressures they feel in trying to conform to white ways and avoid possible discrimination. One study of Korean immigrants found negative effects on their mental health in their first years in the United States, and some significant mental problems later on as well. In addition, research on Asian American teenagers has discovered that they have the highest levels of depression for any racial group. Other studies of both young and old Asian Americans have found relatively high levels of suicide, often the highest among U.S. groups. Such mental-health problems, as well as some physical health problems, can often be reasonably linked, at least in part, to the great stress that comes from dealing with anti-Asian racism and from attempting to conform to white-imposed cultural and social pressures in educational, employment, and other historically white environments.[59]

Continuing Racial Discrimination: Latino Americans

As we have seen in SPLC research cited in the chapter opening, recent field studies reveal that Mexican Americans and other Latinos face much everyday hostility and discrimination, mostly by white Americans. The SPLC study shows that working-class Latinos are often discriminated against by employers who do not pay them what they are owed or who do not provide safe working conditions.[60] Similarly, an earlier study on the West Coast (Los Angeles) found Mexican American and other Latino workers there reporting much workplace discrimination, with better-educated workers actually reporting the most. Moreover, in recent in-depth interviews with more than 100 middle-class Latinos from various nationality groups, José Cobas and I have received many reports of discrimination at the hands of whites. As with Asian Americans, this racial discrimination has ranged from blatant to subtle and covert and is reported for a diverse array of societal arenas, including schools, workplaces, shopping sites, and encounters with police officers.[61]

Recall that in the mid- and late-1990s large numbers of white Californians, many apparently fearful of Latino immigrants, voted in the majority for major ballot propositions designed to abolish government services for immigrants, eradicate affirmative action, and reduce bilingual programs, thereby producing major negative consequences for the lives of Latinos and other Californians of color. Numerous white politicians and voters in other regions have pressed for similar restrictions on immigrants and their children. White hostility to the Spanish language faced by early Latino residents of the Southwest persists today—in the "English only" movement, in white opposition to bilingual education, and in the widespread mocking of the Spanish language and Latino cultures. Consider again Jane Hill's research (Chapter 4, pp. 115–116) on the mock Spanish used by whites in the mass media, for consumer products, and in various other societal settings. Many whites use a wide array of made-up Spanish phrases such as "el cheapo," "hasta banana," and "hasta la vista, baby," language that explicitly or implicitly mocks Latinos and/or their culture. This ridicule typically reveals an underlying racist framing of Latinos, especially Mexican Americans, and their culture.

Numerous government housing and zoning agencies have targeted recent Mexican and other Latino immigrants to their areas. In the South and North, local agencies, usually directed by whites, have implemented discriminatory legislation targeting Latino immigrants, especially those who are undocumented. For example, some local political bodies in the Northeast have developed new health and safety laws limiting the number of people in a house, or have aggressively enforced pre-existing but little-used occupancy restrictions, in order to make Latino immigrants' lives so difficult that they will leave these local communities. One of the ironies of such code enforcement is that these communities often seek and need the low-wage labor that immigrants provide, yet the latter are not welcomed there after the work day is over.[62]

Aggressive targeting of Mexican and other Latino immigrants has meant police discrimination, as the previously noted SPLC report documents. Numerous local police agencies in the South and other areas, sometimes working with federal immigration agencies in special agreements, have enforced

> immigration law in a way that has led to accusations of systematic racial profiling and has made Latino crime victims and witnesses more reluctant to cooperate with police. Such policies have the effect of creating a subclass of people who exist in a shadow economy, beyond the protection of the law.[63]

This common racial profiling, which is often based on stereotyped assumptions from the dominant racial frame, has had an impact well beyond the undocumented immigrants who are officially its targets:

> Even legal residents and U.S. citizens of Latino descent say that racial profiling, bigotry and myriad other forms of discrimination and injustice are staples of their daily lives. "The assumption is that every Latino possibly is undocumented," says one immigrant advocate in North Carolina. "So [discrimination] has spread over into the legal population."[64]

White attacks on Latinos, as with other Americans of color, often take the form of aggressive hate-based crimes. In several U.S. regions hundreds of racially motivated or racially linked crimes targeting Latinos are reported each year. The aforementioned FBI report indicates that 830 Latinos were victims of racially motivated crimes in a recent year, again likely much lower than the actual figure because of under-reporting by police agencies. Racially motivated attacks have ranged from racist graffiti making threats of violence—often painted on homes or businesses or circulated on the Internet—to violent attacks on individuals, such as the racially motivated killing of several Latinos recently in East Coast cities.[65]

Given what some analysts describe as a metaphorical "war" on Latinos in numerous communities, it is not surprising that the SPLC interviewers found that many Latino citizens in southern towns and cities live in great fear of the police and other government agents. Note too that recurring discrimination and the stress from it have had significant health impacts. Increasing numbers of health research studies are demonstrating numerous negative effects on psychological and physical health, similar to effects documented for other Americans of color, from Latinos' everyday struggles with discrimination in many areas of the country.[66]

Other Social Costs of Intermediate Status

Latino and Asian Americans placed into an intermediate or near-white status, or who seek that status for themselves, endure various costs from trying to be white. One such cost may be self-deception. The "model minority" stereotype has been more or less accepted by some Asian Americans, particularly youth growing up in predominantly white suburbs. According to a few researchers, some young Asian Americans have come to think of themselves and their group in terms of the white-crafted model-minority imagery, probably because it appears to be positive. These youth do not yet understand the racist purpose for which this imagery was created, and they apparently do not comprehend the full reality of anti-Asian discrimination. However, as these young people move beyond their own limited friendship groups and school settings into the larger society, such as into white-dominated employment settings, they will probably learn that some whites still target Asian Americans with racist framing and discrimination, which will prevent them from achieving the societal status suggested by the deceptive model minority stereotype.[67]

Research studies indicate that many Latinos and Asian Americans have felt pressured to adjust or abandon their national identities and cultural backgrounds in order to be as white-conforming as they can be. In an important documentary, communications researcher Janice Tanaka has shown the negative impact on Asian Americans of intense pressures for adaptation to white ways. In interviews with third-generation Japanese Americans she found that their second-generation parents—most of whom had been interned as youth (and as U.S. citizens) in barbed-wire "internment" camps by fearful and racist U.S. officials during World War II—were greatly affected by that extremely disruptive and forcible incarceration. After the war the second generation put great pressure on themselves and their children to conform to white norms and perspectives, probably in the hope of keeping that racist outrage from happening to Japanese Americans again. Yet Tanaka found that the effects of this hyper-conformity to whiteness have often been very negative, with significant numbers facing great personal distress, painful self-blame, physical or mental illness, or alcoholism and drug addiction. Some have committed suicide as a result of everyday stress ultimately grounded in the realities of anti-Asian racism.[68]

Today, there is often much pressure on Asian Americans to adapt to whiteness that comes from the mass media and white peer groups, especially in white-majority suburbs, as well as from parents or other relatives. In one interview that I conducted, an Asian American college senior, a second-generation Filipino American, explained the broad impact of racism on herself and her family thus:

> Honestly, I think the way a lot of us [Asian Americans] think about racism is that we don't. I mean, even though it's … something I've thought about a lot, it's still even for me a hard topic to think about. Because it's hard to see, when you don't discuss it often…. To me, racial oppression's like a silent killer.

As this young woman sees it, many Asian Americans try to suppress their consciousness of the silent killer. She also commented on how the pressures work in her important social networks:

> And for me, for Filipinos…. When the kids are born, they check out the nose—it's good if it's pointy, narrow, not too wide—the skin tone—my mom worried that people would say stuff about my sister because she was slightly darker-complected when she was born. I was brought up to think that being called mestizo was this huge compliment. Being called mestizo was like being told "you look more Spanish, that's good, that's beautiful." The idea of "pure" Filipino had negative connotations. "Pure" Filipino means having a non-Spanish, non-Chinese last name, wider nose, darker skin, mountain, backwards…. We grew up thinking white—white is good, not oppressive—if anything, civilizing, educating. Learning about racism is hard to internalize; it's hard to think about, hard to be really convinced that it's going on…. Without the kind of collective memory that blacks have that informs them of their past, their cultural pride—it's easy to get sucked into a white mentality.[69]

This perceptive student has interviewed Filipino Americans in her own research and draws on that research and her own experience to describe the ways in which many Asian Americans have been significantly shaped by systemic racism and the white-to-black racial continuum. Recent research by Rosalind Chou and Joe Feagin examining interviews with 43 middle-class Americans from numerous Asian nationality groups found similar everyday realities. Many of these Asian Americans did not report, for their homes and networks, strong collective memories of whites' racial oppression that has historically targeted Asian Americans. Many described often dealing with contemporary anti-Asian discrimination by prizing whiteness and trying to conform to what they saw as white ways of doing and acting. To a substantial degree, such strategies have reduced discrimination by whites in their everyday lives.[70]

Sociologist Nestor Rodriguez has noted a parallel phenomenon of whiteness pressures among Latinos. Most Latinos, including those up the income ladder, experience recurring racism, but "some do it in a state of denial, that is, they deny the reality of anti-Latino bias, discrimination and prejudices around them. And they push their children into an Anglo-like existence." Increasing social science research documents that such denial of racial bias and conformity to Anglo-whiteness are common responses to anti-Latino racism for many Latinos, especially those who are lighter-skinned and in the middle and upper classes. The pressure to look, dress, talk, and act as white as possible likely does reduce some discrimination, yet it also increases personal or family stress and often reduces a clear recognition of how everyday racism actually operates. This denial and conformity strategy is yet one more destructive consequence of systemic racism.[71]

In addition, first-generation Latino and Asian immigrants, particularly those in modest economic circumstances, often find themselves in a different social position than groups of color that have been in the United States for several generations. Many recent immigrants view other life problems they face as having higher priority, at least for a time, than the racial discrimination they encounter from whites. They must worry greatly about finding shelter and jobs, learning English and local laws, keeping authorities from deporting them, and sending money to families back home. As sociologist Rodriguez has noted:

> they are aware that discrimination exists, but many first-generation migrants see it initially as the cost of being an immigrant and maybe not as disadvantageous as being back home in absolute poverty. They don't usually make good participants of civil rights groups, unless they are dealing with immigrant-related issues or labor issues—then they can organize effectively.[72]

Resisting Racial Oppression

After being in the United States for some time, however, later generations frequently become more willing to organize and take on the racial discrimination they encounter from white Americans. In spite of pressures to conform to whiteness, many Latino and Asian Americans, like the Filipino student above, actively resist the racial hostility and discrimination that oppresses them. For example, during the periodic anti-affirmative action drives by whites in California and other western areas, many Asian and Latino American students have worked aggressively with African American students and others against these conservative and regressive efforts designed to maintain the racial status quo. These young activists have certainly been willing to be viewed as activist students of color, and they have been joined in such efforts by many older Asian and Latino Americans. In spite of pervasive assimilationist and conformity pressures, many Asian and Latino Americans do not deny the reality of continuing racism and openly organize against it in important community and national organizations.

Since the 1960s many Asian and Latino Americans have joined in group-pride and panethnic organizations as a countering response to white racism. Among Mexican Americans, group-pride movements like the La Raza Unida Party and the Brown Berets have pressed for an end to discrimination and accented a perspective sometimes called "Chicanismo." Periodically, groups like the National Council of La Raza have brought together a diverse group of Latinos to work on panethnic issues such as increasing positive representations of Latinos in the media and developing political coalitions. Similarly, pan-Asian civil rights groups have aggressively asserted Asian American interests and concerns about racial discrimination and marginalization. They have pressed for an end to anti-Asian hate crimes, better police protection for Asian communities, a rejection of racist terms like "Oriental" in the press, and effective political organization. In New York and several West Coast cities activists have created important pan-Asian political and university organizations.[73]

Hostility among Subordinated Groups: Using the White Racial Frame

Systemic racism affects everyone caught in its web. It provides the broad and influential social context for relations between all Americans, those defined as white and those defined as not white. Intermediate groups on the society's racial continuum often come to stereotype, frame, and oppress those below them on the ladder, who may in turn retaliate, and these intergroup conflicts generally reinforce the racist system set in place by and for whites. Historically, whites have encouraged groups below them on the racial status ladder to negatively assess and disparage each other. Racial stereotypes, images, and other framing held by people in one racially subordinated group that target people in other subordinated groups are not independent of the larger context of white racism. Many racial stereotypes and prejudices carried in subordinated communities exist because of the dominant racial frame that was originally created by whites to interpret and rationalize white-on-black oppression. All groups of color adapt and conform to many of the attitudes and orientations of the dominant white society, both toward their own group and toward other groups of color. As African American scholar Charles Lawrence has put it, "we use the white man's words to demean ourselves and to disassociate ourselves from our sisters and brothers. And then we turn this self-hate on other racial groups who share with us the ignominy of not being white."[74]

The white-racist system often intentionally fosters racial stereotyping and hostility between groups of color. When those higher on the racial ladder express racist views about those lower, this helps preserve the systemic racism that benefits whites the most. By asserting that one's own group, though subordinated, is still better than those considered lower, members of an in-between group underwrite the racist ladder of privilege. Intergroup stereotyping and hostility among communities of color are very useful for whites who can often play down the significance of their own racist thinking and practice. Whites can thus assert that "everyone is prejudiced."

As we have seen numerous times in previous chapters, racist images, racial stereotypes, and other racist framing are central to systemic racism. What most Americans know about an array of racial and ethnic matters beyond their own experiences and collective memories is mostly what they are taught by mainstream avenues of socialization, such as the movies, television, radio, music videos, websites, and the print media, all of which circulate important elements of the white racial frame across the United States and the globe. When these racially framed images and accompanying discriminatory propensities are brought by Asian, Latino, and other immigrants to the United States, they can become the basis for intergroup hostility and conflict. Racist framing and practices are not just generated within the United States, but are often generated by a now-international white-racist order. Much negativity between groups of color thus reflects the impact of white-generated and systemic racism. As Lawrence has expressed it:

> when a Vietnamese family is driven out of its home in a project by African-American youth, that is white supremacy. When a Korean store owner shoots an African-American teenager in the back of

the head, that is white supremacy. When 33 percent of Latinos agree with the statement, "Even if given a chance, [African-Americans] aren't capable of getting ahead," that is white supremacy.[75]

Positioning one's own group closer to whites frequently involves the articulation of strongly antiblack views and some participation in antiblack discrimination. We have seen this historically in the actions of European immigrants like the Irish as they were seeking to be defined as white. Similarly, in recent years some Latino leaders and other Latinos have actively tried to reposition their group, as Roberto Suro puts it, "on the racial spectrum so that they ended up closer to the side of privilege and whiteness than to the side of color and minority-group status." These leaders and those persuaded by them often attempt to reposition themselves by parroting certain antiblack stereotypes and creating positive stereotypes for their group, such as an accent on a strong work ethic. Suro notes:

> Sometimes implicitly, sometimes explicitly, Latinos endorse one of the most basic tenets of American racism by suggesting that blacks remain at the low end of society as a result of their own failings and inferiority, rather than as a result of circumstances.[76]

For example, one recent survey of Latino immigrants in a North Carolina city with a growing Latino population found that many already held very negative views of African Americans, even more so than local whites. Even though they mostly live in neighborhoods with or near blacks, these Latino respondents were also much more likely to say they had the "most in common" with whites than to say they had the "most in common" with blacks. Given the respondents' substantially negative views of black Americans, the researchers suggested that many may have gotten their racist views before arrival in the United States. This Latino adaptation response in North Carolina seems similar to what some researchers have found for many Mexican Americans in Texas and for many Cuban Americans in Florida—that is, "identification with whites, distancing themselves from blacks, and feeling no responsibility to rectify the continuing inequalities of black Americans."[77]

Recently, one large survey of both Asian and Latino Americans, a majority of them recent immigrants or their children, found large percentages agreeing with a strong racial stereotype of African Americans. Some 47 percent of the Asian American respondents and 44 percent of the Latino respondents agreed with the statement that "I am generally afraid of African Americans because they are responsible for most crime."[78] Not only do nearly half of both groups accept this rather extreme stereotype of African Americans as being responsible "for most crime," but they also signal their fear of African Americans. In this survey the Asian and Latino respondents were also asked how comfortable they were in doing business with other racial groups. In both cases, a majority chose whites—61 percent of the Latinos and 53 percent of the Asian Americans—as the group they were most comfortable with.[79] In these various studies we observe that pressure on Americans of color, and especially immigrants and their children, to orient themselves to whites and whiteness is strong, and probably exists before their arrival in the United States. Indeed, many immigrants bring negative views of black Americans from their home countries. Racist movies and other racist media productions created by U.S. corporations are shown regularly across the globe, including in Asia and Latin America. Apparently, thus, many Asian and Latino immigrants make choices in the direction of whiteness for reasons that are similar to those of earlier European immigrants who historically made similar choices. Many thereby choose whatever privileges they can get from whites and whiteness over building strong multiracial alliances against racism with African Americans.

Significantly, the North Carolina survey cited above found that the level of racial stereotyping of black Americans by Latinos was not reciprocated. While the black respondents in that city did report some anti-Latino views, on the whole they had far more favorable views of Latinos than most of the Latinos had of black Americans. Interestingly, too, a recent Los Angeles study of black views toward Latinos found that their attitudes toward Latinos were shaped more by economic issues than by the movement of large numbers of Latinos into their neighborhoods. In areas where black neighborhoods had seen significant Latino in-migration, the scale of the Latino immigration was not correlated with the level of anti-Latino prejudice among black residents, except where there was a huge socioeconomic gap between the two populations.[80]

In addition, given their many generations of experience with white racism, African Americans seem to be generally more realistic about the racialized character of the proverbial "American dream," and less likely than other Americans of color to accept the conventional rhetoric of the white racial frame in this regard. One survey of African, Asian, and Latino Americans found significant differences in views on societal opportunities. While over half the African American respondents did not think that the American dream ("If you work hard … you will succeed in the United States") was actually available to their group, substantial majorities of the Asian American and Latino respondents thought that the American dream was indeed available for their groups.[81]

We should note too the related issue of the internalization of the white racial frame. Numerous researchers have noted the ways in which oppression becomes *internalized* when Americans of color adopt racially or ethnically stereotyped views in regard to their own group. This internalized oppression often goes unnoticed or under-researched. For example, one study of recent Korean and Vietnamese immigrants found a process of intra-ethnic othering in which some in each group viewed others in stereotyped terms. Thus, those who were "too ethnic" were called and stereotyped by yet other members of their Asian groups by the derogatory term, FOB ("Fresh Off the Boat"). Those who were considered "too assimilated" by other members of these Asian groups were stereotyped and called out as "whitewashed." (Those in the middle were generally considered "normal.") Those Asian Americans labeled FOBs were given that label because they engaged heavily in behavior linked to their home cultures, including traditional ways of dressing, language spoken, and socializing with people like themselves— actions negatively characterized by many whites as well. Those considered whitewashed were those who associated substantially or mostly with whites, who were viewed as aggressively adapting to white ways, and who were giving up the traditional home-country customs. The researchers concluded that, while some of this intra-ethnic othering attempts to resist the status imposed on members of the groups by whites, "it does so by reproducing racial stereotypes and a belief in the essential racial and ethnic differences between whites and Asians."[82]

In addition, recent immigrants from Asia and Latin America have often triggered renewed hostility directed by many whites not only at the immigrants but also at the larger Asian and Latino communities. Because of this negative white reaction, some native-born Asian and Latino Americans have themselves openly expressed resentment toward the newer immigrants from Asia and Latin America. Similarly, some Latino organizations have been critical of, and opposed the continuing immigration of, undocumented Mexicans because the latter have been used by white employers to frustrate the unionization of native-born Latino workers. Such internal group divisions make it more difficult to create group alliances to fight the larger problem of white hostility and discrimination facing these communities.[83]

Conclusion

After land was stolen, often violently, from North America's indigenous peoples, European Americans stole the labor of African Americans. For nearly four centuries those whose stolen labor has been central to the development of prosperity for white Americans—African Americans—are those who have most endured whites' racialized control, segregation, and discrimination. As a group, African Americans may be the most American in their highly blended ancestry. They are among the most American in the amount of time (nearly four centuries) spent working to build the prosperity of the new nation, yet they are also among the *least* American historically in terms of their human rights, privileges, and opportunities. The age-old oppression endured by African Americans is much more than a mental construction in white heads. Their oppressive reality is one that has been economically, physically, socially, and ideologically constructed.

Social science research on torture has found that people can endure much if there appears to be some hope of escape from such severe conditions, but torture is much harder to endure when it has gone on for some time and those tortured feel there is no hope of escaping. Drawing on this insight, one can perhaps understand why African Americans often have a different sense of how burdensome, omnipresent, and imbedded is the system of racist oppression than do other Americans, including some other Americans of color. Today as in the past, black Americans must operate with collective memories of 9-to-15 generations of white racial oppression, with its well-developed antiblack framing and patterns of everyday discrimination. As a group they have an amplified culture of resistance and counter-framing that has enabled them to endure and counter this racialized oppression for nearly four centuries. Many generations of oppression create a deep, critical, and nuanced perspective that may be different from that developed over one-to-three generations of racial discrimination. As we have seen, the majorities in most Asian American and Latino groups are immigrants and the children of immigrants. Some research indicates that, compared with native-born African Americans, many immigrants of color seem less aware of, or downplay, the racial discrimination they face at the hands of whites—in part because they are trying to establish an economic toehold and in part because they compare their current situation with that of the home country, and by this latter standard the U.S. often looks good.

However, it seems likely that as current and future U.S.-born generations of Latinos and Asian Americans come of political age, the barriers and pain of systemic racism will be attacked much more openly, and many more will likely come to share the views of African Americans about openly and aggressively organizing to bring major changes in the racist system. Historically, in organized pursuit of civil rights and equality in the United States, black Americans have usually led the way. Since at least the early 1900s they have forced the passage of all major civil rights laws and the majority of the pivotal executive orders and court decisions protecting or extending antidiscrimination efforts. Latinos, Native Americans, Asian Americans, and others have all been able to use these new civil rights mechanisms to fight discrimination against their own groups, and such efforts will likely continue in the future.

African, Asian, Latino, and Native Americans all have a history of white oppression and of attempts to liberate themselves from that. These groups have all had to struggle hard for human dignity and equality in this society. Since the various forms of racial oppression in the United States have drawn heavily on the white-racist framework created for black Americans, most forms of white-racist attitudes and practices directed against the numerous groups of color reproduce and reinforce each another. Moreover, as we have seen, the character of the racism faced by a group can vary depending on its time of entry into the country, region of entry, size, cultural characteristics, or physical characteristics as perceived by the dominant white group. In earlier periods whites usually placed new Asian or Latino groups near the "black end" of the society's racist continuum and targeted them for racial exploitation and oppression. Later in the process of group interaction, some in groups within these broad umbrella categories—especially those lighter-skinned and more Anglo-conforming—have been moved by whites to an intermediate position or one closer to the "white end" of the racist white-to-black continuum. The purpose of this white placement is often to destroy coalitions between peoples of color, and to thereby protect the old system of white power and privilege.

In the last few decades, this racial process of intermediation has increased in importance, perhaps because the United States is becoming less white in demographic composition. Taking a panoramic view, one might speak of the "Brazilianization" or "Latinamericanization" of the United States. Like other Latin American countries, Brazil's racialization process has called out and distinguished certain mixed-racial groups (with white-African ancestry or white-Indian ancestry) and placed them in a middle status somewhere between those Brazilians mostly of African ancestry and those of mostly European ancestry. The middle groups are socially more acceptable to whites than Afro-Brazilians, who suffer intense racist framing and discrimination.

Possibly, a fully developed tripartite Brazilian pattern—with clearly recognized and named intermediate groups providing a social buffer between whites and blacks—may be the future for the United States. Because of the apparently privileged position of intermediate groups, white Brazilians have long proclaimed their country to be one *not* seriously infected by white racism. And those in the intermediate groups tend to be antagonistic and discriminatory toward Afro-Brazilians at the bottom of the racial ladder. Not surprisingly, many North American whites have taken a similar position, citing the advancements of certain groups in the Asian American and Latino communities, and their in-between and economically enhanced status, as evidence that the United States has become a democracy no longer infected by white racism. Many whites in Brazil and the United States have adopted a similar colorblind position where they claim, falsely as we have seen, that there is no longer a serious problem of white racism in either country.[84]

8
Antiracist Strategies and Solutions
Past, Present, and Future

In the summer of 2009 the U.S. Senate passed a belated and brief resolution apologizing for slavery and Jim Crow segregation:

(1) *Apology for the Enslavement and Segregation of African-Americans.* The Congress (A) acknowledges the fundamental injustice, cruelty, brutality, and inhumanity of slavery and Jim Crow laws; (B) apologizes to African-Americans on behalf of the people of the United States, for the wrongs committed against them and their ancestors who suffered under slavery and Jim Crow laws; (C) expresses its recommitment to the principle that all people are created equal and endowed with inalienable rights to life, liberty, and the pursuit of happiness, and calls on all people of the United States to work toward eliminating racial prejudices, injustices, and discrimination from our society.

(2) *Disclaimer.* Nothing in this resolution (A) authorizes or supports any claim against the United States; or (B) serves as a settlement of any claim against the United States.[1]

Significantly, this non-binding apology accented the "injustice, cruelty, brutality, and inhumanity" of slavery and Jim Crow segregation, yet numerous whites in the Senate insisted on a strongly stated disclaimer to explicitly bar African Americans from seeking compensation and reparations for the role of the U.S. government in these long centuries of recognized oppression. Even the remote possibility of reparations for black Americans is rejected by most white members of Congress. In effect, such an apology operates to salve white consciences, yet provides no commitment to deal with the long-term impacts and continuing negative consequences of racial oppression. Specifically, there is no mention of the need for aggressive and specific congressional action to end racial discrimination.

In the United States the liberal and moderate sectors of the white elite have an inordinate fondness for symbolic resolutions like this apology and for setting up commissions to study U.S. social problems. Over the last century, thus, at least a dozen major government commissions and committees have looked into problems of antiblack and other racism. For example, in 1997 President Bill Clinton set up a seven-member advisory board headed by African American historian John Hope Franklin to start a "national conversation on race." The advisory board heard much testimony about racial and ethnic discrimination. Its final report, *One America in the 21st Century*, presented substantial findings on widespread racist framing and racial discrimination, but concluded with mostly modest solutions. The report did not provide an integrated analysis of how and why institutionalized and systemic racism pervades society, nor did it call for major restructuring of institutions to get rid of that racism.[2] Most importantly, no serious congressional or presidential action was taken to implement the report's most important recommendations, such as significantly increasing the actual enforcement of the current civil rights laws.

Today, U.S. society remains imbedded in a racist system. It was founded as such, and no large-scale action has ever been taken to rebuild this system of racism from that foundation up. From the first decades, European colonists incorporated land theft and slavery into the political–economic process and structure of the new nation. After the Civil War large-scale African American enslavement was replaced by the near slavery of legal segregation in southern states, border states, and some areas of the North, while some legal and much de facto segregation continued in the rest of the North. These institutional arrangements were designed to keep antiblack oppression in place. Periodically, the racist structure has been altered, in the 1860s when slavery was abolished and in the 1960s when legal segregation was replaced by the current system of more informal racial oppression. Other Americans of color have periodically been incorporated into U.S. society by whites operating from within this well-established white-racist framework. The U.S. house of racism has been remodeled somewhat over time—usually in response to protests from those racially oppressed—but its formidable societal foundation remains firmly in place.

What is the likelihood of future societal change on the scale required to replace this persisting racial foundation? On this point, there is some pessimism among leading U.S. intellectuals. For some time, African American analysts have pointed to the great difficulty of bringing large-scale changes in systemic racism. In the 1940s sociologist Oliver Cox noted that "because the racial system in the United States is determined largely by the interests of a powerful political class, no spectacular advance in the status of Negroes could be expected."[3] More recently, leading constitutional scholar Derrick Bell has contended that black people will never gain full equality in this country. Even those herculean efforts we hail as successful will produce no more than temporary "peaks of progress," short-lived victories that slide into irrelevance as racial patterns adapt in ways that maintain white dominance.[4]

Bell has no illusions about how very hard it is to change the foundational realities of this still highly racist society.

Nonetheless, the racist patterns and arrangements of this society do regularly generate open resistance and organized opposition. These oppressive patterns have occasionally been altered to some degree by antiracist movements in the past, and they can conceivably be changed again if the effort is great enough. Historically, other societies have experienced large-scale societal revolutions. Future domination of U.S. society by whites is not automatic. Viewed over the very long term, no hierarchical system is permanent, and such a societal configuration must be constantly buttressed and diligently reinforced by its main beneficiaries. If we think dialectically and discern the social contradictions lying deeply beneath the surface of this society, we see that the racist system has created some seeds of its eventual destruction. Thus, this racist system is legitimated by widely proclaimed ideals of equality and democratic participation, ideals that have provided it with some respect internally and internationally. While the equality ideals have long been used to gloss over its persisting racial oppression and inequalities, they have also been adopted aggressively as bywords for all movements of the socially oppressed. Ideals of equality and democracy are taken very seriously by African Americans and other Americans of color and have regularly spurred them to protest racial oppression. The honed-by-struggle ideals of equality, justice, and civil rights are critical tenets of the antiracist counter-framing that has emerged over centuries of protest, and they are periodically implemented in contemporary antiracist strategies and actions. They have served as important rallying points and have sometimes increased group solidarity. The situation of long-term racial oppression has pressed African Americans—and, sometimes, other Americans of color—to unite for their own survival and, periodically, for large-scale protest.

Demographic Changes and Challenges

Until major crises in this society occur, most whites seem unlikely to see the need for large-scale social justice and egalitarian reforms. They are too constrained by their own social privileges and racial framing, by their personal and group biographies, to see the need for radical structural change in this society's racial patterns. Still, at certain times in human history new social options appear. What complexity (chaos) theory calls "cascading bifurcations" can mean great societal instability and, possibly, a new societal order.[5]

The Coming White Minority

Current population trends alone are creating societal contradictions that will probably lead to a major societal transformation, including the likely reduction of white domination over Americans of color. Today, people of European descent are a modest minority (less than one-fifth) of the world's population and are still decreasing in proportion. Americans of European descent are also decreasing in their proportion of the U.S. population. Since the 1970s a substantial immigration of people of color from Latin America, Asia, and the Caribbean has helped to change the demographic makeup of U.S. society in a more populous and racially and ethnically diverse direction. White Americans are today a statistical minority in central cities of the metropolises of New York City and Chicago, and of the entire metropolitan areas of Los Angeles and Houston. They will soon be a statistical minority in many of the country's largest cities. Whites are a minority of the population in the states of California, Texas, New Mexico, and Hawaii. If future birth and immigration rates are similar to those of today, about half the U.S. population will be Americans of color no later than the 2040s. And by 2050, the Census Bureau estimates, a substantial majority of a U.S. population of 429 million will be Americans of color—with the Latino population increasing rapidly by then to 30 percent, the black population growing more slowly to 15 percent, the Asian American population growing rapidly to 9 percent, and the Indian, Pacific Islander, and native Alaskan populations growing rapidly to a bit more than 2 percent of the total population.[6]

Over the last decade or two, U.S. Latino and Asian populations have grown significantly and spread to more geographical areas, but remain substantially concentrated, with around half of both groups living in just ten metropolitan areas. Latinos are heavily concentrated in New York, Chicago, Miami, and southwestern and western cities, while Asian Americans are concentrated in New York, Chicago, and western cities. This concentration has stayed roughly at this level for two decades. Moreover, the African American population has continued to grow somewhat. Between 2000 and 2007 the African American population continued its shift back to the South, one especially involving younger workers and retirees, with a large-scale migration taking place since the 1990s. In contrast, over the last two decades the white population has had relatively low fertility and immigration rates, and has grown more slowly, percentage-wise, than the Latino, Asian, and black populations. Not surprisingly, between 2000 and 2007 the white population declined in many of the country's largest metropolitan areas, including New York and Los Angeles. Still, some other metropolitan areas in the South and Rocky Mountain states have witnessed a growing white population.[7]

In future decades this significant and ongoing demographic shift will likely bring more pressure for social, economic, and political changes. Today, nearly one-third of our large metropolitan areas have populations under 15 years of age that are more than half children of color. By the mid-2020s a majority of all U.S. elementary school students will be African, Latino, Asian, and Native American. They and their parents will doubtless strive for greater input and fairer representation in the operation, staffing, and curricula of many white-dominated school systems. By the late 2030s, moreover, more than half the working-age population will be workers of color. One has to wonder whether these workers will raise questions about having to support many elderly whites (e.g., by paying substantially into Social Security) who have long maintained patterns of discrimination targeting them. The composition of the voting population will continue to change dramatically. In the 2008 election nearly one-quarter of voters were voters of color, and their votes were essential to the election of the first president of color, Barack Obama. By the late 2020s, moreover, a majority of young adults (aged 18–29), and perhaps of young voters, will likely be people of color. As voting majorities change from majority white, there will probably be significant changes in jury composition, the operation of the criminal justice system, legislatures' composition, and thus some priorities of numerous local and national legislative bodies. Where voting majorities change, we will probably see far fewer white politicians opposing remedial laws for racial discrimination or pressing for new laws restricting Latin American and Asian immigration and government support for new immigrants.[8]

Negative White Responses and Reactions

Increasingly, Americans are becoming aware of these major demographic changes. Indeed, today a substantial number of whites seem to fear a more multiracial future where they will be the statistical minority of the U.S. population—and likely, at least eventually, of entrepreneurs, employees, voters, and political officials. In the 1990s the journalist Dale Maharidge wrote a provocative book, *The Coming White Minority*, focused on significant demographic changes then already evident in California. In his view the reasonable fears of white Californians were underestimated: "Whites dread the unknown and not-so-distant tomorrow when a statistical turning point will be reached that could have very bad consequences for them.... They fear losing not only their jobs but also their culture."[9] Nationally, many whites seem to look at the demographic changes from within the old white racial frame and cannot visualize a

United States highly diverse in racial terms, minority white, and perhaps more democratic and egalitarian.

Moreover, whether Americans of color become substantially more powerful economically and politically in future decades depends on several important factors, including the strength of their political coalitions and the potency of countering measures taken by the white elites and public to maintain whites' great power and privilege in society.

Many whites may respond to their new minority status with various strategies of social resistance. Some may try to enhance racial separation and segregation in residential and other spatial terms. Today we see some evidence of this in the continuing balkanization of U.S. residential patterns. Since the 1970s many whites have moved from large cities with growing populations of color to whiter suburban areas, exurban and rural areas, or guarded-gated communities within cities. From 2000 to the mid-2000s nearly one-third of the country's 361 metropolitan areas saw a decline in their white populations, with the largest losses in New York, San Francisco, and Los Angeles. Some demographic studies show that the largest metropolitan centers—especially the immigrant "magnets" of New York, Los Angeles, San Francisco, Chicago, Washington, and Miami—have gained many new residents from overseas, but have at the same time lost millions of their native-born residents to other cities, large and small. Those leaving include many whites and, increasingly, some native-born residents of color. And many U.S. counties with substantial population growth from domestic (internal) migration have had little or modest growth in the overseas immigrant population, and thus these counties are becoming whiter and older. Whites are also dispersing to an increasing degree to smaller-sized cities and towns. These various trends are creating new spatial patterns of demographic segregation.

In addition, within counties, towns, and cities, this society is still substantially segregated along racial lines. Most white Americans and most Americans of color live largely separate lives in their schools and neighborhoods. The U.S. workforce continues to be substantially divided, with disproportionate numbers of workers of color in lower-paying job categories or facing chronic unemployment, and disproportionate numbers of whites dominating the better-paying, relatively more secure jobs.[10]

There is also significant political separation along racial lines, which the changing demography may be accentuating. Thus, over the last few decades the Democratic Party has become ever-more diverse, with large percentages of black, Latino, and Asian American voters voting for the Democratic Party in recent elections, including the pathbreaking 2008 presidential election. However, in that election the Republican Party won a substantial majority of the white voters, even as they lost the election. This voting pattern was substantially the result of different party strategies. For example, in the 1990s Ralph Reed, an important Republican leader, reviewed the past and future strategies of his party and openly asserted that in the future strategy "you're going to see a new Republican Party that is still primarily white and that is fiscally and morally conservative, but that also is attempting to project an image of racial tolerance and moderation."[11]

Beginning with the 1964 presidential campaign, the Republican Party largely abandoned black voters and strongly targeted the interests of white voters. While the party lost nationwide in 1964, its pro-white "southern" strategy captured five southern states. Reinvigorated by Richard Nixon in the late 1960s, the pro-white strategy captured more white voters, especially in southern and border states, which helped Nixon win the White House. Some Republican strategists have periodically argued that the Republican Party does not need many (or any) black voters and other voters of color in order to win major political victories, but should continue to focus on the interests of white voters.[12] This pro-white strategy was used successfully in the Ronald Reagan and George H.W. Bush campaigns of the 1980s and in the two George W. Bush campaigns in the 2000s. Between the 1960s and the early 2000s, thus, a great many working-class and middle-class whites, particularly in southern and border states, moved into the Republican Party, many substantially because of racial issues.

In the last several presidential election years, as a result, the Republican Party's presidential convention has been overwhelmingly white in the composition of its delegates. At the important 2008 national convention, which nominated two whites for president and vice-president, just 7 percent of Republican Party delegates were delegates of color and only 1.5 percent were African American. In contrast, one-third of the delegates at the 2008 Democratic Party convention were delegates of color, and this Democratic Party convention was the first major U.S. party convention to nominate an African American for president.[13] As we move well into the twenty-first century, the Republican Party remains antagonistic to many civil rights and other social issues of great concern to many voters of color, including voters who are immigrants or their children, and as of now secures only a minority of their votes in most major elections.

Growing White Nationalism and Cyber Hate

For some years now, numerous human rights activists have researched and underscored the national and international growth of a renewed, broad-based white-supremacist movement. In the United States there are now many extreme white-nationalist groups, including older groups like the Ku Klux Klan and a variety of neo-Nazi groups and armed white militias.

Nationally, in the year 2008, the Southern Poverty Law Center counted 926 known groups operating actively across the United States. This number has grown dramatically in recent years, in substantial part because of white extremists' concerns over the growth in Latino and Asian immigration, and over the increasing racial diversity of the U.S. population, and over the election of an African American president.[14]

People in these white-nationalist groups, as well as hundreds of thousands of others who read their literature, sometimes engage in racially motivated crimes. For example, right after the 2008 presidential election there were at least 200 incidents of hate-based vandalism, as well as many threats of violence against President-Elect Obama, more than for any previous U.S. president. Such death threats have continued into Obama's presidency, many likely being racially motivated.[15] White-supremacist leaders have viewed the 2008 election of an African American as an important recruiting tool to bring new whites into their organizations. David Duke, former Klan leader, gave a press conference at which he reportedly asserted that the election

> is a real shock to me and it should be a shock to the community that European Americans now have to fight for our rights, in I guess Obama's "New America."... In Obama's America, do whites have rights?... I don't see him as our President.[16]

In an interview before the election, Duke had argued that half of all whites would be upset if Obama won, and as a result many would move toward the white-supremacist organizations. Indeed, after the election several white-supremacist groups claimed they had seen a strong increase in interest in their groups from whites.[17]

Since the late twentieth century, and especially after the 2008 election, these white-supremacist and other hate-based organizations, both in the United States and overseas, have grown significantly in number and impact. One relatively new activity for some of these groups is the development of active websites, a relatively inexpensive way to spread a racist-hate ideology. The Council of Europe (COE) has estimated there are about 4,000 hate-based websites worldwide, with some 2,500 originating out of the U.S. However, because estimates of hate-based websites vary greatly—from a few hundred to as many as 60,000—one should treat such estimates with caution. Nonetheless, it is clear there are at least several hundred active websites originating from the United States that aggressively spread a white-supremacist ideology and encourage racial violence or other discriminatory actions based on that ideology. One reason for U.S. dominance in setting up the majority of influential white-supremacist websites is the way that the first amendment to the U.S. Constitution is usually interpreted to protect racist hate speech. Most other countries—including Austria, Brazil, Canada, England, France, Germany, Italy, and the Netherlands— significantly restrict white-supremacist and other hate-based speech, usually including online speech, yet most U.S. policymakers still stand behind the notion that extreme white-supremacist speech should be constitutionally protected. (In contrast, much "obscene" speech is *not* constitutionally protected, but actively prohibited in the United States.) This U.S. position insures that it is very difficult to combat white-supremacist speech globally, including online, and makes the U.S. an easy place to print and distribute extremely racist materials and to create white-supremacist websites.[18]

Researcher Jessie Daniels has shown there are two forms of racist-right and other hate-speech websites on the Internet, websites that many people treat as important sources of information. There are the openly white-supremacist sites that "showcase racist propaganda for those outside the organization, including youth; and for those within, use the 'private web' of encrypted messages for communication, command and control." Even more sinister perhaps are the "cloaked" websites, which present themselves as being about the "truth" of racial issues and may seem moderate or pro-civil rights, yet are really working for "a hidden white-supremacist agenda. These sites use a combination of carefully chosen domain names, deceptive graphic user interfaces (GUI), and subtly racist rhetoric that pose a pernicious epistemological threat to racial equality."[19] Given the large and increasing percentages of people, especially young people, who use the Internet as a major source for information, this growth in racist websites is serious and challenging for those who seek to reduce white-supremacist framing and extreme racist activities in the United States and other countries across the globe. More so than other types of controversial speech, such hate-based speech is likely to link to discriminatory action. Historical analyses have revealed that the United States and other countries have long histories of white-supremacist and other hate-based speech motivating aggressive discrimination and physical violence.[20]

We should note too that the hate-based extremist groups and white-supremacist websites often make use of numerous elements of the old white-racist frame that has long been dominant in this society. There is often significant overlapping in the way in which those whites inside these extremist groups and numerous other whites who are opposed to such groups and are members of mainstream social groups actually frame the racial worlds in which they live. Whites of different backgrounds and politics periodically make use of similar racist stereotypes, racist images, or other racist features of the dominant white racial frame. Indeed, once in a while, a member of a white nationalist group even becomes visible as a member of a mainstream political organization. For example, recently an outspoken white supremacist became a member of the Republican Party's Executive Committee in Palm Beach County, Florida.[21]

Black Resistance to Racial Oppression

In the United States systemic racism has developed within a framework of constant protests from its racialized targets. Many whites have traditionally viewed African Americans and many other Americans of color as lazy and unwilling to help themselves, but this is a myth from the white racial frame. For centuries the religious, civic, and civil rights organizations of Americans of color have not only engaged in self-help community projects but also striven to improve the country's general welfare by regularly pressing forward on the goals of racial equality and social justice. Black Americans, in particular, have not quietly accepted oppression as hapless victims. They have regularly fought back, like many other oppressed peoples historically. They protest, survive, and even thrive in spite of the racist subjugation they have long endured. For centuries black Americans have taken much strength from the collective heritage transmitted through their extended families and other social and community networks. The knowledge carried there includes numerous positive values and perspectives on life. Living in a society with a dominant white-European-oriented culture has forced black Americans, as well as other Americans of color, to become bicultural. They have had to know white society well and become experts on how to respond to whites' discriminatory actions. As we discussed in previous chapters, this necessary expertise includes antiracist counter-framing and learned strategies of protest against oppression passed across many generations. The contemporary home culture of African Americans stems partly from the collective heritage that Africans brought with them, and partly from centuries of experience with systemic racism in North America.[22]

A comprehensive theory of systemic racism recognizes the impact of resistance strategies developed by black Americans and other Americans of color on the type and character of the continuing arrangements of oppression. Out of their experience with everyday racism has come a strong counter-framing and consciousness that regularly leads to significant protests and occasional large-scale revolts. To this stage in U.S. history, significant alterations in systemic racism have only come when black Americans and their allies, including other Americans of color, have organized and battled for change. U.S. society has usually moved backward when that pressure ebbs.

Past and Present Patterns of Resistance

African American resistance began in the earliest days of slavery. Those enslaved responded in many ways—ranging from passive acquiescence, to flight on a large scale, to attacks on slaveholders and their property, to insurrections. Slave revolts and conspiracies to revolt averaged one per year over more than two centuries of slavery. Moreover, in the early decades of the nineteenth century black and white abolitionists held many protest demonstrations against slavery and created militant antislavery organizations—thereby helping to bring about the abolition of slavery. The growing abolitionism was generated in part "by the slave unrest for which rebels and swelling numbers of runaways supplied tangible evidence."[23]

After the Civil War, black Americans engaged in extensive political and community organizing. In the late 1860s and 1870s the Reconstruction South developed significant multiracial democracy—with many black men (but no women) in many areas participating in local and state politics. State constitutional conventions and legislatures included many black delegates, and 22 black men served in the U.S. House and Senate. Non-elite whites and blacks worked together to bring much progressive change, such as public schools and prison reforms, to the formerly oligarchical South. However, this experiment in democracy was soon repressed by the many killings and terrorist actions of thousands of whites led by the southern gentry and working through new white terrorist organizations like the Ku Klux Klan.

A new civil rights movement was born in the early 1900s, soon taking the form of the National Association for the Advancement of Colored People (NAACP). After decades of legal efforts and organizing by the NAACP and other black organizations laid much of the groundwork, there was an important spurt in civil rights protests from the 1940s to the 1970s, with many black men, women, and children participating in numerous local and national protests for freedom and justice. One strategy was the boycott, such as the one that targeted segregated buses in Montgomery, Alabama, and brought Rosa Parks, the seamstress who refused to be segregated on a bus, and Dr. Martin Luther King, Jr., who was asked by local black activists to lead the movement, to national attention as leaders in the reinvigorated civil rights movement.[24]

Soon thereafter came many sit-ins, freedom rides, and other demonstrations by African Americans challenging much legal segregation in the South and much informal segregation in the North. New organizations oriented toward greater political and economic power for black Americans included the Student Nonviolent Coordinating Committee (SNCC), the Congress of Racial Equality (CORE), and the Black Panthers. Often rooted in a strong base of black churches and civic organizations, this activism provided money and mobilized people, which enabled civil rights organizations to achieve successes in forcing a dismantling of official Jim Crow segregation. One lesson added to the book of resistance strategies by this civil rights movement was that destruction of systemic racism in the United States would require more than speeches and traditional U.S. politics. **Nonviolent civil disobedience** was an important new strategy that African Americans developed for dealing with both official and informal racism. Dr. King and other black leaders became the critical U.S. theorists of the counter-frame idea that significant change only comes from creative social disruptions, especially those carried out by strong indigenous grassroots organizations.[25]

Successes and Limitations

Many victories came out of the 1950s–1960s civil rights movement, including passage of major laws prohibiting discrimination in such areas as employment, voting, and housing. The 1964 Civil Rights Act, perhaps the most important, prohibited discrimination in many areas. Title I set down protections for voting in elections. Title II asserted:

> All persons shall be entitled to the full and equal enjoyment of the goods, services, facilities, privileges, advantages, and accommodations of any place of public accommodation ... without discrimination or segregation on the ground of race, color, religion, or national origin.

Title III required desegregation of public facilities operated by governments. Title IV authorized federal action to encourage desegregation of schools, and Title VI prohibited discrimination in programs receiving federal assistance. Title VII prohibited discrimination in employment. It became illegal for an employer (1) to "refuse to hire or to discharge any individual or otherwise discriminate against any individual with respect to his compensation, terms, conditions, or privileges of employment, because of such individual's race, color, religion, sex, or national origin"; or (2) to

> limit, segregate or classify his employees in any way which would deprive or tend to deprive any individual of employment opportunities or otherwise adversely affect his status as an employee, because of such individual's race, color, religion, sex, or national origin.[26]

Title VIII required the collection of voting statistics.

The many black Americans and other Americans actively protesting in the civil rights movement had pressured the mostly white legislators to pass one of the most strongly worded antidiscrimination laws in any country. Pressures building from the civil rights movement also prodded some white judges in federal courts to act, albeit often slowly and grudgingly, against an array of manifestations of structural racism, such as school segregation.

Nonetheless, in the intervening years these civil rights laws and court desegregation decisions have frequently been overwhelmed by the scale of the racial discrimination they attempt to deal with. These laws were mostly crafted by the white political elite, usually in the face of grassroots protests from the 1950s to the 1970s. The laws were never intended to uproot systemic racism. While they got rid of official Jim Crow segregation, they have often been weakly enforced and for the most part have been ineffective in ending most informal discrimination. Each year, researchers and civil rights enforcers estimate, millions of acts of racial discrimination are perpetrated by whites against Americans of color. Still, today, most are *not* countered and substantially remedied by the effective enforcement of civil rights laws. Local, state, and federal agencies with civil rights responsibilities usually have neither the resources and staff nor, all too often, the will to vigorously enforce antidiscrimination laws. Moreover, state agencies like the New York Division of Human Rights and federal agencies such as the Equal Employment Opportunity Commission typically have such a large backlog of cases that most victims of discrimination cannot achieve timely and appropriate remedies. All local, state, and federal agencies dealing with discrimination complaints process fewer than 100,000 or so cases each year, and most of these are resolved with little in the way of serious penalties for discriminators.

As they have been enforced—or, more accurately, weakly enforced—over several decades, the civil rights laws can even contribute to the persistence of racial discrimination by making it difficult to file a successful complaint against a discriminator. The procedures are often lengthy and bureaucratic. By providing a strong rhetoric of equal opportunity, these laws allow most white Americans to assume that the problem of serious racial discrimination has largely been solved. Unquestionably, a first step in a renewed antiracist strategy for dismantling systemic racism would be an aggressive program of enforcing current civil rights laws.[27]

Community Control as a Strategy

Between the 1960s and today the civil rights movement has generally declined in number of public protests and in public visibility. One reason is that, at least for a time, civil rights laws, progressive court decisions, and affirmative-action efforts suggested a societal commitment to real racial change. Another reason was the hiring or co-optation of many middle-class African Americans, who had formerly been a major source of civil rights activists, in corporations and government agencies where they had largely been absent. Yet another was government repression of more radical change-oriented groups such as the organized police campaign against the Black Panthers, a militant black group calling for an end to police brutality and an increase in black political and economic control over black communities. Historically, the more the pressure builds from below, the more action the white elite takes to repress or reduce that grassroots pressure.

Government-sponsored civil rights progress came to a standstill, even backtracked, in the 1980s and early 1990s, and again in the first eight years of the 2000s, when enforcement of civil rights laws and the implementation of remedial programs for discrimination were cut back or eliminated under the conservative administrations of Ronald Reagan, George H.W. Bush, and George W. Bush. For example, a draft report of the U.S. Commission on Civil Rights summarized George W. Bush's civil rights record in the 2000s as one designed "to carry out official duties, not to promote initiatives or plans for improving opportunity. President Bush has implemented policies that have retreated from long-established civil rights promises in each of these areas."[28]

Yet, even in the difficult period since the 1980s, black civil rights and other organizations have periodically responded with public demonstrations for expanded civil rights and social support programs in Washington, D.C., and other cities. Since the 1980s there have been numerous local protests against racism and for community solidarity, as well as a few national demonstrations, such as the 1995 Million Man March in Washington, D.C., a march accenting the need for black solidarity. Local protests often focus on incidents of antiblack violence and other major discrimination, such as in the January 2009 protests in Oakland, California, over the killing of an unarmed black man by a BART transit system police officer. There have also been numerous efforts to organize black workers against exploitative employers and to organize against the waste dumps and other environmental hazards near black communities.[29]

Dissatisfaction with stalled progress or backtracking on the official commitments to racial desegregation has periodically led black activists, organizers, and intellectuals to press for separatist and cultural–nationalist strategies. During the 1920s and 1930s, for example, there was an outpouring of novels, music, and other arts celebrating African American traditions and interests—the Harlem Renaissance. Coupled with this cultural renaissance was an accent on expanding black businesses and community institutions. In organizations like the Nation of Islam since the 1940s, numerous African Americans have rejected racial integration as the goal and instead accented a black community control or separatist strategy. Sometimes, this strategy has been coupled with a call for direct reparations for nearly four centuries of racial oppression.[30]

Periodically since the 1960s many African Americans have shown a renewed interest in black community control or separatist strategies. A *New York Times* reporter, Isabel Wilkerson, interviewed numerous middle-class black Americans in Los Angeles after a major riot in the 1990s. They were angry over police brutality and other white racism issues. As a group, they were becoming increasingly interested in the idea of buying from black businesses and in greater black solidarity. In addition, in a major 1990s policy-oriented book *Integration or Separation?* constitutional scholar Roy Brooks documented the drawbacks of the racial-integration strategy as actually practiced. He has argued there and in other works since that African Americans should keep the traditional integration strategy, but couple it with strong community-focused strategies that have long been necessary for their long-term economic and psychological well-being.[31]

Working in the tradition of Malcolm X and W.E.B. Du Bois, numerous black scholars and community leaders have periodically reiterated the importance of African values and traditional perspectives for African Americans. They reject myths of European cultural superiority and call for African Americans, as anthropologist Marimba Ani puts it, to refocus their "energies toward the recreation of cultural alternatives informed by ancestral visions of a future that celebrates Africanness."[32] In this Afrocentric perspective societal revolution begins not with open warfare but with a counter-framing, a counter-hegemony of ideas created by the oppressed. African Americans have not been alone in developing this resistance perspective. For example, a major counter-framing that rejects European myths and assertions of cultural superiority has been asserted by Native American groups for all the centuries of European intrusion and dominance in North America, as Native Americans too have strongly resisted white colonization of lands and minds.

Some Individual Strategies of Resistance

As the 1960s civil rights movement demonstrated, successful antioppression movements usually require a shattering of negative racial images in the minds of the oppressed themselves. How to increase this self-consciousness remains an ongoing task for antiracist struggles. Consciousness raising among black Americans, as well as among other Americans of color, includes self-inquiry into one's own attitudes as well as a parallel dialogue with others. The African revolutionary Frantz Fanon cogently stressed that an "authentic national liberation exists only to the precise degree to which the individual has irreversibly begun his own liberation."[33]

Many African Americans have pioneered in this process of individual liberation. Since several researchers have documented these individual strategies for dealing with discrimination in detail elsewhere, let us note just one major example here. In a national study of middle-class respondents, a black professional explained her approach to whites, saying:

> I know I have very little tolerance for white people who expect me to change my behavior to make them comfortable. They don't change their behavior to make me comfortable. I am who I am. Either they sit with me and work with me respecting that, or you can't sit and work together.

After indicating that she does not generally tolerate racist attitudes or remarks, she then adds:

> Then there are other people, who are personal friends, who may make a racist statement, and it's really based on their ignorance and their lack of understanding, and I'll take the time to deal with it. There's a young white woman that I work with now, and she's really not worked with a lot of different people of color, and she uses the term, "you people," and I bring it to her attention, And she's like, "oh, oh," and so it's an education, we're working together. But I don't generally accommodate white people's conflicts.

Like most African Americans, she tailors her response to expressed racist attitudes to fit the situation and the person.[34]

Over a lifetime of much experience with whites, black Americans typically develop a counter-framing to the white racial frame and an array of countering strategies to fight whites' racist attitudes and practices. Sometimes in interview studies they speak of withdrawing to fight another day. At other times, they describe open confrontations with white discriminators, with all the costs that can entail. As in the above account, they often distinguish among whites, taking time to educate those who seem to be open to change. Like many others, this woman has seen to her own liberation from racial oppression.[35]

The Equality Ideal: Black Support, White Resistance

From the 1600s to the present, the racial subordination of African Americans and other Americans of color has contradicted the ideals enshrined in the Declaration of Independence—the emphasis on "all men are created equal" and on the inalienable rights of "life, liberty, and the pursuit of happiness." As white men with property, however, the founders had in mind their own freedom and equality in regard to British political control. However, once the genie of freedom was let out of the bottle, many other Americans have pressed for full inclusion under these great human ideals of liberty, justice, and equality.

For centuries, thus, African Americans have regularly forced white Americans to confront or implement these grand ideals. Perhaps the first great manifesto for full human equality in U.S. history was the 1829 *Appeal to the Coloured Citizens of the World* by black abolitionist David Walker.

In this widely circulated manifesto, Walker quoted the words "all men are created equal" from the Declaration of Independence and then added for his white readers this:

> Compare your own language above, extracted from your Declaration of Independence, with your cruelties and murders inflicted by your cruel and unmerciful fathers and yourselves on our fathers and on us—men who have never given your fathers or you the least provocation!... I ask you candidly, was your sufferings under Great Britain, one hundredth part as cruel and tyrannical as you have rendered ours under you? Some of you, no doubt, believe that we will never throw off your murderous government and "provide new guards for our future security."[36]

He then assured his white readers that black Americans would indeed take strong action to achieve freedom, equality, and justice. Walker's manifesto created great fear among slaveholders, who realistically saw it as an incitement to revolution. A bounty was placed on Walker's head by slaveholding interests, and he may have been poisoned in June 1830 for his militant advocacy of liberty and justice for all.

After the Civil War black Americans again pressed very hard to secure meaningful freedom and equality, including the right to vote and hold office, equal treatment in public accommodations, fair economic opportunities, and just treatment in the judicial system. Leaders like Frederick Douglass and Sojourner Truth forcefully and aggressively enunciated these ideals of liberty and justice for all. Moreover, in the early 1900s, new civil rights movements emerged, and yet more black leaders spoke out for implementation of these ideals. For example, in a 1902 lecture to a Quaker group, Anna Julia Cooper, a leading activist for the poor and an early African American feminist, noted how

> dragged against his will over thousands of miles of unknown waters to a strange land among strange peoples, the Negro was transplanted to this continent in order to produce chattels and beasts of burden for a nation "conceived in liberty and dedicated to the proposition that all men are created equal."

Elsewhere, she added that black men and women are endowed with the inalienable rights of "Life, Liberty, and the pursuit of Happiness" and thus have a "right to grow up, to develop, to reason and to live" just like white Americans.[37]

During the 1950s and 1960s the United States again witnessed a reinvigorated movement accenting these historical ideals. The hundreds of thousands of participants in these antiracist movements were greatly influenced by national and international ideals of social justice and equal rights. Just before his 1968 assassination, Dr. Martin Luther King, Jr. passionately argued for racial equality. He noted that a major problem was getting whites to understand the meaning of the black struggle for liberty, for there is "not even a common language when the term 'equality' is used. Negro and white have a fundamentally different definition." Dr. King added that black Americans

> have proceeded from a premise that equality means what it says, and they have taken white Americans at their word when they talked of it as an objective. But most whites in America in 1967, including many persons of goodwill, proceed from a premise that equality is a loose expression for improvement. White America is not even psychologically organized to close the gap—essentially it seeks only to make it less painful and less obvious but in most respects to retain it.[38]

Because of centuries of black pressure, as well as the rise of movements among other people of color, the white public's understanding of equality and the color line has slowly been transformed from the idea of the founders that only white men (later, whites) had a right to liberty, justice, and political representation to a much broader view. Recent surveys suggest that the white majority now holds this view: in principle, all men and women have a right to legal and political equality, as well as to equal opportunities in employment, housing, and education. However, as we have seen previously, for the white majority this extension and understanding of equality dates only from the 1970s and today does not mean that most whites wish to see a truly egalitarian societal reality, or even thorough racial integration. Today, as in the recent past, a majority support equality only if that means some chances for individual opportunity and improvement. The majority do not yet accept the goal of substantial group equality in all historically white institutional areas and, thus, do not support specific government actions designed to implement much greater racial equality.[39]

Indeed, a majority of whites believe that in many areas African Americans already have equality. For example, one national survey found that 61 percent of the white respondents felt the average black person had health care access equal to or better than that of the average white person. Half also felt that black Americans had a level of education similar to or better than that of whites and that, on average, whites and blacks were about as well off in the jobs they held. As we have seen in previous chapters, such white views are quite incorrect. Altogether, some 70 percent of the whites in this survey held one or more erroneous beliefs about white–black differentials in contemporary life conditions. Moreover, another recent national survey found that most whites thought the United States was now living up to the liberty-and-justice ideals of the Pledge of

Allegiance. In contrast, more than half the black respondents in the poll felt the country was *not* living up to these ideals.[40] In yet another national survey more than 80 percent of the black respondents reported widespread racial discrimination in at least one major societal area. Only one-fifth felt things were better today for black Americans than five years ago, and just 44 percent felt that life would be better for them in the future.[41]

For most black men and women, the central goal remains real political, social, and economic equality, including being treated fairly and justly in all societal institutions. As Ralph Ellison long ago expressed it, the goal is creation of real democracy in which a black person will be "free to define himself for what he is and, within the large framework of that democracy, for what he desires to be."[42]

White Responses to Pressure for Change

Since the 1960s civil rights revolution white Americans, including the elite, have faced a recurring ideological and moral crisis. They have had to confront a growth of strong liberty-and-justice and other antiracist ideas among African Americans, as well as among other Americans fighting against persisting racism. Protest against white dominance and hegemony includes not only overt confrontation with the dominant group but also the development of a strong counter-frame—in the case of black Americans, an antiracist counter-frame generated over a very long period of fighting white oppression. Periodically, this antiracist counter-framing has helped to generate an ideological or moral crisis for many white Americans.

Remedial Strategies: Moderates and Liberals

On occasion, faced with pressures for racial desegregation, moderate members of the white elite have been willing to accept some meaningful changes. From the 1940s to the 1960s an accent on modest black integration and some anti-segregation action was the orientation of the elite's moderate wing, although not of the elite as a whole nor of the white public. Reflecting the social sciences of the 1940s, Gunnar Myrdal argued in *An American Dilemma* that biological racism was being discredited and antiblack discrimination should now be remedied. Myrdal's solution accented the need for ethical changes by individual whites. One solution was to reeducate whites to view racial prejudice as against American ideals. Myrdal and his associates pressed for gradual, one-way integration of black Americans into white society. It would be, he believed, "to the advantage of American Negroes as individuals and as a group to become assimilated into American culture, to acquire the traits held in esteem by the dominant white Americans."[43] Such one-way assimilation, however, does not aim at remaking basic institutions.

278 · Antiracist Strategies and Solutions

By the 1950s the white elite and public were confronted by black pro-testors risking their lives in the new strategy of nonviolent confrontation and civil disobedience. By making moderate desegregation and other policy concessions to these pressures in the 1950s and 1960s, whites probably averted more serious protests and more extensive societal changes. The new civil rights laws eliminated official Jim Crow segregation, and remedial programs for discrimination began a gradual process of placing some, often token or modest, numbers of African Americans, other Americans of color, and white women in historically white male workplaces and other institutional settings. However, for the most part white moderates and liberals have only sought to eliminate the most blatant forms of racial discrimination and to provide some increased societal opportunities.

The much-criticized affirmative action (a term originally meaning just positive action) programs of recent decades were initially created by white men in the moderate or liberal wing of the white elite. Since these programs were first put into effect to deal with discrimination—mostly by white men at or near the top of corporations, universities, and other major organizations—these programs have typically involved modest, often successful efforts to bring some people of color and white women into major institutions where they had historically been excluded. These affirmative action programs have the look of going significantly beyond just equality of opportunity, but actually they have mostly opened up opportunities to those who are highly qualified.

Recent research shows that the serious use of affirmative action programs, together with designating specific organizational responsibility for them, is still an effective way of diversifying U.S. workforces. One research evaluation of corporate employment diversity efforts at the managerial level looked at several different strategies. The researchers found that diversity training programs were the least effective approach to increasing a corporation's percentage of black and female managers. Mentoring and networking programs also showed less significant effects in increasing managerial diversity than organizational programs accenting "accountability, authority, and expertise (affirmative action plans, diversity committees and taskforces, diversity managers and departments)." Concrete plans and managerial accountability are very important in making real changes in managerial diversity. Even so, the study also found that even the best affirmative action programs had rather modest effects on corporate diversity.[44]

From the viewpoint of even the more supportive whites, government affirmative action and similar policies were designed to be modest and temporary, and to get the job opportunity game to work in the private and public sectors for Americans of color. In recent years most critics of these affirmative action programs seem to have forgotten, or wish to forget, the fact that they were originally created by relatively liberal *white* male politicians and officials as a modest, and often paternalistic, response to pressures from black and other protesters seeking civil rights changes in the 1950s–1960s era. Not surprisingly given their origin, only a few of the implemented affirmative action and other antidiscrimination programs have seriously challenged the white male domination of most historically white institutions.

Conservative Strategies Persist

The conservative political resurgence since the 1980s has periodically involved attacks on and removal of numerous antidiscrimination programs. The conservative ideological attack, with its continuing denial of significant racism, its assertion of white innocence, and its romanticizing of the country's racial past, has frequently been accompanied by political actions that have often moved the U.S. government and private organizations away from modest attempts at desegregation and other racial change.

In recent decades conservative white politicians have been influential on racial matters at all levels of government. Conservative intellectuals have helped in getting conservative politicians elected and in preparing backtracking legislation, and they have participated actively in shaping and manipulating the views and inclinations of the general public by serving as op-ed writers in major newspapers, appearing as experts on major news programs and influential talk shows, and writing best-selling books. Recall the extensive development of conservative theories about black Americans (see Chapter 3, pp. 85–88). Especially significant is the conservative tendency to ignore systemic-racism factors and blame the targets of discrimination for the failure of remedial and support programs. In addition to developing notions of black "family pathology" and black inferiority in values or intelligence, some conservatives have even engaged in attacks on the ideal of equality.[45]

Conservative commentaries drawing on the "IQ test" literature continue to plague the scientific community and the public discussion. Note that the distinguished physical scientist James Watson has argued recently that conventional IQ-test data demonstrate that blacks are actually less intelligent than whites. Watson has also hypothesized that, because a little research suggests that melanin (which creates skin color) extracts enhance the sex drive that, therefore, dark-skinned people must have a greater sex drive than lighter-skinned people. This type of unreflective, white-framed approach to the biology of "race" is an old approach, one that most scientists of all types used in the more overtly racist, early decades of the twentieth century. However, in recent decades the overwhelming majority of physical and social scientists have abandoned this blatant biological racism.[46]

Since the 1970s, as part of the conservative resurgence against government actions to reduce racial inequalities, powerful whites in government and business have cut back or ended numerous antidiscrimination programs. For example, most U.S. companies now do little significant training of their white and other employees for interracial cooperation and management. One study found that less than one-fifth of human-resource specialists in large companies reported that diversity training was provided to employees in most jobs.[47]

As I noted previously, most affirmative action and other antidiscrimination programs were originally intended to alter the racist system only in modest ways and usually for a short period of time. In recent decades numerous conservatives have moved aggressively to weaken or destroy even this moderate level of remedial action. Since the 1970s they have filed major lawsuits, including those that have resulted in Supreme Court decisions dismantling affirmative action, such as the 1989 *Croson* decision noted in Chapter 5 (see pp. 145–147). Several recent cases have continued to weaken antidiscrimination programs further. For example, decided by a conservative-controlled Supreme Court in the early 2000s, two major University of Michigan cases (*Gratz* v. *Bollinger* and *Grutter* v. *Bollinger*) effectively limited attempts in higher education to improve lagging diversity in U.S. colleges and universities. In these decisions the high court significantly limited the use of remedial action aimed at diversifying college admissions, though it did allow racial characteristics to be used alongside numerous other factors in carefully crafted college admissions procedures.[48]

Over recent decades a conservative Supreme Court has rejected the argument, well-documented in social science research, that institutional racism is the immediate context and shaper of individual racism. The Court's conservatives have argued that the civil rights created by the Fourteenth Amendment to the U.S. Constitution are only for individuals and cannot be used to destroy institutional patterns of discrimination. Since the 1980s, a string of cases from this conservative high court have treated the white interest in keeping white privilege and power as more important than the interests of Americans of color in eradicating institutional racism.[49]

Indeed, federal judges have often ignored existing data in this regard. Take the common claim that affirmative action in the area of college scholarships has greatly hurt white students because students of color get a huge share of them. Yet General Accounting Office data show clearly that 96 percent of undergraduate scholarship money involves no consideration of race, and that far less than 1 percent (0.25 percent) of all undergraduate scholarship money is linked to scholarships just for minority applicants.[50] Once again, as we have seen many times previously, preferential treatment for white Americans has long been central, institutionalized, and legitimate. It is action to remedy longstanding discrimination against Americans of color that has been controversial and difficult to implement.

A Major Remedial Program: Significant Changes

In recent years many U.S. analysts, especially conservative analysts, have regularly criticized the government programs developed as part of the liberal elite response to the civil rights movement, including affirmative action programs, programs to provide education, and programs creating job opportunities. In the view of these analysts, these programs of government intervention have not brought the significant changes that were promised, should be cataloged as failures and abandoned, or violate merit procedures and are unfair to white Americans.

However, most such critics ignore some important programs of remedial action against discrimination that have brought substantial organizational changes, including their implications for issues of merit in the larger society. For example, consider the substantial efforts at job and other racial desegregation in the U.S. Army. Today the army, which has the largest proportion (26.3 percent) of black personnel in the military, is the most desegregated of the larger historically white institutions in U.S. society. In recent studies the proportion of black Americans among U.S. Army officers (11 percent) has been shown to be significantly higher than it is among executives in most large U.S. corporations. Today, the thousands of black army officers constitute the largest group of black executives in any historically white organization. African Americans also make up a disproportionate percentage of the important sergeant ranks in the army, a proportion higher than that for comparable supervisors in most other U.S. workplaces. (Their percentages in the U.S. Navy are also now large and growing.) In addition, surveys indicate that black personnel generally see intergroup relations as significantly better in the army than in the larger society.[51]

How was this desegregation of an organization with a very long history of intense and well-institutionalized racial segregation accomplished? The explanation lies in the fact that the armed forces were ordered to desegregate by an executive order issued by President Harry Truman in 1948. Linked to this is the fact that the army is an authoritarian organization that has in recent decades punished overt discrimination by white personnel and often rewarded white officers who have worked for significant racial desegregation. The army has required courses on racial, ethnic, and gender issues, and diversity in units is often taken into account in personnel decisions. Interestingly, too, the army approach accents conventional merit procedures. To meet the problem of enlistees without the skills necessary to move up the ranks—a common problem for civilian employers as well—the army has developed a strong array of compensatory education programs. Rather than lower standards, the army has often set up major programs to bring personal skills to levels necessary for satisfactory performance and promotion. These educational programs are usually well-crafted and relatively brief, and have generally been successful in providing many black personnel and other personnel of color with the skills necessary to meet military entrance and promotion standards. Given real opportunities, black Americans have excelled in the job structure of a historically white institution. In addition, the U.S. military requires significant diversity training for all its officers and enlisted personnel. There are also spin-off effects from the military desegregation programs. For example, the most racially integrated towns and cities in the United States are generally those near military bases.[52]

The desegregation of the army demonstrates that some conservative views of government intervention as useless in dealing with racial discrimination are wrong-headed. Army programs demonstrate that much more can be done to reduce and remedy historic discrimination, even without a complete restructuring of society. In the enforcement of antidiscrimination laws and the desegregation of everyday operations, military leaders and ordinary personnel have often accomplished much more than white executives and managers in most other government agencies, in large corporations and most other businesses, or in most unions. Once the changes were well underway, moreover, they developed a critical mass of black personnel in the army, which in turn has fueled further changes in institutional racism there. Developing a critical mass that can perpetuate changes is essential to a long-term antiracist strategy. Nonetheless, much remains to be done. The Armed Forces Equal Opportunity Survey shows there is still much subtle and covert discrimination, and some blatant discrimination, in all military branches. However, in spite of these continuing problems, the 1964 Civil Rights Act has been implemented more effectively in numerous military organizations than in most areas of the civilian society.[53]

Antiracist Strategies Today

One classic study of racial prejudice, *The Authoritarian Personality* (1950), concluded that the racist views of whites vary with social setting: "What people say and, to a lesser degree, what they really think depends very largely upon the climate of opinion in which they are living; but when that climate changes, some individuals adapt themselves more quickly than others."[54] The social context can restrict or encourage the possibility that whites (and others) will take action against systemic racism and for a society that is more humane, egalitarian, and just. Historical conditions and the existing social structure set limits on what individuals can do, but they are not all-determining. Today, even within a society thoroughly grounded in white racism, a significant number of whites are working actively with Americans of color to destroy that racism in their own lives and in the larger society.

Some Strategies in Dealing with Whites

At lecture sessions I have done over many years, some whites ask, usually in frustration and after they have become more consciously aware that racial hostility and discrimination are commonplace across the country: "What can I do to bring change? I am only one individual." The answer to this may lie in the old idea that one person, whatever her or his social status, can help to topple a system if action is taken at the right place and time. One person's actions can often make a difference. The actions of a relative few can reduce or end great societal evils. Consider the European Holocaust. It might not have happened if a modest number of individuals had taken action to stop it at the right point in time. Sociologist Zygmunt Bauman has suggested:

> Evil is not all powerful. It can be resisted. The testimony of the few who did resist shatters the authority of the logic of self-preservation. It shows it for what it is in the end—a choice. One wonders how many people must defy that logic for evil to be incapacitated. Is there a magic threshold of defiance beyond which the technology of evil grinds to a halt?[55]

This is the important practical question. During the 1950s–1960s civil rights movement only a modest percentage of black Americans, and a very small percentage of other Americans, ignored the logic of self-preservation and actively participated in the organized protests against Jim Crow. Today, likewise, we need more people who will ignore self-preservation and act to disrupt individual and group framing and actions that reinforce the persisting racial hierarchy. With such individual and small group efforts, we might well be able to reach the "threshold of defiance" that permanently destabilizes the system of racial oppression.

One barrier for most whites is their significant lack of empathy for the situations of those across the color line. Racism requires in its oppressors and discriminators a lack of recognition of the humanity of the racialized others. Systemic racism, thus, involves the social alexithymia discussed previously. Being an oppressor in a racist society typically requires a significantly reduced ability to understand or relate to the emotions, such as recurring pain, of those targeted by racial hostility and discrimination.

Whites who change in this regard seem to develop through at least three stages: *sympathy, empathy,* and *autopathy.* The initial stage, sympathy, is important but limited. It typically involves a willingness to set aside some racist stereotypes, images, and hostility, and the development of a friendly if variable interest in what is happening to the racialized others. Numerous whites have moved into this stage since the 1960s civil rights movement. Empathy is a much more advanced stage, in that it requires a developed ability to routinely reject numerous distancing stereotypes and imagery, plus a sustained capacity to see and feel some of the pain of those in the oppressed group. Autopathy is yet a third stage. Autopathic understandings and feelings occur when a white person has intentionally put herself or himself, if partially, into the racist world of the oppressed—and not only receives racist hostility from other whites but also personally feels some pain that comes from being enmeshed in racist conditions central to the lives of oppressed others. This case of feeling racism's pain more directly often comes when whites are close friends, lovers, parents, or other relatives of blacks (or other people of color) who are direct and daily targets of racism. Accounts by white parents of black children reveal the great autopathic pain the former frequently endure as they confront the everyday racism faced by their children.[56]

Today the challenge for those seeking to expand antiracist strategies and actions includes the creation of conditions where more whites will have to confront the reality of the pain that systemic racism has caused Americans of color, especially those with whom they come into regular contact. A large-scale educational effort—one that is candid and blunt about the past and present reality of racist framing and racist practices—seems required if more than a handful of whites are ever to move into these important stages of empathy and autopathy.

Can Education Make a Difference?

Over more than four decades of teaching experience with thousands of students, I have found that, until whites have substantial instruction in the history and contemporary reality of racial oppression, most reject the important understandings and interpretations they need to be supportive of major changes in our racist system. Substantially changing the centuries-old white racial frame and actions generated by it will require much new effort, including new educational strategies. Today, very few Americans have had even a brief Stereotyping 101 or Racism 101 course anywhere in their educations, from kindergarten to college or graduate school.[57]

By means of well-constructed 101 courses like these, whites, and many others, can be made aware of the reality of the white racial frame deeply imbedded in their minds. In addition, they can be taught the importance of reframing away from the old white racial frame to an operational and sincere liberty-and-justice framing of society. In my view generating a sincere acceptance of this liberty-and-justice frame, and dramatically increasing action out of it, will require a process of renewed education in which white individuals and their important networks move toward understanding how our system of white racial privilege and power was created, and how whites routinely help to maintain it today. Such education will need to probe deeply into the racist character and structure of U.S. society, and it will require a purposeful unlearning of the mythology and framing most whites have used to paper over the continuing reality of racial discrimination in all sectors of this society. As we saw earlier, collective forgetting is central to the way in which most whites have dealt with the history of U.S. racism (p. 218). Typical high school and college textbooks mostly neglect or downplay our racist history. Learning more about the harsh reality of U.S. history—about its oppression, brutality, and unjust impoverishment for Americans of color, and its unjust enrichment and privileges for whites—is likely to be critical to the goal of increasing the number of whites (and others) who will actively join antiracist efforts at local and national levels.[58]

As of now, this important educational project is clearly in an early stage. One optimistic finding from recent research is that even modest educational steps can make some difference. For example, one recent study involved two groups of white children aged 6–11. Each group was given just six 20-minute daily history lessons providing biographical information on historically important African Americans. One white group got biographies with explicit discussions of racial discrimination faced by the person under consideration, while the other white group got the same biographies without references to discrimination. Before and after the lessons, researchers gave these children an evaluative scale designed to measure positive and negative views of black and white Americans. The white children who had the brief racial-discrimination lessons had significantly more positive attitudes and less negative attitudes about black Americans than the group that had not gotten such lessons. In addition, the children getting the discrimination lessons also revealed in the testing that they were more inclined than the others to racial fairness and, among the older children, had more racial guilt.[59] Clearly, such research suggests that even brief historical lessons about discrimination may have some modest positive effects on younger whites' racial attitudes, including activation of their sense of responsibility for a racist society.

The usefulness of racial guilt has been debated, but a few other studies also suggest it may have positive effects. Some research on white college students has shown that the extent of their feelings of guilt about apparently racist views predicts their interest in participating in prejudice-reducing behavior. In one study those with more racial guilt were more likely to desire to participate in reading prejudice-reducing articles and thus in "rectifying the transgression that originally produced the guilt."[60] The generation of the emotion of racialized guilt can conceivably play a beneficial role in stimulating positive action against racism.

Yet other modest educational strategies have been shown to have some important positive effects. Teaching people in one racial group how to see complexity and nuances in people in other groups may be another useful step in breaking down stereotypes and other racial framing. For example, in one Canadian study psychological researchers showed 264 photos of Chinese, black, and white male faces to 20 whites. After they had been trained for ten hours on seeing nuanced and subtle differences in these particular human faces, the volunteers were less likely to associate negative words like "hate" with black faces than they were before the training. One researcher suggests that such training in seeing facial differences might reduce racial profiling by police and other officials: "It's beneficial even if it doesn't affect their unconscious bias because it's still good to have them tell individuals apart better than before, and a side benefit might be that it affects how much they stereotype."[61] One common problem in the micro-actions of everyday racism is the way in which members of one group, especially the dominant white group, operate out of a racial frame that sees little difference in racial out-groups, indeed a framing that often insists that "they all look alike."

In addition, other recent research has examined which strategies and experiences seem to break down racial isolation in various high school and college settings. The character of interracial contacts, including friendships, seems important. For example, one research study found that positive interracial experiences in desegregated high school settings, such as having significant interracial friendships, increased the likelihood of having meaningful interracial friendships later on in college settings.[62] Another study interviewed students at eight University of California campuses. Students were asked about how they "gained a deeper understanding" of the views of students who differed from them in religious beliefs, political opinions, nationality, race and ethnicity, and sexual orientation. Interestingly, the researchers found that discussions that improved student understandings "more commonly occurred (about 60% reporting frequent) where the topic was race/ethnicity and nationality—student differences that were more apparent because of visual differences or accent." The students themselves made this connection between changed views and visible group characteristics. The reality of racial–ethnic diversity in college and other organizational settings like this can have, under the right circumstances (for example, equal status contacts), some positive effects on what people learn and understand about those unlike themselves.[63]

Interracial Organizations Working Against Racism

Group action is also essential. Antiracist action began in the first centuries of North American development. Multiracial groups have periodically helped to bring about social changes, as the 1840s–1850s abolitionists and 1950s–1960s civil rights activists demonstrated. Some whites have given their lives for antiracist movements. In October 1859, John Brown, a white abolitionist, led a small band of whites and blacks in an attempt to seize weapons at a federal arsenal at Harper's Ferry, with the goal of arming enslaved black Americans and facilitating rebellion against slavery. Today, one required step is for all levels of U.S. education to offer courses that discuss the actions of antiracist activists like John Brown. Radical abolitionists constituted one of the first multiracial groups to struggle aggressively against systemic racism. John Brown's lucid comment on his sentence of death for his efforts indicates his commitment to racial justice:

> Now, if it is deemed necessary that I should forfeit my life for the furtherance of the ends of justice, and mingle my blood further with the blood of my children and with the blood of millions in this slave country whose rights are disregarded by wicked, cruel, and unjust enactments,—I submit, so let it be done![64]

Since the antislavery efforts of the diverse Harper's Ferry band in 1859, a long line of whites, blacks, and others of color have worked together, often against enormous opposition, to bring expanded liberty and justice to this country. Recall the creation of the NAACP in the early 1900s, an organization seeking to fight racial exclusion. For many years this organization, which has constantly worked against systemic racism, has had both black and white officials in its leadership and/or membership. It celebrated its one-hundredth anniversary in 2009, with President Barack Obama as keynote speaker and with a racially diverse audience. Its then-chair, Julian Bond, made clear in his interviews and speeches that the social justice and racial equality goals of the organization had not yet been met, and that much work on racial discrimination and inequality still lay ahead.[65] We should note too that not only the NAACP efforts, but also other organizational efforts in the black-led civil rights movement of the 1950s and 1960s, involved participants from an array of racial and ethnic groups, including numerous whites. This movement had significant success in bringing down official segregation. In a social system like ours there seem to be only a few high leverage points from which to precipitate lasting changes, and U.S. history suggests that large coalitions of black and non-black Americans working against systemic racism can create such high leverage points for change in society.

In recent decades antiracist whites have helped to organize or have joined in grassroots organizations working against systemic racism. For example, dozens of groups called the "Institutes for the Healing of Racism" regularly hold seminars and dialogues on issues of racism in various U.S. cities. These multiracial groups work locally to heighten the awareness of racism, educate citizens about how to fight racial hostility and discrimination, and provide dialogue across local racial group boundaries. These antiracist groups have dealt openly with racist framing and institutional racism in their own lives and areas.[66]

Typical of the range of current antiracist organizations are the People's Institute for Survival and Beyond (PI) and Antiracist Action (ARA). Located in New Orleans and created by black activists, PI is a community-oriented group that sets up "Undoing Racism" workshops to train people in community and nonprofit organizations. These multiracial workshops—which have trained thousands of people, many of them whites, since the 1980s—are designed to help officials in organizations and community activists better understand racism and cultural diversity and to show them how they can "undo racism" in their lives and organizations. Taking a somewhat different tack, the substantially white ARA groups, about 200 as of 2009, have worked aggressively against racism in numerous cities in the United States and Canada. Originally established to combat neo-Nazi and Klan organizations, ARA groups have developed other antiracist programs. For example, their Copwatch program attempts to reduce police brutality by having members take video devices into the streets to record police actions in their dealings with citizens of color. While their objectives have varied, other antiracist organizations have also pressed for changes in systemic racism over the last few decades. A brief sampling includes the Dismantling Racism Program of the National Conference (St. Louis), the Anti-Racism Institute of Clergy and Laity Concerned (Chicago), the Northwest Coalition Against Malicious Harassment, the Southern Empowerment Project, and the Committee Against Anti-Asian Violence. We should note too that a number of these antiracist organizations, as well as established civil rights groups like the NAACP and Urban League, have played important roles in openly countering the racist accusations and charges that have been made against President Barack Obama and in helping to secure his election as president in 2008.[67]

One next step in a broad antiracist strategy for the United States would be to expand greatly the number and size of these and other antiracist organizations and to connect them into a national association working against the many aspects of systemic racism. Today, as in the past, broad multiracial organizations working against racial and ethnic oppression seem to be necessary. Coalitions have been attempted in the past. For example, since the 1980s the Reverend Jesse Jackson, a black civil rights leader, has worked with people from numerous racial and ethnic groups, including many whites, to build the Rainbow Coalition (later Rainbow-PUSH). This influential organization, based in Chicago, has pressed since the 1980s for social justice goals such as: better jobs and government job creation; more aggressive government efforts against racism, sexism, and homophobia; and government efforts to protect the environment. For a decade the organization helped to win some progressive electoral battles in several states and supported Jesse Jackson's pioneering bids for the U.S. presidency in 1984 and 1988.[68] Most recently, the organization has continued to focus major efforts on the persisting unemployment, home foreclosures, health care problems, and higher-education issues facing African Americans and other Americans of color across the country.

A New Constitutional Convention: an Idea Whose Time Has Come?

In 1787, some 55 white men met in Philadelphia and wrote a Constitution for what was seen as the first democratic nation. They met at the end of a long revolutionary struggle and often articulated their perspective using strong language about human equality and freedom. However, they had a very restricted view of those grand ideas. As we saw in Chapter 1, this Constitutional Convention did not include white women, African Americans, or Native Americans, who collectively made up a substantial majority of the population. Nor did it include representation for white men with little property. The representatives of less than 5 percent of the population framed a new constitution that has governed, with some amendments, the United States since the late eighteenth century. The document created by these propertied white men reflected their racial, class, and gender interests. While some of these interests encompassed the desires of all Americans to be free of the tyrannies of Europe—such as the constitutional prohibition of aristocratic titles and of a state religion—it took strong protests in the colonies from ordinary Americans before a Bill of Rights was added by the elite to their new Constitution.[69]

The 1858 Constitution

Not one of the original Constitutional Convention's delegates saw African Americans and Native Americans as human beings whose views, interests, and perspectives should be seriously considered. How then should African Americans and Native Americans, whose ancestors were present in large numbers in the country but excluded at the convention and whose enslavement was ratified by the Constitution, regard the document? Why should they accept the authority of a Constitution their ancestors played no part in making? As I see it, this undemocratic Constitution and its often racially biased tradition of pro-white interpretation over the intervening years should be replaced, for this tradition has constrained progressive change toward equality and justice for too long. All attempts to fully eradicate systemic racism since the late 1700s have been constrained by this document and interpretations of it by the mostly white judges and members of Congress holding office since that time. Significant attempts at societal change—scattered court decisions knocking down some discrimination and new civil rights laws—have been made within this white-framed and white-dominated societal context and, thus, have come only slowly and with enough deficiencies, such as weak enforcement, to insure that the underlying system of racial oppression has not been eliminated. The U.S. democratic project yet remains to be fully accomplished.

Significantly, only one multiracial group of Americans has, to my knowledge, tried to formulate and implement an antiracist constitution and declaration of independence. On May 8, 1858, more than a year before the previously mentioned Harper's Ferry raid, John Brown and his allies, black and white, met in Chatham, Canada, to formulate a new constitution to govern the small band of revolutionaries fighting for liberty—a constitution looking forward to a new antiracist nation of the United States. A total of 12 white Americans and 33 black Americans (some having fled to Canada) were present at this convention. The preamble to the pathbreaking provisional constitution they created read as follows:

> Whereas slavery, throughout its entire existence in the United States, is none other than a most barbarous, unprovoked and unjustifiable war of one portion of its citizens upon another portion ... in utter disregard and violation of those eternal and self-evident truths set forth in our Declaration of Independence: therefore, we, citizens of the United States, and the oppressed people who, by a recent decision of the Supreme Court, are declared to have no rights which the white man is bound to respect, together with all other people degraded by the laws thereof, do, for the time being, ordain and establish ourselves the following provisional constitution and ordinances, the better to protect our persons, property, lives, and liberties, and to govern our actions.[70]

Their radical declaration of independence further insisted "that the Slaves are, & of right ought to be ... free." Their new constitution and declaration of independence appear to be the only ones in U.S. history to be prepared by the representatives of oppressed African Americans, with their interests in liberty and justice substantially in mind.[71]

A New Constitutional Convention

Over recent decades, the U.S. government has a history of pressuring certain undemocratic countries to develop democratic constitutional conventions or commissions and, thus, democratic constitutions. For example, in 2005 numerous U.S. officials and political commentators put great pressure on the new Iraqi officials who replaced U.S.-deposed dictator Saddam Hussein to develop a constitutional Commission that would represent all the people of Iraq and create a new democratic constitution. There was much U.S. insistence that all major religious and ethnic groups in Iraq have representation, that women be represented, and that women's rights, minority rights, and religious rights be clearly recognized in the new Constitution. Among the 55 members of this constitutional Commission were indeed male and female representatives of most major groups in Iraq, although some were significantly underrepresented. The final Iraqi Constitution, approved in a national referendum, describes the country as a "democratic, federal, representative republic" and a "multiethnic, multi-religious country." The Constitution specifically lists an array of protected human rights, among them equality before law, equal opportunity, privacy, right to counsel, presumption of innocence, freedom of speech and press, the right to vote, economic and cultural liberty, the right to work, ownership of personal property, and at least a dozen more human rights. Significantly, this constitution explicitly bans racial discrimination and prohibits groups from propagating racism.[72]

Contemporary U.S. analysts have debated the meaning of these provisions and whether they can be fully implemented in a country with no strong history of democracy. Whether Iraq can become a true democracy at this time remains to be seen, but what is relevant for our purposes here is that many U.S. government officials and prominent commentators pressured the Iraqis to set up a constitutional Commission representing all major groups of Iraqis and to craft a new constitution with a full array of strong human rights protections. In stark contrast, however, the United States has *never* had such a constitutional convention or commission that represented all (or even much) of the population, nor has it developed a U.S. Constitution with nearly as large an array of explicit human rights protections as this Iraqi constitution provides. It is hard to see how the United States can insist on being the world's premier democracy without having its own political constitution made in at least as democratic a fashion as the U.S.-pressured Iraqi constitution.

Given this historical background, it seems time for the United States to have another constitutional convention, one that fairly represents all Americans. The old racialized foundation of the U.S. socio-political system needs to be replaced if the persisting realities of racial hostility and discrimination are to be thoroughly removed, just as the sinking foundation of a dilapidated old building must be replaced. A new constitutional convention is required not only to address issues of human rights and restitution for racially oppressed groups, but also to ensure that the governing document of the new multiracial democracy is actually produced by representatives of all the people of this country. The egalitarian and democratic ideas associated with the U.S. Bill of Rights and U.S. civil rights laws could well be points for important discussion at this new convention. However, as I see it, no existing U.S. laws should automatically be part of a new constitution because the meaning of these laws usually rests on their interpretation by the current, mostly white-dominated, judiciary.

What would be a more adequate set of starting points in beginning the debate on a constitution for a true multiracial democracy? The new convention might use the United Nation's Universal Declaration of Human Rights and related human rights documents that have expanded that declaration, including those on women's rights. First ratified in 1948 by the United Nations, this extraordinarily important international declaration today represents a growing consensus across the globe on what human rights are essential for a truly healthy society (see below, pp. 303–305). Without respect for a broad array of fundamental human rights there can be no real democracy. Thus, the official call for the new constitutional convention might indicate a grounding of its discussions in a mutual respect for the broad human rights of all Americans and in a mutual respect for the plurality of U.S. cultures and heritages.

Some experienced civil rights scholars and leaders have opposed the idea of a new constitutional convention because they fear the white majority there might even roll back existing civil rights protections. For example, the constitutional scholar Roy Brooks has criticized an earlier framing of this idea of a new convention because it "would open debate and reconsideration of the existing document, and the consequences could be dire."[73] He and others fear that in a society where many whites are still firmly operating out of a white-racist framing such a new convention might be dominated by whites who would consider restricting existing rights such as free speech and reproductive rights.

These fears might be reasonable if the new convention were to be dominated just by white male conservatives. However, in my hypothetical scenario the convention would *not* take place unless those who write the new constitution are fully representative of *all* sectors of the current population. No other arrangement will create the necessary conditions for full and open debates on matters of concern to all the American people. If the convention were to be held today, this stipulation would mean that white men would be about 32 percent of the delegates, instead of the 100 percent representation they had at the first convention. In addition, that 32 percent would include a much more diverse array of white men—such as labor union and gay rights activists—than those at the first convention. In addition, nearly 30 percent of the delegates would be Americans of color, and women would make up a little more than half of the delegates. These changes alone would make a contemporary convention dramatically different from the 1787 convention.

Some readers may also wonder if the average citizen or politician, who may be relatively ignorant of political and legal matters and history, would have the ability to deal intelligently and critically with issues of government as complex and difficult as those faced by the first constitutional convention—and certainly those faced by a new constitutional convention. One partial solution for this difficulty would be to require a process of intensive, open, and critical political education for all those who are delegates to this new convention, indeed perhaps for the entire U.S. population. In addition, prior to calling an official constitutional convention, those committed to the creation of a diverse and full democracy might press for trial conventions to test how such a truly representative convention might operate in dealing with the array of difficult decisionmaking, human rights, and related political issues. Indeed, there could be a practice convention in each major region, which might well generate important human rights and other important political debates in every area. The final convention might thus have its political and legal agenda shaped by the collective wisdom and decisions emanating from these previous regional deliberations.

A truly representative assembly would insure that, for the first time in U.S. history, the white majority hears much discussion of, and faces pressure to take seriously, the group interests and rights of Americans of color. This assembly will necessarily be diverse enough that many decisions on key constitutional provisions will likely have to be negotiated among the diverse contending groups. Constitutional decisions will require a consideration of the originally excluded interests of women and Americans of color, as well as of the more recently asserted interests of gay, lesbian, disabled, and other Americans. As with the first convention, the debates will probably be quite revealing and educational, not only for delegates but for the country as a whole. These constitutional debates would likely remove the smokescreen disguising the current undemocratic reality of U.S. society and show unequivocally how racial, class, gender, heterosexist, and other forms of exploitation and discrimination operate to the detriment of many Americans. A true democracy is one in which all people not only are represented but also have a significant and fair input into the creation of its laws and political institutions. Indeed, as now structured, with antique political institutions such as a U.S. Senate elected on the basis of territory not population and an unelected Supreme Court, the U.S. political system is much less democratic than numerous European political systems.[74] Of course, a new constitutional convention would be only a first step. A truly democratic constitution becomes the political basis on which to build and operate an array of effective democratic policies and institutions.

For all its possible difficulties, a new constitutional convention seems required not only to guarantee full human rights for previously excluded Americans but also to insure that the foundational document of this country is actually made by the representatives of all Americans. Such a convention also seems an important part of a reinvigorated antiracist strategy to build a truly just and egalitarian foundation for the United States. Equally as important to this antiracist strategy is the symbolism and reality of having a truly representative national assembly making the nation's actual constitution. Once those who have never actively participated in U.S. politics see that their representatives have been actively involved in making the founding document, commitment to and involvement in the new democracy will likely increase substantially. A strongly and truly democratic constitution—with broad citizen participation in its associated institutions and recurring citizen activism on behalf of its asserted human rights—seems the only real guarantee of full liberty, equality, and social justice for the United States.

Restitution and Reparations for Racism

As yet, no major group of white Americans has taken on the responsibility to call for reparations for the past and continuing negative impact of slavery, segregation, and contemporary racism on African Americans. For the most part, white leaders and rank-and-file whites have rejected proposals for large-scale reparations for those who have suffered from systemic racism. Recall the summer 2009 apology from the U.S. Senate for slavery and Jim Crow segregation. (The U.S. House passed a somewhat similar resolution in 2008.) This modest Senate apology includes a white-generated disclaimer explicitly barring black Americans from seeking reparations for nearly four centuries of racial oppression in this country. Thus, an apology like this operates, in effect, to play down the current seriousness and continuing negative consequences of this racial oppression.

Once there is a new democratic constitution in place, a comprehensive antiracist strategy would require an early addressing of reparations for the damage done by centuries of white-imposed oppression to African Americans and other Americans of color. Let us now consider here some of the arguments over such reparations for African Americans, the group most often discussed in this regard.

Some Arguments Against Reparations

Today, as in the past, many white Americans reject the idea that whites should have to pay with strong antidiscrimination programs like affirmative action for the persisting negative consequences brought on African Americans by the legacies of slavery and Jim Crow segregation, which operated before they were born. A common reaction is, "Let bygones be bygones." This view is documented in recent research on opposition to affirmative action efforts. In one study white respondents were given a hypothetical scenario with a white person having a slightly higher merit score than a black person applying for a job, but with the black person being hired. Evaluating this situation, most whites were opposed to the qualified black person being hired. They used reasoning like "merit should be foremost," "the past is the past," and "two wrongs don't make a right." However, on other survey questions these same whites gave abstract support for doing something about the difficult societal situation faced by black Americans, but this support gave way when white applicants had slightly better conventional test scores. In this study, most whites did not think that the recent racist past should affect employment decisions in the present.[75]

In many whites' view of this society the unjust enrichments gained by whites over earlier centuries should be forgotten. Collective forgetting is one way in which most handle the tension between the values of liberty and justice and the long history of racial oppression. However, there are major problems in the argument that whites today should not be accountable for what their ancestors did, as many say, "hundreds of years ago." Indeed, slavery ended less than 150 years ago, and today many black Americans are only a few generations removed from their enslaved ancestors. In addition, the near-slavery of Jim Crow segregation only came to an end in the late 1960s, well within the lifetimes of a great many white and black Americans alive today.

Many white Americans are inconsistent in regard to what parts of our past history they wish to be acknowledged and accepted, and what parts they wish to ignore and forget. In the thinking of most whites, the actions of our famous "founding fathers" and later prominent political leaders that have benefited whites are given great weight and legitimacy. Such actions include the making of a U.S. Constitution and the subsequent court decisions that actively interpreted that Constitution in the interest of whites. However, according to the prevailing view, the racially oppressive actions by the same white founders and later leaders should be forgotten or forgiven by those whose ancestors were victimized by their oppressive actions. Not surprisingly, a majority of whites do not see the earlier structures of oppression as relevant to present-day inequalities. Nonetheless, these whites will insist that black Americans and other Americans of color accept the U.S. Constitution and the laws created by whites as fully binding on them, even though they had no say in the laws' creation. The legal scholar Richard Delgado has summarized this point well in the form of a comment from a black professor in a constructed dialogue: Most whites insist that blacks

> owe obligations arising out of that social contract, but no obligation is owed to us arising from the abuse we suffered in connection with it. Ahistorical young conservatives want the benefit of social compliance from blacks with a system that provides young whites with security, schools, and liberty. But they don't want to pay for it by recognizing a debt they owe blacks arising from their forefathers' wrongs.[76]

In addition, some white analysts have argued that reparations for African Americans would not be fair for those whites whose ancestors immigrated to the United States after the slavery era. However, this common view overlooks the massive discrimination faced by black Americans under Jim Crow segregation after slavery, as well as contemporary discrimination. Much antiblack discrimination has been carried out, or colluded in, by later white immigrants and their children and grandchildren. Yet other anti-reparations arguments by conservatives include the argument that African Americans are better off in the United States, even with their enslavement, than they would have been in Africa without slavery. Among other problems, however, this view conveniently ignores the extensive European imperialism and intensive colonization that has long devastated and impoverished much of Africa, political–economic operations and consequences still quite evident across Africa today. It is likely that Africans would be prosperous today if they had not lost tens of millions of mostly younger people over centuries to the Atlantic slavery system and if they had maintained full control over their many mineral and other valuable resources that have often been lost to past and present Western imperialism.[77]

The Case for Restitution and Reparations

In the Charter of the Nuremberg Tribunal convened to deal with the Nazi war crimes after World War II, "crimes against humanity" were defined as "murder, extermination, enslavement, deportation, and other inhuman acts committed against any civilian population ... whether or not in violation of the domestic law of the country where perpetrated."[78] As we showed in previous chapters, white Europeans and white Americans have a long tradition of such crimes against humanity. Large-scale enslavement and extensive oppression of Africans across the Atlantic basin for centuries was, and remains, one of the most serious "crimes against humanity."

Most whites have benefited from centuries of racial oppression and the transmission of many racial privileges and substantial amounts of ill-gotten wealth from earlier oppression to later generations. Enslaved

Africans and African Americans created much wealth and capital that spurred not only the economic development of southern areas of this country, but also the industrial revolution in the United States and much of Europe. "Western production levels were transformed," the scholar Ali Mazrui informs us. "But so were Western living standards, life expectancy, population growth, and the globalization of capitalism. How do we measure such repercussions of slavery?"[79] The current prosperity, relatively long life expectancies, and relatively high living standards of whites as a group in the United States, as well as in the West generally, are ultimately and substantially rooted in the agony, exploitation, and impoverishment of those who were colonized and enslaved, as well as in the oppression and misery of their descendants under legal segregation and contemporary discrimination. As we have shown throughout this book, over several centuries white Americans as individuals, families, and communities have done much damage to African Americans. This damage is not just in the past, for African Americans today suffer from many psychological, economic, political, and other social costs that are the consequences of past and/or present racism.

Recently, researchers Jonathan Kaplan and Andrew Valls have suggested that one can base a strong case for black reparations today just on the reality and impact of blatant housing discrimination over the last decades of the Jim Crow segregation era—discrimination that often persists in a less overt form in our contemporary era. For a lengthy period racial segregation in housing was forced or reinforced by federal laws and government agency regulations mandating discrimination against Americans of color. Whites who implemented the huge federal home-ownership programs after World War II, such as the FHA and VA programs, built blatant racial discrimination into their operation. The FHA program had an underwriting manual that encouraged racially exclusionary housing covenants for new subdivisions, and the VA housing program had similar discriminatory regulations. White members of Congress made sure these large-scale programs were run by local white officials whose racist views often affected decisions about housing loans for black Americans and other Americans of color. Not until the 1980s were all aspects of this operational discrimination fully removed. Even then, much housing discrimination by local government officials and private individuals has continued by informal means. Housing discrimination was not even officially banned until the 1968 Civil Rights Act and its later amendments were passed.[80]

Significantly, the government housing legislation passed after World War II enabled a very large number of white families to move into the middle-class in the decades since that war—with the resulting substantial build-up of housing equities being a major source of resources and wealth many whites have passed along to children and grandchildren. In contrast, because of this substantial government-supported or government-enforced discrimination in housing, as well as in other institutional areas, black families were usually unable to secure adequate housing and to build up housing equity and related resources for their children and grandchildren. The currently huge wealth gap between white and black Americans is substantially the result of such government-supported blatant discrimination in the recent and distant past. Thus, one can today quantify some of what is owed to many still-living older black Americans who suffered years under official housing discrimination and other official and overt discrimination.[81]

This housing example effectively counters some whites' arguments that racial oppression was in some far distant past and that it is not possible to identify the perpetrators or victims for significant compensation. It also shows some problems with a related argument some whites have made against reparations for racism. They argue that institutional discrimination against African Americans is too impersonal for the development of concrete remedies. In several federal court cases, thus, judges have asserted the view that, while there may be societal discrimination, no one can determine who in particular is responsible and who has benefited. However, the housing example is one where one can often identify who in particular was actually responsible and who in particular was actually harmed—and what some of the significant long-term costs actually were, and indeed are today.

Recall that in traditional Western law the concept of unjust enrichment includes not only receiving benefits that justly belong to another but also the obligation to make full *restitution* to the victims. Numerous court decisions have provided remedies measured more by the gain to a defendant than by a plaintiff's loss. The defendant must give up the unjust enrichment, including substantial gains often made from it.[82] However, the law on such remedies has traditionally ignored group claims against unjust enrichment, and systemic racism involves unjust injuries to a very large group. An antiracist strategy might extend the remedies law to conditions of group oppression. Whites whose families have been in North America for generations, which is the majority, generally benefit today from significant racial advantages that their ancestors gained, often including gains under slavery and/or Jim Crow segregation. A majority have benefited from economic, political, and educational discrimination that favored their ancestors—and still favors themselves today (see Chapter 5, pp. 143–185). As with individual remedies, group remedies should encompass stopping the unjust extraction of benefits now and in the future as well as making restitution to the victim group for past actions. Restitution and reparations are inadequate without stopping the racialized processes that distribute, maintain, and increase the ill-gotten gains for both present and future generations of whites.

Occasionally, a few federal judges have recognized the principle of large-scale restitution as relevant to eliminating the effects of past racial discrimination. In *Larry Williams* et al. v. *City of New Orleans* et al., the savvy appellate justice John Wisdom argued, in a partially dissenting opinion, that the U.S. Congress that crafted the antislavery (thirteenth, fourteenth, fifteenth) amendments to the U.S. Constitution and a major civil rights act after the Civil War fully intended to grant the federal government power

> to provide for remedial action aimed at eliminating the present effects of past discrimination against blacks as a class ... the thirteenth amendment is an affirmative grant of power to eliminate slavery along with its "badges and incidents" and to establish universal civil freedom. The amendment envisions affirmative action aimed at blacks as a race. When a present discriminatory effect upon blacks as a class can be linked with a discriminatory practice against blacks as a race under the slavery system, the present effect may be eradicated under the auspices of the thirteenth amendment.[83]

Given this important historical argument, one can understand why many whites wish to *break* the historical link to large-scale past oppression. A full recognition of that linkage creates great pressure for significant compensation and restitution in the present.

Some Government Restitution and Reparations

Most white Americans appear to consider significant reparations for group-based damages suffered by black Americans to be a radical and undesirable public policy. However, white political leaders, white judges, and even ordinary whites have on occasion accepted the principle of reparations for past damages done to certain social groups. For example, U.S. courts have required corporations to compensate the deformed children of mothers who in the past took harmful drugs during their pregnancies without knowing of the drug's side-effects. The courts held that such harm done to later generations was foreseeable by the corporate executives in power at that earlier point. The argument that those executives are now gone was not allowed to get the corporations off the hook. Harmed children received significant compensation even though the damage from problematical corporate decisions became evident only years later. This compensation principle is similar to the one asserted by those arguing for reparations for African Americans, whose current socioeconomic conditions often reflect the significant damage done by earlier generations of whites.[84]

Significantly, the U.S. government has justifiably been active since World War II in efforts to pressure the German government to make large-scale reparations (many billions) to Jewish and other victims of the Nazi Holocaust, even though no one in the current German government making the reparations was part of earlier Nazi governments. Occasionally, moreover, U.S. political leaders have recognized a reparations principle in regard to discriminatory action taken against U.S. citizens. Belatedly, thus, the federal government agreed to pay some modest reparations to the Japanese Americans wrongfully imprisoned in U.S. internment camps during World War II. In 1987 Congress passed a law not only containing an apology to these Japanese Americans but also providing $1.2 billion in reparations.

With actions like this in mind, Roy Brooks has argued that to redress its role in the enslavement and segregating of African Americans, the U.S. government must not only provide an official apology for that oppression—which the U.S. House and Senate belatedly did in 2008–2009—but also support that apology with substantial reparations. Brooks terms this combination an *atonement* formula: "Apology and reparation—plus forgiveness leads to racial reconciliation." Interestingly, numerous other governments have made strong apologies for their involvement in racial oppression, including the apology by the post-war German government to Jews who had survived the Holocaust, the apology of Queen Elizabeth of Great Britain to the Maori people of New Zealand, and the apology of the South African government for apartheid. In several cases, moreover, significant reparations for government crimes have been provided. Because many governments have had to face the implications of the Nazi Holocaust during World War II, the ideas of apology and reparations for racial oppression are now clear to many people across the globe. A formal government apology begins to "set the record straight" on the impact of slavery and Jim Crow, but only significant and concrete reparations will transform the "rhetoric of the apology into a meaningful, material reality."[85]

Specific Proposals for Reparations

From the earliest days of abolitionist activity in the eighteenth and nineteenth centuries black leaders and their white allies argued that abolition of slavery and citizenship for African Americans were not enough. Thus, at an 1865 Republican convention, one congressional leader, Thaddeus Stevens, called for the taking of 400 million acres from former slaveholders and providing that to freed African Americans. Another abolitionist, Senator Charles Sumner (Massachusetts), also called for land grants to those recently enslaved. In their view legal equality alone would not eradicate the "large disparities of wealth, status, and power."[86] In the years 1866–1867 reparations legislation was brought before Congress, but failed. After the southern white oligarchy of former slaveholders resumed control in the 1870s, little was heard on the matter of such compensation or restitution for those freed from slavery. A century passed, and then since the 1960s civil rights movement the idea of reparations has had a resurgence. Dr. Martin Luther King, Jr. called for significant compensation for slavery, segregation, and continuing discrimination.[87]

Over recent decades scholars and activists have developed several international campaigns for reparations to Africans or African Americans. Recall the 1994 petition by Nation of Islam leaders to the United Nations for reparations for antiblack racism. And in 1992 a dozen experts selected by the Organization of African Unity developed a campaign for African reparations from Western countries like those provided by the German government to Holocaust survivors. Moreover, in 1996 the British House of Lords had a serious debate on the impact of slavery on Africa and Africans, with a few members proposing the idea of reparations to African countries from Great Britain and other colonial nations. Lord Anthony Gifford defended the idea that international law requires those who commit crimes against humanity, including enslavement, to make reparations to their victims or their descendants. There is no statute of limitations for crimes against humanity, so the still-harmed descendants of earlier victims of oppression deserve substantial reparations. He offered a procedure:

> The claim would be brought on behalf of all Africans, in Africa and in the Diaspora, who suffer the consequences of the crime, through the agency of an appropriate representative body.... The claim would be brought against the governments of those countries which promoted and were enriched by the African slave trade and the institution of slavery.... The amount of the claim would be assessed by experts in each aspect of life and in each region, affected by the institution of slavery.[88]

Such a debate needs to be held in the U.S. Congress. Every year since 1989 Congressman John Conyers, Jr. (Michigan) has introduced a bill in Congress to set up a commission to investigate the continuing impact of slavery on black Americans and examine the possibility of concrete reparations for slavery and its lasting impact. A key feature of the commission would be to educate the public, especially the white public, on the often hidden racist realities of U.S. history. While Conyers has been unable yet to secure hearings on his bill, he has gotten numerous congressional co-sponsors and continued to work patiently for a public discussion of meaningful reparations for centuries of systemic racism.[89]

In the case of African Americans, reparations might take several different but interrelated forms. One type of action would be the gradual transfer of an appropriate amount of compensating wealth from white communities to black communities, a transfer linked to particular remedial goals. For instance, the National Coalition of Blacks for Reparations in America (N'COBRA) has sought nearly $400 million in reparations—not just individual compensation but provision of group programs enabling black communities to prosper collectively over the long term. One way to make substantial restitution is to provide well-funded and extensive government support programs, over several generations, at the local and state levels for upgrading the education, job training, housing opportunities, and incomes of black Americans as individuals. A similar program could provide government resources to significantly upgrade major public facilities, including public schools, in all black communities. Yet other actions would guarantee representative political participation in all local, state, and national legislatures, so that black Americans could have an appropriate voice in significant government decisions. Such programs would be critical steps in a comprehensive strategy designed to restore African Americans to the place they would have been, had not trillions of dollars in wealth and uncounted other resources been taken from them by means of slavery, Jim Crow segregation, and contemporary discrimination.[90]

Numerous opponents of reparations have argued that there is no money available on such a scale. However, various recent government expenditures demonstrate that the issue is not principally the amount of money. For example, the federal government quickly found more than a trillion dollars to bail out private financial and related institutions in the 2008–2010 economic recession, with little difficulty and little debate before doing it. The federal government has also found trillions for military defense programs and overseas actions that were later judged to be dubious or unnecessary. Given such huge expenditures, the federal government, which was heavily involved in creating and maintaining the slavery and Jim Crow systems, can likely find the substantial amount of money needed to meet this country's moral and restorative obligations to long oppressed African Americans, Native Americans, and other Americans of color.

Note too that well-planned and well-distributed reparations and other restoration programs may be a better government option than the intentionally limited remedial programs of the past, such as affirmative action, which was initially the creation of white elites responding to civil rights protests. Substantial economic reparations can more easily be seen as direct compensation for the great economic damages suffered at the hands of discriminatory whites over several centuries—and thus not as a government "handout," a common view many whites have of current remedial programs. Even the beginning of meaningful reparations would have significance beyond the monetary compensation, for it would constitute dramatic societal symbolism, a serious recognition of the damage done by whites during long centuries of racial oppression.[91]

Building a Real Democracy

It appears that relatively few white Americans have ever envisaged for the United States the possibility of a truly just and egalitarian democracy grounded solidly in respect for a full array of human rights. Certainly, the original white founders did not conceive of such a possibility, even in the long run. Nor did later prominent white leaders such as Presidents Abraham Lincoln, Woodrow Wilson, Franklin D. Roosevelt, and Dwight D. Eisenhower envision that type of multiracial democratic future. Most contemporary white political leaders also do not seem to have that fully democratic future in mind. However, as the United States and the world change demographically and dramatically in coming decades, whites everywhere will face ever-greater pressures to create and participate in new or reinvigorated sociopolitical systems that move greatly in the direction of being non-racist, just, and egalitarian.

An International Standard for Expanded Rights

As another phase in a comprehensive racial-change strategy, Americans might be pressed to think futuristically in terms of what an authentic democracy might be like. Americans, especially white Americans, might be pressured to step outside the existing U.S. system, as best they can, to think carefully about an ideal fair, just, and fully humane society. To evaluate the U.S. system and suggest a replacement, we might begin by drawing on the international rights perspective as described in such documents as the Universal Declaration of Human Rights—a perspective that views every person as having a broad range of basic rights by virtue of being human. The idea that basic human rights *transcend* the boundaries and authority of any particular society or government was actually articulated by Thomas Jefferson and his fellow revolutionaries. Today, we need to extend this idea well beyond what the elitist founders envisioned. The international perspective on human rights was greatly strengthened by the Nuremberg trials of Nazi government officials after World War II. These trials established the principle that "crimes against humanity" are condemned by human principles higher than the norms and laws of any particular nation-state.[92]

The struggle to deal with the Nazi Holocaust, together with ongoing struggles for human rights by people in many countries—including African Americans in the United States—led to the pathbreaking Universal Declaration of Human Rights adopted in late 1948 by the United Nations General Assembly with no negative votes and eight abstentions. This important international agreement stipulates in Article 1 that "all human beings are born free and equal in dignity and rights," and in Article 7 that "all are equal before the law and are entitled without any discrimination to equal protection of the law." Article 8 further asserts, "Everyone has the right to an effective remedy ... for acts violating the fundamental rights," and Article 25 states that these rights extend to everyday life: "Everyone has the right to a standard of living adequate for the health and well-being of himself and his family, including food, clothing, housing." Since 1948 numerous international covenants on economic, social, and political rights have been signed by most United Nations members, and agencies like the UN Commission on Human Rights have been established to monitor human rights globally. The UN International Convention on the Elimination of All Forms of Racial Discrimination (CERD), put in force in 1969, specifically requires governments to make illegal the dissemination of ideas of racial superiority and the operation of organizations set up to promote discrimination. This convention, first ratified by some nations in the 1960s, was ratified by the United States only in 1994. Today CERD commits the U.S. and other governments to "adopt all necessary measures for speedily eliminating racial discrimination in all its forms and manifestations." These agreements provide some legal support for implementation of the human rights principles of the Universal Declaration of Human Rights. However, top U.S. government officials in the relevant agencies have *not* yet undertaken to live up to this international obligation to rid the United States of all forms and manifestations of racial discrimination.[93]

In the mid-1970s two additional agreements—the International Covenant on Economic, Social and Cultural Rights (ICESCR) and the International Covenant on Civil and Political Rights (ICCPR)—were approved by many countries and added to the Universal Declaration of Human Rights to create what is often termed an International Bill of Human Rights. However, while the ICESCR was signed by the U.S. government in 1979, it has not yet been ratified by the U.S. Senate. The U.S. Senate did ratify the ICCPR in 1992, but with 14 reservations, declarations, and understandings, so many that much of that Covenant was thereby invalidated for the United States. Nonetheless, these United Nations covenants represent major international responses to, as Judith Blau and Alberto Moncada suggest, "genocide, oppressive labor practices, the antiapartheid movement, national independence movements, liberation movements of colonized people, and atrocities committed against civilians" and to the "civil rights movement in America, the feminist movement, and the newly empowered voices of indigenous groups and landless peasants."[94] Thus, even without full U.S. participation, these important agreements signal a very important and increasing international consensus on the array of human rights necessary for a healthy society.

International Pressure for Change

Since its adoption the Universal Declaration of Human Rights (UDHR) has been used in crafting many international agreements, and major provisions have become part of international law. Originally implemented to spell out the meaning of the key terms "human rights" and "fundamental freedoms" in the UN Charter, it is binding on countries like the United States that became UN members. Leading legal scholars view this document as the "foundational international instrument of the human rights movement."[95] Most international documents on human rights at least allude to this important declaration. Court systems in numerous nations have cited the declaration—on occasion in overturning patterns of discrimination. At least 69 national constitutions take note of the UDHR and "twenty-four constitutions expressly incorporate its provisions."[96]

In contrast, U.S. judges and other officials have made much less use of the declaration than those in numerous other countries. Only a few U.S. court judges have occasionally been willing to take this international statement of human rights seriously. Indeed, much of the U.S. judicial and political leadership has been quite nationalistic and generally lacking in commitment to much of the international human rights perspective. Louis Henkin, a leading international legal scholar, has noted that the U.S. government "has not been a pillar of human rights, but a 'flying buttress'—supporting them from the outside, but declining itself to accept the obligations of the human rights regime."[97]

The comprehensive human rights perspective expressed in these UN documents draws not only on progressive human rights traditions of Europeans but also from the human rights perspectives of Native, African, Latino, and Asian Americans, and of other peoples around the globe. The UN human rights agreements strongly affirm that human beings have rights independent of particular governments and press governments to incorporate fundamental rights into everyday operations. They provide an internationally legitimated standard that can be used to judge systemic racism everywhere, including in the United States. As noted above, they can be the basis for significant discussion if the United States has a new and more democratic constitutional convention. Implementing this egalitarian standard of human interaction by new institutionalized arrangements to effect real democracy could dramatically restructure or eliminate current racist institutions in the United States.

Major change away from our racist institutions will require much more than one-way integration of racially subordinated people into existing white-dominated institutions. A multifaceted restructuring, mutual integration, and mutual adaptation are critical—among European Americans, African Americans, and all other Americans of color. Dr. Martin Luther King, Jr. once spoke of the movement of black Americans to be "creative dissenters who will call our beloved nation to a higher destiny," and not just to seek to integrate "into existing values of American society."[98] A democratically restructured U.S. society will require new human rights commitments, which could lead to the higher societal destiny that Dr. King contemplated.

Certain human needs seem universal: the need for personal self-respect, for substantial control over one's own life, for significant group self-management, and for access to the necessities of material life. Significantly, the U.S. Constitution has never had an economic bill of rights, even though civil rights and labor leaders have pressed to expand these rights since at least the 1960s. Conservative interests have fought against any such expansion of rights. Significantly, however, in his 1944 State of the Union address, the revered World War II era president President Franklin D. Roosevelt pressed for an "Economic Bill of Rights."[99] Roosevelt conceived of an expanded U.S. bill of rights that would include economic and social rights for all regardless of race, class, or religion. In a complete and authentic democracy, as he stated the matter, there would need to be full respect for the diversity of individuals, communities, and cultures.

Links with Other Antioppression Efforts

Ultimately, a truly robust U.S. democracy is impossible without an elimination of all major types of human oppression. Significant destruction of systemic racism, once begun, is likely to be corrosive of other types of societal oppression. In this relatively short book, even as I have tried to dig deeply into one major type of social oppression in this country, I have periodically discussed, albeit too briefly, some connections between racial, class, and gender oppression. Numerous scholars have noted the important interconnections and interrelationships between these important types of societal oppression. For instance, Sandra Harding has argued that "We should think of race, class and gender as interlocking; one cannot dislodge one piece without disturbing the others."[100] Not only racist structures, but capitalistic, sexist, heterosexist, ageist, and bureaucratic–authoritarian arrangements will have to be dismantled in this country if the lives of individuals and the functioning of their communities are to be truly democratic and rid of antihuman oppression.

Historically, Marxist analysis and activism have played perhaps the greatest role in generating protest movements against societal oppression in the Americas and elsewhere over the last century or so. Labor movements, many inspired by Marxist analysis, have brought improvements to the lives of workers in numerous capitalistic countries. Clearly, all Americans need access to sufficient economic, housing, and other social resources. Labor progressives have long argued that a full-fledged economic democracy is a requisite step in destroying the class structures of economic oppression and exploitation.[101]

Historically, as we have seen, there are strong similarities and cross-cutting linkages between antiracist struggles and class struggles in the United States. Ordinary workers, including white workers, are still greatly exploited by the capitalist class, which is regularly assisted by most U.S. political and intellectual elites. White and other workers usually have little role in how their workplaces are run, and always have little role in how the general capitalistic economy operates. However, as we have seen in earlier chapters, the white elite has worked hard to secure the acceptance of the existing racial and class hierarchies by white workers by offering them the "public and psychological wage of whiteness." As a result, white workers as a group have had more socioeconomic privileges and opportunities than black workers and many other workers of color. A successful antiracist coalition across the color line will need to deal with the majority of white workers' commitments to racial framing, privileges, and practices. Ultimately, many aspects of societal oppression will have to be dealt with, including not only antiblack and other racist framing and actions among white male and female workers but also sexist framing and actions among men, including men of color, and heterosexist framing and actions among whites and people of color.[102]

There are still multiple societal oppressions, and no one analysis can adequately deal with all these major oppressions. The research evidence I have presented throughout this book shows clearly and unmistakably that systemic racism remains central to the foundation of this society. I have argued here that a better and comprehensive understanding of this racism's history, framing, character, operation, and maintenance is essential to making sense of this society generally and to destroying persisting racial oppression in its contemporary forms. Having set this task, by no means do I downplay the importance of analyzing and eradicating the other types of social oppression central to U.S. society, including class exploitation, sexism, and heterosexism.

Over the last century there has been some conflict between those in one group struggling against a particular type of societal oppression and those in another group contending against yet other societal oppression, and so far there has been relatively little joining together in more general antioppression efforts and coalitions. Yet at the heart of each of these societal movements for change seem to be certain paramount issues that can be accented by all those seeking to build successful coalitions now and in the future. Perhaps the most important idea held in common is that of ridding the society of oppressive domination by one group over another, together with the related idea of meaningful democracy and self-determination to the fullest extent possible for every group. With great effort and new imagination in collective organizing, perhaps this shared vision of a country ultimately free of such societal oppression and domination can be used to build successful intergroup coalitions in the near future.

Conclusion

Antiracism is more than a theoretical framework organizing, explaining, and interpreting the realities of systemic racism. Now and in the past, active antiracism has encompassed an array of individual and group strategies to eradicate both individual and systemic racism. Many have studied racial oppression: the point is to eradicate it.

The eradication of systemic racism requires more than removing a few racial inequalities. Steps in the direction of removing discrimination and inequalities are very important and improve people's lives. However, a substantial reduction in, or full eradication of, systemic racism will require uprooting and replacing the existing hierarchy of racialized power and privilege. A developed antiracist strategy will need to move beyond reforms in current institutions to complete elimination of existing systems of racialized power. One analysis of U.S. liberatory strategies concluded that "oppressors cannot renounce their power and privilege *within* a racist relationship; they must *abandon* that relationship."[103]

Historically, oppression leads to conflict, and major conflict frequently leads to significant change. Most progressive developments in human rights in U.S. and global history have come after large-scale protests, people's movements, civil disobedience, open conflict, and/or societal revolutions. As Paul Lauren notes, from the

> emancipation of slaves after the French Revolution and United States Civil War to the gaining of independence by colonial peoples after World Wars I and II, the cause of human rights invariably has required some drastic upheaval to shift power away from those unwilling to share it voluntarily.[104]

Theorists and activists committed to an antiracist, liberty-and-justice framing of society cannot prove there will be societal change again, but can act on the assumption it is likely. As Ben Agger has noted about critical social theory, the

> future is a risk, a choice, framed by the past, the legacy of which is difficult to overcome. But critical social theorists … are certain that the past and present do not neatly extend into the future without any slippage.[105]

Human agency is possible in spite of oppressive structures, but must be regularly supported and regenerated.

Why should whites support major changes in the racist system? One reason is general but essential: whites have a moral obligation to take action, as individuals and as a group, to overturn the systemic racism they and their ancestors have created, and make meaningful the liberty-and-justice framing of society they often proclaim. There are also practical benefits. Some are small-scale benefits for whites as individuals. For example, one study of 50 white students found that interracial interactions were especially difficult for those among them who held very strong racial prejudices. Interactions with people of other racial groups resulted in very prejudiced whites being more likely than other whites to perform poorly on color/word-matching tasks.[106] Thus, educational efforts that break down a white individual's racist framing and its many prejudices may conceivably give him or her better interactive skills and comfort in interracial interactions in an ever-diversifying United States.

There are group advantages as well. Systemic racism has created significant racial inequalities in education and job skills, which in reality affect not only those racially subordinated but the country as a whole. Recently, Brookings Institution analysts noted that wide racial disparities in educational attainment do not just affect certain Americans of color, but now greatly threaten the country's "future economic growth, as well as the broader promise of upward mobility in American society."[107] In a situation where more highly educated workers are badly needed, the society as a whole benefits when more of its people gain strong "human capital" such as advanced education. W.E.B. Du Bois once argued that systems of oppression that exclude some people inevitably miss out on "vast stores" of human wisdom. When Americans of color are oppressed in this country's major institutions, not only do they suffer greatly, but the white-controlled institutions and whites within them often suffer significantly. Excluding many people of color has meant excluding much human knowledge, creativity, and understanding from society generally. A society that ignores such great stores of human knowledge and ability irresponsibly risks its future. Indeed, this problem can now regularly be seen in white policymakers' poor decisions on the domestic scene, as well as in their poor decisions about foreign policy, such as in regard to ill-advised military invasions overseas.[108]

If there is no real societal change in the near future, pressures for change will increase dramatically as whites become an ever-smaller minority of the U.S. population over the twenty-first century. As Abraham Lincoln once predicted, a "house divided against itself cannot stand." At the time, Lincoln's metaphor accented the centrality and contradictions of slavery in U.S. society. We can extend it today to the reality of a country still inegalitarian and racially divided because of "slavery unwilling to die." The question hanging over white Americans is this: do they wish to face increased societal conflicts for themselves, their children, or their grandchildren? During the 1960s civil rights movements numerous black leaders and a few white leaders pointed out that without social justice there can be *no* lasting public order. This is still the long-term reality. Without social justice the United States will never achieve a truly democratic and stable social order.

African Americans remain at the center of the U.S. system of racial oppression, and their antiracist counter-framing and consciousness have substantial potential for continuing challenges to our racist order. Fortunately for U.S. progress on multiracial democracy, African Americans have developed large-scale change movements a few times in U.S. history, and smaller-scale movements numerous times, and there will doubtless be more such movements in the future. While large-scale liberation movements have come and gone, strong efforts against U.S. racism have never disappeared. As a group, black Americans have not retreated to an enervating pessimism but have slowly pressed onward. While some have become more conservative and moved away from traditional civil rights efforts, many others continue to participate in civil rights, civic, and religious organizations working to eradicate racism, to get civil rights laws enforced, and to secure better living conditions for all Americans. Historically, this country has seen periods when black American protests have changed what the white elites and public see as in their own best interests. "The destabilizing effects of protest and resistance can alter the cost–benefit calculus so that change favorable to blacks actually comes to be in the interest of dominant forces."[109] This was true during the abolitionist period from the 1830s to the 1860s and again during the civil rights movements and rioting of the period from the 1950s to the early 1970s. Perhaps it can be so again.

In addition, the major efforts of African Americans to free themselves from societal oppression have often stimulated other Americans of color to do the same. Inspired by black efforts, or acting on their own, the latter have frequently reacted strongly to the white discrimination that specifically targets them. Today, there are numerous antiracist and civil rights groups, including the American Indian Movement, the Mexican American Legal Defense and Education Fund, the Puerto Rican Legal Defense Fund, the Japanese American Citizens League, the Asian American Legal Defense Fund, and the Organization of Chinese Americans. These and other similar groups are working now for change in U.S. patterns of racial oppression. To take just one example, today Native American activists are organizing local protest movements and fighting numerous legal battles to force the federal government to honor its hundreds of legal treaties. Moreover, the groups listed above are joined by an array of other organizations also pressing for social justice, including women's rights organizations and gay and lesbian organizations. One major challenge for U.S. progressives today is to build united coalitions against the numerous types of established oppression.

The world of which the U.S. is a part is dramatically changing. Numerous social contradictions have emerged out of the global racial order originally created to legitimate imperialistic aspirations and colonial expansion of European countries. These international dynamics created social and political structures that, then as now, have created and imbedded a strong racist framing with its negative images and ideologies of racial subordination. International relations, global markets, global financial institutions, and multinational corporations—along with shifts in new technologies—are all racialized, with white perspectives and the European and U.S. corporate class usually at their core. For centuries these Eurocentric institutions have been globalizing, dominant, and resistant to change. Today, however, there is substantial ferment against social oppressions across the globe. Over the next century neither the U.S. nor the world is likely to stay the same. Over the next century many groups and countries will almost certainly move farther out from under the dominance of white Americans and Europeans. People of color and those who question oppression everywhere are regularly organizing for change. In recent years we have seen strong antiracism movements in South Africa and Brazil, and renewed labor movements in numerous countries such as South Africa, Brazil, China, and Nigeria. Even in Europe, including in England and France, racially oppressed groups are uniting and questioning the old imperialist powers at their core.

Today, people of African descent remain the globe's largest racially oppressed group, a group now resident in many countries. In the 1980s and 1990s we saw a systemically racist society, the Republic of South Africa, move from white to black political control and begin to change the rest of its social and economic structure of racism (apartheid). Few analysts predicted such a sea change, and even though South Africa still faces many serious challenges before it attains full political and economic democracy, it has changed faster and more substantially than Western analysts had predicted. The possibility of a global democratic order rid of white racism remains only a dream, but the South African revolution shows that it is a powerful dream. More changes in the world's racist system will likely come as the human spirit conquers the continuing realities of oppression, however daunting they may be. The chair of the Special United Nations Committee against Apartheid once expressed this futuristic hope: the "world can never be governed by force, never by fear, never by power. In the end what governs is the spirit and what conquers is the mind."[110]

Notes

Introduction

1 Janet Kornblum, "Richards: 'I Lost My Temper Onstage,'" *USA Today*, November 20, 2006, www.usatoday.com/life/people/2006-11-20-michael-richards_x.htm (accessed September 4, 2009); Allen Salkin, "Comedy on the Hot Seat," *New York Times*, December 3, 2006, www.nytimes.com/2006/12/03/fashion/03comedy.html (accessed September 4, 2009).

2 "Imus Called Women's Basketball Team 'Nappy-headed Hostility,'" *MediaMatters*, April 7, 2007, http://mediamatters.org/items/200704040011 (accessed November 7, 2008); on surveys, see "Race and Ethnicity," www.pollingreport.com/race.htm (accessed February 27, 2009).

3 Jane H. Hill, *The Everyday Language of White Racism* (New York: Wiley-Blackwell, 2008), pp. 134–157.

4 Paul M. Sniderman and Thomas Piazza, *The Scar of Race* (Cambridge, MA: Harvard University Press, 1993), pp. 5, 175; Dinesh D'Souza, *The End of Racism: Principles for a Multiracial Society* (New York: Free Press, 1995), pp. 70–87.

5 "President-Elect Obama: the Voters Rebuke Republicans for Economic Failure," *Wall Street Journal*, November 5, 2008, http://online.wsj.com/article/SB122586244657800863.html (accessed December 28, 2008).

6 C.L.R. James, *American Civilization*, ed. Anna Grimshaw and Keith Hart (Cambridge, MA: Blackwell, 1993), p. 201.

7 James Madison, quoted in Michael P. Rogin, *Fathers and Children: Andrew Jackson and the Subjugation of the American Indian* (New York: Knopf, 1975), p. 319.

1 Systemic Racism: A Comprehensive Perspective

1 National Archives and Records Administration, *Framers of the Constitution* (Washington, D.C.: National Archives Trust Fund Board, 1986).

2 Max Farrand, ed., *Records of the Federal Convention of 1787*, vol. 1 (New Haven: Yale University, 1911), p. 486.

3 Herbert Aptheker, *Early Years of the Republic: From the End of the Revolution to the First Administration of Washington (1783–1793)* (New York: International Publishers, 1976), pp. 74–95.

4 Ibid., pp. 55–57.

5 William Lee Miller, *Arguing about Slavery: the Great Battle in the United States Congress* (New York: Knopf, 1996), p. 21.

6 Farrand, *Records*, vol. 1, 587; William M. Wiecek, *The Sources of Antislavery Constitutionalism in America, 1760–1848* (Ithaca: Cornell University Press, 1977), p. 15.

7 James Madison, Alexander Hamilton, and John Jay, *The Federalist Papers*, ed. Isaac Kramnick (New York: Viking Penguin, 1987). This quote is from number 54.

8 James Madison, quoted in Michael P. Rogin, *Fathers and Children: Andrew Jackson and the Subjugation of the American Indian* (New York: Knopf, 1975), p. 319. See also Paul Jennings, "A Colored Man's Reminiscences of James Madison," *White House History* 1 (1983): 46–51.

9 W.E.B. Du Bois, *The Suppression of the African Slave Trade to the United States of America, 1638–1870* (New York: Schocken Books, 1969), pp. 54–62; Donald Robinson, *Slavery in the Structure of American Politics* (New York: Norton, 1979), p. 71.

10 Robert A. Rutland, ed., *The Papers of George Mason: 1725–1792*, vol. 3 (Chapel Hill: University of North Carolina Press, 1970), pp. 965–966.

11 Paul Finkelman, "Slavery and the Constitutional Convention," in *Beyond Confederation: Origins of the Constitution and American National Identity*, eds. Richard Beeman, Stephen Botein, and Edward C. Carter (Chapel Hill: University of North Carolina Press, 1987), p. 225.

12 Aptheker, *Early Years of the Republic*, p. 93.

13 Donald E. Lively, *The Constitution and Race* (New York: Praeger, 1992), pp. 4–5. Lively draws on research by William M. Wiecek.

14 F. Nwabueze Okoye, "Chattel Slavery as the Nightmare of the American Revolutionaries," *William and Mary Quarterly* 37 (January 1980): 13.

15 John Dickinson, *Letters from a Farmer in Pennsylvania to the Inhabitants of the British Colonies* (Philadelphia, 1768), p. 38, quoted in Okoye, "Chattel Slavery as the Nightmare of the American Revolutionaries," p. 3. Emphasis in original.

16 Benjamin B. Ringer, *"We the People" and Others* (New York: Tavistock, 1983), pp. 130–131.

17 Quotes are from William Lloyd Garrison, "A Compact with Hell," in *The United States Constitution*, eds. Bertell Ollman and Jonathan Birnbaum (New York: New York University Press, 1990), p. 96.

18 I draw on several sources, especially Dennis Cauchon, "For Founding Fathers, Slave Ownership Common; Practice Went Unquestioned by Many Admired Historical Figures," *USA Today*, March 9, 1998, p. 8A.

19 Herbert Aptheker, *The Unfolding Drama: Studies in U.S. History*, ed. Bettina Aptheker (New York: International Publishers, 1978), p. 100.

20 William M. Wiecek, "The Origins of the Law of Slavery in British North America," *Cardozo Law Review* 17 (May 1996): 1791.

21 "1000 Commemorate One Va. Man's Freeing of Slaves 72 Years Early," *Marietta Times*, July 29, 1991, p. A1; Andrew Levy, *The First Emancipator: Slavery, Religion, and the Quiet Revolution of Robert Carter* (New York: Random House, 2007).

22 Aptheker, *Early Years of the Republic*, p. 93.

23 W.E.B. Du Bois, *The World and Africa* (New York: International Publishers, 1965 [1946]), p. 23.

24 Frederick Douglass, "The Color Line," *North American Review* (June 1881), as excerpted in *Jones et ux. v. Alfred H. Mayer Co.*, 392 U.S. 409, 446–47 (1968). Emphasis added.

25 W.E.B. Du Bois, *Darkwater* (1920), as reprinted in *The Oxford W.E.B. Du Bois Reader*, ed. Eric J. Sundquist (New York: Oxford, 1996), p. 504.

26 Ida B. Wells-Barnett, *A Red Record*, as excerpted in Patricia Madoo Lengermann and Jill Niebrugge-Brantley, eds., *The Women Founders: Sociology and Social Theory, 1830–1930* (New York: McGraw-Hill, 1998), p. 177.

27 Oliver C. Cox, *Caste, Class, and Race* (Garden City: Doubleday, 1948), p. 344.

28 Kwame Ture [Stokely Carmichael] and Charles V. Hamilton, *Black Power: the Politics of Liberation in America* (New York: Vintage, 1967). See also Bob Blauner, *Racial Oppression in America* (New York: Harper and Row, 1972).

29 Du Bois, *The World and Africa*, p. 37.

30 See Theodore Cross, *The Black Power Imperative: Racial Inequality and the Politics of Nonviolence* (New York: Faulkner, 1984), p. 510; Patricia Williams, *The Alchemy of Race and Rights* (Cambridge, MA: Harvard University Press, 1991), p. 101; Ian Ayres and Fredrick E. Vars, "When Does Private Discrimination Justify Public Affirmative Action?" *Columbia Law Review* 98 (November 1998): 1598–1610; Richard Delgado, *The Coming Race War?* (New York: New York University Press, 1996), pp. 104–105.

31 James A. Ballentine, *Ballentine's Law Dictionary*, 3rd edn, ed. William S. Anderson (San Francisco: Bancroft-Whiteney, 1969), p. 1320.

32 "Abraham Lincoln's Second Inaugural Address," wikisource, http://en.wikisource.org/wiki/Abraham_Lincoln%27s_Second_Inaugural_Address (accessed July 1, 2009).

33 Philomena Essed, *Understanding Everyday Racism* (Newbury Park: Sage, 1991), p. 37; Bertell Ollman, *Alienation: Marx's Conception of Man in Capitalist Society*, 2nd edn. (Cambridge: Cambridge University Press, 1976).

34 I am influenced here by Catharine A. MacKinnon, *Toward a Feminist Theory of the State* (Cambridge, MA: Harvard University Press, 1989), pp. 3–5.

35 Melvin M. Leiman, *The Political Economy of Racism: a History* (London: Pluto Press, 1993); William Julius Wilson, *The Declining Significance of Race: Blacks and Changing American Institutions* (Chicago: University of Chicago Press, 1978); Jim Sleeper, *The Closest of Strangers: Liberalism and the Politics of Race in New York* (New York: Norton, 1990); William Julius Wilson, *More Than Just Race: Being Black and Poor in the Inner City* (New York: W.W. Norton, 2009).

36 Michael Omi and Howard Winant, *Racial Formation in the United States: From the 1960s to the 1990s*, 2nd edn. (New York: Routledge, 1994), p. 48.

37 Robert Miles, *Racism* (London: Routledge, 1989).

38 Jorge Klor de Alva, Earl Shorris, and Cornel West, "Our Next Race Question: the Uneasiness Between Blacks and Latinos," in *Critical White Studies: Looking Behind the Mirror*, eds. Richard Delgado and Jean Stefancic (Philadelphia: Temple University Press, 1997), p. 485.

39 Dole comments on *Meet the Press*, NBC Television, February 5, 1995.

40 I am indebted to Sidney Willhelm for discussion here.

41 Iris Young, *Justice and the Politics of Difference* (Princeton: Princeton University Press, 1990), p. 52.

42 Brian K. Bucks, Arthur B. Kennickell, Traci L. Mach, and Kevin B. Moore, "Changes in U.S. Family Finances from 2004 to 2007: Evidence from the Survey of Consumer Finances," *Federal Reserve Bulletin* 95 (February 2009): A1–A55.

43 Joe R. Feagin and Clairece Y. Feagin, *Racial and Ethnic Relations*, 8th edn. (Upper Saddle River: Prentice Hall, 2008), chapters 3–4; Karen Brodkin, *How the Jews Became White Folks: and What that Says about Race in America* (New Brunswick: Rutgers University Press, 1998).

44 Edward Ball, *Slaves in the Family* (New York: Ballantine Books, 1999), p. 14.

45 Martin J. Katz, "The Economics of Discrimination: the Three Fallacies of Croson," *Yale Law Journal* 100 (January 1991): 1041–1044; Melvin L. Oliver and Thomas M. Shapiro, "Creating an Opportunity Society," *American Prospect* 18 (May 2007), pp. A27–A28.

46 Jeffrey M. Timberlake, "Racial and Ethnic Inequality in the Duration of Children's Exposure to Neighborhood Poverty and Affluence," *Social Problems* 54 (August 2007): 319–342.

47 Joe R. Feagin, Kevin Early, and Karyn D. McKinney, "The Many Costs of Discrimination," unpublished paper, University of Florida, 1999.

48 W.E.B. Du Bois, *Black Reconstruction in America 1860–1880* (New York: Atheneum, 1992 [1935]), p. 700.

49 Theodore Allen, *The Invention of the White Race: Racial Oppression and Social Control* (London: Verso, 1994), pp. 19–21.

50 Ibid., p. 143; Du Bois, *Black Reconstruction in America 1860–1880*, p. 27.

51 Louise Michele Newman, *White Women's Rights: the Racial Origins of Feminism in the United States* (New York: Oxford University Press, 1999), pp. 179–85; bell hooks, *Feminist Theory: From Margin to Center* (Boston: South End Press, 1984), pp. 6–51.

52 Joe R. Feagin, *The White Racial Frame: Centuries of Racial Framing and Counter-Framing* (New York: Routledge, 2010).

53 Du Bois, *Darkwater* (1920), as reprinted in *The Oxford W.E.B. Du Bois Reader*, pp. 497–498.

54 See Ronald T. Takaki, *Iron Cages: Race and Culture in 19th Century America* (New York: Oxford University Press, 1990), pp. 4–15.
55 Benjamin Franklin, "Observations Concerning the Increase of Mankind, Peopling of Countries, Etc." (1751), as quoted in *Benjamin Franklin: a Biography in His Own Words*, ed. Thomas Fleming (New York: Harper and Row, 1972), pp. 105–106. I use modern capitalization.
56 See Robert S. Feldman, *Social Psychology* (Englewood Cliffs: Prentice-Hall, 1995), p. 94.
57 Oliver C. Cox, *Elements and Social Dynamics* (Detroit: Wayne University Press, 1976), pp. xxxi, 393.

2 Slavery Unwilling to Die: The Historical Development of Systemic Racism

1 "Charles Joyner on the Middle Passage," PBS, www.pbs.org/wgbh/aia/part1/1i3067.html (accessed July 6, 2009).
2 United Nations, "Convention on the Prevention and Punishment of Genocide," *The United Nations and Human Rights, 1945–1995* (New York: United Nations Department of Public Information, 1995), p. 151.
3 David E. Stannard, *The American Holocaust: Columbus and the Conquest of the New World* (New York: Oxford University Press, 1992); Charles W. Mills, *The Racial Contract* (Ithaca: Cornell University Press, 1997), pp. 98, 155.
4 William T. Hagan, *American Indians* (Chicago: University of Chicago Press, 1961), p. 14. See also pp. 12–15. An earlier version of this section is in Joe R. Feagin and Clairece B. Feagin, *Racial and Ethnic Relations*, 8th edn. (Upper Saddle River: Prentice-Hall, 1999), chapters 7 and 8.
5 They are quoted in Michael P. Rogin, *Fathers and Children: Andrew Jackson and the Subjugation of the American Indian* (New York: Knopf, 1975), p. 319; Winthrop D. Jordan, *White Over Black: American Attitudes Toward the Negro, 1550–1812* (Chapel Hill: University of North Carolina Press, 1968), pp. 239–241.
6 Benjamin B. Ringer, *"We the People" and Others* (New York: Tavistock, 1983), pp. 134–138.
7 *Dred Scott v. John F.A. Sandford*, 60 U.S. 393, 403–404, 408 (1857).
8 Ringer, *"We the People" and Others*, p. 36.
9 Robin Blackburn, *The Making of New World Slavery: From the Baroque to the Modern, 1492–1800* (London: Verso, 1997), p. 10.
10 A. Leon Higginbotham, Jr., *Shades of Freedom: Racial Politics and the Presumptions of the American Legal Process* (New York: Oxford University Press, 1996), pp. 14–51.
11 Forrest G. Wood, *The Arrogance of Faith: Christianity and Race in America from the Colonial Era to the Twentieth Century* (New York: Knopf, 1990), p. xviii.
12 Higginbotham, *Shades of Freedom*, p. xxiii; Lawrence M. Friedman, *A History of American Law* (New York: Simon and Schuster, 1973), pp. 72–76, 192–200; Herbert Aptheker, *American Negro Slave Revolts* (New York: International Publishers, 1943), pp. 53–78.
13 Thomas Jefferson, as quoted in Peter M. Bergman, *The Chronological History of the Negro in America* (New York: Harper & Row, 1969), p. 52.
14 Walter Johnson, "Slavery, Reparations, and the Mythic March of Freedom," *Raritan* 27 (2007): 41–67; M'Baye Gueye, "A Continent of Fear," *UNESCO Courier* 47(1994): 16. On numbers, see Philip D. Curtin, *The African Slave Trade: a Census* (Madison: University of Wisconsin Press, 1968); Joseph E. Inikori, ed., *Forced Migration* (New York: Africana Publishing, 1982), pp. 19–33.
15 Blackburn, *The Making of New World Slavery*, p. 19; Herbert Aptheker, *The Colonial Era* (New York: International Publishers, 1959), pp. 18–39.
16 Ronald Segal, *The Black Diaspora* (New York: Farrar, Straus and Giroux, 1995),

pp. 58–59; Kenneth S. Greenberg, *Honor and Slavery* (Princeton: Princeton University Press, 1996).

17 Peter J. Parish, *Slavery: History and Historians* (New York: Harper and Row, 1989), p. 129; see also pp. 126–132.

18 Elizabeth Fox-Genovese, *Within the Plantation Household: Black and White Women of the Old South* (Chapel Hill: University of North Carolina Press, 1988), p. 24.

19 See Kenneth Stampp, *The Peculiar Institution: Slavery in the Ante-Bellum South* (New York: Vintage Books, 1956); Robert W. Roel and Stanley Engerman, *Time on the Cross: the Economics of American Negro Slavery* (Boston: Little, Brown, 1974).

20 Lorenzo J. Greene, *The Negro in Colonial New England* (New York: Atheneum, 1969), pp. 68–69.

21 Ronald Bailey, "The Other Side of Slavery," *Agricultural History* 68 (spring 1994): 36.

22 James W. Loewen, *Lies My Teacher Told Me: Everything Your American History Textbook Got Wrong* (New York: The New Press, 1995), p. 135.

23 A. Leon Higginbotham, Jr., *In the Matter of Color* (New York: Oxford University Press, 1978), pp. 63–70, 144–149. An earlier discussion is in Joe R. Feagin, "Slavery Unwilling to Die: the Background of Black Oppression in the 1980s," *Journal of Black Studies* 17 (December 1986): 173–200. See also Ringer, *"We the People" and Others*, p. 533.

24 John R. McKivigan, "The Northern Churches and the Moral Problem of Slavery," in *The Meaning of Slavery in the North*, eds. David Roediger and Martin H. Blatt (New York: Garland, 1998), pp. 77–94.

25 Olaudah Equiano, "The Interesting Narrative of the Life of Olaudah Equiano," in *Afro-American History*, ed. Thomas R. Frazier (New York: Harcourt, Brace & World, 1970), pp. 18–20. There is debate on the Equiano biography, but not Middle Passage conditions. See Adam Hochschild, *Bury the Chains: Prophets and Rebels in the Fight to Free an Empire's Slaves* (Boston: Houghton Mifflin, 2006).

26 Stephanie Smallwood, *Saltwater Slavery* (Cambridge, MA: Harvard University Press, 2007), p. 68.

27 William Wells Brown, *From Fugitive Slave to Free Man*, ed. William L. Andrews (New York: Mentor Books, 1993 [1847]), p. 30.

28 See T. Lindsay Baker and Julie P. Baker, eds., *The WPA Oklahoma Slave Narratives* (Norman: University of Oklahoma Press, 1996).

29 David Brown and Clive Webb, *Race in the American South: From Slavery to Civil Rights* (Gainesville: University of Florida Press, 2007), p. 138. See also Patricia Morton, "Introduction," in *Discovering the Women in Slavery*, ed. Patricia Morton (Athens: University of Georgia Press, 1996), pp. 7–8.

30 Patricia J. Williams, *The Alchemy of Race and Rights* (Cambridge, MA: Harvard University Press, 1991), pp. 154–156.

31 Melton A. McLaurin, *Celia: a Slave* (Athens: University of Georgia Press, 1991).

32 The three-quarters-white Hemings was half-sister of Jefferson's wife. Jerry Fresia, *Toward an American Revolution: Exposing the Constitution and Other Illusions* (Boston: South End, 1988), pp. 1–2; Dinitia Smith and Nicholas Wade, "DNA Evidence Links Thomas Jefferson to Slave's Offspring," *Gainesville Sun*, November 1, 1998, p. 4A.

33 James Parton, quoted in Paul Finkelman, *Slavery and the Founders: Race and Liberty in the Age of Jefferson* (Armonk: M.E. Sharpe, 1996), p. 143.

34 Jordan, *White Over Black*, p. 153.

35 S.E. Anderson, *The Black Holocaust* (New York: Writers and Readers Press, 1995), pp. 156–158.

36 I am indebted here to discussions with Holly Hanson. See John Thornton, *Africa and Africans in the Making of the Atlantic World, 1400–1680* (New York: Cambridge University Press, 1992), pp. 5–9; Molefi Kete Asante, "The Wonders of Africa," post to Discussion List for African American Studies (H-Afro-Am), November 1999. See also

Dinesh D'Souza, *The End of Racism: Principles for a Multiracial Society* (New York: Free Press, 1995), pp. 70–87; Stanley M. Elkins, *A Problem in American Institutional and Intellectual Life* (New York: Grosset and Dunlap, 1963), pp. 96–97.

37 W.E.B. Du Bois, *Darkwater* (1920), as reprinted in *The Oxford W.E.B. Du Bois Reader*, ed. Eric J. Sundquist (New York: Oxford, 1996), p. 504.

38 W.E.B. Du Bois, *Black Reconstruction in America 1860–1880* (New York: Atheneum, 1992 [1935]), p. 10.

39 See John Willinsky, *Learning to Divide the World: Education at Empire's End* (Minneapolis: University of Minnesota Press, 1998), p. 191.

40 Rafael Tammariello, "The Slave Trade," *Las Vegas Review-Journal* (February 8, 1998): 1E.

41 J. H. Parry and P.M. Sherlock, *A Short History of the West Indies*, 3rd edn. (New York: St. Martin's Press, 1971), pp. 110–111. See also William M. Wiecek, *The Sources of Antislavery Constitutionalism in America, 1760–1848* (Ithaca: Cornell University Press, 1977), pp. 15–16.

42 William M. Wiecek, "The Origins of the Law of Slavery in British North America," *Cardozo Law Review* 17 (May 1996): 1739; Eric Williams, *Capitalism and Slavery* (Chapel Hill: University of North Carolina Press, 1994 [1944]), pp. 98–107; Douglass C. North, *The Economic Growth of the United States, 1790–1860* (Englewood Cliffs: Prentice-Hall, 1961), pp. 38–45; Bailey, "The Other Side of Slavery," p. 40; Blackburn, *The Making of New World Slavery*, chapter 12; Anderson, *The Black Holocaust*, p. 19; Barbara L. Solow and Stanley L. Engerman, "British Capitalism and Caribbean Slavery: the Legacy of Eric Williams: an Introduction," in *British Capitalism and Caribbean Slavery: The Legacy of Eric Williams* (Cambridge: Cambridge University Press, 1987), pp. 8–9.

43 Williams, *Capitalism and Slavery*, p. 52. See also Wilson E. Williams, *Africa and the Rise of Capitalism* (New York: AMS Press, 1975 [1938]), pp. 23–25.

44 Solow and Engerman, "British Capitalism and Caribbean Slavery," pp. 5–7; Ronald Bailey, "'Those Valuable People, the Africans,'" in *The Meaning of Slavery in the North*, eds. Roediger and Blatt, p. 11.

45 Fred Bateman and Thomas Weiss, *A Deplorable Scarcity: the Failure of Industrialization in the Slave Economy* (Chapel Hill: University of North Carolina Press, 1981); Stanley Lebergott, *The Americans: an Economic Record* (New York: Norton, 1984); Robert S. Browne, "Achieving Parity Through Reparations," in *The Wealth of Races: the Present Value of Benefits from Past Injustices*, ed. Richard F. America (New York: Greenwood Press, 1990), pp. 201–202.

46 North, *The Economic Growth of the United States, 1790–1860*, p. 63.

47 Bailey, "'Those Valuable People, the Africans,'" in *The Meaning of Slavery in the North*, eds. Roediger and Blatt, pp. 14, 19. I draw here on North, *The Economic Growth of the United States, 1790–1860*, p. 63; and Ronald T. Takaki, *Iron Cages: Race and Culture in 19th-Century America* (New York: Oxford University Press, 1990), p. 78.

48 North, *The Economic Growth of the United States*, 1790–1860, p. 41; Takaki, *Iron Cages*, p. 77; Browne, "Achieving Parity Through Reparations," p. 201; Segal, *The Black Diaspora*, pp. 56–58.

49 Ali A. Mazrui, "Who Should Pay for Slavery? Reparations to Africa," *World Press Review* 8 (August 1993): 22. I also draw on North, *The Economic Growth of the United States, 1790–1860*, p. 122.

50 Herbert Aptheker, *The Unfolding Drama: Studies in U.S. History*, ed. Bettina Aptheker (New York: International Publishers, 1978), p. 84; Segal, *The Black Diaspora*, p. 58.

51 Fritz Hirschfeld, *George Washington and Slavery: a Documentary Portrayal* (Columbia: University of Missouri Press, 1997), p. 236. I also draw here on pp. 16, 37, 49, 68–69.

52 Takaki, *Iron Cages*, pp. 43–54.

53 Edmund S. Morgan, *American Slavery, American Freedom: the Ordeal of Virginia* (New

York: Norton, 1975), p. 5. See Derrick Bell, "White Supremacy in America: its Legal Legacy, its Economic Costs," in *Critical White Studies: Looking Behind the Mirror*, eds. Richard Delgado and Jean Stefancic (Philadelphia: Temple University Press, 1997), p. 596.

54 *Merriam-Webster's Collegiate Dictionary*, 10th edn. (Springfield: Merriam-Webster, 1993), p. 901. See Jack Niemonen, "The Role of the State in the Sociology of Racial and Ethnic Relations: Some Theoretical Considerations," *Free Inquiry in Creative Sociology* 23 (May 1995): 28.

55 William Lee Miller, *Arguing About Slavery: the Great Battle in the United States Congress* (New York: Knopf, 1996), p. 13; Loewen, *Lies My Teacher Told Me*, pp. 143–146.

56 Aptheker, *The Unfolding Drama*, p. 83.

57 John Hope Franklin, *From Slavery to Freedom*, 4th edn. (New York: Knopf, 1984), pp. 250–253.

58 Stetson Kennedy, *After Appomattox: How the South Won the War* (Gainesville: University Press of Florida, 1995), p. 3. See Cedric J. Robinson, *Black Movements in America* (New York: Routledge, 1997), pp. 86–88.

59 Kennedy, *After Appomattox*, pp. 3–4.

60 *Civil Rights Cases*, 109 U.S., 62–63 (1883).

61 Ruth Thompson-Miller and Joe R. Feagin, "The Reality and Impact of Legal Segregation in the United States," in *Handbook of the Sociology of Racial and Ethnic Relations*, eds. Hernán Vera and Joe R. Feagin (New York: Springer Science, 2007), pp. 455–464; John W. Cell, *The Highest State of White Supremacy: the Origins of Segregation in South Africa and the American South* (Cambridge: Cambridge University Press, 1982), pp. 168–170.

62 *Plessy v. Ferguson*, 163 U.S. 537, 552–553, 563 (1896).

63 Trudier Harris, *Exorcising Blackness: Historical and Literary Lynching and Burning Rituals* (Bloomington: Indiana University Press, 1984), p. 7.

64 The quotes are from Nedra Tyre, "You All Are a Bunch of Nigger Lovers," in *Red Wine First* (New York: Simon and Schuster, 1947), pp. 120–122, as quoted in Harris, *Exorcising Blackness*, p. 10.

65 Sidney Willhelm, personal communication, July 1998; Melvin L. Oliver and Thomas M. Shapiro, *Black Wealth/White Wealth: a New Perspective on Racial Equality* (New York: Routledge, 1995), pp. 14–15.

66 Oliver and Shapiro, *Black Wealth, White Wealth*, p. 14.

67 Du Bois, *Black Reconstruction*, p. 602.

68 Pete Daniel, *The Shadow of Slavery: Peonage in the South, 1901–1969* (Urbana: University of Illinois Press, 1972), p. ix; Feagin, "Slavery Unwilling to Die," pp. 173–200.

69 John Egerton, *Speak Now Against the Day: the Generation Before the Civil Rights Movement in the South* (Chapel Hill: University of North Carolina Press, 1994), pp. 29–30.

70 Ringer, *"We the People" and Others*, p. 535.

71 Bob Blauner, *Racial Oppression in America* (New York: Harper and Row, 1972), p. 64.

72 Arthur I. Waskow, *From Race Riot to Sit-In, 1919 and the 1960s* (Garden City: Doubleday, 1966), pp. 209–240; David Chalmers, *Hooded Americanism: the History of the Ku Klux Klan* (Durham: Duke University Press, 1987 [1965]), pp. 200–250.

73 Gunnar Myrdal, *An American Dilemma*, vol. 1 (New York: McGraw-Hill, 1964 [1944]), p. 240.

74 Harvard Sitkoff, *A New Deal for Blacks: the Emergence of Civil Rights as a National Issue* (New York: Oxford, 1978), pp. 37–38.

75 C.G. Wye, "The New Deal and the Negro Community," *Journal of American History* 59 (December 1972): 630–640; Nancy J. Weiss, *Farewell to the Party of Lincoln: Black Politics in the Age of FDR* (Princeton: Princeton University Press, 1983), p. 119.

76 David Brown and Clive Webb, *Race in the American South: From Slavery to Civil Rights* (Gainesville: University of Florida Press, 2007), pp. 193–196.

77 Ibid. See Richard Wright, *Black Boy* (New York: HarperCollins, 1993 [1944–1945]), p. 231.
78 William H. Harris, *The Harder We Run: Black Workers Since the Civil War* (New York: Oxford University Press, 1982), pp. 124–131.
79 Harris, *The Harder We Run*, p. 131.
80 Sidney M. Willhelm, *Who Needs the Negro?* (Cambridge, MA: Schenkman, 1970); Sidney M. Willhelm, *Black in a White America* (Cambridge, MA: Schenkman, 1983). I also draw on Willhelm's presentation at Syracuse University, June 10, 1998.
81 *Jones et ux. v. Alfred H. Mayer Co.*, 392 U. S. 409, 442–443 (1968).
82 Ibid., pp. 446–447.

3 The White Racial Frame: A Social Force

1 Thomas Jefferson, *Notes on the State of Virginia*, ed. Frank Shuffelton (New York: Penguin, 1999 [1785]), pp. 147–148.
2 W.E.B. Du Bois, *Dusk of Dawn: an Essay Toward an Autobiography of a Race Concept* (New Brunswick: Transaction Books, 1984 [1940]), p. 144.
3 Karl Marx and Friederich Engels, *The German Ideology*, ed. R. Pascal (New York: International Publishers, 1947), p. 39.
4 Kenneth O'Reilly, *Nixon's Piano: Presidents and Racial Politics from Washington to Clinton* (New York: Free Press, 1995), p. 11.
5 Oliver C. Cox, *Caste, Class, and Race* (Garden City: Doubleday, 1948), pp. 331–334; Joe R. Feagin and Clairece B. Feagin, *Racial and Ethnic Relations*, 8th edn. (Upper Saddle River: Prentice-Hall, 2008).
6 Ronald T. Takaki, *Iron Cages: Race and Culture in 19th-Century America* (Oxford: Oxford University Press, 1990), pp. 11–14.
7 Marimba Ani, Yurugu, *An African-Centered Critique of European Cultural Thought and Behavior* (Trenton: Africa World Press, 1994), pp. 348, 482–484; Edward W. Said, *Orientalism* (New York: Vintage Books, 1979), pp. 6–7.
8 Takaki, *Iron Cages*, pp. 12–14.
9 James Fenimore Cooper, *The Last of the Mohicans* (1826), as quoted in Emily Morison Beck, ed., *John Bartlett's Familiar Quotations*, 15th edn. (Boston: Little Brown, 1980), p. 463.
10 Winthrop D. Jordan, *White Over Black: American Attitudes Toward the Negro, 1550–1812* (Chapel Hill: University of North Carolina Press, 1968), pp. 18–19.
11 A. Leon Higginbotham, Jr., *Shades of Freedom: Racial Politics and the Presumptions of the American Legal Process* (New York: Oxford University Press, 1996), p. 119.
12 Jordan, *White Over Black*, p. 12. I draw on Michael Banton, *Racial and Ethnic Competition* (Cambridge: Cambridge University Press, 1983), pp. 37–38.
13 Jordan, *White Over Black*, p. 96. See also pp. 94–96.
14 Manning Marable, *Black American Politics* (London: New Left Books, 1985), p. 5; Higginbotham, *Shades of Freedom*, p. 11.
15 Tomás Almaguer, *Racial Fault Lines* (Berkeley and Los Angeles: University of California Press, 1994), p. 28; Takaki, *Iron Cages*, pp. 30–34.
16 William M. Wiecek, "The Origins of the Law of Slavery in British North America," *Cardozo Law Review* 17 (May 1996): 1777; see also Edmund S. Morgan, *American Slavery, American Freedom: the Ordeal of Virginia* (New York: Norton, 1975), pp. 3–20.
17 See Frances Lee Ansley, "Stirring the Ashes: Race, Class and the Future of Civil Rights Scholarship," *Cornell Law Review* 74 (September 1989): 993.
18 Samuel Hopkins, quoted in Jordan, *White Over Black*, p. 276; emphasis added.
19 A. Leon Higginbotham, Jr. and Barbara K. Kopytoff, "Racial Purity and Interracial Sex in the Law of Colonial and Antebellum Virginia," *Georgetown Law Journal* 77 (August 1989): 1671.
20 Benjamin Franklin, quoted in Takaki, *Iron Cages*, p. 50; see also Claude-Anne Lopez

and Eugenia W. Herbert, *The Private Franklin: the Man and His Family* (New York: Norton, 1975), pp. 194–195.

21 George Frederickson, *The Black Image in the White Mind* (Hanover: Wesleyan University Press, 1971), p. 282.

22 Joel Kovel, *White Racism: a Psychohistory*, rev. edn. (New York: Columbia University Press, 1984), pp. xli–xlvii.

23 Cox, *Caste, Class, and Race*, p. 332.

24 See Lewis R. Gordon, *Her Majesty's Other Children: Sketches of Racism from a Neocolonial Age* (Lanham: Rowman & Littlefield, 1997), p. 55.

25 Audrey Smedley, *Race in North America* (Boulder: Westview Press, 1993), p. 303.

26 Pieterse, *White on Black*, p. 41.

27 Jefferson, *Notes on the State of Virginia*, pp. 145–148.

28 Benjamin Schwarz, "What Jefferson Helps Explain," *Atlantic Monthly*, March 1997, n.p., quoted from www.theatlantic.com.

29 Immanuel Kant, *Gesammelte Schiften*, as quoted in Emmanuel C. Eze, "The Color of Reason: the Idea of 'Race' in Kant's Anthropology," in *Postcolonial African Philosophy: a Critical Reader*, ed. Emmanuel C. Eze (London: Blackwell, 1997), pp. 130, 118.

30 Ibid., p. 118.

31 William H. Tucker, *The Science and Politics of Racial Research* (Urbana: University of Illinois Press, 1994), pp. 8–9; Ivan Hannaford, *Race: the History of an Idea in the West* (Baltimore: Johns Hopkins University Press, 1996), pp. 205–207.

32 Smedley, *Race in North America*, p. 26.

33 Fredrickson, *The Black Image in the White Mind*, p. 48.

34 Jan N. Pieterse, *White on Black: Images of Africa and Blacks in Western Popular Culture* (New Haven: Yale University Press, 1992), p. 60. The quote is from p. 34.

35 Arthur de Gobineau, *Selected Political Writings*, ed. M.D. Biddiss (New York: Harper & Row, 1970), p. 136.

36 Tucker, *The Science and Politics of Racial Research*, p. 23. See also Allan Chase, *The Legacy of Malthus: the Social Costs of the New Scientific Racism* (New York: Knopf, 1977), pp. 91–94.

37 *Dred Scott v. John F.A. Sandford*, 60 U.S. 393, 407–408 (1857).

38 Abraham Lincoln, "The Sixth Joint Debate at Quincy, October 13, 1858," in *The Lincoln–Douglas Debates: the First Complete, Unexpurgated Text*, ed. Harold Holzer (New York: HarperCollins, 1993), p. 283.

39 Andrew Johnson, quoted in Ani, *Yurugu*, p. 299.

40 James Brooks, quoted in Tucker, *The Science and Politics of Racial Research*, p. 25.

41 *Plessy v. Ferguson*, 163 U.S. 537, 560 (1896).

42 Ian F. Haney Lopez, *White By Law: the Legal Construction of Race* (New York: New York University Press, 1996), pp. 1–7, 203–227.

43 Charles Darwin, as quoted in Frederickson, *The Black Image in the White Mind*, p. 230.

44 M.G. Delaney is cited in Stephen Jay Gould, *Hen's Teeth and Horse's Toes* (New York: Norton, 1983), pp. 21–22. See Joe R. Feagin, *Subordinating the Poor: Welfare and American Beliefs* (Englewood Cliffs: Prentice-Hall, 1975), pp. 35–36; Frederick L. Hoffman, "Vital Statistics of the Negro," *Arena* 5 (April 1892): 542, cited in Frederickson, *The Black Image in the White Mind*, pp. 250–251.

45 John Higham, *Strangers in the Land* (New York: Atheneum, 1963), pp. 96–152; Tucker, *The Science and Politics of Racial Research*, p. 35.

46 Carl C. Brigham, *A Study of American Intelligence* (Princeton: Princeton University Press, 1923), pp. 124–125, 177–210.

47 Madison Grant, *The Passing of the Great Race* (New York: Charles Scribner's Sons, 1916).

48 Lothrop Stoddard, *The Rising Tide of Color: Against White World-Supremacy* (New York: Scribner's, 1920), p. 3.

49 Tucker, *The Science and Politics of Racial Research*, p. 93.

50 Theodore Cross, *Black Power Imperative: Racial Inequality and the Politics of Non-violence* (New York: Faulkner, 1984), p. 157.

51 Magnus Hirschfeld, *Racism*, trans. and ed. by Eden and Cedar Paul (London: V. Gollancz, 1938). The book was originally published in German in 1933.

52 Warren G. Harding and Calvin Coolidge, quoted in Tucker, *The Science and Politics of Racial Research*, p. 93.

53 Rudyard Kipling, "The White Man's Burden," in *Rudyard Kipling's Verse: Inclusive Edition 1885–1926* (New York: Doubleday, Doran and Co., 1929), pp. 373–374.

54 Theodore W. Allen, *The Invention of the White Race* (New York: Verso, 1994), pp. 21–50, 184; Cox, *Caste, Class, and Race*, pp. 575–576, 578.

55 David R. Roediger, *The Wages of Whiteness: Race and the Making of the American Working Class* (London: Verso, 1991), p. 127.

56 S. Derek Turner and Mark Cooper, "Out of the Picture: Minority and Female TV Station Ownership in the United States," freepress 2006, www.freepress.net (accessed February 26, 2009); S. Derek Turner, "Off the Dial: Female and Minority Radio Station Ownership in the United States: How FCC Policy and Media Consolidation Diminished Diversity on the Public Airwaves," freepress 2007, www.freepress.net (accessed February 26, 2009); David K. Shipler, "Blacks in the Newsroom," *Columbia Journalism Review* (May/June 1998): 26–29; Robert M. Entman *et al.*, *Mass Media and Reconciliation: a Report to the Advisory Board and Staff, The President's Initiative on Race* (Washington, D.C., 1998).

57 Edward Herman, "The Propaganda Model Revisited," *Monthly Review* 48 (July 1996): 115; Sidney Blumenthal, *The Rise of the Counter-Establishment* (New York: Times Books, 1986), pp. 4–11, 133–170; Peter Steinfels, *The Neoconservatives: the Men Who are Changing America's Politics* (New York: Touchstone, 1979), pp. 214–277.

58 Franklin D. Gilliam, Jr. and Shanto Iyengar, "Prime Suspects: the Effects of Local News on the Viewing Public," University of California at Los Angeles, unpublished paper, n.d.

59 Richard Cohen, "Ignorant, Apathetic and Smug," *Washington Post*, February 2, 1996, p. A19; Bobbie Harville, "History: Knowledge is Lacking; Americans' Understanding of the Country's History is Thin, a New Survey Reveals," *Dayton Daily News*, July 14, 1996, p. 15A.

60 James W. Loewen, *Lies My Teacher Told Me: Everything Your American History Textbook Got Wrong* (New York: The New Press, 1995).

61 Qingwen Dong and Arthur Phillip Murrillo, "The Impact of Television Viewing on Young Adults' Stereotypes Towards Hispanic Americans," *Human Communication* 10 (2007): 33–44.

62 Lerone Bennett, *Confrontation: Black and White* (Baltimore: Penguin, 1965), pp. 187–188.

63 John H. Franklin, *From Slavery to Freedom*, 4th edn. (New York: Knopf, 1974), p. 421; Derrick Bell, "*Brown v. Board of Education* and the Interest Convergence Dilemma," *Harvard Law Review* 93 (1980): 518.

64 *Brown v. Board of Education of Topeka*, 347 U.S. 483 (1954).

65 Thomas Ferguson and Joel Rodgers, *Right Turn: The Decline of the Democrats and the Future of American Politics* (New York: Hill and Wang, 1986), pp. 55–56.

66 Samuel P. Huntington, "The Erosion of American National Interests," *Foreign Affairs* (September/October 1997): 28.

67 *Report of the National Advisory Commission on Civil Disorders* (Washington, D.C.: U.S. Government Printing Office, 1968), pp. 1, 5.

68 Ferguson and Rodgers, *Right Turn*, pp. 65–66.

69 *City of Richmond, Virginia v. J.A. Croson Co.*, 488 U.S. 469 (1989); see also *Adarand Constructors, Inc. v. Pena*, 515 U.S. 200 (1995).

70 Barbara J. Flagg, "'Was Blind But Now I See': White Race Consciousness and the

Requirement of Discriminatory Intent," *Michigan Law Review* 91 (1993): 953; Wendy Moore, *Reproducing Racism* (Lanham: Rowman & Littlefield, 2008).

71 Larry T. Reynolds, *Reflexive Sociology: Working Papers in Self-Critical Analysis* (Rockport: Rockport Institute Press, 1999), pp. 141–145.

72 Arthur R. Jensen, "How Much Can We Boost IQ and Scholastic Achievement?" *Harvard Educational Review* 39 (1969): 1–123.

73 Richard J. Herrnstein and Charles Murray, *The Bell Curve: Intelligence and Class Structure in American Life* (New York: Free Press, 1994), pp. 295–316; Jean Stefancic and Richard Delgado, *No Mercy: How Conservative Think Tanks and Foundations Changed America's Social Agenda* (Philadelphia: Temple University Press, 1996), p. 34.

74 "Nobel Winner in 'Racist' Claim Row," CNN.com, October 18, 2007, http://edition. cnn.com/2007/TECH/science/10/18/science.race/index.html?iref=mpstoryview (accessed January 20, 2009).

75 Jessie Daniels and Amy J. Schulz, "Constructing Whiteness in Health Disparities Research," in *Health and Illness at the Intersections of Gender, Race and Class*, eds. A.J. Schulz and L. Mullings (San Francisco: Jossey-Bass, 2006), pp. 89–127. One example is N. Risch, E. Burchard, E. Ziv, and H. Tang, "Categorization of Humans in Biomedical Research: Genes, Race, and Disease," *Genome Biology* 7 (2002), http://genomebiology. com/2002/3/7/comment/2007 (accessed March 15, 2005).

76 Daniels and Schulz, "Constructing Whiteness in Health Disparities Research."

77 Daniel P. Moynihan, *The Negro Family: the Case for National Action* (Washington, D.C.: U.S. Government Printing Office, 1965), p. 5.

78 Ellen K. Coughlin, "Worsening Plight of the Underclass Catches Attention," *Chronicle of Higher Education*, March 1988, p. A5. See Joe R. Feagin and Leslie Inniss, "The Black Underclass Ideology in Race Relations Analysis," *Social Justice* 16 (winter 1989): 12–34.

79 Juan Williams, *Enough: the Phony Leaders, Dead-End Movements, and Culture of Failure that are Undermining Black America – and What We Can Do About It* (New York: Three Rivers Press, 2007); Bill Cosby and Alvin F. Poussaint, *Come On People: on the Path from Victims to Victors* (New York: Thomas Nelson, 2007).

80 Anthony Farley, "The Black Body as Fetish Object," *Oregon Law Review* 76 (fall 1997): 522–526.

81 Joe R. Feagin and Eileen O'Brien, *White Men on Race* (Boston: Beacon, 2003); Rhonda Levine, "The Souls of Elite White Men: White Racial Identity and the Logic of Thinking on Race," paper presented at annual meeting, Hawaiian Sociological Association, February 14, 1998.

82 Glenn Adams, Teceta Thomas Tormala, and Laurie T. O'Brien, "The Effect of Self-Affirmation on Perception of Racism," *Journal of Experimental Psychology* 42 (2006): 616–626. Italics added.

83 "President-Elect Obama: the Voters Rebuke Republicans for Economic Failure," *Wall Street Journal*, November 5, 2008, http://online.wsj.com/article/SB122586244657 800863.html (accessed December 28, 2008).

84 Ibid.

85 Jane H. Hill, *The Everyday Language of White Racism* (New York: Wiley-Blackwell, 2008), p. 180. See also pp. 134–157.

86 Hernán Vera and Andrew Gordon, *Screen Saviors: Hollywood Fictions of Whiteness* (Lanham: Rowman & Littlefield, 2003); Cedric J. Robinson, *Black Movements in America* (New York: Routledge, 1997), p. 12.

87 Hernán Vera and Andrew Gordon, "Sincere Fictions of the White Self in the American Cinema: 1915–1998," unpublished paper, University of Florida, 1998.

88 Dinesh D'Souza, *The End of Racism: Principles for a Multiracial Society* (New York: Free Press, 1995), p. 113.

89 William Henry III, *In Defense of Elitism* (New York: Doubleday, 1994).

90 Kristin Collins, "Plantation Tours Downplay Slavery: Study," *Chicago Sun-Times*, February 11, 2009, www.suntimes.com/news/nation/1424984,w-plantations-slavery-joel-lane-museum021109. article (accessed March 13, 2009). The South Carolina government brochure is "South Carolina: Smiling Faces, Beautiful Places," n.d.

91 Jacqueline Soteropoulos, "Skeptics Put Cops on Trial: the American Public Isn't Giving Government or Police Officers the Blind Trust it Once Did," *Tampa Tribune*, April 17, 1995, p. A1. I draw on Nick Mrozinske, "Derivational Thinking and Racism," unpublished research paper, University of Florida, fall 1998

92 Mrozinske, "Derivational Thinking and Racism." The search algorithm did not allow for the word "whites" alone because this picks up individual surnames.

93 Edward Ball, *Slaves in the Family* (New York: Ballantine Books, 1999), p. 13.

94 Feagin and O'Brien, *White Men on Race*.

95 Patrick Buchanan, as quoted in Clarence Page, "U.S. Media Should Stop Abetting Intolerance," *Toronto Star*, December 27, 1991, p. A27.

96 Patrick Buchanan, as quoted in John Dillin, "Immigration Joins List of 92 Issues," *Christian Science Monitor*, December 17, 1991, 6.

97 Patrick J. Buchanan, "A Brief for Whitey," March 21, 2008, www.buchanan.org (accessed March 31, 2008).

98 Peter Brimelow, *Alien Nation: Common Sense about America's Immigration Disaster* (New York: Random House, 1995), pp. 10, 59. See also "VDARE.COM," http://en.wikipedia.org/wiki/VDARE (accessed April 30, 2009).

99 Huntington, "The Erosion of American National Interests," p. 28. See Arthur Schlesinger, Jr., *The Disuniting of America: Reflections on a Multicultural Society* (New York: Norton, 1991), pp. 13, 124–125.

100 Frank Furedi, *The Silent War: Imperialism and the Changing Perception of Race* (New Brunswick: Rutgers University Press, 1998), p. 1.

101 George Lakoff and M. Johnson, *Metaphors We Live By* (Chicago: University of Chicago Press, 1980), p. 158.

4 Contemporary Racial Framing: White Americans

1 J.L. Eberhardt, P.A. Goff, V.J. Purdie, and P.G. Davies, "Seeing Black: Race, Crime, and Visual Processing," *Journal of Personality and Social Psychology*, 87 (2004): 876–893.

2 Herbert Blumer, "Race Prejudice as a Sense of Group Position," *Pacific Sociological Review* 1 (spring 1958): 3–7.

3 Gordon Allport, *The Nature of Prejudice*, abridged edn. (New York: Anchor Books, 1958), p. 10. See Teun A. van Dijk, *Discourse, Racism and Ideology* (La Laguna: RCEI Ediciones, 1996), pp. 49–50.

4 David R. Roediger, *The Wages of Whiteness: Race and the Making of the American Working Class* (London: Verso, 1991), pp. 96–121.

5 Surveys are cited in Richard Morin, "Unconventional Wisdom: New Facts and Hot Stats from the Social Sciences," *Washington Post*, April 6, 1997, p. C5.

6 William Brink and Louis Harris, *The Negro Revolution in America* (New York: Simon and Schuster, 1964), pp. 140–143; see also William Brink and Louis Harris, *Black and White* (New York: Simon and Schuster, 1966), pp. 109, 136.

7 For surveys, see Howard Schuman, Charlotte Steeh, and Lawrence Bobo, *Racial Attitudes in America: Trends and Interpretations* (Cambridge, MA: Harvard University Press, 1985), pp. 71–162; Herbert H. Hyman and Paul B. Sheatsley, "Attitudes Toward Desegregation," *Scientific American* 211 (July 1964): 16–22; Glenn Firebaugh and K.F. Davis, "Trends in Antiblack Prejudice, 1972–1984: Region and Cohort Effects," *American Journal of Sociology* 94 (1988): 251–272.

8 Lincoln Quillian, "New Approaches to Understanding Racial Prejudice and Discrimination," *Annual Review of Sociology* 32 (2006): 299–328.

9   See John F. Dovidio *et al.*, "Stereotyping, Prejudice, and Discrimination: Another Look," in *Stereotypes and Stereotyping*, eds. C. Neil Macrae, Miles Hewstone, and Charles Stangor (New York: Guilford, 1995), pp. 276–319.

10 See Andrew Scott Baron and Mahzarin R. Banaji, "The Development of Implicit Attitudes: Evidence of Race Evaluations From Ages 6 and 10 and Adulthood," *Psychological Science* 17 (2006): 52–53; John F. Dovidio, John C. Brigham, Blair T. Johnson, and Samuel L. Gaertner, "Stereotyping, Prejudice, and Discrimination: Another Look," in *Stereotypes and Stereotyping*, eds. C. Neil Macrae, Miles Hewstone, and Charles Stangor (New York: Guilford, 1995), pp. 276–319; Sonja M.B. Givens and Jennifer L. Monahan, "Priming Mammies, Jezebels, and Other Controlling Images: an Examination of the Influence of Mediated Stereotypes on Perceptions of an African American Woman," *Media Psychology* 7 (2005), pp. 102–103.

11 Eduardo Bonilla-Silva and Tyrone A. Forman, "'I Am Not a Racist But…': Mapping White College Students' Racial Ideology in the U.S.A.," *Discourse and Society* 11 (2000): 51–86.

12 Nilanjana Dasgupta, Debbie E. McGhee, Anthony G. Greenwald, and Mahzarin R. Banaji, "Automatic Preference for White Americans: Eliminating the Familiarity Explanation," *Journal of Experimental Social Psychology* 36 (2000): 316–328; Shankar Vedantam, "Many Americans Believe They Are Not Prejudiced: Now a New Test Provides Powerful Evidence that a Majority of Us Really Are," *Washington Post Magazine*, January 23, 2005, p. W12.

13 The research is summarized in Vedantam, "Many Americans Believe They Are Not Prejudiced," p. W12; Associated Press, "Racism Studies Find Rational Part of Brain Can Override Prejudice," www.beliefnet.com/story/156/story_15664_1.html (accessed November 28, 2004).

14 Baron and Banaji, "The Development of Implicit Attitudes," pp. 52–53.

15 Leslie Houts Picca and Joe R. Feagin, *Two Faced Racism: Whites in the Backstage and Frontstage* (New York: Routledge, 2007). See Joe R. Feagin, Hernán Vera, and Pinar Batur, *White Racism: the Basics*, 2nd edn. (New York: Routledge, 2001), pp. 186–253.

16 I am indebted to Christiana Otto for discussions here. See also Feagin, Vera, and Batur, *White Racism*.

17 General Social Survey, National Opinion Research Center, Chicago, Illinois, 1994. For current examples, see Jackie Gilbert, Norma Carr-Ruffino, John M. Ivancevich, and Millicent Lownes-Jackson, "An Empirical Examination of Inter-Ethnic Stereotypes: Comparing Asian American and African American Employees," *Public Personnel Management* (summer 2003): 252–259.

18 Sut Jhally and Justin Lewis, *Enlightened Racism* (Boulder: Westview Press, 1992), p. 95. See also pp. 96–110.

19 Thomas F. Pettigrew, "The Ultimate Attribution Error: Extending Allport's Cognitive Analysis of Prejudice," *Personality and Social Psychology Bulletin* 5 (1979): 461–476. I draw on the research summary in Robert S. Feldman, *Social Psychology* (Englewood Cliffs: Prentice-Hall, 1995), pp. 91–92.

20 Patricia Hill Collins, *Black Feminist Thought: Knowledge, Consciousness, and the Politics of Empowerment* (Boston: Unwin Hyman, 1990), p. 67. I draw here on Yanick St. Jean and Joe R. Feagin, *Double Burden: Black Women and Everyday Racism* (Armonk: M.E. Sharpe, 1998), chapters 3–4.

21 See Jan N. Pieterse, *White on Black: Images of Africa and Blacks in Western Popular Culture* (New Haven: Yale University Press, 1992).

22 Joya Misra, Stephanie Moller, and Marina Karides, "Envisioning Dependency: Changing Media Depictions of Welfare in the 20th Century," *Social Problems* 50 (2003): 482–504. See also Maureen Dowd, "Americans Like G.O.P. Agenda But Split on How to Reach Goals," *New York Times*, December 15, 1994, pp. A1, A24; Derrick Z. Jackson, "Unspoken During Race Talk," *Boston Globe*, December 5, 1997, p. A27.

23 Joshua J. Dyck and Laura S. Hussey, "The End of Welfare as We Know It? Durable Attitudes in a Changing Information Environment," *Public Opinion Quarterly*, November 22, 2008, advance access online version, http://poq.oxfordjournals.org/cgi/content/abstract/nfn053v1 (accessed May 11, 2009).

24 Anthony E.O. King and Terrence T. Allen, "Personal Characteristics of the Ideal African American Marriage Partner: a Survey of Adult Black Men and Women," *Journal of Black Studies* 39 (2009): 570–588. The quote is from the abstract.

25 Diane Roberts, *The Myth of Aunt Jemima: Representations of Race and Region* (New York: Routledge, 1994), p. 5.

26 Marci Bounds Littlefield, "The Media as a System of Racialization: Exploring Images of African American Women and the New Racism," *American Behavioral Scientist* 51 (January 2008): 675–685; Patricia Hill Collins, *Black Sexual Politics* (New York: Routledge, 2005); Joe R. Feagin and Melvin P. Sikes, *Living With Racism: the Black Middle-Class Experience* (Boston: Beacon Press, 1994).

27 WDSU.com, "Candidate Apologizes for 'Buckwheat' Remark," WDSU.com, November 12, 2007, www.wdsu.com/news/14573933/detail.html (accessed April 11, 2008).

28 St. Jean and Feagin, *Double Burden*, pp. 90–91.

29 Adia Harvey Wingfield, *Doing Business With Beauty: Black Women, Hair Salons, and the Racial Enclave Economy* (Lanham: Rowman and Littlefield, 2008).

30 See Mark Warr, "Dangerous Situations: Social Context and Fear of Victimization," *Social Forces* 68 (1990): 905–906.

31 Earl Warren, quoted in Theodore Cross, *Black Power Imperative: Racial Inequality and the Politics of Nonviolence* (New York: Faulkner, 1984), pp. 157–158.

32 "Bennett Under Fire for Remarks on Black Crime," CNN.com, September 30, 2005, www.cnn.com/2005/POLITICS/09/30/bennett.comments/index.html (accessed January 20, 2009).

33 For example, D'Souza, *The End of Racism*, pp. 245–272.

34 Joe R. Feagin and Hernán Vera, *White Racism: the Basics* (New York: Routledge, 1995), p. 159.

35 Lev S. Vygotsky, *Mind in Society: the Development of Higher Psychological Processes*, eds. M. Cole, V. John-Steiner, S. Scribner, and E. Souberman (Cambridge, MA: Harvard University Press, 1978). I draw here on Steven Shaffer, "Resurrecting the Linguistic Relativity Hypothesis," www.scshaffer.com/files/scsshaffer-lrh.pdf (accessed February 6, 2006), pp. 2–17.

36 P.R. Klite, R.A. Bardwell, and J. Salzman, "Local TV News: Getting Away with Murder," *Press/Politics* 2 (1997): 102–112; Franklin D. Gilliam, Jr. and Shanto Iyengar, "Prime Suspects: the Effects of Local News on the Viewing Public," unpublished research paper, University of California (Los Angeles), n.d.

37 Travis L. Dixon and D. Linz, "Overrepresentation and Underrepresentation of African Americans and Latinos as Lawbreakers on Television Shows," *Journal of Communication* 50 (2000): 131–154; Travis L. Dixon and D. Linz, "Television News, Prejudicial Pretrial Publicity, and the Depiction of Race," *Journal of Broadcasting and Electronic Media* 46 (2002): 112–136. I also draw on the research summary in Mary Beth Oliver, "African American Men as 'Criminal and Dangerous': Implications of Media Portrayals of Crime on the 'Criminalization' of African American Men," *Journal of African American Studies* 7 (2003): 6–7.

38 Oliver, "African American Men as 'Criminal and Dangerous,'" pp. 8–9.

39 Travis L. Dixon, "Crime News and Racialized Beliefs: Understanding the Relationship Between Local News Viewing and Perceptions of African Americans and Crime," *Journal of Communication* 58 (March 2008): 106–125.

40 Eberhardt, Goff, Purdie, and Davies, "Seeing Black: Race, Crime, and Visual Processing," pp. 876–893.

41 Katheryn Russell, *The Color of Crime: Racial Hoaxes, White Fear, Black Protectionism,*

Police Harassment, and Other Macroaggressions (New York: New York University Press, 1998), pp. 69–93 and passim.

42 Gilliam and Iyengar, "Prime Suspects," p. 17.

43 Bruce Western, *Punishment and Inequality in America* (New York: Russell Sage Foundation, 2006). See Robert B. Hill *et al.*, *Research on the African American Family: a Holistic Perspective* (Westport: Auburn House, 1993).

44 See Manning Marable, "Incarceration vs. Education: Reproducing Racism and Poverty in America," *Urban Habitat*, fall 2008, www.urbanhabitat.org/node/2808 (accessed June 29, 2009).

45 James A. Rada, "Color Blind-Sided: Racial Bias in Network Television's Coverage of Professional Football Games," *Howard Journal of Communications* 7 (July–September 1996): 234–236.

46 Abby L. Ferber, "The Construction of Black Masculinity: White Supremacy Now and Then," *Journal of Sport and Social Issues* 31 (2007): 22.

47 See Charles Gallagher, "Miscounting Race: Explaining Whites' Misperceptions of Racial Group Size," *Sociological Perspectives* 46 (2003): 381–396; see also Priscilla Labovitz, "Just the Facts," *New York Times*, March 25, 1996, p. A2.

48 Charles A. Gallagher, "Living in Color: Perceptions of Racial Group Size," unpublished research paper, Georgia State University, 1999.

49 Picca and Feagin, *Two Faced Racism*.

50 Tim Cox, "Rights Groups Cautious about 'Odd Couple' Appearances," United Press International, November 22, 1988.

51 Kenneth O'Reilly, *Nixon's Piano: Presidents and Racial Politics from Washington to Clinton* (New York: Free Press, 1995), pp. 6–7; Bruce Oudes, ed., *From: The President: President Nixon's Secret Files* (New York: Harper and Row, 1989), p. 451.

52 These examples are from http://novusordo.com, as cited in Margaret Ronkin and Helen E. Karn, "Mock Ebonics: Linguistic Racism in Parodies of Ebonics on the Internet," *Journal of Sociolinguistics* 3 (August 1999): 360–380.

53 Bonnie Henry, "What Will I Do With $21 Mil?" *Arizona Daily Star*, January 19, 1997, p. J1.

54 Jane H. Hill, *The Everyday Language of White Racism* (New York: Wiley-Blackwell, 2008), especially pp. 134–157; Rosalind Chou and Joe Feagin, *The Myth of the Model Minority* (Boulder: Paradigm Books, 2008), chapter 1.

55 Rosina Lippi-Green, *English with an Accent* (New York: Routledge, 1997), p. 201.

56 See Adia Harvey Wingfield and Joe R. Feagin, *Yes We Can: White Racial Framing and the 2008 Presidential Campaign* (New York: Routledge, 2010), especially chapters 1–5.

57 I draw from *Merriam-Webster's Collegiate Dictionary*, 10th edn. (Springfield: Merriam Webster, 1993), pp. 118, 1348; and Robert B. Moore, "Racist Stereotyping in the English Language," in *Racism and Sexism: an Integrated Study*, ed. Paula S. Rothenberg (New York: St. Martin's Press, 1988), pp. 270–271.

58 Thomas Greenfield, as quoted in Moore, "Racist Stereotyping in the English Language," p. 273.

59 Joanna Russ, *How to Suppress Women's Writing* (Austin: University of Texas Press, 1983), pp. 17–25. I am indebted to Nick Mrozinske for this point.

60 Toni Morrison, *Playing in the Dark: Whiteness and the Literary Imagination* (New York: Vintage Books, 1992), pp. 63–65.

61 No name was given. The spelling and punctuation are per the original letter.

62 "Baseball Committee Formed to Investigate Racist, Ethnic Remarks Made by Cincinnati Reds Owner," *The Ethnic NewsWatch*, December 9, 1992, p. 1.

63 James R. Kluegel and Eliot R. Smith, *Beliefs About Inequality* (New York: Aldine de Gruyter, 1986), pp. 186–187.

64 Pew Research Center, "Blacks See Growing Values Gap Between Poor and Middle Class: Optimism about Black Progress Declines," November 13, 2007, http://pewsocialtrends.

org/pubs/700/black-public-opinion (accessed May 5, 2008). The survey was done with National Public Radio.

65 "Race and Ethnicity," www.pollingreport.com/race.htm (accessed February 27, 2009).

66 All the surveys are reported in "Race and Ethnicity," www.pollingreport.com/race.htm (accessed February 27, 2009).

67 Feagin and Vera, *White Racism*, pp. 160–161.

68 George V. Gushue and Madonna G. Constantine, "Colorblind Racial Attitudes and White Racial Identity Attitudes in Psychology Trainees," *Professional Psychology: Research and Practice* 38 (2007): 321–328; Eduardo Bonilla-Silva, *Racism Without Racists*, 2nd edn. (Lanham: Rowman and Littlefield, 2006); Leslie Carr, *"Colorblind" Racism* (Thousand Oaks: Sage, 1997).

69 Jerome M. Culp, Jr., "Water Buffalo and Diversity: Naming Names and Reclaiming the Racial Discourse," *Connecticut Law Review* 26 (fall 1993): 209.

70 Patricia G. Devine, "Stereotypes and Prejudice: their Automatic and Controlled Components," *Journal of Personality and Social Psychology* 56 (1989): 15–16. I draw on the summary of Devine's work in Feldman, *Social Psychology*, p. 97.

71 David O. Sears, "Symbolic Racism," in *Eliminating Racism*, eds. Phyllis A. Katz and Dalmas A. Taylor (New York: Plenum, 1988), pp. 55–58; Lawrence Bobo, "Group Conflict, Prejudice, and the Paradox of Contemporary Racial Attitudes," in *Eliminating Racism*, eds. Katz and Taylor, pp. 99–101; Michael Hughes, "Symbolic Racism, Old-Fashioned Racism, and Whites' Opposition to Affirmative Action," in *Racial Attitudes in the 1990s: Continuity and Change*, eds. Steven A. Tuch and Jack K. Martin (Westport: Praeger, 1997), pp. 73–74.

72 Lawrence Bobo, James R. Kluegel, and Ryan A. Smith, "Laissez-Faire Racism: The Crystallization of a Kinder, Gentler, Antiblack Ideology," in *Racial Attitudes in the 1990s: Continuity and Change*, eds. Steven A. Tuch and Jack K. Martin (Westport: Praeger, 1997), pp. 25, 39.

73 See surveys reported at www.pollingreport.com/race.htm (accessed June 29, 2009); Quillian, "New Approaches to Understanding Racial Prejudice and Discrimination," pp. 299–328.

74 Sidney Verba and Gary R. Orren, *Equality in America: the View from the Top* (Cambridge, MA: Harvard University Press, 1985), p. 63.

75 Quoted from the survey report at "Race and Ethnicity," www.pollingreport.com/race. htm (accessed February 27, 2009).

76 Smith, "Bridging the Gulf Between Blacks & Whites," p. A1; and Jeffrey M. Jones, "Race, Ideology, and Support for Affirmative Action: Personal Politics Has Little to do with Blacks' Support," Gallup Poll, August 2005, www.gallup.com (accessed May 27, 2008).

77 Robert J. Blendon *et al.*, "The Public and the President's Commission on Race," *The Public Perspective* (February 1998): 66.

78 Christine Reyna, P.J. Henry, William Korfmacher, and Amanda Tucker, "Examining the Principles in Principled Conservatism: the Role of Responsibility Stereotypes as Cues for Deservingness in Racial Policy Decisions," *Journal of Personality and Social Psychology* 90 (2005): 109–128.

79 Ruth Frankenberg, *White Women, Race Matters* (Minneapolis: University of Minnesota Press, 1993), pp. 228–229; Karyn D. McKinney, *Being White: Stories of Race and Racism* (New York: Routledge, 2005).

80 Survey results are cited in Blendon *et al.*, "The Public and the President's Commission on Race," p. 66.

81 Marimba Ani, *Yurugu: an African-Centered Critique of European Cultural Thought and Behavior* (Trenton: Africa World Press, 1994), p. 294.

82 See Theodor W. Adorno *et al.*, *The Authoritarian Personality* (New York: Harper, 1950), pp. 248–279; Thomas F. Pettigrew, *Racially Separate or Together?* (New York: McGraw-

Hill, 1971), pp. 131–135; Robin M. Williams, Jr., *Strangers Next Door* (Englewood Cliffs: Prentice-Hall, 1964), pp. 110–113.

83 John Briggs and F. David Peat, *Turbulent Mirror: an Illustrated Guide to Chaos Theory and the Science of Wholeness* (New York: Harper & Row, 1990), p. 154.

84 Maurice Halbwachs, *On Collective Memory*, ed. and trans. by L. Coser (Chicago: University of Chicago Press, 1992), pp. 38, 52. I build on ideas I introduced in Picca and Feagin, *Two Faced Racism*, chapter 1.

85 Feldman, *Social Psychology*, p. 399.

86 Feagin and Vera, *White Racism*, p. 149. The poll is by CBS polls, as reported at http://db.cbs.com/prd1 (accessed May 1999).

87 Bonilla-Silva, *Racism Without Racists*.

88 The quote is from a research summary by Siri Carpenter, "Buried Prejudice: the Bigot in Your Brain," *Scientific American* (May 2008), www.sciam.com/article.cfm?id=buried-prejudice-the-bigot-in-your-brain (accessed June 1, 2008). See also Vygotsky, *Mind in Society*; Steven Shaffer, "Resurrecting the Linguistic Relativity Hypothesis," www.scshaffer.com/files/scsshaffer-lrh.pdf (accessed February 6, 2006), pp. 2–17.

89 Debra Van Ausdale and Joe R. Feagin, "Using Racial and Ethnic Concepts: the Critical Case of Very Young Children," *American Sociological Review* 61 (October 1996): 779–793. See also Jean Piaget, *The Moral Judgment of the Child* (Glencoe: The Free Press, 1932).

90 Joseph Carroll, "Who Are the People in Your Neighborhood? South Reports Highest Proportion of Blacks; West Reports Highest Number of Hispanics, Recent Immigrants," Gallup Poll, July 2005, www.gallup.com/poll/17293/Who-People-Your-Neighborhood.aspx (accessed March 2, 2009).

91 Isabel Wilkerson, "The Tallest Fence: Feelings on Race in a White Neighborhood," *New York Times*, June 21, 1992, section 1, p. 18.

92 Heidi McGlothlin and Melanie Killen, "Intergroup Attitudes of European American Children Attending Ethnically Homogeneous Schools," *Child Development* 77 (September/October 2006): 1375–1386.

93 Feldman, *Social Psychology*, p. 90; Jim Sidanius, Felicia Pratto, and Lawrence Bobo, "Racism, Conservatism, Affirmative Action, and Intellectual Sophistication," *Journal of Personality and Social Psychology* 70 (1996): 487.

94 Cara A. Talaska, Susan T. Fiske, and Shelly Chaiken, "Legitimating Racial Discrimination: Emotions, Not Beliefs, Best Predict Discrimination in a Meta-Analysis," *Social Justice Research* 21 (2008): 263–296.

95 Laurie A. Rudman and Richard D. Ashmore, "Discrimination and the Implicit Association Test," *Group Processes & Intergroup Relations* 10 (2007): 359–372.

96 Russell H. Fazio *et al.*, "Variability in Automatic Activation as an Unobtrusive Measure of Racial Attitudes: a Bona Fide Pipeline?" *Journal of Personality and Social Psychology* 69 (1995): 1025–1026.

97 Bridget C. Dunton and Russell H. Fazio, "An Individual Difference Measure of Motivation to Control Prejudiced Reactions," *Personality and Social Psychology Bulletin* 23 (March 1997): 316–326.

98 Richard J. Barnet and John Cavanagh, *Global Dreams: Imperial Corporations and the New World Order* (New York: Touchstone, 1994), p. 138. I draw on Joe R. Feagin and Pinar Batur-Vanderlippe, "The Globalization of Racism and Antiracism: France, South Africa and the United States," unpublished manuscript, University of Florida, 1996; and Robert W. McChesney, "The New Global Media: it's a Small World of Big Conglomerates," *The Nation*, November 29, 1999, www.hartfordwp.com/archives/29/053.html (accessed July 3, 2008).

99 Jeffrey K. Lyons, "Media Globalization and its Effect upon International Communities: Seeking a Communication Theory Perspective," *Global Media Journal*, 4 (fall 2005), http://lass.calumet.purdue.edu/cca/gmj/fa05/gmj-fa05-lyons.htm (accessed May 14, 2009). Lyons draws on research by Robert W. McChesney.

100 Pinar Batur-Van der Lippe, "Centering on Global Racism and Anti-Racism," *Sociological Spectrum* 19 (1999): 467–484.
101 Yarrow Dunham, Andrew S. Baron, and Mahzarin R. Banaji, "From American City to Japanese Village: a Cross-Cultural Investigation of Implicit Race Attitudes," *Child Development* 77 (2006): 1268–1281; Yuki Fujioka, "Television Portrayals and African-American Stereotypes: Examination of Television Effects When Direct Contact is Lacking," *Journalism and Mass Communication Quarterly* 76 (spring 1999): 52–75.
102 Hsiao-Chuan Hsia, "Imported Racism and Indigenous Biases: the Impacts of the U.S. Media on Taiwanese Images of African Americans," paper presented at meeting of American Sociological Association, August 5–9, 1994, Los Angeles.
103 Alexis Tan, Lingling Zhang, Yungying Zhang, and Francis Dalisay, "Stereotypes of African Americans in China and Media Use," paper presented at the Annual Meeting of the Association for Education in Journalism and Mass Communication, Washington, D.C., August 8, 2007.
104 Nestor Rodriguez, personal communication with the author.

5 Racial Oppression Today: Everyday Practice

1 The study was done by Marianne Bertrand and Sendhil Mullainathan and is summarized in David Wessel, "Racial Discrimination: Still at Work in the U.S.," *The Wall Street Journal Online*, at www.careerjournal.com/myc/diversity/20030916-wessel.html (accessed May 26, 2005). See Pamela Mendels, "Up for Evaluation," *Newsday*, June 13, 1995, p. 6.
2 See Kwame Ture [Stokely Carmichael] and Charles Hamilton, *Black Power* (New York: Random House, 1967); the older approach is in Gordon Allport, *The Nature of Prejudice*, abridged edn. (New York: Anchor Books, 1958).
3 Philomena Essed, *Understanding Everyday Racism* (Newbury Park: Sage, 1991), p. 50.
4 United Nations, "Convention on the Prevention and Punishment of Genocide," in *The United Nations and Human Rights, 1945–1995* (New York: United Nations Department of Public Information, 1995), pp. 219–225.
5 Amani Nuru-Jeter *et al.*, "'It's The Skin You're In': African-American Women Talk About their Experiences of Racism," *Maternal and Child Health Journal* 13 (2009): 32. See also pp. 33–39.
6 Joe R. Feagin and Melvin P. Sikes, *Living With Racism: the Black Middle-Class Experience* (Boston: Beacon Press, 1994), p. 54.
7 John O. Calmore, "To Make Wrong Right: the Necessary and Proper Aspirations of Fair Housing," in *The State of Black America 1989* (New York: National Urban League, 1989), p. 89.
8 The lead researcher was Kerry Kawakami. I draw on summaries of the study in "Racism: What We Say Doesn't Match What We Do," www.msnbc.msn.com/id/28563183/ (accessed June 29, 2009); and in "Study Finds Gap Between What We Say, Do About Racism," www.freep.com/article/20090108/NEWS07/90108092/1118/RSS (accessed March 13, 2009).
9 Leslie Houts Picca and Joe R. Feagin, *Two Faced Racism: Whites in the Backstage and Frontstage* (New York: Routledge, 2007).
10 Joe R. Feagin, Hernán Vera, and Nikitah Imani, *The Agony of Education: Black Students at White Colleges and Universities* (New York: Routledge, 1996); Joe R. Feagin and Karyn D. McKinney, *The Many Costs of Racism* (Lanham: Rowman & Littlefield, 2003; and Joe R. Feagin, *Systemic Racism: a Theory of Oppression* (New York: Routledge, 2006).
11 Gallup Organization, *Blacks and Whites Still Perceive Local Treatment of Blacks Differently* (Princeton: Gallup Organization, 2003), www.gallup.com/poll/8476/Blacks-Whites-Still-Perceive-Local-Treatment-Blacks-Differently.aspx (accessed January 18, 2008); Gallup Organization, *Black–White Relations 2001 Update* (Princeton: Gallup

Organization, 2001), pp. 1–24, at www.gallup.com/poll/9901/BlackWhite-Relations-United-States-2001-Update.aspx (accessed May 15, 2009).

12 Josephine Louie, "We Don't Feel Welcome Here: African Americans and Hispanics in Metro Boston," Harvard University Civil Rights Project, research report, April 25, 2005, pp. i–iii.

13 Lee Sigelman and Susan Welch, *Black Americans' Views of Racial Inequality: the Dream Deferred* (Cambridge: Cambridge University Press, 1991), p. 59.

14 Chandler Davison and Bernard Grofman, eds., *The Quiet Revolution in the South: the Impact of the Voting Rights Act 1965–1990* (Princeton: Princeton University Press, 1994); Chandler Davidson, Tanya Dunlap, Gale Kenny, and Benjamin Wise, *Republican Ballot Security Programs: Vote Protection or Minority Vote Suppression – Or Both?* Report to Center for Voting Rights & Protection, September 2004.

15 Davidson, Dunlap, Kenny, and Wise, *Republican Ballot Security Programs.*

16 *City of Richmond, Virginia* v. *J.A. Croson Co.*, 488 U.S. 469 (1989).

17 Michel Rosenfeld, "Decoding Richmond: Affirmative Action and the Elusive Meaning of Constitutional Equality," *Michigan Law Review* 87 (June 1989): 1762.

18 *City of Richmond, Virginia* v. *J.A.Croson Co.*, 488 U.S. 469, 503 (1989).

19 Martin J. Katz, "The Economics of Discrimination: the Three Fallacies of Croson," *Yale Law Journal* 100 (January 1991): 1044.

20 *City of Richmond, Virginia* v. *J.A. Croson Co.*, 488 U.S. 469, 552–553 (1989).

21 Jerome McCristal Culp Jr., "Understanding the Racial Discourse of Justice Rehnquist," *Rutgers Law Journal* 25 (spring 1994): 604. See Matthew Smith, "Bridging the Gulf Between Blacks & Whites," *Pittsburgh Post-Gazette*, April 7, 1996, p. A1.

22 Gunnar Myrdal, *An American Dilemma*, vol. I (New York: McGraw-Hill, 1964 [1944]); Joe R. Feagin and Harlan Hahn, *Ghetto Revolts* (New York: Macmillan, 1973).

23 Gallup Organization, *A Downturn in Black Perceptions of Racial Harmony* (Princeton: Gallup Organization, 2007), www.gallup.com/poll/28072/Downturn-Black-Perceptions-Racial-Harmony.aspx (accessed January 18, 2008); Gallup Organization, *Black–White Relations 2001 Update* (Princeton: Gallup Organization, 2001), pp. 1–24.

24 Kim Lersch and Joe R. Feagin, "Violent Police–Citizen Encounters: an Analysis of Major Newspaper Accounts," *Critical Sociology* 22 (1996): 29–49.

25 ACLU, "Racial Profiling Alert," www.aclu.org/racialjustice/racialprofiling/index.html (accessed May 15, 2009).

26 The data are cited in S.B. Duke, "Casualties of War," *Reason* (1994): 20–27.

27 ACLU, "Racial Profiling Alert," April 2006, www.aclu.org/racialjustice/racialprofiling/2 8283res20060401.html (accessed May 15, 2009).

28 ACLU, "Landmark Settlement Reached With Maryland State Police In 'Driving While Black' Case," www.aclu.org/racialjustice/racialprofiling/34753prs20080402.html (accessed May 15, 2009).

29 Michael R. Cogan, "The Drug Enforcement Agency's Use of Drug Courier Profiles: One Size Fits All," *Catholic University Law Review* 41 (1992): 943–946; David Harris, *Driving While Black: Racial Profiling on Our Nation's Highways* (New York: American Civil Liberties Union, 1999), as cited at www.lwvcincinnati.org/publications/Driving_While_Black.html (accessed February 2, 2006).

30 "U.N. Expert Calls on U.S. to Address Ongoing Issues of Racism," May 8, 2008, http://news.prnewswire.com/DisplayReleaseContent.aspx?ACCT=ind_focus.story&STORY=/www/story/05–08–2009/0005022751&EDATE= (accessed May 15, 2009).

31 Ian Ayres and Joel Waldfogel, "A Market Test for Race Discrimination in Bail Setting," *Stanford Law Review* 46 (May 1994): 993. See also p. 994.

32 David L. Lewis, "Bias in Drug Sentences," *The National Law Journal* (February 5, 1996): p. A19.

33 Julie Rawe, "Congress's Bad Drug Habit," *Time*, November 19, 2007, p. 60; and Devlin Barrett, "Attorney General Wants Review of Cocaine Sentences," *Washington Post*, June

24, 2009, www.washingtonpost.com/wp-dyn/content/article/2009/06/24/AR20090624
03215.html (accessed June 30, 2009).

34 Glenn L. Pierce and Michael L. Radelet, "The Impact of Legally Inappropriate Factors
on Death Sentencing for California Homicides, 1990–1999," *Santa Clara Law Review*
46 (2005): 1–49. Recently there were 3,316 people on death row.

35 Amnesty International, *United States of America: Rights for All* (London: Amnesty
International Publications, 1998), pp. 3, 109–110; Susan Estrich, *Real Rape*
(Cambridge, MA: Harvard University Press, 1987), p. 107; Michael J. Carter, "Charges
of Racism Offer New Evidence," InterPress Service, www.ipsnews.net/news.asp?
idnews=42514 (accessed March 19, 2009). The Houston research was conducted by
Scott Phillips.

36 See "Innocence Project," Wikipedia, http://en.wikipedia.org/wiki/Capital_punish-
ment_in_the_United_States#endnote_2 (accessed May 15, 2009).

37 Amnesty International, *United States of America: Rights for All*, p. 110.

38 William E. Martin and Peter N. Thompson, "Judicial Toleration of Racial Bias in the
Minnesota Justice System," *Hamline Law Review* 25 (winter 2002): 235–270.

39 Roger Boesche, "How White People Riot: Quietly, at the Ballot Box," *Baltimore Sun*,
October 15, 1995, p. 3F.

40 Feagin and Hahn, *Ghetto Revolts*, pp. 78–81.

41 FBI, "Hate Crime Statistics," October 2008, www.fbi.gov/ucr/hc2007/victims.htm
(accessed May 17, 2009).

42 Mark Potok, "Diversity and its Discontents," *Intelligence Report*, spring 2009, www.spl-
center.org/intel/intelreport/article.jsp?aid=1010 (accessed May 17, 2009).

43 Thomas Fields-Meyer *et al.*, "One Deadly Night: Deep in the Woods of East Texas,
James Byrd Died a Terrible Death, Leaving a Town and a Nation in Shock," *People*, June
29, 1998, p. 46; Howard Chua-Eoan and Hilary Hylton-Austin, "Beneath The Surface:
a 'New South' Town is Haunted by 'Deep South' Ghosts – And a Fresh, Ugly Murder,"
Time, June 22, 1998, p. 34. The *New York Times* article is dissected in Les Payne,
"Exploitation and Dismissal of a Victim," *Newsday*, June 21, 1998, p. B6.

44 Gary Harki, "Six Arrested, Charged in Woman's Weeklong Torture," *Charleston Gazette*,
September 11, 2007, p. 1A.

45 Sophia Hong, "New Noose Incident in Hempstead Town Building," *Newsday*, January
11, 2008, p. A22.

46 Paul Vitello, "Few Answers About Nooses, But Much Talk of Jim Crow," October 21,
2007, www.nytimes.com/2007/10/21/nyregion/21noose.html?ex=1350705600&en=2b
dea5e2571dfa16&ei=5124&partner=permalink&exprod=permalink (accessed May 17,
2009).

47 Klanwatch Project, *False Patriots: the Threat of Antigovernment Extremists* (Montgomery: Southern Poverty Law Center, 1996), pp. 3–5; Potok, "Diversity and its Discontents."

48 Anonymous, "Ethnic Diversity Grows, Neighborhood Integration Lags Behind,"
unpublished research report, Lewis Mumford Center, University at Albany, April 3,
2001, n.p. The figures are weighted for population size.

49 Ibid. See John R. Logan, Brian J. Stults, and Reynolds Farley, "Segregation of Minorities
in the Metropolis: Two Decades of Change," unpublished research paper, Center for
Social and Demographic Analysis, University of Albany, n.d., p. 11. For older data, see
Douglas S. Massey and Nancy A. Denton, *American Apartheid: Segregation and the
Making of the Underclass* (Cambridge, MA: Harvard University Press, 1993).

50 Richard D. Alba, John R. Logan, and Brian J. Stults, "How Segregated Are Middle-Class
African Americans?" *Social Problems* 47 (November 2000): 543–558.

51 See also Joe R. Feagin, "Excluding Blacks and Others from Housing: the Foundation of
White Racism," *Cityscape* 4 (1999): 79–91.

52 *Jones et ux. v. Alfred H. Mayer Co.*, 392 U.S. 441–443 (1968).

53 Ibid., p. 445 (1968).

54 Stephen G. Meyer, *As Long As They Don't Move Next Door: Segregation and Racial Conflict in American Neighborhoods* (Lanham: Rowman & Littlefield, 2000), p. 8.

55 Massey and Denton, *American Apartheid*, pp. 92–94; Farai Chideya, *The Color of Our Future* (New York: William Morrow, 1999), p. 132.

56 "The Multi-City Study of Urban Inequality," Russell Sage Foundation Newsletter, fall 1999, p. 2; Margery Austin Turner, Raymond J. Struyk, and John Yinger, *Housing Discrimination Study: Synthesis* (Washington, D.C.: U.S. Government Printing Office, 1991), pp. ii–viii; Fair Housing Action Center, Inc., "Greater New Orleans Rental Audit," New Orleans, 1996; San Antonio Fair Housing Council, "San Antonio Metropolitan Area Rental Audit 1997," San Antonio, 1997. See also Fair Housing Council of Greater Washington, as reported in Caroline E. Mayer, "Minorities Said to Face Bias in House Hunting; Study Finds Blacks, Hispanics Treated Worse," *Washington Post*, April 9, 1997, p. C9.

57 Shanna L. Smith, National Fair Housing Alliance, "Testimony Before the House Financial Services Committee, Subcommittee on Housing and Community Opportunity," February 28, 2006, www.house.gov/financialservices/media/pdf/022806ss.pdf. (accessed May 18, 2009).

58 Adrian G. Carpusor and William E. Loges, "Rental Discrimination and Ethnicity in Names," *Journal of Applied Social Psychology* 36 (April 2006): 934–952.

59 Vincent J. Roscigno, Diana L. Karafin, and Griff Tester, "The Complexities and Processes of Racial Housing Discrimination," *Social Problems* 56 (February 2009): 49–69. The quote is on p. 67.

60 Martin D. Abravanel and Mary K. Cunningham, *How Much Do We Know? Public Awareness of the Nation's Fair Housing Laws* (Washington, D.C.: U.S. Department of Housing and Urban Development, 2002), p. 20.

61 See Stephen Thernstrom and Abigail Thernstrom, *America in Black and White: One Nation, Indivisible, Race in Modern America* (New York: Simon and Schuster, 1997).

62 Maria Krysan and Reynolds Farley, "The Residential Preferences of Blacks: Do They Explain Persistent Segregation?" *Social Forces* 80 (March 2002): 937–980; Camille Zubrinsky Charles, "Residential Segregation in Los Angeles," in *Prismatic Metropolis: Inequality in Los Angeles*, eds. Lawrence D. Bobo, Melvin L. Oliver, James H. Johnson, and Abel Valenzuela (New York: Russell Sage, 2000), pp. 204–205.

63 Meyer, *As Long As They Don't Move Next Door*, pp. 219–220.

64 Krysan and Farley, "The Residential Preferences of Blacks: Do They Explain Persistent Segregation?" pp. 937–980; see also Reynolds Farley, Elaine Fielding, and Maria Krysan, "The Residential Preferences of Blacks and Whites: a Four-Metropolis Analysis," *Housing Policy Debate* 8 (1997): 763–800.

65 Shanna L. Smith and Cathy Clous, "Documenting Discrimination by Homeowners Insurance Companies Through Testing," in *Insurance Redlining: Disinvestment, Reinvestment, and the Evolving Role of Financial Institutions*, ed. Gregory D. Squires (Washington, D.C.: Urban Institute Press, 1997), pp. 106–117; John Goering and Ron Wienk, "An Overview," in *Mortgage Lending, Racial Discrimination, and Federal Policy*, eds. J. Goering and R. Wienk (Washington, D.C.: Urban Institute Press, 1996), pp. 16–19.

66 Gregory D. Squires, personal communication; see Sunwoong Kim and Gregory D. Squires, "The Color of Money and the People Who Lent It," *Journal of Housing Research* 9 (1998): 271–284.

67 Trevor Delaney, "Subprime Lenders Under Fire," *Black Enterprise* (October 2007): 31–32; Vikas Bajaj and Ford Fessenden, "What's Behind the Race Gap?" *New York Times*, November 4, 2007, p. 16.

68 Ibid.

69 Joe Sims, "How Racism Sparked Capitalism's Financial Crisis," *People's Weekly World Newspaper*, www.pww.org/article/articleview/14364 (accessed March 19, 2009).

70 "Dallas Officials Twice as Likely to Raze Black Homes," *Houston Chronicle*, September 14, 1998, p. 14A.

71 Joe R. Feagin and Robert Parker, *Building American Cities* (Englewood Cliffs: Prentice-Hall, 1990), chapter 5; Leland T. Saito, *The Politics of Exclusion: the Failure of Race-Neutral Policies in Urban America* (Palo Alto: Stanford University Press, 2009).

72 Shanna L. Smith, National Fair Housing Alliance, personal communication with the author, June 9, 1997; National Fair Housing Alliance, *Fair Housing Enforcement: Time for a Change*, May 1, 2009, Washington, D.C.; National Commission on Fair Housing and Equal Opportunity, Report, 2008, as summarized in Gary Orfield, *Reviving the Goal of an Integrated Society: a 21st-Century Challenge* (Los Angeles: UCLA Civil Rights Project, 2009), p. 5.

73 Feagin and Parker, *Building American Cities*, chapter 8.

74 Derrick Bell, "Property Rights in Whiteness – their Legal Legacy, their Economic Costs," in *Critical Race Theory: the Cutting Edge*, ed. Richard Delgado (Philadelphia: Temple University Press, 1995), p. 75.

75 Gallup Organization, *Black–White Relations 2001 Update* (Princeton: Gallup Organization, 2001), pp. 1–24, at www.gallup.com/poll/9901/BlackWhite-Relations-United-States-2001-Update.aspx (accessed May 15, 2009); Josephine Louie, "We Don't Feel Welcome Here: African Americans and Hispanics in Metro Boston," Harvard University Civil Rights Project, research report, April 25, 2005, pp. i–iii. See also Lawrence Bobo and Susan A. Suh, "Surveying Racial Discrimination: Analyses from a Multi-ethnic Labor Market," unpublished research report, Department of Sociology, University of California at Los Angeles, August 1, 1995.

76 Alfred W. Blumrosen *et al.*, *Employment Discrimination Against Women and Minorities in Georgia* (Newark: Rutgers University S.I. Newhouse Center for Law and Justice, 1999).

77 Devah Pager, "The Mark of a Criminal Record," *American Journal of Sociology* 108 (March 2008): 937–975. I also draw on a research summary in Wessel, "Racial Discrimination: Still at Work in the U.S"; and on Devah Pager and Lincoln Quillian, "Walking the Talk: What Employers Say Versus What They Do," *American Sociological Review* 70 (June 2005): 355–380.

78 Marc Bendick, Jr., "Situation Testing for Employment Discrimination in the United States of America," *Revue Horizons Stratégiques*, Centre D'analyse Stratégique, July 2007, pp. 6–18.

79 Margaret M. Zamudio and Michael I. Lichter, "Bad Attitudes and Good Soldiers: Soft Skills as a Code for Tractability in the Hiring of Immigrant Latina/os over Native Blacks in the Hotel Industry," *Social Problems* 55 (November 2008): 573–589.

80 Marc Bendick, Jr., "Race–Ethnic Employment Discrimination in Upscale Restaurants: Evidence from Paired Comparison Testing," Bendick and Egan Economic Consultants, Washington, D.C., February 2009; Jennifer Lee, "Racial Bias Seen in Hiring of Waiters," *New York Times*, March 31, 2009, http://cityroom.blogs.nytimes.com/2009/03/31/racial-bias-seen-in-hiring-of-waiters/?hp (accessed April 7, 2009).

81 I draw on "The Multi-City Study of Urban Inequality," pp. 1–3, and its supplement.

82 Marc Bendick Jr., *Discrimination Against Racial/Ethnic Minorities in the United States: Empirical Findings from Situation Testing* (Geneva: International Labor Office, 1996), p. 24.

83 Deirdre A. Royster, *Race and the Invisible Hand: How White Networks Exclude Black Men from Blue-Collar Jobs* (Los Angeles: University of California Press, 2003).

84 Donald Tomaskovic-Devey, M. Thomas, and K. Johnson, "Race and the Accumulation of Human Capital Across the Career: a Theoretical Model and Fixed-effects Application," *American Journal of Sociology* 111 (2005): 58–89.

85 Bobo and Suh, "Surveying Racial Discrimination: Analyses from a Multiethnic Labor Market." See Lawrence Bobo *et al.*, "Work Orientation, Job Discrimination, and Ethnicity: a Focus Group Perspective," in *Research in the Sociology of Work*, eds. Richard L. Simpson and Ida H. Simpson (Stamford: JAI Press, 1995), pp. 81–82.

86 "Locked Out: the Lack of Gender and Ethnic Diversity on Cable News Continues," *Media Matters*, May 7, 2007, http://mediamatters.org/reports/200705070003 (accessed May 26, 2009).

87 Marc Bendick, Jr. and Mary Lou Egan, "Research Perspectives on Race and Employment in the Advertising Industry," Bendick and Egan Economic Consultants, Inc., Washington, D.C., January 2009, p. 1.

88 Ibid., p. 1.

89 Stuart Elliott, "Advertising: a Lawyer's Call for a Greater Black Presence in Agencies," *New York Times*, January 8, 2009, www.nytimes.com/2009/01/09/business/media/09adco.html?_r=1 (accessed April 7, 2009).

90 Marc Bendick, Jr., Mary Lou Egan, and Louis Lanier, "The 'Business Case for Diversity' and the Pernicious Practice of Matching Employees to Customers," paper presented at Tenth International Human Resource Management Conference, Santa Fe, NM, June 2009, p. 12. Italics added.

91 The report is cited in Tim Wise, "Commentary," http://academic.udayton.edu/race/01race/white10.htm (accessed November 24, 2004).

92 The Bureau of Labor Statistics data are summarized in Orfield, *Reviving the Goal of an Integrated Society*, p. 5.

93 James H. Johnson, Jr., Grover C. Burthey, III, and Kevin Ghorm, "Economic Globalization and the Future of Black America," *Journal of Black Studies* 38 (2008): 883–899; see also Willhelm, *Black in a White America*, p. 345.

94 Marc Bendick, Jr., Mary Lou Egan, and Suzanne Lofhjelm, "Workforce Diversity Training: From Anti-Discrimination Compliance to Organization Development," *Human Resource Planning* 24 (2001): 10–25.

95 Jacquelyn Scarville *et al.*, *Armed Forces Equal Opportunity Survey* (Arlington: Defense Manpower Data Center, 1999), pp. 46–78; Office of the Under Secretary of Defense Personnel and Readiness, *Career Progression of Minority and Women Officers* (Washington, D.C.: Department of Defense, 1999), pp. 83–85.

96 Jesse Washington, "Study: Networking Hinders Black Women Executives," Associated Press, January 7, 2009, www.foxnews.com/wires/2009Jan07/0,4670,BlackWomenExecutives,00.html (accessed March 19, 2009).

97 Benjamin P. Bowser, *The Black Middle Class: Social Mobility – and Vulnerability* (Boulder: Lynne Rienner Publishers, 2007), p. 140.

98 Scarville *et al.*, *Armed Forces Equal Opportunity Survey*, pp. 46–78.

99 "Suit Against Microsoft for its Plantation Mentality," *Invisible America*, January 5, 2001, www.invisibleamerica.com/microseg.html (accessed February 5, 2001).

100 Bendick, Egan, and Lofhjelm, *The Documentation and Evaluation of Anti-Discrimination Training in the United States*, p. 9; and *The Race Relations Reporter*, December 15, 1996, p. 1.

101 Ellen Neuborne, "March of Time Yields Little Progress for Many Blacks," *USA Today*, November 25, 1996, p. 3B.

102 William C. Rhoden, *Forty Million Dollar Slaves: the Rise, Fall, and Redemption of the Black Athlete* (New York: Three Rivers Press, 2007). The quote is from the cover text. See also "Vital Statistics," *The Journal of Blacks in Higher Education* (summer 2008), www.jbhe.com/vital/60_index.html (accessed April 6, 2009). On debates on Major League baseball, see Allen Barra, *Brushbacks and Knockdowns: the Greatest Baseball Debates of Two Centuries* (New York: Thomas Dunne Books, 2004).

103 Melvin L. Oliver and Thomas M. Shapiro, *Black Wealth/White Wealth: a New Perspective on Racial Equality* (New York: Routledge, 1995), pp. 36–50; Thomas M. Shapiro, *The Hidden Cost of Being African American: How Wealth Perpetuates Inequality* (New York: Oxford University Press, 2004), p. 31.

104 Martin J. Katz, "The Economics of Discrimination: the Three Fallacies of Croson," *Yale Law Journal* 100 (January 1991): 1044.

105 Maria Enchautegui *et al.*, *Do Minority-Owned Businesses Get a Fair Share of Government Contracts?* (Washington, D.C.: Urban Institute Press, 1996), p. 51; Timothy Bates

and William D Bradford, "Venture-Capital Investment in Minority Business," *Journal of Money, Credit & Banking* 40 (March–April 2008): 489–503.

106 Enchautegui *et al.*, *Do Minority-Owned Businesses Get a Fair Share of Government Contracts?*; Timothy Bates, *Strategies for the Black Worker* (Washington, D.C.: Joint Center for Political and Economic Studies, 1997).

107 Adia Harvey Wingfield, personal communication. See Adia Harvey Wingfield, *Doing Business With Beauty: Black Women, Hair Salons, and the Racial Enclave Economy* (Lanham: Rowman and Littlefield, 2008).

108 "Vital Statistics," *The Journal of Blacks in Higher Education*. On the impact of housing on school segregation, see this earlier study: Diana Pearce, "Breaking Down Barriers: New Evidence on the Impact of Metropolitan School Desegregation on Housing Patterns," research report, School of Law, Catholic University, 1980, pp. 48–53.

109 John R. Logan, *Choosing Segregation: Racial Imbalance in American Public Schools, 1990–2000*, unpublished research report, Lewis Mumford Center, University at Albany, March 29, 2002, n.p.

110 Orfield, *Reviving the Goal of an Integrated Society*, pp. 3–6.

111 Bruce Oudes, ed., *From: The President: President Nixon's Secret Files* (New York: Harper and Row, 1989), p. 451.

112 *Milliken* v. *Bradley*, 418 U.S. 717, 782 (1974).

113 *Board of Education of Oklahoma* v. *Dowell 488* U.S. 237 (1991); *Freeman* v. *Pitts*, 503 U.S. 467 (1992).

114 Zeus Leonardo, *Race, Whiteness, and Education* (New York: Routledge, 2009), p. 10.

115 Orfield, *Reviving the Goal of an Integrated Society*, pp. 3–6; "Vital Statistics," *The Journal of Blacks in Higher Education*.

116 New York ACORN Schools Office, *Secret Apartheid: a Report on Racial Discrimination Against Black and Latino Parents and Children in the New York City Public Schools* (New York: ACORN, 1996).

117 David N. Figlio, "Names, Expectations and the Black–White Test Score Gap," National Bureau of Economic Research Working Paper, March 2005, www.nber.org/papers/w11195 (accessed May 22, 2009); "University Of Florida Economist Finds That Black Children's Names Hinder Their Educational Development," *The Journal of Blacks in Higher Education Weekly Bulletin* (May 26, 2005): 1.

118 "Vital Statistics," *The Journal of Blacks in Higher Education*.

119 Tukufu Zuberi and Eduardo Bonilla-Silva, eds., *White Logic, White Methods* (Lanham: Rowman & Littlefield, 2008).

120 Richard Delgado, *The Coming Race War?* (New York: New York University Press, 1996), p. 71.

121 "Vital Statistics," *The Journal of Blacks in Higher Education*.

122 See Hope Landrine and Elizabeth A. Klonoff, "The Schedule of Racist Events: a Measure of Racial Discrimination and a Study of its Negative Physical and Mental Health Consequences," *Journal of Black Psychology* 22, 2 (1996): 144–168. See also Joe R. Feagin, Hernán Vera, and Nikitah Imani, *The Agony of Education: Black Students at White Colleges and Universities* (New York: Routledge, 1996); Urban Affairs Programs, *The Graduate School Climate at MSU* (East Lansing: Michigan State University Office of the Provost, 1995).

123 Leslie Houts Picca and Joe R. Feagin, "Experiences of Students of Color," University of Dayton, unpublished research, 2009.

124 Daren Briscoe and Evan Thomas, "Hate on Campus," *Newsweek*, November 28, 2005, p. 41.

125 C. Richard King and David J. Leonard, "The Rise of the Ghetto-Fabulous Party," *Colorlines Magazine*, October 5, 2007, www.diverseeducation.com/artman/publish/article_9687.shtml (accessed May 22, 2009).

126 This list is compiled from my reading and Tim Wise, "Majoring in Minstrelsy: White Students, Blackface and the Failure of Mainstream Multiculturalism," June 22, 2007, www.lipmagazine.org/~timwise/minstrelsy.html (accessed May 22, 2009); and from King and Leonard, "The Rise of the Ghetto-Fabulous Party."

127 Jennifer C. Mueller, Danielle Dirks, and Leslie Houts Picca, "Unmasking Racism: Halloween Costuming and Engagement of the Racial Other," *Qualitative Sociology* 30 (2007): 315–335.

128 Ibid. I am indebted to Jennifer Mueller and Rosalind Chou for these class data. See Rosalind Chou, "Racist Frame is Still Firmly in the Minds of Educated Whites," www. racismreview.com (accessed May 22, 2009).

129 Emily Goodell, Emma Fidel, and Nathan Swire, "E-mail on Kim Stirs Controversy," http://thedartmouth.com/2009/03/05/news/email/print (accessed May 22, 2009). Also see "Tufts Official Says Racial Parody Was Harassing, Hostile, and an Exercise of Free Speech," *Chronicle of Higher Education*, August 27, 2007, http://chronicle.com/news/ article/2929/tufts-official-says-racial-parody-was-harassing-hostile-and-an-exercise-of-free-speech (accessed May 20, 2009).

130 Tamara Towles-Schwen and Russell H. Fazio, "Automatically Activated Racial Attitudes as Predictors of the Success of Interracial Roommate Relationships," *Journal of Experimental Social Psychology* 42 (2006): 698–705.

131 Joe R. Feagin, *The White Racial Frame: Centuries of Racial Framing and Counter-Framing* (New York: Routledge, 2010).

132 Cynthia Willming, "Leisure-travel Behaviors of College-educated African Americans and Perceived Racial Discrimination," unpublished Ph.D. dissertation, University of Florida, 2001. I draw on the summary in Danielle Dirks and Stephen K. Rice, "'Dining while Black': Tipping as Social Artifact," *Cornell Hotel & Restaurant Administration Quarterly* 45 (February 2004): 30–47. See also Gallup Organization, *Black–White Relations 2001 Update*; Gallup, *Black/White Relations in the United States*, pp. 29–30, 108–110.

133 See citations in Jerome D. Williams, May O. Lwin, Anne-Marie G. Hakstian, and Velma A.R. Gooding, "Assessing Perceived Discrimination in 'Brick and Mortar' Retail Settings Using a Power–Responsibility Equilibrium Framework," in *Brick & Mortar Shopping in the 21st Century*, ed. Tina Lowrey (Mahwah: Lawrence Erlbaum, 2007), pp. 172–179.

134 New Jersey Citizen Action, "New Report Highlights Impact of Hidden Practice of Auto Finance Markup on New Jersey Consumers," press release, February 23, 2005, www.njcitizenaction.org/craautofinancpress.html. See also the older study in Ian Ayres, "Fair Driving: Gender and Race Discrimination in Retail Car Negotiations," *Harvard Law Review* 104 (February 1991): 820, 829–830.

135 Thomas L. Ainscough and Carol M. Motley, "Will You Help Me, Please? The Effects of Race, Gender and Manner of Dress on Retail Service," *Marketing Letters* 11 (2000): 129–135; Anne-Marie G. Harris, "Shopping While Black: Applying 42 U.S.C. 1981 to Cases of Consumer Racial Profiling," *Boston College Third World Law Journal* 23 (2003): 1.

136 Harris, "Shopping While Black," p. 1. I have deleted note numbers.

137 Tyan P. Dominguez, "Race, Racism, and Racial Disparities in Adverse Birth Outcomes," *Clinical Obstetrics and Gynecology* 51 (June 2008): 360–370; Tyan P. Dominguez *et al.*, "Stress in African American Pregnancies: Testing the Roles of Various Stress Concepts in Prediction of Birth Outcomes," *Annals of Behavioral Medicine* 29 (2005): 12–21; Tyan P. Dominguez *et al.*, "Racial Differences in Birth Outcomes: the Role of General, Pregnancy, and Racism Stress," *Health Psychology* 27 (2008): 194–203.

138 Eric L. Krakauer, Christopher Crenner, and Ken Fox, "Barriers to Optimum End-of-life Care for Minority Patients," *Journal of the American Geriatric Society* 50 (2002): 182–190. "Mental Health Care Doesn't Meet Standards, Study Finds," *Research Matters*, www. researchmatters.harvard.edu/story.php?article_id=108 (accessed May 26, 2005); "Minority

Patients Face Barriers To Optimum End-Of-Life Care," *Research Matters*, Harvard University, www.researchmatters.harvard.edu/story.php?article_id=361 (May 26, 2005).

139 Kevin A. Schulman *et al.*, "The Effect of Race and Sex on Physicians' Recommendations for Cardiac Catheterization," *New England Journal of Medicine* (February 25, 1999): 618–626; Peter B. Bach *et al.*, "Racial Differences in the Treatment of Early-Stage Lung Cancer," *New England Journal of Medicine* (October 14, 1999): 1198–1205.

140 The studies are reported in Vanessa Housing, "Doctors in Study Prefer Whites to Blacks: UW Researchers Take a Look at Physician Biases," SeattlePI.com, October 29, 2008, http://seattlepi.nwsource.com/local/385343_doctorbias29.html?source=rss (accessed April 6, 2009).

141 Alexander R. Green *et al.*, "Implicit Bias Among Physicians and its Prediction of Thrombolysis Decisions for Black and White Patients," *Journal of General and Internal Medicine* 24 (January 2009): 137–140.

142 See, for example, John F. Dovidio, "The Subtlety of Racism," *Training and Development* (April 1993): 51–55; Faye Crosby *et al.*, "Recent Unobtrusive Studies of Black and White Discrimination and Prejudice: a Literature Review," *Psychological Bulletin* 87 (1980): 546; Delgado, *The Coming Race War?*, p. 17.

143 Bullard is quoted in Cynthia Gordy, "Troubled Waters," *Essence*, July 2007, pp. 146–176. The data are also from this article.

144 Paul Mohai and Robin Saha, "Racial Inequality in the Distribution of Hazardous Waste: a National-Level Reassessment," *Social Problems* 54 (August 2007): 343–370.

145 Quoted in Benjamin B. Ringer, *"We the People" and Others* (New York: Tavistock, 1983), p. 327.

6 White Privileges and Black Burdens: Still Systemic Racism

1 Joe R. Feagin and Melvin P. Sikes, *Living with Racism: the Black Middle-Class Experience* (Boston: Beacon Press, 1994), pp. 295–296; Joe R. Feagin and Karyn D. McKinney, *The Many Costs of Racism* (Lanham: Rowman & Littlefield, 2003), pp. 39–64.

2 Karyn D. McKinney, "'I Really Felt White': Turning Points in Whiteness Through Interracial Contact," *Social Identities* 12 (2006): 183; Joyce E. King, "Dysconscious Racism: Ideology, Identity, and the Miseducation of Teachers," *Journal of Negro Education* 60 (1991): 135. I am indebted to Nancy DiTomaso for comments.

3 McKinney, "'I Really Felt White': Turning Points in Whiteness Through Interracial Contact," p. 183 and passim.

4 Jane Lazarre, *Beyond the Whiteness of Whiteness* (Durham: Duke University Press, 1996), p. 41.

5 Nyla R. Branscombe, Michael T. Schmitt, and Kristin Schiffhauer, "Racial Attitudes in Response to Thoughts of White Privilege," *European Journal of Social Psychology* 37 (2007): 203–215. The quote is on p. 213.

6 Frances Lee Ansley, "Stirring the Ashes: Race, Class and the Future of Civil Rights Scholarship," *Cornell Law Review* 74 (September 1989): 1035.

7 See Theodore Cross, *The Black Power Imperative: Racial Inequality and the Politics of Nonviolence* (New York: Faulkner, 1984), p. 510.

8 David R. Roediger, *The Wages of Whiteness: Race and the Making of the American Working Class* (London: Verso, 1991), p. 12; see also Joe R. Feagin, Clairece B. Feagin, and David Baker, *Social Problems*, 6th edn. (Upper Saddle River: Prentice-Hall, 2005), pp. 462–463, 500.

9 Kenneth W. Smallwood, "The Folklore of Preferential Treatment," unpublished manuscript, Southfield, Michigan, 1985; Cross, *The Black Power Imperative*, pp. 515–518.

10 Irving Kristol, "The Negro Today is Like the Immigrant of Yesterday," *New York Times Magazine*, September 11, 1966, pp. 50–51, 124–412.

11 Theodore Hershberg *et al.*, "A Tale of Three Cities: Blacks, Immigrants, and Opportu-

nity in Philadelphia: 1850–1880, 1930, 1970," in *Philadelphia*, ed. Theodore Hershberg (New York: Oxford University Press, 1981), pp. 462–464.

12 Herbert Hill, "The Racial Practices of Organized Labor – the Age of Gompers and After," in *Employment, Race and Poverty*, eds. Arthur M. Ross and Herbert Hill (New York: Harcourt, Brace & World, 1967), p. 365; Stanley B. Greenberg, *Race and State in Capitalist Development* (New Haven: Yale University Press, 1980), p. 349.

13 Joe R. Feagin, *Systemic Racism: a Theory of Oppression* (New York: Routledge, 2006), pp. 199–207; Joe R. Feagin, Kevin Early, and Karyn D. McKinney, "The Many Costs of Discrimination: the Case of Middle-Class African Americans," *Indiana Law Review* 34 (2001): 1313–1360.

14 For details see Cross, *The Black Power Imperative*, pp. 515–518; Melvin L. Oliver and Thomas M. Shapiro, *Black Wealth/White Wealth: a New Perspective on Racial Inequality* (New York: Routledge, 1995), pp. 36–45.

15 Ira Katznelson, *When Affirmative Action was White: an Untold History of Racial Inequality in Twentieth-Century America* (New York: W.W. Norton, 2005), p. 38ff.

16 Ibid., pp. 38–39; David Roediger, *Working Toward Whiteness* (New York: Basic Books, 2005).

17 Harvard Sitkoff, *A New Deal for Blacks* (New York: Oxford University Press, 1978); Joe R. Feagin, "Slavery Unwilling to Die: the Background of Black Oppression in the 1980s," *Journal of Black Studies* 17 (December 1986): 173–200; Cross, *The Black Power Imperative*, p. 515.

18 Erika Hayes James and Lynn Perry Wooten, *2004 Census of African Americans on Boards of Directors of Fortune 500 Companies* (Institute for Leadership Development and Research, 2004), pp. 5–9; Jesse Washington, "Study: Networking Hinders Black Women Executives," Associated Press, January 7, 2009, www.foxnews.com/wires/2009 Jan07/0,4670,BlackWomenExecutives,00.html (accessed March 19, 2009).

19 "'Babyface' Look Can Help Black CEOs, Study Says," MSNBC, May 8, 2009, http://today.msnbc.msn.com/id/30642824 (accessed May 27, 2009). Robert Livingston is the researcher.

20 Matthew Miller and Duncan Greenberg, "The Forbes 400," *Forbes*, September 9, 2008, www.forbes.com (accessed May 27, 2009).

21 *Dred Scott* v. *John F.A. Sandford*, 60 U.S. 393, 407 (1857). Emphasis added.

22 Mary Beth Norton, *Liberty's Daughters* (Boston: Little, Brown, 1980); Edmund S. Morgan, *American Slavery, American Freedom: the Ordeal of Virginia* (New York: Norton, 1975), p. 165.

23 U.S. Census Bureau, "U.S. Census Bureau Household Income Rises, Poverty Rate Unchanged, Number of Uninsured Down," August 26, 2008, www.census.gov/Press-Release/www/releases/archives/income_wealth/012528.html (accessed May 27, 2009); Graduate Minority Student Project, University of California (Berkeley), "Statistics of Racism in the United States: Income, Health, and Rights," http://struggle4reparations.com/starkey/rep_sta.html (accessed May 27, 2009).

24 U.S. Census Bureau, "U.S. Census Bureau Household Income Rises, Poverty Rate Unchanged, Number of Uninsured Down."

25 Brian K. Bucks, Arthur B. Kennickell, Traci L. Mach, and Kevin B. Moore, "Changes in U.S. Family Finances from 2004 to 2007: Evidence from the Survey of Consumer Finances," *Federal Reserve Bulletin* 95 (February 2009): pp. A1–A55.

26 Thomas M. Shapiro, *The Hidden Cost of Being African American: How Wealth Perpetuates Inequality* (New York: Oxford University Press, 2004), p. 31.

27 National Urban League, *The State of Black America 2009* (New York: National Urban League, 2009), pp. 1–2.

28 James Marketti, "Estimated Present Value of Income Diverted During Slavery," in *The Wealth of Races: the Present Value of Benefits from Past Injustices*, ed. Richard F. America (New York: Greenwood, 1990), p. 118.

29 Roger L. Ransom and Richard Sutch, "Growth and Welfare in the American South in the Nineteenth Century," in *Market Institutions and Economic Progress in the New South 1865–1900*, eds. Gary Walton and James Shepherd (New York: Academic Press, 1981), pp. 150–151; David H. Swinton, "Racial Inequality and Reparations," in *The Wealth of Races*, ed. America, p. 156.

30 William A. Darity, Jr., "Forty Acres and a Mule: Placing the Price Tag on Oppression," in *The Wealth of Races*, ed. America, p. 11. Total figures have been put at $10–24 trillion by Richard America and Jack White. See Kevin Merida, "Did Freedom Alone Pay a Nation's Debt?" *The Washington Post*, November 23, 1999, p. C1.

31 Stephen J. DeCanio, "Accumulation and Discrimination in the Postbellum South," in *Market Institutions and Economic Progress in the New South 1865–1900*, eds. Walton and Shepherd, p. 105; see also pp. 103–125.

32 Swinton, "Racial Equality and Reparations," p. 157.

33 Martin J. Katz, "The Economics of Discrimination: the Three Fallacies of *Croson*," *Yale Law Journal* 100 (January 1991): 1041–1045.

34 Shapiro, *The Hidden Cost of Being African American*, pp. 30–51; Oliver and Shapiro, *Black Wealth/White Wealth*, pp. 36–50.

35 Melvin L. Oliver and Thomas M. Shapiro, "Creating an Opportunity Society," *American Prospect* 18 (May 2007), p. A27. See Shapiro, *The Hidden Cost of Being African American*, pp. 70–72; Benjamin P. Bowser, *The Black Middle Class: Social Mobility – and Vulnerability* (Boulder: Lynne Rienner Publishers, 2007), p. 87.

36 Andrew Hacker, *Two Nations: Black and White, Separate, Hostile, Unequal* (New York: Scribner's, 1992), pp. 31–32.

37 Patricia J. Williams, "Alchemical Notes: Reconstructing Ideals from Deconstructed Rights," *Harvard Civil Rights and Civil Liberties Review* 22 (1987): 415.

38 Ellis Cashmore, *The Black Culture Industry* (New York: Routledge, 1997), pp. 1, 3.

39 I am indebted to comments here from Charity Clay.

40 Martin Luther King, Jr., *Where Do We Go from Here? Chaos or Community?* (New York: Bantam Books, 1967), p. 122.

41 Joe R. Feagin, *The White Racial Frame: Centuries of Racial Framing and Counter-Framing* (New York: Routledge, 2010), chapters 6 and 7; Feagin and Sikes, *Living with Racism: the Black Middle Class Experience*.

42 Feagin, *The White Racial Frame*, pp. 133–136. See Judith Lichtenberg, "Racism in the Head, Racism in the World," *Philosophy and Public Policy* 12 (spring/summer 1992): 4.

43 Ruth Thompson-Miller and Joe R. Feagin, "Continuing Injuries of Racism: Counseling in a Racist Context," *The Counseling Psychologist* 35 (2007): 106–115. See Joe R. Feagin and Karyn D. McKinney, *The Many Costs of Racism* (Lanham: Rowman & Littlefield, 2003), pp. 46–120; Yanick St. Jean and Joe R. Feagin, *Double Burden: Black Women and Everyday Racism* (Armonk: M.E. Sharpe, 1998).

44 Claude M. Steele and Joshua Aronson, "Stereotype Threat and the Intellectual Test Performance of African Americans," *Journal of Personality and Social Psychology* 69 (1995): 797–811. See also Feagin and McKinney, *The Many Costs of Racism*, pp. 39–64; Claude M. Steele, "A Threat in the Air: How Stereotypes Shape Intellectual Identity and Performance," *American Psychologist* (June 1997): 627.

45 See Antonio Gramsci, *Letters from Prison: Antonio Gramsci*, ed. Lynne Lawner (New York: Harper Colophon, 1975 [1932]); Catharine A. MacKinnon, *Toward a Feminist Theory of the State* (Cambridge, MA: Harvard University Press, 1989), p. 8.

46 Vanessa Hazell and Juanne Clarke, "Race and Gender in the Media: a Content Analysis of Advertisements in Two Mainstream Black Magazines," *Journal of Black Studies* 39 (2008): 5–21.

47 William H. Grier and Price M. Cobbs, *Black Rage* (New York: Basic Books, 1968), p. 4.

48 Feagin and Sikes, *Living with Racism*, p. 294. See also Feagin and McKinney, *The Many Costs of Racism*, pp. 39–52, 142–145.

49 Alexander Thomas and Samuel Sillen, *The Theory and Application of Symbolic Interactionism* (Boston: Houghton-Mifflin, 1977), p. 54.

50 Teletia R. Taylor *et al.*, "Racial Discrimination and Breast Cancer Incidence in US Black Women," *American Journal of Epidemiology* 1 (2007): 46–54. See also Nancy Krieger, "Embodying Inequality: a Review of Concepts, Measures, and Methods for Studying Health Consequences of Discrimination," *International Journal of Health Services* 29 (1999): 295–352.

51 Feagin and McKinney, *The Many Costs of Racism*, p. 78. See also Thompson-Miller and Feagin, "Continuing Injuries of Racism: Counseling in a Racist Context," pp. 106–115.

52 This study by Nancy Krieger is summarized in Amanda Husted, "Discrimination Can Pose Health Risk for Blacks and Homosexuals," *Atlanta Journal and Constitution* (November 1, 1994): D22. Those who reported no discrimination had blood pressure as high as those who reported much discrimination, which Krieger interprets to mean the former are under-reporting. See Rosalind M. Peters, "Racism and Hypertension Among African Americans," *Western Journal of Nursing Research* 26 (2004): 612–631.

53 See V.R. Clark, "The Perilous Effects of Racism on Blacks," *Ethnicity and Disease* 11 (fall 2001): 769–772.

54 Sharon B. Wyatt *et al.*, "Racism and Cardiovascular Disease in African Americans," *American Journal of Medical Science* 325 (June 2003): 315–331. Italics omitted.

55 James Oakes, *The Ruling Race: a History of American Slaveholders* (New York: Vintage Books, 1983); Kenneth M. Stampp, *The Peculiar Institution: Slavery in the Ante-Bellum South* (New York: Vintage Books, 1956), pp. 318–321; Thomas F. Pettigrew, *A Profile of the Negro American* (Princeton: Van Nostrand, 1964), p. 99; Amadu Jacky Kaba, "Life Expectancy, Death Rates, Geography, and Black People: a Statistical World Overview," *Journal of Black Studies* 39 (2009): 337–347.

56 Rodney Coates, personal communication with the author, November 9, 1995. For a similar image of sexism, see Marilyn Frye, *The Politics of Reality* (Freedom: Crossing Press, 1983), p. 4.

57 Tyrone A. Forman, "The Social Psychological Costs of Racial Segmentation: a Study of African Americans' Well-Being," unpublished research paper, University of Michigan, 1999, p. 24.

58 "Concurring opinion" in *Jones et ux.* v. *Alfred H. Mayer Co.*, 392 U.S. 409, 445 (1968).

59 See Marc Bendick, Jr., *Discrimination Against Racial/Ethnic Minorities in the United States: Empirical Findings from Situation Testing* (Geneva: International Labour Office, 1996), p. 23; John O. Calmore, "To Make Wrong Right: The Necessary and Proper Aspirations of Fair Housing," in *The State of Black America 1989* (New York: National Urban League, 1989), p. 89.

60 Gunnar Myrdal, *An American Dilemma*, vol. 1 (New York: McGraw-Hill, 1964 [1944]), p. 4.

61 Oliver C. Cox, *Caste, Class, and Race: a Study in Social Dynamics* (New York: Doubleday, 1948), p. 531.

62 Michael Hughes, "Symbolic Racism, Old-Fashioned Racism, and Whites' Opposition to Affirmative Action," in *Racial Attitudes in the 1990s: Continuity and Change*, eds. Steven A. Tuch and Jack K. Martin (Westport: Praeger, 1997), pp. 73–74; Joe R. Feagin and Eileen O'Brien, *White Men on Race: Power, Privilege and the Shaping of Cultural Consciousness* (Boston: Beacon, 2003).

63 William Lee Miller, *Arguing about Slavery: the Great Battle in the United States Congress* (New York: Knopf, 1996), p. 10.

64 James W. Button, Barbara A. Rienzo, and Ken Wald, "Politics and School Health

Reform: Factors Influencing the Success of School-Based Health Care," unpublished research paper, University of Florida, 1999.

65 Quoted in George J. Church, "The Boom Towns," *Time*, June 15, 1987, p. 17. This section draws on discussions with Gregory D. Squires.

66 See F. James Davis, *Who is Black?* (University Park: Pennsylvania State University Press, 1991), pp. 21–22.

67 Ibid., p. 22; Shirlee Taylor Haizlip, "Are There Any Truly Black (or White) Americans?" *Los Angeles Times*, February 20, 1994, p. M3; Mario de Valdes y Cocom, "Secret Daughter: the Blurred Racial Lines of Famous Families," January 1999, www.pbs.org/wgbh/pages/Frontline/shows/secret/famous (accessed July 23, 1999).

68 Bliss Broyard, *One Drop: My Father's Hidden Life – a Story of Race and Family Secrets* (Boston: Back Bay Books, 2007); Edward Ball, *Slaves in the Family* (New York: Ballantine Books, 1999); Henry Wiencek, *The Hairstons: an American Family in Black and White* (New York: St. Martin's Press, 1999); see also Mackey Alston's documentary film, *Family Name* (1998).

69 Lewis R. Gordon, *Bad Faith and Antiblack Racism* (Atlantic Highlands: Humanities Press, 1995), pp. 183–184. I am indebted to Bernice McNair Barnett and Hernán Vera for discussions here.

70 "List of countries by Human Development Index," Wikipedia, http://en.wikipedia.org/wiki/List_of_countries_by_Human_Development_Index (accessed June 5, 2009); "American Human Development Index by Gender, Race, and Region," *American Human Development Report 2008–9*, http://verifiable.com/data_sets/2003 (accessed June 5, 2009).

7 Systemic Racism: Other Americans of Color

1 Southern Poverty Law Center, *Under Siege: Life for Low-Income Latinos in the South* (Montgomery: SPLC, 2009), p. 4.

2 See Yolanda Flores-Niemann, "Social Ecological Contexts of Prejudice Between Hispanics and Blacks," in *Race, Ethnicity, and Nationality in the United States: Toward the Twenty-First Century*, ed. Paul Wong (Boulder: Westview Press, 1999), p. 170; Eduardo Luna, "How the Black/White Paradigm Renders Mexicans/Mexican Americans and Discrimination Against Them Invisible," *Berkeley La Raza Law Journal* (fall 2003), pp. 226, 230.

3 I draw here on Joe R. Feagin and Clairece B. Feagin, *Racial and Ethnic Relations*, 8th edn. (Upper Saddle River: Prentice-Hall, 2008), chapters 7–11.

4 Michael Omi and Howard Winant, *Racial Formation in the United States* (New York: Routledge, 1986).

5 This estimate assumes a birth rate of about 40 live births per 1,000 persons under slavery for the period. Estimating this birth rate for the varying black population over the period – the black population grew from about half-a-million in 1776 to about 4.2 million in 1865 – one gets about six million births as a low-end estimate. I am indebted to Doug Deal for helping me estimate the six million figure.

6 I base this rough calculation on estimates of the "crude birth rate" for each year in this entire period. On Native Americans, see Vine Deloria, *Custer Died for Your Sins: an Indian Manifesto* (London: Macmillan, 1969).

7 See Ellis Cose, *Colorblind: Seeing Beyond Race in a Race-Obsessed World* (New York: HarperCollins, 1997).

8 Jorge Klor de Alva, Earl Shorris, and Cornel West, "Our Next Race Question: The Uneasiness Between Blacks and Latinos," in *Critical White Studies: Looking Behind the Mirror*, eds. Richard Delgado and Jean Stefancic (Philadelphia: Temple University Press, 1997), p. 485; Deloria, *Custer Died for Your Sins*, p. 8.

9 See Kenneth O'Reilly, *Nixon's Piano: Presidents and Racial Politics from Washington to Clinton* (New York: Free Press, 1995).

10 Jessie Daniels, *White Lies: Race, Class, Gender, and Sexuality in White Supremacist Discourse* (New York: Routledge, 1997); Jessie Daniels, personal communication with the author, 1999.

11 Ruth Frankenberg, *White Women, Race Matters* (Minneapolis: University of Minnesota Press, 1993), p. 12. See also Joe R. Feagin and Hernán Vera, *White Racism: the Basics* (New York: Routledge, 1995); Joe R. Feagin, *Systemic Racism: a Theory of Oppression* (New York: Routledge, 2006).

12 Lewis R. Gordon, *Her Majesty's Other Children: Sketches of Racism from a Neocolonial Age* (Lanham: Rowman and Littlefield, 1997), pp. 5, 53.

13 Frank Wu, "Neither Black Nor White: Asian Americans and Affirmative Action," *Boston College Third World Law Journal* 15 (1995): 249–250. See Janine Young Kim, "Are Asians Black? The Asian-American Civil Rights Agenda and the Contemporary Significance of the Black–White Paradigm," *Yale Law Journal* 108 (June 1999): 2385–2413.

14 Tomás Almaguer, *Racial Fault Lines* (Berkeley and Los Angeles: University of California Press, 1994), pp. 7, 210.

15 Feagin and Feagin, *Racial and Ethnic Relations*, chapters 10–11.

16 Ronald T. Takaki, *Strangers from a Different Shore: a History of Asian Americans* (Boston: Little, Brown, 1989), p. 100. This section draws on pp. 99–104.

17 Ibid., p. 101; see *Gong Lum* v. *Rice*, 275 U.S. 78, 85 (1927).

18 *People* v. *Hall*, 4 Cal. 399 (1854). See Takaki, *Strangers from a Different Shore*, p. 102; Benjamin B. Ringer, *"We the People" and Others* (New York: Tavistock, 1983), p. 382.

19 James W. Loewen, *The Mississippi Chinese: Between Black and White* (Cambridge, MA: Harvard University Press, 1971), pp. 58–68.

20 Takaki, *Strangers from a Different Shore*, p. 101.

21 Ibid.

22 *Plessy* v. *Ferguson*, 163 U.S. 537, 561 (1896).

23 Claire Jean Kim, "The Racial Triangulation of Asian Americans," *Politics and Society* 27 (March 1999): 105–138.

24 Gary Y. Okihiro, *Margins and Mainstreams: Asians in American History and Culture* (Seattle: University of Washington Press, 1994), p. 34.

25 Edward K. Strong, Jr., *The Second-Generation Japanese Problem* (Stanford: Stanford University Press, 1934), p. 133. See also Miriam Sharma, "Labor Migration and Class Formation Among the Filipinos in Hawaii, 1940–1946," in *Labor Immigration Under Capitalism*, eds. Lucie Cheng and Edna Bonacich (Berkeley and Los Angeles: University of California Press, 1984), pp. 583–593.

26 George Frederickson, *The Black Image in the White Mind* (Hanover: Wesleyan University Press, 1971), p. 305.

27 *In re Ah Yup*, 1 F. cas. 223 (C.C.D.Cal. 1878); Ian F. Haney Lopez, *White By Law: the Legal Construction of Race* (New York: New York University Press, 1996), pp. 1–7, 203–227.

28 James J. Scheurich and Michelle D. Young, "Coloring Epistemologies: Are Our Research Epistemologies Racially Biased?" *Educational Researcher* 26 (May 1997): 7. See Mario de Valdes y Cocom, "Secret Daughter: the Blurred Racial Lines of Famous Families," January 1999, www.pbs.org/wgbh/pages/frontline/shows/secret/famous (accessed June 30, 2009).

29 John C. Calhoun, quoted in Frederickson, *The Black Image in the White Mind*, p. 136.

30 Abel G. Rubio, *Stolen Heritage* (Austin: Eakin Press, 1986).

31 Joan Moore, *Mexican Americans*, 2nd edn. (Englewood Cliffs: Prentice-Hall, 1976), p. 108.

32 Feagin and Feagin, *Racial and Ethnic Relations*, chapter 8.

33 Lopez, *White By Law*, p. 61.

34 Allen, *The Invention of the White Race*, p. 27; Feagin and Feagin, *Racial and Ethnic Relations*, chapter 8.

35 Feagin and Feagin, *Racial and Ethnic Relations*, chapter 8; Nestor Rodriguez, personal communication with the author.

36 Oliver C. Cox, *Caste, Class, and Race: a Study in Social Dynamics* (New York: Doubleday, 1948), p. 349.

37 Roberto Suro, *Strangers Among Us: How Latino Immigration is Transforming America* (New York: Knopf, 1998), pp. 81–82; Feagin and Feagin, *Racial and Ethnic Relations*, chapters 8–11.

38 See the white-framed arguments of Dinesh D'Souza, *The End of Racism: Principles for a Multiracial Society* (New York: Free Press, 1995), p. 300.

39 Rosalind Chou and Joe R. Feagin, *The Myth of the Model Minority* (Boulder: Paradigm Books, 2008).

40 John Liu, personal communication with the author. See also "Voters Don't Rank Immigration as a Priority Issue," *Rasmussen Reports*, April 14, 2009, www.rasmussen-reports.com/public_content/politics/general_politics/voters_don_t_rank_immigration_as_a_priority_issue (accessed June 9, 2009).

41 Jorge M. Chavez and Doris Marie Provine, "Race and the Response of State Legislatures to Unauthorized Immigrants," *Annals of the American Association of Political and Social Science* 623 (May 2009): 79–92.

42 Nathan Glazer, *We Are All Multiculturalists Now* (Cambridge, MA: Harvard University Press, 1997), p. 149.

43 Andrew Hacker, *Two Nations: Black and White, Separate, Hostile, Unequal* (New York: Scribner's, 1992), p. 16.

44 See Michael Lind, *The Next American Nation: the New Nationalism and the Fourth American Revolution* (New York: Free Press, 1995), pp. 115–116.

45 Ewa A. Golebiowska, "The Contours and Etiology of Whites' Attitudes Toward Black–White Interracial Marriage," *Journal of Black Studies* 38 (2007): 268–287. The white percentages willing to say to pollsters they are opposed to intermarriages are probably lower than actual percentages. See also General Social Survey, National Opinion Research Center, Chicago, Illinois, 1990.

46 U.S. Census Bureau, "America's Families and Living Arrangements: 2006," www.census.gov/population/www/socdemo/hh-fam/cps2006.html (accessed June 9, 2009), "New Trends in Interracial Marriage," PRNewswire, www.prnewswire.com/cgi-bin/stories.pl?ACCT=104&STORY=/www/story/03–08–2007/0004542097&EDATE= (accessed June 10, 2009). See also Gordon, *Her Majesty's Other Children*, p. 69.

47 Leland Saito, personal communication, fall 1998; Milton M. Gordon, *Assimilation in American Life* (New York: Oxford University Press, 1964); Julie Montgomery, "Cyber Brides: the Internet and the Asian Commodity," unpublished Master's paper, University of Florida, 1999; C.N. Le, "The Public and Private Sides of Ethnicity," www.asian-nation.org/interracial.shtml (accessed June 9, 2009).

48 Peter Brimelow, *Alien Nation: Common Sense About America's Immigration Disaster* (New York: Random House, 1995), pp. 10, 59.

49 For example, Samuel P. Huntington, "The Erosion of American National Interests," *Foreign Affairs* (September/October 1997): 28.

50 Joe R. Feagin and Danielle Dirks, "Who is White? College Students' Assessments of Key US Racial and Ethnic Groups," unpublished manuscript, Texas A&M University, 2004. A study of Canadian students by Doug Daniels reveals the same. See Maurice Berger, *White Lies: Race and the Myths of Whiteness* (New York: Farrar, Strauss, and Giroux, 1999), pp. 41–42.

51 Tatcho Mindiola, Nestor Rodriguez, and Yolanda Flores-Niemann, "Intergroup Relations Between African Americans and Hispanics in Harris County," unpublished research report, Center for Mexican American Studies, University of Houston, 1996; U.S. Bureau of the Census, *1997 Community Survey Profile – Houston City*, 1997; and Pew Hispanic Center and Kaiser Family Foundation, *2002 National Survey of Latinos*

(Washington, D.C.: Pew Hispanic Center/Kaiser Family Foundation, 2002), pp. 31–33.

52 Rosalind S. Chou and Joe R. Feagin, *The Myth of the Model Minority: Asian Americans Facing Racism* (Boulder: Paradigm Books, 2008).

53 Jennifer Lee and Frank D. Bean, "Reinventing the Color Line: Immigration and America's New Racial/Ethnic Divide," *Social Forces* 86 (December 2007): 577–579.

54 For detailed discussions of discrimination facing groups of color, see Feagin and Feagin, *Racial and Ethnic Relations*, chapters 4–11.

55 New America Media, *Deep Divisions, Shared Destiny: a Poll of African Americans, Hispanics, and Asian Americans on Race Relations* (San Francisco: New America Media, 2007), pp. 6–8, 11.

56 Chou and Feagin, *The Myth of the Model Minority*. See also Min Zhou, *Chinatown: the Socioeconomic Potential of an Urban Enclave* (Philadelphia: Temple University Press, 1992); Pyong Gap Min, ed., *Asian Americans: Contemporary Trends and Issues* (Thousand Oaks: Sage, 1995); Paul Ong, ed., *Economic Diversity: Issues and Policies* (Los Angeles: Leadership Education for Asian Pacifics, 1994); Cliff Cheng, "Are Asian American Employees a Model Minority or Just a Minority?" *Journal of Applied Behavioral Science* 33 (September 1997): 277–290.

57 FBI, "Hate Crime Statistics," October 2008, www.fbi.gov/ucr/hc2007/victims.htm (accessed May 17, 2009); U.S. Commission on Civil Rights, *Civil Rights Issues Facing Asian Americans in the 1990s* (Washington, D.C.: U.S. Government Printing Office, 1992).

58 Leland Saito, personal communication with the author, fall 1998. See Leland Saito, *Race and Politics: Asian Americans, Latinos, and Whites in a Los Angeles Suburb* (Urbana: University of Illinois Press, 1998), pp. 39–54.

59 I summarize here in part from Chou and Feagin, *The Myth of the Model Minority*, chapter 1. See Won Moo Hurh, "Adaptation Stages and Mental Health of Korean Male Immigrants in the United States," *International Migration Review* 24 (1990): 456–477; Center for Medicaid Services, *Medicaid Managed Care Enrollment Report: Depression Diagnoses for Adolescent Youth* (Medicaid Statistics Publications, 2002); C. Browne and A. Broderick, "Asian and Pacific Island Elders: Issues for Social Work Practice and Education," *Social Work* 39 (1994): 252–259; Laura Harder, "Asian Americans Commit Half of Suicides at Cornell," *The Cornell Daily Sun*, March 29, 2005, p. 1; Elizabeth Cohen, "Push to Achieve Tied to Suicide in Asian-American Women," www.cnn.com/2007/HEALTH/05/16/asian.suicides/index.html (accessed May 16, 2007).

60 Southern Poverty Law Center, *Under Siege*, pp. 3–6.

61 José Cobas and Joe R. Feagin, "Latinos/as and the White Racial Frame," *Sociological Inquiry* 78 (February 2008): 39–53. The Los Angeles study is Bobo and Suh, "Surveying Racial Discrimination."

62 National Fair Housing Advocate, "Farmworkers Represented by CRLA and the County of Riverside Settle Major Fair Housing Case," www.fairhousing.com/news_archive/releases/crla5–23–00.html (accessed March 1, 2001); Dan Rozek, "Elgin Denies Housing Bias against Hispanics," *Chicago Sun-Times*, October 3, 2000, p. 32; "Center Calls for the Rejection of Anti-Immigrant Ordinances," *Southern Poverty Law Center Report*, September 2006, p. 3.

63 Southern Poverty Law Center, *Under Siege*, p. 5.

64 Ibid.

65 FBI, "Hate Crime Statistics"; Southern Poverty Law Center, *Under Siege*.

66 Michael Smart, "Racism Associated with Disturbed Sleep and Depression in Latinos, BYU Study Shows," January 30, 2006, http://byunews.byu.edu/archive06-Jan-steffen.aspx (accessed April 6, 2009); Gilbert C. Gee, Andrew Ryan, David J. Laflamme, and Jeanie Holt, "Self-Reported Discrimination and Mental Health Status Among African Descendants, Mexican Americans, and Other Latinos in the New Hampshire REACH

2010 Initiative," *American Journal of Public Health* 26 (October 2006): 1821–1828; José Cobas, Jorge Duany, and Joe R. Feagin, eds., *How the United States Racializes Latinos: At Home and Abroad* (Boulder: Paradigm Books, 2009).

67 Leland Saito, personal communication with the author, fall 1998; Chou and Feagin, *The Myth of the Model Minority*, passim.

68 *When You're Smiling: the Deadly Legacy of Internment*, produced and directed by Janice D. Tanaka, Visual Communications, 1999.

69 Interview by Joe Feagin, fall 1998. Used by permission.

70 Chou and Feagin, *The Myth of the Model Minority*, pp. 3–23; see also Karen Pyke, "Vietnamese Parents and their Children: Pressures of Assimilation," unpublished research paper, University of Florida, 1999.

71 Nestor Rodriguez, personal communication; Cobas, Duany, and Feagin, *How the United States Racializes Latinos*.

72 Nestor Rodriguez, e-mail communication, fall 1998.

73 Yen Lee Espiritu, *Asian American Panethnicity* (Philadelphia: Temple University Press, 1992); José Cobas and Joe R. Feagin, "Language Oppression and Resistance: Latinos in the United States," *Ethnic and Racial Studies* 31 (February 2008): 390–410.

74 Charles R. Lawrence III, "Race, Multiculturalism, and the Jurisprudence of Transformation," *Stanford Law Review* 47 (May 1995): 829.

75 Ibid.

76 Suro, *Strangers Among Us*, pp. 251–252, 254.

77 Paula D. McClain *et al.*, "Racial Distancing in a Southern City: Latino Immigrants' Views of Black Americans," *The Journal of Politics* 68 (August 2006): 581–582. On Mexican and Cuban Americans, see Tatcho Mindiola, Yolanda F. Niemann, and Nestor Rodriguez, *Black–Brown Relations and Stereotypes* (Austin: University of Texas Press, 2002); Feagin and Feagin, *Racial and Ethnic Relations*, chapter 9.

78 New America Media, *Deep Divisions, Shared Destiny*, pp. 6–8, 11. See also Chou and Feagin, *The Myth of the Model Minority*, pp. 170–215.

79 New America Media, *Deep Divisions, Shared Destiny*, pp. 6–8, 11; Tyrone Foreman and Nadia Kim, "Beyond Black and White: Asian Americans' Attitudes Toward Blacks and Latinos," unpublished report, University of Michigan, 1999, pp. 17–23.

80 Claudine Gay, "Seeing Difference: the Effect of Economic Disparity on Blacks' Attitudes Toward Latinos," *American Journal of Political Science* 50 (October 2006), pp. 982, 990, 994–995.

81 New America Media, *Deep Divisions, Shared Destiny*, pp. 6–8, 11.

82 Karen Pyke and Tran Dang, "'FOB' and 'Whitewashed': Identity and Internalized Racism Among Second Generation Asian Americans," *Qualitative Sociology* 26 (summer 2003): 168.

83 Saito, *Race and Politics*, p. 59. See also David Gutierrez, *Walls and Minors: Mexican Americans, Mexican Immigrants, and the Politics of Ethnicity* (Berkeley: University of California Press, 1995).

84 See France Winddance Twine, *Racism in a Racial Democracy: the Maintenance of White Supremacy in Brazil* (New Brunswick: Rutgers University Press, 1998); Leone Campos de Sousa and Paulo Nascimento, "Brazilian National Identity at a Crossroads: the Myth of Racial Democracy and the Development of Black Identity," *International Journal of Politics, Culture, and Society* 19 (June 2008): 129–143.

8 Antiracist Strategies and Solutions: Past, Present, and Future

1 The full resolution is at www.opencongress.org/bill/111-sc26/text (accessed June 24, 2009).

2 Advisory Board on Race, *One America in the 21st Century: Forging a New Future* (Washington, D.C.: U.S. Government Printing Office, 1998).

3   Oliver C. Cox, *Caste, Class, and Race: a Study in Social Dynamics* (New York: Doubleday, 1948), p. 571.

4   Derrick Bell, *Faces at the Bottom of the Well* (New York: Basic Books, 1992), p. 12; italics omitted. See also Derrick Bell, *Race, Racism, and the Law*, 6th edn. (New York: Aspen Publishers, 2008).

5   John Briggs and F. David Peat, *Turbulent Mirror: an Illustrated Guide to Chaos Theory and the Science of Wholeness* (New York: Harper & Row, 1990), p. 177.

6   Steve H. Murdock, *An America Challenged: Population Change and the Future of the United States* (Boulder: Westview Press, 1995), pp. 33–47; U.S. Census Bureau, "An Older and More Diverse Nation by Midcentury," August 2008, www.census.gov/Press-Release/www/releases/archives/population/012496.html (accessed June 12, 2009).

7   William H. Frey, Alan Berube, Audrey Singer, and Jill H. Wilson, "Getting Current: Recent Demographic Trends in Metropolitan America," Brookings Institution, www.brookings.edu/reports/2009/~/media/Files/rc/reports/2009/03_metro_demographic_trends/03_metro_demographic_trends.pdf (accessed June 12, 2009).

8   Joe R. Feagin, "The Future of U.S. Society in an Era of Racism, Group Segregation, and Demographic Revolution," in *Sociology for the 21st Century: Continuities and Cutting Edges*, ed. Janet Abu-Lughod (Chicago: University of Chicago Press, 1999); U.S. Census Bureau, "An Older and More Diverse Nation by Midcentury," August 2008, www.census.gov/Press-Release/www/releases/archives/population/012496.html (accessed June 12, 2009); William H. Frey, "Diversity Spreads Out," Brookings Institution, www.frey-demographer.org/reports/Brook06.pdf (accessed June 19, 2009).

9   Dale Maharidge, *The Coming White Minority: California's Eruptions and America's Future* (New York: Random House, 1996), p. 11.

10 Bill Moyers, *A World of Ideas*, ed. Betty S. Flowers (New York: Doubleday, 1989), p. 283; William H. Frey, "Domestic and Immigrant Migrants: Where Do They Go?" *Current*, January 22, 1997, n.p.; Frey, "Diversity Spreads Out"; William H. Frey, "Metropolitan Magnets for International and Domestic Migrants," www.frey-demographer.org/reports/Brook3-2.pdf (accessed June 19, 2009).

11 Quoted in Kevin Sack, "South's Embrace of G.O.P. is Near a Turning Point," *New York Times*, March 16, 1998, p. A1. I am indebted here to suggestions from Chandler Davidson.

12 Kevin Phillips, *The Emerging Republican Majority* (New Rochelle: Arlington House, 1969).

13 Paul Jenkins, "The GOP's White Supremacy," *Huffington Post*, December 28, 2008, www.huffingtonpost.com/paul-jenkins/the-gops-white-supremacy_b_153823.html (accessed December 29, 2008); James Wright, "Black Republicans Ponder Their Future," *Afro-American Newspapers*, November 24, 2008, http://news.newamericamedia.org/news/view_article.html?article_id= (accessed December 18, 2008).

14 Southern Poverty Law Center, "Hate Group Numbers Up By 54% Since 2000," www.splcenter.org/news/item.jsp?aid=366 (accessed June 19, 2009).

15 Greg Mitchell, "Racial Incidents and Threats Against Obama Soar," November 15, 2008, www.huffingtonpost.com/greg-mitchell/racial-incidents-and-thre_b_144061.html (accessed December 29, 2008).

16 Duke is quoted in "David Duke Holds Memphis News Conference," http://whitereference.blogspot.com/2008/11/dr-david-duke-holds-memphis-news.html (accessed December 26, 2008).

17 Sonia Scherr, "Hate Groups Claim Obama Win is Sparking Recruitment Surge," *Hatewatch*, November 6, 2008, www.splcenter.org/blog/2008/11/06/hate-groups-claim-obama-win-is-sparking-recruitment-surge (accessed December 26, 2008).

18 Jessie Daniels, *Cyber Racism* (Lanham: Rowman and Littlefield, 2009), pp. 5–6. I am also indebted here to extensive discussions with Daniels.

19 Jessie Daniels, "Race, Civil Rights, and Hate Speech in the Digital Era," in *Learning Race*

and Ethnicity: Youth and Digital Media, ed. Anna Everett (Cambridge, MA: MIT Press, 2008), p. 129.

20 Alexander Tsesis, *Destructive Messages: How Hate Speech Paves the Way for Harmful Social Movements* (New York: NYU Press, 2002). See also Jennifer M. Pendleton, "Review of *Destructive Messages*," *Harvard Human Rights Journal* 16 (spring 2003): 312–314.

21 James Wright, "Black Republicans Ponder Their Future," *Afro Newspapers*, November 24, 2008, http://news.newamericamedia.org/news/view_article.html?article_id= (accessed December 18, 2008); Alexander Burns, "Steele: 'How Do You Like Me Now?'" *Politico*, January 30, 2009, http://dyn.politico.com/printstory.cfm?uuid=2A1BA222–18FE-70B2-A83323D0DB01F7E4 (accessed February 9, 2009).

22 See Bonnie L. Mitchell and Joe R. Feagin, "America's Racial–Ethnic Cultures: Opposition Within a Mythical Melting Pot," in *Toward the Multicultural University*, eds. Benjamin Bowser, Terry Jones, and Gale Auletta-Young (Westport: Praeger, 1995), pp. 65–86.

23 Merton L. Dillon, *Slavery Attacked: Southern Slaves and their Allies, 1619–1865* (Baton Rouge: Louisiana State University Press, 1990), p. 269; Herbert Aptheker, *American Negro Slave Revolts* (New York: International Publishers, 1952), pp. 162–163.

24 Robin D.G. Kelley, *Race Rebels: Culture, Politics, and the Black Working Class* (New York: Free Press, 1994).

25 Aldon Morris, *The Origins of the Civil Rights Movement: Black Communities Organizing for Change* (New York: Free Press, 1984); Joe R. Feagin and Clairece B. Feagin, *Racial and Ethnic Relations*, 8th edn. (Upper Saddle River: Prentice-Hall, 2008), chapter 7.

26 I draw quotes from this law as reprinted in Benjamin B. Ringer, *"We the People" and Others* (New York: Tavistock, 1983), pp. 311–330. See Supreme Court cases like *Brown v. Board of Education of Topeka*, 347 U.S. 483, 493 (1954) and the institutional racism case, *Griggs v. Duke Power Co.*, 401 U.S. 424 (1971).

27 See Roy Brooks, *Rethinking the American Race Problem* (Berkeley and Los Angeles: University of California, 1990), p. 105.

28 Office of Civil Rights Evaluation, U.S. Commission on Civil Rights Redefining Rights in America, "The Civil Rights Record of the George W. Bush Administration, 2001–2004," www.thememoryhole.org/pol/usccr_redefining_rights.pdf (accessed April 12, 2005).

29 See, for example, Carol Amoruso, "We ACT for Environmental Justice," *Third Force*, November/December 1997, 18–21; "Examine-BART Cop Arrested," NBC BayArea News, www.nbcbayarea.com/news/local/BART-Shooting-Officer-Arrested-Taken-Back-to-Oakland.html (accessed July 21, 2009).

30 Linda Jones, "Closing the Books on Slavery? African American Groups Seek Reparations on Ancestors' Behalf," *Dallas Morning News*, June 15, 1996, p. 1C.

31 Isabel Wilkerson, "Middle-Class But Not Feeling Equal, Blacks Reflect on Los Angeles Strife," *New York Times*, May 4, 1993, p. A20; Roy Brooks, *Integration or Separation? A Strategy for Racial Equality* (Cambridge, MA: Harvard University Press, 1996).

32 Marimba Ani, *Yurugu: an African-Centered Critique of European Cultural Thought and Behavior* (Trenton: Africa World Press, 1994), p. 570. See Molefi Kete Asante, *The Afrocentric Idea* (Philadelphia: Temple University Press, 1987).

33 Frantz Fanon, *Toward the African Revolution* (New York: Grove Press, 1967), p. 103.

34 Joe R. Feagin and Melvin P. Sikes, *Living with Racism: the Black Middle-Class Experience* (Boston: Beacon Press, 1994), pp. 286–287. See also Joe R. Feagin, *Systemic Racism: a Theory of Oppression* (New York: Routledge, 2006); Joe R. Feagin and Karyn McKinney, *The Many Costs of Racism* (Lanham: Rowman and Littlefield, 2003); Kenneth Bolton and Joe R. Feagin, *Black in Blue: Black Police Officers in White Departments* (New York: Routledge, 2004); Ruth Thompson-Miller and Joe R. Feagin, "Continuing Injuries of Racism: Counseling in a Racist Context," *The Counseling Psychologist* 35 (2007): 106–115.

35 See Feagin and McKinney, *The Many Costs of Racism*; Thompson-Miller and Feagin, "Continuing Injuries of Racism."

36 David Walker, *Appeal to the Coloured Citizens of the World*, ed. Charles M.Wiltse (New York: Hill and Wang, 1965), p. 75.

37 Anna Julia Cooper, *The Voice of Anna Julia Cooper*, eds. Charles Lemert and Esme Bhan (Lanham: Rowman and Littlefield, 1998), pp. 207, 212.

38 Quotes are from Martin Luther King, Jr., *Where Do We Go from Here? Chaos or Community?* (New York: Bantam Books, 1967), p. 9.

39 On earlier decades, see Howard Schuman, Charlotte Steeh, and Lawrence Bobo, *Racial Attitudes in America: Trends and Interpretations* (Cambridge, MA: Harvard University Press, 1985), pp. 182–189; Mary R. Jackman, *The Velvet Glove: Paternalism and Conflict in Gender, Class, and Race Relations* (Berkeley: University of California Press, 1994), pp. 231–241. For recent views, see discussion in Jennifer Hochschild, "Ambivalence About Equality in the United States or, Did Tocqueville Get it Wrong and Why Does that Matter?" *Social Justice Research* 19 (March 2006): 43–62.

40 Richard Morin, "Misperceptions Cloud Whites' View of Blacks," *Washington Post*, July 11, 2001, p. A01. For countering data, see Feagin and Feagin, *Racial And Ethnic Relations*, pp. 178–189; Rasmussen Reports, "What They Told Us: Reviewing Last Week's Key Polls," www.rasmussenreports.com/public_content/lifestyle/general_lifestyle/82_ say_u_s_is_best_place_to_live_41_say_u_s_lacks_liberty_and_justice_for_all (accessed July 6, 2008).

41 Pew Research Center, "Blacks See Growing Values Gap Between Poor and Middle Class: Optimism about Black Progress Declines," November 13, 2007, http://pewsocialtrends. org/pubs/700/black-public-opinion (accessed May 5, 2008). The survey was done with National Public Radio.

42 Ralph Ellison, *Shadow and Act* (New York: Random House, 1964), p. 304.

43 Gunnar Myrdal, *An American Dilemma*, vol. 2 (New York: McGraw-Hill, 1964), p. 929. I also draw here on Walter A. Jackson, *Gunnar Myrdal and America's Conscience: Social Engineering and Racial Liberalism, 1938–1987* (Chapel Hill: University of North Carolina Press, 1990), pp. 11–15, 369–370.

44 Alexandra Kalev, Frank Dobbin, and Erin Kelly, "Best Practices or Best Guesses? Assessing the Efficacy of Corporate Affirmative Action and Diversity Policies," *American Sociological Review* 71 (August 2006): 589–617.

45 Peter Steinfels, *The Neoconservatives* (New York: Touchstone, 1979), p. 6. See also Stephan Thernstrom and Abigail Thernstrom, *America in Black and White: One Nation Indivisible* (New York: Simon & Schuster, 1999); Abigail Thernstrom and Stephan Thernstrom, *No Excuses: Closing the Racial Gap in Learning* (New York: Simon & Schuster; 2004). On equality, see Irving Kristol, "Thoughts on Equality and Egalitarianism," in *Income Distribution*, ed. Colin D. Campbell (Washington, D.C.: American Enterprise Institute, 1977), p. 42; Daniel Bell, *The Coming of Post-Industrial Society* (New York: Basic Books, 1973), p. 453.

46 "Nobel Winner in 'Racist' Claim Row," CNN.com, October 18, 2007, http://edition. cnn.com/2007/TECH/science/10/18/science.race/index.html?iref=mpstoryview (accessed January 20, 2009); and "James D. Watson," Wikipedia, http://en.wikipedia. org/wiki/James_D._Watson#Political_activism (accessed January 20, 2009).

47 Marc Bendick, Jr., Mary Lou Egan, and Suzanne Lofhjelm, *The Documentation and Evaluation of Anti-Discrimination Training in the United States* (Geneva: International Labour Office, 1998), p. 17.

48 Susan W. Kaufmann, "The History and Impact of State Initiatives to Eliminate Affirmative Action," *New Directions for Teaching and Learning 2007* (fall 2007): 4–5; Caryn, Meyers Fliegler, "Dim Days For Affirmative Action," *University Business* 10 (February 2007), p. 13. See *Grutter* v. *Bollinger*, 539 U.S. 306 (2003) and *Gratz* v. *Bollinger*, 539 U.S. 244 (2003).

49 Cheryl I. Harris, "Whiteness as Property," *Harvard Law Review* 106 (June 1993): 1707.

50 U.S. General Accounting Office, *Information on Minority Targeted Scholarships* (Washington, D.C.: U.S. Government Printing Office, 1994). I am indebted to Tim Wise for noting these data.

51 Charles C. Moskos and John S. Butler, *All That We Can Be: Black Leadership and Racial Integration the Army Way* (New York: Basic Books, 1996), pp. 5–8; Mike Prior, "Sixty Years after Integration, Opportunities Abound for Minority Soldiers," Armed Forces Press Service, July 28, 2008, www.defenselink.mil/news/newsarticle.aspx?id=50615 (accessed July 2, 2009). See also Nelson Lim, Michelle Cho, and Kimberly Curry, *Planning for Diversity: Options and Recommendations for DOD Leaders* (Santa Monica: RAND, 2008).

52 See Moskos and Butler, *All That We Can Be*, pp. 2, 74. Current data are in Prior, "Sixty Years after Integration, Opportunities Abound for Minority Soldiers."

53 Jacquelyn Scarville *et al.*, *Armed Forces Equal Opportunity Survey* (Arlington: Defense Manpower Data Center, 1999), pp. 46–50, 150–153.

54 Theodor W. Adorno *et al.*, *The Authoritarian Personality* (New York: Harper, 1950), p. 4. See Patricia G. Devine, "Stereotypes and Prejudice: their Automatic and Controlled Components," *Journal of Personality and Social Psychology* 56 (1989): 15.

55 Zygmunt Bauman, *Modernity and the Holocaust* (Ithaca: Cornell University Press, 1989), p. 207.

56 I am indebted to discussions here with Sharon Rush. See Sharon Rush, *Loving Across the Color Line* (Lanham: Rowman and Littlefield, 2000); Jane Lazarre, *Beyond the Whiteness of Whiteness* (Durham: Duke University Press, 1996); Becky V. Thompson, *Mothering Without a Compass: White Mother's Love, Black Son's Courage* (Minneapolis: University of Minnesota Press, 2000).

57 I summarize the detailed discussion in Joe R. Feagin, *The White Racial Frame: Centuries of Racial Framing and Counter-Framing* (New York: Routledge, 2010).

58 See James W. Loewen, *Lies My Teacher Told Me: Everything Your American History Textbook Got Wrong* (New York: The New Press, 1995), p. 163; James W. Loewen, *Teaching What Really Happened: How to Avoid the Tyranny of Textbooks and Get Students Excited About Doing History* (New York: Teachers' College Press, 2009).

59 Julie M. Hughes, Rebecca S. Bigler, and Sheri R. Levy, "Consequences of Learning About Historical Racism Among European American and African American Children," *Child Development* 78 (November/December 2007): 1689–1705. The quote is on p. 1695.

60 David M. Amodio, Patricia G. Devine, and Eddie Harmon-Jones, "A Dynamic Model of Guilt: Implications for Motivation and Self Regulation in the Context of Prejudice," *Psychological Science* 18 (June 2007): 524–530.

61 As reported in C. Eugene Emery, "Brown Study Counteracts Racial Stereotypes," www.projo.com/education/content/BROWN_FACES_02–15–09_9LD9Q76_v10.1da8fe3.html (accessed April 7, 2009).

62 Elizabeth Stearns, Claudia Buchmann, and Kara Bonneau, "Interracial Friendships in the Transition to College: Do Birds of a Feather Flock Together Once They Leave the Nest?" *Sociology Of Education* 82 (April 2009): 175–195.

63 "Student Experience in the Research University," University of California, http://cshe.berkeley.edu/research/seru (accessed May 22, 2009).

64 Cedric J. Robinson, *Black Movements in America* (New York: Routledge, 1997), p. 63.

65 "Interview with Julian Bond," *Democracy Now*, July 21, 2009.

66 Nathan Rutstein, *From a Gnat to an Eagle: the Story of Nathan Rutstein*, ed. Carolyn Kerner Stein (Wilmette: Bahai Publishing, 2008); Nathan Rutstein, *Racism: Unraveling the Fear* (Washington, D.C.: The Global Classroom, 1993), pp. 225–228; National Resource Center for the Healing of Racism, www.nrchr.org/index.php (accessed June 23, 2009).

67 Eileen O'Brien, *Whites Confront Racism* (Boulder: Rowman and Littlefield, 2001);

Michael Omi, "(E)racism: Emergent Practices of Antiracist Organizations," paper presented at American Sociological Association Meetings, San Francisco, CA, August 1998. See the websites for People's Institute at www.pisab.org/index.cfm?nodeid=2 (accessed June 23, 2009); and for Antiracist Action at http://antiracistaction.org (accessed June 23, 2009). See also Adia Harvey Wingfield and Joe R. Feagin, *Yes We Can: White Racial Framing and the 2008 Presidential Campaign* (New York: Routledge, 2010).

68 The Rainbow-Push Coalition website describes their goals and actions, at www.rainbowpush.org/about (accessed June 23, 2009).

69 An early version of this argument appears in Joe R. Feagin and Hernán Vera, *White Racism: the Basics* (New York: Routledge, 1995), pp. 188–191.

70 W.E.B. Du Bois, *John Brown* (New York: International Publishers, 1962), pp. 263–264.

71 Ibid., pp. 264–265. I use modern spelling.

72 See Ibrahim al-Marashi, "Iraq's Constitutional Debate," *Meria*, http://meria.idc.ac.il/journal/2005/issue3/jv9no3a8.html (accessed June 24, 2009); "Constitution of Iraq," http://en.wikipedia.org/wiki/Iraqi_Constitution (accessed June 24, 2009).

73 Brooks, *Integration or Separation*, p. 115. I am indebted here to discussions with Roy Brooks.

74 See Joe R. Feagin, "Heeding Black Voices: the Court, Brown, and Challenges in Building a Multiracial Democracy," *University of Pittsburgh Law Review* 66 (fall 2004): 57–81; Joe R. Feagin and Bernice M. Barnett, "Success and Failure: How Systemic Racism Trumped the *Brown* v. *Board of Education* Decision," *University of Illinois Law Review* (2004): 1099–1130.

75 Brent Barry and Eduardo Bonilla-Silva, "'They Should Hire the One with the Best Score': White Sensitivity Qualification Differences in Affirmative Action Hiring Decisions," *Ethnic and Racial Studies* 31 (February 2008): 215–242.

76 Richard Delgado, *The Coming Race War?* (New York: New York University Press, 1996), p. 10.

77 Roy L. Brooks, *Atonement and Forgiveness: a New Model for Black Reparations* (Los Angeles: University of California Press, 2004), pp. 188, 194; Joe R. Feagin, "Documenting the Costs of Slavery, Segregation, and Contemporary Discrimination: Are Reparations in Order for African Americans?" *Harvard Black Letter Law Journal* 20 (2004): 49–80.

78 Lord Anthony Gifford, "The Legal Basis of the Claim for Reparations," paper presented to First Pan-African Congress on Reparations, Abuja, Federal Republic of Nigeria, April 27–29, 1993.

79 Ali A. Mazrui, "Who Should Pay for Slavery? Reparations to Africa," *World Press Review* 8 (August 1993): 22.

80 Jonathan Kaplan and Andrew Valls, "Housing Discrimination as a Basis for Black Reparations," *Public Affairs Quarterly* 21 (July 2007): 255–270.

81 Ibid., especially p. 268.

82 Andrew Kull, "Rationalizing Restitution," *California Law Review* 83 (October 1995): 1191–1198.

83 *Larry Williams*, et al. v. *The City Of New Orleans*, et al., 729 F. 2d 1554, 1577 (1984).

84 Delgado, *The Coming Race War?*, p. 103.

85 Brooks, *Atonement and Forgiveness*, pp. xii–xiv, 142. I extend here earlier arguments in Leslie Houts Picca and Joe R. Feagin, *Two Faced Racism: Whites in the Backstage and Frontstage* (New York: Routledge, 2007), pp. 271–272.

86 Rhonda V. Magee, "The Master's Tools, from the Bottom Up: Responses to African-American Reparations Theory in Mainstream and Outsider Remedies Discourse," *Virginia Law Review* 79 (May 1993): 886. Sumner is quoted in Magee, "The Master's Tools, from the Bottom Up," p. 887.

87 Martin Luther King, Jr., *Why We Can't Wait* (New York: Signet Books, 1963).

88 Gifford, "The Legal Basis of the Claim for Reparations."

89 See John Conyers, Jr., statements on reparations bill, http://conyers.house.gov/index.

cfm?FuseAction=Issues.Home&Issue_id=06007167-19b9-b4b1-125c-df3de5ec97f8 (accessed June 25, 2009); Kevin Merida, "Did Freedom Alone Pay a Nation's Debt?" *The Washington Post*, November 23, 1999, p. C1.

90 See their website: www.ncobra.org.

91 See Feagin, "Documenting the Costs of Slavery, Segregation, and Contemporary Discrimination," pp. 50–79.

92 Gideon Sjoberg *et al.*, "Ethics, Human Rights and Sociological Inquiry: Genocide, Politicide and Other Issues of Organizational Power," *American Sociologist* 26 (spring 1995): 11–13.

93 United Nations, *The United Nations and Human Rights, 1945–1995* (New York: United Nations Department of Public Information, 1995), pp. 33, 153–155, 219–225.

94 Judith Blau and Alberto Moncada, *Human Rights: Beyond the Liberal Vision* (Lanham: Rowman & Littlefield, 2005), p. 63; "The Universal Declaration of Human Rights," http://en.wikipedia.org/wiki/Universal_declaration_of_human_rights#cite_note-1 (accessed June 26, 2009).

95 Louis Henkin, Sarah H. Cleveland, Laurence R. Helfer, Gerald L. Newman, and Diana F. Orentlicher, *Human Rights* (New York: Foundation Press, 2009), p. 216. I am indebted here to suggestions by Roy Brooks.

96 Ibid., citing Tom Ginsburg, Svitlana Chernykh, and Zachary Elkins, "Commitment and Diffusion: How and Why National Constitutions Incorporate International Law," *University of Illinois Law Review* (2008): 201, 208.

97 Ibid., quoting Louis Henkin, *The Age of Rights* (New York: Columbia University Press, 1990), p. 76. See also Hurst Hannum, "The Status and Future of the Customary International Law of Human Rights: the Status of the Universal Declaration of Human Rights in National and International Law," *Georgia Journal of International and Comparative Law* 25 (fall 1995/winter 1996): 287–320; "Universal Declaration of Human Rights," Wikipedia, http://en.wikipedia.org/wiki/Universal_Declaration_of_Human_Rights (accessed July 22, 2009).

98 Quoted in Sidney M. Willhelm, *Black in a White America* (Cambridge, MA: Schenkman, 1983), p. 352.

99 Franklin Roosevelt, "State of the Union," www.presidency.ucsb.edu/ws/index.php?pid=16518 (accessed February 28, 2005).

100 Sandra Harding, "Taking Responsibility for our Own Gender, Race, Class: Transforming Science and the Social Studies of Science," *Rethinking Marxism* (fall 1989): 14.

101 See Melvin M. Leiman, *Political Economy of Racism* (London: Pluto Press, 1993), pp. 7–9, 313.

102 On racial lines in the feminist movement, see Louise Michele Newman, *White Women's Rights: the Racial Origins of Feminism in the United States* (New York: Oxford University Press, 1999), pp. 179–185. See also W.E.B. Du Bois, *Black Reconstruction in America 1860–1880* (New York: Atheneum, 1992 [1935]), p. 30.

103 Michael Albert *et al.*, *Liberating Theory* (Boston: South End Press, 1986), p. 2.

104 Paul G. Lauren, *Power and Prejudice: the Politics and Diplomacy of Racial Discrimination* (Boulder: Westview Press, 1988), p. 285.

105 Ben Agger, *Critical Social Theories: an Introduction* (Boulder: Westview, 1998), p. 9.

106 Jennifer A. Richeson and J. Nicole Shelton, "When Prejudice Does Not Pay: Effects of Interracial Contact on Executive Function," *Psychological Science* 14 (May 2003): 287–290.

107 William H. Frey, Alan Berube, Audrey Singer, and Jill H. Wilson, "Getting Current: Recent Demographic Trends in Metropolitan America," Brookings Institution, www.brookings.edu/reports/2009/~/media/Files/rc/reports/2009/03_metro_demographic_trends/03_metro_demographic_trends.pdf (accessed June 12, 2009). The quote is from p. 21.

108 See W.E.B. Du Bois, "On the Ruling of Men," in *The Oxford W.E.B. Du Bois Reader*, ed.

Eric J. Sundquist (New York: Oxford University Press, 1996), pp. 555–557; and Feagin, *The White Racial Frame.*

109 Frances Lee Ansley, "Stirring the Ashes: Race, Class and the Future of Civil Rights Scholarship," *Cornell Law Review* 74 (September 1989): 1002.

110 Quoted in Lauren, *Power and Prejudice,* p. 288.

Index

Terms in **bold** are followed by a brief definition.